# A Ruined Land

By the same author

*To Gettysburg and Beyond*
*The Civil War*
*Reconstruction and Reaction*
*Where America Stands*

# A Ruined Land

## The End of the Civil War

### Michael Golay

**John Wiley & Sons, Inc.**
New York • Chichester • Weinheim • Brisbane • Singapore • Toronto

*For Julie and the girls, again*

Library of Congress Cataloging-in-Publication Data:

Golay, Michael.
    A ruined land : the end of the Civil War / Michael Golay.
        p.   cm.
    Includes bibliographical references (p. 369) and index.
    ISBN 0-471-18367-9 (acid-free paper)
        1. United States—History—Civil War, 1861–1865—Social aspects.
    2. United States—History—Civil War, 1861–1865—Peace.
    3. Reconstruction. 4. United States—Politics and government—
    1865–1869.  I. Title.
    E488.9.068   1999
    973.7′14—dc21                                                99-35591

Printed in the United States of America
10  9  8  7  6  5  4  3  2  1

# Contents

# Illustrations

# Author's Note

THIS NARRATIVE FOLLOWS a dozen or so representative men and women for a short reach along the river of history. A strong current carries them downstream. Most simply drift and try to stay afloat, though a visionary few try to pull against the flow. Two or three powerful figures might have overcome the current or even changed the river's course. Their sins, omissions, and fumbled opportunities compounded the tragedy of the Civil War and its violent, chaotic aftermath, and are our legacy.

A few words of acknowledgment. *A Ruined Land* is based on personal histories drawn from primary sources, many of them unpublished. My thanks go to librarians and special collections archivists at the Boston Public Library, Bowdoin College, the University of California at Berkeley, the Concord (Mass.) Free Public Library, Duke University, the Georgia Historical Society, the Indiana Historical Society, the Indiana State Library, the Massachusetts Historical Society, the Massachusetts State Library, Phillips Exeter Academy, the South Caroliniana Library at the University of South Carolina, the Southern Historical Collection at the University of North Carolina at Chapel Hill, and Wheaton (Mass.) College.

Thanks, too, are due my agent, Edward W. Knappman of Chester, Connecticut; my editor at John Wiley & Sons, Hana Lane; and especially my wife, Julie Quinn.

—Michael Golay
Exeter, N.H.
September 1998

# Time Line

## 1863

*January 1.* President Lincoln's Emancipation Proclamation frees all slaves in Confederate territory.

## 1864

*July 2.* Congress approves the Wade-Davis Reconstruction plan; Lincoln pocket-vetoes it.

*November 8.* Lincoln wins election to a second term.

*November 15.* General William T. Sherman's army leaves Atlanta on the first stage of the March to the Sea.

*November 30.* Federal forces repulse a Confederate attack at Franklin, Tennessee, with heavy losses.

Confederates turn back a Union assault at Honey Hill near Grahamville, South Carolina.

*December 13.* A Federal assault carries Fort McAllister in the Savannah defenses, allowing Sherman to open a seaborne supply line for his army.

*December 15–16.* Union forces attack and nearly destroy the Confederate Army of Tennessee at Nashville.

*December 18.* Lincoln issues a call for an additional 300,000 Union troops.

*December 20–21.* The Confederates evacuate Savannah during the night. Federal troops occupy the city in the morning.

*December 25.* A Federal assault force withdraws after failing to carry Fort Fisher near Wilmington, North Carolina.

## 1865

*January.* Sherman transfers part of the army from Savannah to Port Royal Island, South Carolina, in preparation for the Campaign of the Carolinas.

*January 9.* War Secretary Edwin Stanton arrives in Savannah to confer with Sherman and admonish the general for the alleged mistreatment of former slaves trailing his columns.

*January 15.* Federal naval and land forces capture Fort Fisher.

*January 16.* Sherman issues Special Orders Number 15 setting aside land in coastal South Carolina, Georgia, and Florida for black settlement.

*January 19.* President Jefferson Davis names General Robert E. Lee commander in chief of the Confederate land forces.

*January 31.* The U.S. House approves a proposed constitutional amendment abolishing slavery throughout the United States and its territories.

*February 1.* Sherman advances into interior South Carolina.

*February 3.* Lincoln and Secretary of State William Seward meet with Confederate peace commissioners Alexander Stephens, John A. Campbell, and Robert M.T. Hunter aboard the *River Queen* off Hampton Roads, Virginia. The talks are inconclusive.

*February 17.* Union forces under Oliver Otis Howard enter Columbia. That night, wind-fanned fires consume the heart of the South Carolina capital.

The Confederates evacuate Charleston.

*February 21.* Confederate forces withdraw from Wilmington, the last important Confederate East Coast port.

*March 3.* Congress establishes the Bureau of Refugees, Freedmen, and Abandoned Lands—the Freedmen's Bureau.

*March 4.* Lincoln is inaugurated for his second term.

*March 13.* Davis signs a measure for the enlistment of slaves in the Confederate army.

*March 16.* Sherman's left wing defeats a portion of General Joseph E. Johnston's Confederate army at Averasboro, North Carolina.

*March 19–22.* Confederates withdraw toward Raleigh after three days of inconclusive fighting near Bentonville, North Carolina.

*March 22.* The Union general J. H. Wilson launches his cavalry raid to Selma, Alabama.

*March 25.* The Army of Northern Virginia attacks at Fort Stedman near Petersburg and is repulsed; it is Lee's last offensive operation.

*March 27–28.* Lincoln, General Ulysses S. Grant, Sherman, and Admiral David D. Porter confer at City Point, Virginia.

*March 29.* Grant opens the last campaign by sending General Philip Sheridan against the Confederate right south of Petersburg.

*April 1.* Sheridan's forces rout the Confederates at Five Forks and turn Lee's right.

*April 2.* Lee announces he will evacuate Richmond.

*April 2–3.* Confederates withdraw from Richmond; fires ravage the heart of the city; Federal troops enter the rebel capital.

*April 4.* Lincoln tours occupied Richmond.

*April 6.* Sheridan cuts off and destroys a third of Lee's retreating army at Sayler's Creek, Virginia.

*April 9.* Lee surrenders to Grant at Appomattox Court House, Virginia.

*April 11.* In a speech on a White House balcony, Lincoln proposes the franchise for black soldiers and "intelligent" blacks. It is his last speech.

*April 12.* Union forces occupy Mobile, Alabama.

*April 14.* Lincoln is shot at Ford's Theater in Washington, D.C.

*April 15.* Lincoln dies at 7:22 A.M. Andrew Johnson takes the presidential oath of office later in the day.

*April 18.* Sherman and Johnston reach a surrender agreement near Durham, North Carolina, that touches on questions of political restoration. Sherman sends the agreement to Washington for approval.

*April 24.* Grant arrives in Raleigh with word the cabinet has rejected the Johnston settlement. Sherman prepares to resume the campaign.

*April 26.* Johnston surrenders to Sherman on terms identical to those Grant gave Lee.

Federal troops surround a tobacco barn near Port Royal, Virginia, and call on John Wilkes Booth, Lincoln's assassin, to surrender. A soldier fires at Booth and mortally wounds him.

*April 27.* The steamboat *Sultana* explodes on the Mississippi; more than twelve hundred repatriated Union prisoners of war perish.

*April 30.* Union general E. R. S. Canby and Confederate general Richard Taylor reach a truce agreement near Mobile.

*May 1.* Johnson orders the appointment of a military commission to try the eight Lincoln conspirators.

*May 2.* Johnson offers a $100,000 reward for capture of Jefferson Davis.

*May 4.* Taylor surrenders Confederate troops in Alabama, Mississippi, and east Louisiana.

*May 10.* Johnson declares the armed insurrection "virtually at an end."

A detachment of the Fourth Michigan Cavalry captures Davis near Irwinville, Georgia.

A military court in Washington formally charges the Lincoln conspirators.

*May 15.* Howard takes charge of the Freedmen's Bureau.

*May 22.* Johnson declares all Southern seaports except four in Texas open for trade effective July 1.

*May 23–24.* The Union armies parade in the Grand Review in Washington.

*May 29.* Johnson issues an amnesty covering most Confederates.

A separate presidential proclamation restores civil rule in North Carolina.

*June 2.* Edmund Kirby Smith surrenders his Trans-Mississippi army, the last substantial body of Confederate troops.

*June 13.* Johnson appoints Benjamin F. Perry provisional governor of South Carolina.

*June 30.* The eight Lincoln conspirators are found guilty; four are sentenced to hang, the others to prison terms.

*July 7.* Lincoln conspirators George Atzerodt, David Herold, Lewis Paine, and Mary Surratt are hanged in Washington.

*August 14.* A Mississippi state constitutional convention convenes.

*September 13.* South Carolina's state constitutional convention meets.

*October 2.* A former Confederate general, Benjamin G. Humphreys, is elected governor of Mississippi.

*October 18.* James L. Orr, a former Confederate senator, is elected governor of South Carolina.

*November 10.* Andersonville Prison commandant Henry Wirz is executed after a war crimes trial.

*December 2.* The Mississippi legislature enacts a Black Code.

*December 4.* Congress refuses to seat former Confederates elected to the House and Senate.

*December 15.* Alabama enacts a Black Code.

*December 18.* The Thirteenth Amendment abolishing slavery is ratified.

*December 21.* The South Carolina legislature enacts a Black Code.


## 1866

*February 8.* Congress passes the Southern Homestead Act.

*February 19.* Johnson vetoes a bill renewing the Freedmen's Bureau.

*February 28.* Virginia enacts a Black Code.

*April 9.* Congress approves the Civil Rights Act over Johnson's veto.

*April 26.* Johnson officially declares the Civil War at an end.

*May 1.* A race riot erupts in Memphis, Tennessee.

*June 13.* Congress passes the Fourteenth Amendment.

*July 16.* Congress overrides the president's veto and extends the life of the Freedmen's Bureau.

*July 30.* A race riot racks New Orleans.

*August 14.* A National Union Convention meets in Philadelphia in support of Johnson's Reconstruction policy.

*August 28.* Johnson sets out on his "Swing around the Circle" campaign tour.

*September.* Maine votes; the returns are overwhelmingly Republican.

*October–November.* Republicans sweep to an election victory that will give them a Congress proof against Johnson's vetoes.


## 1867

*March 2.* Congress passes the first of three Military Reconstruction Acts.

## 1868

*February 24.* Congress impeaches Andrew Johnson.

*April 16.* Ex-Union Army officer Robert K. Scott of Ohio is elected governor of South Carolina.

*May 16.* The Senate finds Johnson not guilty at his impeachment trial.

*July 9.* South Carolina is readmitted to the Union under the congressional Reconstruction Acts.

*July 25.* Congress votes to shut down the Freedmen's Bureau on January 1, 1869.

*July 28.* The Fourteenth Amendment is ratified.

## 1873

*September 18.* The failure of Jay Cooke & Company touches off the Panic of 1873. Economic depression lasts several years.

## 1874

*August–September.* White League outbreaks convulse Louisiana.

*October 15.* Daniel H. Chamberlain of Massachusetts is elected governor of South Carolina.

## 1875

*November 2.* Conservative Democrats take control of the Mississippi legislature and "redeem" the state.

## 1876

*July 8.* White vigilantes murder five unarmed black militiamen in Hamburg, South Carolina.

*September 6.* Black Republicans attack white and black Democrats in Charleston; a race riot erupts.

*November 7.* Former Confederate general Wade Hampton is elected governor of South Carolina.

Rutherford B. Hayes and Samuel Tilden deadlock in the election for the presidency.

## 1877

*February 8.* An electoral commission awards disputed electoral votes to Hayes.

*April 10.* Federal troops are withdrawn from South Carolina and Hampton becomes governor.

# Cast of Characters

ADAMS, Charles Francis Jr. (1835–1915), Massachusetts. Union soldier, First Massachusetts Cavalry, commanding officer, Fifth Massachusetts Cavalry, patrician, skeptical, driven, from a leading American political family, among the first to enter abandoned Richmond, April 1865.

BARTLETT, Edward (1842–1914), Massachusetts. Union soldier, Forty-fourth Massachusetts, Fifth Massachusetts Cavalry, well-meaning, hard-working, naive, a veteran of the triumphal entry into Richmond, April 1865, and the Army of Observation, Texas, 1865.

ELLIOTT, Emily (1829–1889), South Carolina. Member of a prominent planter family, appalled observer of the collapse of the family fortune, impatient, capable, underemployed, feminist manqué.

ELLIOTT, William (1832–1867), South Carolina. Confederate soldier, conscription officer, 1863–1865, younger brother of Emily Elliott, ailing and overmatched master of The Bluff plantation, 1865–1866.

EWELL, Richard (1817–1872), Virginia. Confederate soldier, colorful, eccentric, enfeebled commander of Second Corps, Army of Northern Virginia, 1863–1864, defenses of Richmond, 1864–1865, surrendered at Sayler's Creek, April 1865, imprisoned four months in Fort Warren, Boston Harbor, 1865.

FOX, Charles (1833–1895), Massachusetts. Union soldier, Thirteenth Massachusetts, Fifty-fifth Massachusetts, diligent, self-critical veteran of Second Bull Run and Antietam, 1862, Honey Hill, 1864, committed to the black troops he commanded but a far from popular figure with them.

FOX, John (1836–1920), Massachusetts. Union soldier, Second Massachusetts, March to the Sea and Siege of Savannah, 1864, Campaign of the Carolinas, 1865, Charles Fox's younger brother, ebullient personality, recorder in his letters home of vivid and lively wartime scenes.

HOWARD, Oliver Otis (1830–1909), Maine. Union soldier, devout, humorless, well-intentioned commander of Sherman's Army of the Tennessee, 1864–1865, commissioner, Bureau of Freedmen, Refugees, and Abandoned Lands (the Freedmen's Bureau), 1865–1868.

JOHNSTONE, Mary Elliott (1824–1900), South Carolina. Wartime widow, lonely, overworked, self-sacrificing, enduring mother of six.

JULIAN, George (1817–1899), Indiana. Quaker-descended Radical Republican congressman, member of the Joint Committee on the Conduct of the War, vain, doctrinaire champion of unconditional civil rights for African Americans and women, leading opponent of the postwar policies of Andrew Johnson.

LeCONTE, Emma (1847–1932), Georgia. Bright, serious, moody diarist with a keen eye for detail, witness of the Columbia, South Carolina, fire, February 1865, and of the Federal occupation of Columbia, adoring daughter of scientist/educator Joseph LeConte.

LeCONTE, Joseph (1823–1901), Georgia. College professor, Confederate government chemist in Columbia, South Carolina, intelligent, clever, of joyous disposition, slave-owning master of Syfax plantation, Liberty County, Georgia.

McLAWS, Lafayette (1821–1897), Georgia. Confederate soldier, veteran, respected division commander under Lee, out of favor after 1863, dour, trouble-prone commander of the South Carolina Low Country defenses, 1865.

MANIGAULT, Charles (1795–1874), South Carolina. Planter-trader, canny patriarch of a large family, apolitical, prewar owner of two hundred slaves, master of Marshlands, Silk Hope, Gowrie plantations, preserver of a substantial property amid the wreck of war.

MANIGAULT, Louis (1828–1899), South Carolina. Planter son of Charles Manigault, traveler, collector, and connoisseur, proprietor of Gowrie plantation, Georgia, secretary to Confederate medical department inspector of Andersonville prison camp, 1864.

MORSE, Charles (1839–1926), Massachusetts. Union soldier, Second Massachusetts Infantry, cool, clear-sighted veteran of the March to the Sea and Siege of Savannah, 1864, Campaign of the Carolinas, 1865, wounded at Averasboro, North Carolina, 1865.

SAXTON, Rufus (1824–1908), Massachusetts. Union soldier, veteran of the Port Royal Expedition, 1861, abolitionist and offensively virtuous inspector of settlements, South Carolina Sea Islands, 1862–1865, assistant commissioner, Freedmen's Bureau, 1865–1866.

STORROW, Samuel (1843–1865), Massachusetts. Union soldier, Forty-fourth Massachusetts, 1862, Second Massachusetts. 1864–1865, Harvard dropout, patriotic, eager, full of promise, doomed veteran of the March to the Sea and the Siege of Savannah, 1864, Campaign of the Carolinas, 1865. Killed in action, Averasboro, North Carolina, 1865.

TOWNE, Laura (1825–1901), Pennsylvania. Volunteer schoolteacher, homeopathic physician, philanthropist, heroine by any standard and near-saint, too, a leading citizen of Saint Helena Island, South Carolina, from 1862.

TROTTER, James Monroe (1842–1892), Mississippi. Slave-born Union soldier, commissioned second lieutenant, Fifty-fifth Massachusetts, July 1865, smart, ambitious, impatient veteran of Honey Hill, South Carolina, 1864, and the occupation of Orangeburg, South Carolina, 1865.

WALLACE, Lewis (1827–1905), Indiana. Union soldier, jurist, author, adventurer, dilettante only too eager to please his superiors, division commander, Shiloh, Tennessee, 1862, commander Eighth Corps, Baltimore, 1864–1865, member, Lincoln conspirators' military commission, president, Andersonville war crimes military commission, election observer, Florida, 1876.

# Part One

# War and Revolution

## November 1864–January 1865

We do all stand in the front ranks
of the battle every moment of our lives;
Where there is a brave man there is
the thickest of the fight—
there is the post of honor.

Henry David Thoreau
*Journal*

# 1

# Honey Hill

VENTING CLOUDS OF OILY SMOKE, the troop transports cast off from Hilton Head, glided into the Broad River, and vanished behind streamers of fog drifting in off the Atlantic. The fog thickened and settled, merging sky, land, and tidewater. The *Cosmopolitan*, carrying the expedition commander, Brigadier General John Hatch, fell out of line and anchored to await daybreak. Other vessels blundered on through the opaque night. The *Canonicus*, with the engineer battalion, turned up a blind channel, hopelessly lost in the murk. At first light, on a falling tide, the *Mary Boardman*, the Fifty-fifth Massachusetts Infantry (Colored) aboard, ran gently into the muddy bank. The pilot, more skilled than the others or luckier, struck the shore just downstream from the objective: the landing at Boyd's Neck, ten miles below the Charleston & Savannah Railroad.

Hatch, a West Point–trained cavalryman, commanded the newly formed Coast Division, assembled toward the end of November 1864 at Hilton Head in the Union-occupied South Carolina Sea Islands. His orders were to march inland and cut the railroad, which conveyed reinforcements and supplies to Confederate forces contesting the advance of Sherman's army through Georgia toward Savannah and the sea.

General Hatch massed fifty-five hundred men for the expedition, stray units of the Department of the South: a dozen infantry regiments with supporting cavalry and artillery. The African American Fifty-fourth and Fifty-fifth Massachusetts had been summoned from the siege lines around Charleston. The Thirty-fourth U.S. Colored Troops were South Carolina men, former slaves. Four other black regiments withdrawn from coastwise garrisons, five white regiments, and a naval brigade of five hundred sailors and marines completed the Coast Division's order of battle.

The Fifty-fifth Massachusetts had marched to the Folly Island jetty on Sunday, November 27, 1864, and boarded two coastal steamers for the short voyage to Hilton Head. Along with rations and ammunition, the regiment carried shelter tents and thick blankets, too, for an unseasonable cold had descended upon the Low Country: heavy frost for two nights past, and a skim of ice on the water pails in the morning.

Lieutenant Colonel Charles Fox, commanding the Fifty-fifth, felt his spirits lift that morning with the purposeful confusion of breaking camp. The son of a Unitarian parson in the Boston horsecar suburb of Dorchester, he had experienced hard service in the Army of the Potomac with the old Thirteenth Massachusetts: the Shenandoah Valley, the Second Bull Run campaign, Antietam. The Fifty-fifth, one of the first of the African American regiments, had seen limited action so far, skirmishes on Charleston's outwork islands mostly, and a profitless expedition to north Florida early in 1864. It came as a relief to escape the saw-grass waste of Folly Island, the furious stinging of the sand flies, and the interminable fatigues of the Charleston siege. The inviolate city itself lay hidden from camp behind a screen of dunes. In the middle distance, beyond Morris Island, battered Fort Sumter formed a squalid hump under its pall of mingled brick dust and smoke from cooking fires, a symbol of the rebellion and a prize long just out of Union reach.

Charley Fox judged the Fifty-fifth Massachusetts battleworthy now, fully recovered from a near mutiny over the issue of equal pay. Breaking a straightforward pledge, the War Department had tendered black enlistees $10 a month, $3 less than whites received, with another $3 taken out for clothing. The two Massachusetts regiments refused to accept the lighter pay packets. "I am not willing to fight for anything less than the white man fights for," announced Corporal John Payne, an Ohio schoolteacher serving with the Fifty-fifth. "If a white man cannot support his family on seven dollars per month I cannot support mine on the same amount." In July, seventy-four soldiers petitioned President Lincoln for full pay or discharge. "If immediate steps are not taken to Relieve us we will resort to more stringent measures," they wrote. Rumors reached Fox that the men were prepared to stack arms and refuse duty. Massachusetts governor John Andrew lobbied Congress to make up the $3 shortfall. The Commonwealth legislature voted to cover the difference and bill the Federal Treasury. Sergeant James Trotter, a Mississippi-born former slave and an unofficial regimental spokesman, replied that the Fifty-fifth appreciated the gesture, but rejected the compromise.[1]

"The men all say that they will not take anything but the full pay from the government while they are in the field," Sergeant William Logan wrote Edward Kinsley, a Boston merchant who had "adopted" the Fifty-fifth (he sent regular parcels of newspapers and tobacco to the sergeant's mess and donated a clarinet to the regimental band) and acted as the soldiers' banker. "They say it would not be right for the state to pay what the government owes them unless she chooses to draw us home and pay us the whole amount."[2]

The Fifty-fifth Massachusetts served without compensation for sixteen months altogether. The government relented finally, dispatching an army paymaster to Folly Island to deal out greenbacks at the rate of $13 a month. Trotter returned from an early-autumn furlough to find an astonishing change in the collective mood. "I tell you that the 55th Reg't seemed an entire new set of men from those I left," he wrote Kinsley. Trotter noted, too, that within a couple of weeks the two Massachusetts black regiments posted upwards of $100,000 home to their wives and children.[3]

So the Fifty-fifth took the field with an important battle honor already won. Colonel Fox felt more than a professional interest in the regiment's readiness, the expedition's objective, and General Sherman's whereabouts. When last heard from, his brother John, a company commander in the Second Massachusetts, had been in Atlanta with Sherman's Twentieth Corps. The surviving soldier brothers Fox (a third, Tom, died of wounds a few weeks after Gettysburg) hadn't met for two years. Charley looked forward to a Christmastime reunion

Lieutenant Colonel Charles B. Fox, commanding officer of
the Fifty-fifth Massachusetts (Colored). The endless war
had taken a psychological toll on Fox, a veteran of hard fighting with the Army of the Potomac in Virginia. "One would
scarcely imagine the fearful scenes [of Honey Hill] were possible," he wrote in December 1864, "or that the men would
be ready to re-enact them." (Massachusetts Historical Society)

in Savannah or Charleston. Then came "reliable" word that the western army had veered to the north and converted Augusta, Georgia,
into a ruin. "It seems almost too good to be true," Fox wrote home.
It was, so he learned; all the same, John could hardly be far off now.[4]

The Fifty-fifth Massachusetts had come ashore at Hilton Head
on Monday the twenty-eighth, rested for a few hours, then reboarded
the steamer for the ghostly glide up the Broad River. The troops

clambered up the greasy bank early Tuesday and joined other Second Brigade units collecting at Boyd's Neck under the protection of navy double-ender gunboats that had found a path through the encircling fog. Hatch's headquarters boat hove into view in the forenoon. When the engineers with the landing stage for troops, guns, and animals failed to appear, the First Brigade infantry landed anyway. The men were lightered ashore in small boats, and the horses and mules were lowered over the side to swim for it. The brigade then marched off, but unwittingly in the wrong direction, and away from the objective, the Grahamville halt on the Charleston & Savannah.[5]

These misadventures frayed Hatch's nerves. The First Brigade discovered its error and doubled back, and other units arrived as the afternoon wore on. Hatch might have pushed inland with these troops. Instead, he sent word for the van—the Naval Brigade with eight sailor-drawn light cannon—to halt for the night at a sandy crossroads eight miles below the railroad.[6]

The advance resumed at sunrise on Wednesday the thirtieth, the column moving westward along a narrow road through a dark, neglected country of bogs, withered grass and gaunt trees. A breeze sprang up early and tore holes in the fog. After a while a figure appeared in the road—a slave sent down from Grahamville to call hogs as a warning of the Yankee approach. A detail of the Fifty-fifth Massachusetts took him in custody.

First Brigade skirmishers encountered Confederate light forces a mile or so beyond a ramshackle meetinghouse called Bolan's Church. Dense woods crowded the track to the left. The terrain opened up to the right, though the rebels were here setting fields of broom sedge and cotton stubble alight as they scampered back. The column pushed on through the roar, heat, and stinging smoke of the fires. The sun had nearly climbed to the overhead before the skirmishers, tired and scorched, caught sight of what appeared to be a formidable earthwork. The road crossed a swampy creek just ahead, then bent sharply to the left around the base of a thirty-foot-high bluff—Honey Hill, according to Hatch's sketch map. Evidently the brigadier and his staff had known nothing of this strongpoint; anyhow, nobody mentioned it to Colonel Edward Potter, commanding the First Brigade. Nevertheless, Potter reeled in the skirmish line and signaled the charge.[7]

The attack went off just as Confederate reinforcements were reaching the battlefield. For two weeks these troops, a division of Georgia militia, had retreated steadily before Sherman. They were jaded—"almost broken down by fatigue and want of rest," reported their commander, Major General Gustavus Smith. Even so, and over the protests of the men, who reminded their officers that, by law, Georgia forces were not to be sent beyond the state's borders, Smith had agreed to go into South Carolina to drive the Yankees back to their gunboats and hold the railroad until the regulars turned up.[8]

Smith's fourteen hundred infantry rode to Grahamville along the warped rails of the Charleston & Savannah, jumping down from the flatcars at daybreak Wednesday and double-timing to Honey Hill. Smith carried out a hurried deployment, then allowed the men a short rest. Potter's line of battle emerged from the swamp 150 yards to his front around eleven o'clock.

Georgia infantry and the dug-in cannon swept the road, stopping the initial charge short of the redoubt. The Federals flailed about in dense undergrowth and standing water under a pelting fire. Hatch sent for the Second Brigade under Colonel Alfred Hartwell to move up in support of Potter. Hartwell formed the Fifty-fifth Massachusetts and part of the Fifty-fourth Massachusetts in a double column in the road, here built up to form a causeway through the bog. Mishearing Hartwell, Charley Fox led three of his companies into a woods off to the right, away from the main action. The other five companies advanced at a jog trot four abreast up the causeway into a blast of Confederate fire.

The attackers flinched, rallied, and surged forward a few rods,* were stopped, rallied again. Canister tore into the mounted group at the head of the column, cutting men down, Hartwell wrote later from a Beaufort hospital, "like grass by a mowing machine." A ball pierced Hartwell's hand; then his horse reared and toppled over onto him. As he fought free of the terrified horse a musket ball ripped into his boot heel, searing his ankle. He regained his feet; a spent grapeshot knocked him down again. A canister slug struck Captain William Crane in the forehead, killing him instantly. A moment later Crane's

---

*A rod measures five and a half yards.

friend Winthrop Boynton dropped to the ground dead. The color sergeant, Richard King, fell, his lifeblood draining out of him and mingling with the blood of Winthrop and Crane. James Trotter was hit. Within five minutes, a hundred officers and men of the Fifty-fifth lay dead, dying, or wounded.[9]

Trailing infantry, stretcher-bearers, supernumeraries, company officers, and befuddled aides milled aimlessly on the causeway in the immediate rear of the fight. Nobody seemed to have the least idea of what to do next.

"Charge, charge!" shouted a flustered lieutenant colonel.

"Where?"

"Charge!" he repeated, wildly waving his arms in the direction of the Confederate redoubt.[10]

Two companies of the Fifty-fourth Massachusetts obediently moved off through a thicket of vines and catbrier. Shaking out into line on a wooded rise overlooking the creek, they lay low against a heavy, accurate fusillade. Dense flights of minié balls passed overhead. Some of the men, veterans of a misbegotten assault on Fort Wagner near Charleston sixteen months ago, swore afterward they had never experienced a hotter fire. And their tormentors were not Confederate veterans at all, only tired, surly, half-mutinous militia.

A lull fell over the battlefield with the collapse of Hartwell's effort. Fox left his three companies in the ooze along the creek and went off in search of the rest of the regiment. He learned on the causeway that Hartwell had delegated the brigade command to him. A few minutes later General Hatch sent word to suspend the attack. Toward sundown, when a captured rebel reported that regular infantry had reached Grahamville, Hatch ordered a retreat to Boyd's Neck, where the lead-colored gunboats lay at their moorings.[11]

Potter organized the withdrawal, which came off without incident in the gathered dusk. Details from the Fifty-fourth and Fifty-fifth collected the wounded—always an urgent task for African American troops, for the Confederates were known as a matter of common practice to deal with blacks red-handed on the battlefield. Improvising stretchers from muskets, shelter tents, and blankets, they carried men too hurt to walk rearward to a makeshift aid station at Bolan's Church. The temperature fell sharply with nightfall. Troops massed at the crossroads around great bonfires of fence rails and brushwood.

Fogbound in every sense, Hatch had thoroughly mismanaged the engagement at Honey Hill, showing off an encyclopedic ignorance of the terrain, the enemy, and the capabilities of his own troops. Coast Division losses for the day added up to 91 killed, 629 wounded, and 26 missing. Confederate casualties amounted to 8 killed, 42 wounded.

"The affair was a repulse owing entirely to the strong position held by the enemy and our want of ammunition," Hatch reported. Major General John Foster, commanding the Department of the South, accepted the explanation without comment. Survivors of the battle knew better. "There appears to have been a lack of foresight in the preparations," a company commander in the Fifty-fourth Massachusetts remarked dryly. Everyone wondered why Hatch had persisted in funneling troops down the narrow causeway into the heaviest concentration of enemy fire. "Hatch, why in hell didn't you flank them on the right?" Sherman himself would ask, riding over the battlefield with the chapfallen brigadier a few weeks later.[12]

"We have been driven back," Charley Fox wrote his wife, Mary, from under the navy's guns at Boyd's Neck, "and whatever may be said, for the time badly whipped. It seems almost wonderful that I am alive."[13]

THE PORT ROYAL MISSIONARIES heard the gunfire at Honey Hill and saw columns of smoke rising into the sky to the northwest. They had made friends with officers of the black regiments, and some of the men in the ranks were native Sea Islanders. Judging by the din, the fighting off toward the railroad was no mere skirmish. The missionaries went about their affairs in the mild, quiet light of that short last afternoon of November and anxiously awaited word of the outcome.

Hundreds of Northerners—Treasury agents, parsons, schoolteachers, traders, bagmen, sharps, and cotton speculators—had infiltrated the Union-occupied South Carolina Sea Islands since 1862. Some came in pursuit of cotton profits, and for the thrill of authority over former slaves. A few came to serve, to work out their humanitarian designs in the island enterprise known as the Port Royal Experiment.

The teachers and clergymen—New Englanders, New Yorkers, and Pennsylvanians mostly—sought to uplift and make citizens of the emancipated people. Naive, sentimental, visionary, they regarded themselves, in the phrase of an ally and admirer, Brigadier General

Rufus Saxton, as the advance installment of "a great national atonement" for the evil of slavery. "We've come to do antislavery work," Pennsylvanian Laura Towne had announced on her arrival in the spring of 1862, "and we think it noble work and mean to do it earnestly." They styled themselves Gideon's Band; they were a herald or pledge of better times for an emerging race.[14]

From the outset, the Gideonites clashed with the soldiers and the cotton traders. The common run of government men struck them as uncouth characters of doubtful honesty. They loathed the speculators. For their part, the army officers and Treasury men derided the volunteers as humbugs, frauds, and quacks, fuzzy-minded amateurs who spoiled the Gullah locals and wasted the government's time.

Even soldiers of liberal inclination were chary of the missionaries. Charles Francis Adams Jr. was raised on abolition. It had been practically a proprietorial issue in his family. Adams's grandfather,* a scourge of slaveholders, defended fifty-three murderous slave mutineers of the *Amistad* and won their freedom in 1841. His father, the elder CFA, ran for the vice presidency on the original Free-Soil ticket in 1848. Time had softened the senior Adams's views, and he sought accommodation with the South on the eve of secession. His son, faced now with the actual experience of emancipation, found himself ambivalent, too.

Adams reached Beaufort on Port Royal Island with the First Massachusetts Cavalry in January 1862, only a few weeks after a Union expeditionary force had seized the region. A reluctant soldier, he had agonized for months before volunteering. At the least, the army offered escape from a slack, stultifying law practice. His father, now United States minister to Britain, tried to dissuade him. There could be no glory in fighting one's own countrymen. But the prospect of glory counted for less than the bite of the Adams conscience: that awkward, inconvenient, and uncomfortable sense of inherited obligation.

"For years our family has talked of slavery and of the South, and been most prominent in the contest of words," Charles wrote his father a few weeks after the rebel attack on Fort Sumter, "and now

---

*John Quincy Adams, the sixth U.S. president.

that it has come to blows, does it become us to stand aloof from the conflict?"[15]

Yet he idled away the spring and summer of 1861. He saw friends and acquaintances off to Virginia with the Second Massachusetts. In his silent office, with its stacks of law books with pages uncut and the dust thick on the blinds, he thumbed restlessly through the newspapers and argued out the case with himself.

"Why do I stay home?"[16]

He settled the question during a long October gallop through the Braintree Woods. The blaze of red and gold had faded to somber russet by then, matching his mood. The formalities were hastily arranged, and on December 28, 1861, he stood on a railroad siding at Readville, Massachusetts, in a cold drizzle of rain while the First Massachusetts Cavalry loaded onto the cars for the first stage of the trip to Port Royal.

"I felt neither regretful nor sentimental," Adams wrote in retrospect. "I asked only to get away."[17]

The first signs of upheaval in the Sea Islands shook him badly. On picket duty on one of the outlying islands, he cantered up to an abandoned plantation house to find the garden filled with rubbish, with splintered furniture and scraps of letters and books from the ransacked library moldering in the grass.

"I wandered round and looked out at the view and wondered why this people had brought all this on themselves," he wrote his mother, "and yet I couldn't but pity them. For I thought how I should feel to see such sights at Quincy."[18]

War was chaos itself; now the ultra-abolitionists were fomenting revolution. "Edward Pierce arrived here on Sunday in command of forty missionaries," Adams wrote his father in March 1862. "They had better have kept away; things are not ripe for them yet and they are trying to force the course of nature."[19] Let the radicals stand aside while the army crushed the rebellion. They could practice their schemes later, after the war had been won.

"There is no abolitionism in the army," he went on. "The ultras in their eagerness have spoiled it all."[20]

Adams and the First Massachusetts Cavalry were ordered away to the Virginia front in August 1862. With the arrival of the first African American regiments in 1863 and 1864, the Port Royal missionaries encountered soldiers of a more sympathetic bent. Some of the white officers of the black units (for now, all the officers were white) were birds of passage. A fair number, though, were committed emancipationists who shared the Gideonites' exalted view of the war's purpose and meaning. The Brahmin abolitionist Robert Gould Shaw had been killed, martyred, leading the Fifty-fourth Massachusetts at Fort Wagner. A son of William Lloyd Garrison himself served as a subaltern in the Fifty-fifth.

Word spread swiftly that the Grahamville expedition had miscarried. The Gideonites thus learned firsthand how fragile a soldier's life could be. "We know that hundreds of wounded men are coming to Beaufort," Laura Towne wrote her family in Pennsylvania. "We met a pleasant gentleman at Coffin Point last Sunday—a Captain Crane, and to-day we hear he is dead."[21]

Miss Towne had found her true vocation in the Sea Islands. Thirty-nine years old in 1864, she had studied homeopathic medicine for a season, then drifted into teaching, supplementing a token charity school income with what she ironically termed "dowry money" from her father, a well-to-do cotton and sugar trader. By 1861 she and a teacher friend, Ellen Murray, were settled in Newport, Rhode Island, joined in the domestic arrangement nineteenth-century New Englanders dubbed a "Boston marriage."

The war, with its implication of freedom for the South's 4 million slaves, stirred visions of heroic exertion in Laura Towne. Army and government service were closed to her, as to most women. Ladylike pastimes such as sewing comforters for the troops, however important, were an insufficient outlet for her energies and ambition. "We had a fine war sermon from Mr. Brooks," she wrote her sisters at home at Oakshade, near Philadelphia, a few weeks after the outbreak of war. "Really the little meek man seemed a cool six-footer, ready for any enemy." Robust, strong-willed, formidably intelligent, she felt just that way herself.

Towne landed at Hilton Head in April 1862 with one of the first of the missionary contingents. Ellen Murray joined her a few weeks later and they took up residence at the Oaks Plantation on Saint Helena Island, where former slaves were raising cotton for the U.S. Treasury under Edward Pierce's supervision. Laura managed Pierce's household. Ellen taught ABC's to the grown people on the place.

Laura Towne, teacher and physician, shown here with pupils
on Saint Helena Island, South Carolina, in 1866. Towne
and her companion, Ellen Murray, found their true vocation
among the former slaves of the Sea Islands. They kept mostly
to themselves and their work, though Towne admitted she
found white Southerners pleasant enough so far as they went.
But "our ways are not their ways," she wrote, "and it is bothersome to know them."

Before the war, the South Carolina Sea Islands—Port Royal,
Ladies', Saint Helena, Hilton Head, Fripp, Edisto, and others lying
between Charleston and Savannah—had produced the world's finest
long-staple cotton. The planters fled to the mainland with the arrival
of Union troops in November 1861, leaving their Gullah slaves behind, as many as ten thousand men, women, and children. In U.S.

government jargon the Gullahs were contrabands—people in a state of transition, no longer enslaved nor yet entirely free.

The Treasury Department intended at first only to supervise the contrabands in their traditional task. This answered two purposes, or seemed to: former slaves were to be paid wages and so could support themselves, and government sales of the cotton they produced would defray some of the cost of the war. Pierce, a Boston businessman, and other plantation superintendents came into the islands under Treasury colors. Teachers and parsons from the private abolition societies presently followed.

For the Gideonites, the Sea Islands were a laboratory for a grand experiment in free labor, education, and citizenship. The cotton superintendents regarded the labor question as paramount and sought to run the abandoned plantations as profit-making enterprises. In the economic miracle they foresaw, former slaves would evolve into a bucolic version of Yankee mill hands, industrious wage earners turning out bumper harvests of the cash crop for Northern investors.

The missionary ultras believed that schooling, land ownership, and political activity would create a new class of independent, self-sufficient citizen out of the shambles of slavery. "God's program," according to the Reverend Mansfield French, "involves freedom in its largest sense—free soil, free schools, free ballot boxes, free representation."[22] The cotton men, so the ultras charged, regarded the Gullahs as a permanent helotry, a source of field labor and fit for little more.

The Gideonites gained an unlooked-for ally in General Saxton, the military governor of Port Royal and (unusually for a soldier) a true believer in black emancipation. His abolitionism had come down to him from his father, an irascible radical of a familiar New England pattern. The Saxtons were an established family in the old Pioneer Valley town of Deerfield, Massachusetts. A lawyer by trade, Jonathan Saxton neglected his clients in favor of advanced social causes: abolition, utopian settlements, temperance, the Short-Skirts League. He counted George Ripley, the Brook Farm visionary, as a friend and reserved a place among Ripley's Associationists for Rufus. Doubtless in reaction to his father's radicalism, the boy followed a different drummer. Winning appointment to the U.S. Military Academy at West Point, he handed down the Brook Farm billet to his younger brother Willard.[23]

Saxton graduated eighteenth out of forty-three in the West Point class of 1849. A Coastal Survey assignment brought him to the Sea Islands in the 1850s, where he had a first up-close look at slavery. He returned at the end of '61 with the Port Royal Expedition. The War Department detailed him a few months later to oversee the abandoned island plantations, put them in cotton-growing order, and protect the Gullahs and mainland refugees flowing into the Federal lines from rebel reprisal.

With the appointment, Saxton rose in one long step from captain to brigadier. His rivals suggested that he had lobbied for the post for the jump in rank. He always denied the charge. "I would have preferred being in the field," he once said, "but I was ordered to do this thing, and I have tried to do it faithfully, till the Government gave me something else to do. I was educated in its school and for its service, and I thought it my business to do whatever it required."[24] Whatever the motive, the family radicalism soon percolated to the surface. Saxton came to regard the Port Royal governorship as a sacred trust. The Sea Islands could be a model, he believed, for emancipation efforts everywhere.

The Gideonites were skeptical at first. Saxton, forty years old in 1864, struck them as just another regular soldier, clannish, narrow-minded, and remote. "It is a great pity that he does not come onto the plantations himself and learn something, personally, of their state and wants," one remarked.[25] But they soon discovered that the holy fire burned within him.

"He is a thoroughgoing Abolitionist," schoolmaster Arthur Sumner wrote of Saxton. "It is delightful to hear a military man express so strong a confidence in Absolute Truth, and let the consequences take care of themselves."[26]

Saxton supplied Gullah families with cloth, farm tools, seed, forage from government stores, and draft animals from government corrals. He abetted their efforts to acquire land. He exposed and hounded corrupt, incompetent, or abusive plantation superintendents. Vain and temperamental, he used to fly out savagely at subordinates who crossed him. When the Treasury agent A. S. Hitchcock recommended chain gangs and workhouses for indigent former slaves, Saxton—through his brother Willard, one of his aides—fired off a scathing rebuke:

The west side of Bay Street, the main thoroughfare in Beaufort, South Carolina, chief town of the Sea Islands, on a quiet winter's day in 1862 or 1863. Federal forces developed Beaufort as a garrison town, with recruiting depots, hospitals, commissary storehouses, and, for soldiers and officials unlucky enough to die there, a cemetery. (U.S. Army Military History Institute)

> Your letter is false, and as cowardly as false, because it is calculated, under a pretended garb of friendship, to misrepresent a downtrodden and oppressed people. General Saxton directs me to express to you his sincere regrets that his Dep't, or his work, has ever been cursed with such an agent as yourself.[27]

In due course the peremptory brigadier found romance as well as a calling in the Sea Islands. Rumors of his courtship of the striking Matilda Thompson, a Philadelphia schoolteacher whose journalist brother edited the radical Beaufort *New South*, titillated the close-knit volunteer community. "The general does not deny it when accused," Towne reported.[28] By force of habit Saxton directed his brother, as aide and factotum, to arrange matters for him.

Willard Saxton handed over Rufus's written proposal of marriage at the end of a long canter through oak woods with Miss Thompson, an accomplished equestrienne. Distractedly stroking the neck of the lathered and blowing horse, she opened the note and read it through. Then she read it again, more carefully this time.

"'Good-bye, brother,' she said as I left," Willard wrote in his journal that night, "& she rode back & I rode home, the bearer of the glorious news of his success."[29]

Parson French joined the couple in Saint Helena's Church, Beaufort, in March 1863. The marriage sealed Saxton's alliance with the Gideonites. French became a key Saxton loyalist. Towne trusted him wholly. She even named a horse after him. The teachers discovered that he could be relied upon for material as well as moral support. When Elizabeth Botume asked Saxton for stuff for her sewing classes, he responded with a donation of yards of a heavy hickory-brown twill from a warehouse full of confiscated cloth originally intended for Confederate army uniforms.

The Gullahs, their ambitions fixed on land, thought highly enough of Saxton to make him a gift of a ceremonial sword on the first anniversary of the Emancipation Proclamation, January 1, 1864. They appreciated, too, his strong backing of the missionary schools. Saxton took every opportunity to show them off to Northern visitors. A steady stream flowed through Lizzie Botume's school just outside Beaufort: evangelists, reformers of every description, ethnographers and ethnologists, musicologists, collectors of folklore, curiosity seekers.

A Yankee officer with one group catechized the students about their religious beliefs.

"Children, who is Jesus Christ?" he asked.

"General Saxby!" one of the boys shouted.[30]

The Gullahs, as it happened, venerated no one among the Gideonites. They knew them far too well for that. The volunteers were intimately mixed up in their lives at school, in the settlements, and on the plantations. From the first, the Gullahs and the missionaries tested one another's endurance, patience, and faith.

The teachers found the Gullahs' English and West African patois impenetrable. Eccentric use of pronouns, multiple proper names for the same person, and a queer if expressive jargon created a babel of misunderstanding. "I never knew whether they were talking of boys or girls," Lizzie Botume confessed. "They spoke of all as 'him.'" Teacher Harriet Ware puzzled over why one of her little pupils should be called "Rode." His mother explained that she had delivered him along the sandy verge of the highway on invasion day in 1861 when the concussive effect of the Yankee bombardment sent her into an early labor.[31]

Gullahs believed in the evil eye, in witches, and in spirits. They dreaded being alone after dark, or sleeping alone. "'The hag will ride we,'" they would whisper. The Gullahs' uninhibited expression of their religion, a folk amalgam of African fetish and Protestant Christianity, shocked even the calm, tolerant Laura Towne—anyhow at first. "I never saw anything so savage," she remarked after witnessing a "shout"—the prolonged, intense and sweaty dance that followed praise meetings on some plantations.[32]

The islanders mistrusted white people congenitally. Associating cotton with slavery, they went grudgingly into the fields; their resistance vexed the superintendents, who could achieve nothing without reliable labor. For their part, the local people found the Northern obsession irksome. "The Yankees preach nothing but cotton, cotton!" a Gullah complained to Towne. She took his point: "The negroes can see plainly enough that the proceeds of the cotton will never get into their black pockets."[33] Exotic, quirky, independent, the Gullahs chafed under Yankee tutelage and resisted Yankee ways.

The Gideonites were volunteers, though, and most of them met hardship and frustration with courage and spirit. They had left behind tranquil lives in the North, exchanging feather beds and fancywork counterpanes for mattress ticking stuffed with cornhusks or Spanish moss, and good order for the prospect of war. For some, the first shocks of slavery were severe beyond imagining. Nothing, Towne discovered, cast the Peculiar Institution in a truer light than the physical scars it left on its victims.

"Loretta showed me her back, arms and breast today," she wrote her sisters at Oakshade. "In many places there were ridges as high and long as my little finger and everywhere marks of the whip. She said that her children had been killed inside her by the whip. She says it was because when heavy with child she could not do the full work of a field hand. I suspect her also of being rather apt to resist and rather smart in speaking her mind, poor thing."[34]

The missionaries adapted slowly, too, to the Sea Islands climate. They lived in dread of malaria, typhoid, and yellow jack. Summer sun parboiled, oppressed, and enervated them; winter east wind, fog, and rain brought on streaming colds and ague chills. Essentials—flypaper, army hardtack, salt junk and sardines, tea, sugar, and salt—were often in short supply, sometimes unavailable altogether.

And there was a whiff of danger. Through most of the war, the threat of a Secesh return seemed real enough, even if the fighting soldiers were disdainful. ("Our pickets stand and gaze placidly at the pickets of the enemy on the shore opposite," Charles Adams once wrote. "About three times a week one party or the other tries to cross in boats and gets fired at, but no one ever seems to be hurt.")[35] Mainland Confederates launched raids into the islands to reclaim abandoned cotton or carry off contrabands. With the Union army preoccupied in Virginia, forces were rarely available to defend the outlying plantations.

At first glance, the islands struck most Northerners as a forlorn country. For hours on end only the monotonous booming of the surf, the dry rasp of the wind in the palmettos, or the sudden shriek of wildfowl in the myrtle broke the exhausted silence. The hot reek of salt grass suffused the air. In the pestilential heat of late summer, Hilton Head might just as well have been a Devil's Island–style penal settlement, or a leper colony.

A long, swaying wooden wharf ran out from a muddy foreshore. Army camps, storehouses, and sutlers' huts (Robber's Row, in soldier argot) straggled along the riverfront. Stands of wind-bent pine rose from the low sandhills behind the camps. Out in the islands the plantations were untidy, the great houses deserted and derelict, and the black settlements squalid, a slum of shacks hammered together out of rough-sawn pine boards with tiny openings for windows and floors of mingled sand and lime.

The languid beauty of the Low Country revealed itself in gradual stages, after the clamor of arrival had died down: on the journey into the islands from Beaufort, say, in the flare of an October sunset with the voices of the boatmen floating over a tidal inlet:

> Jesus make de blind to see,
> Jesus make de cripple walk,
> Jesus make de deaf to hear,
> Walk in, kind Jesus!
> No man can hender me.[36]

The tall, spiky palmettos, once one grew used to them, had a sort of homely charm. "They stand alone in the cotton-fields like our elms in a meadow," Harriet Ware wrote, "though there are fewer of them, and they are stiff and straight."[37] The island roads wound through groves of evergreen live oak hung seductively with long gray draperies of Spanish moss, through which the sun cast shadows of fantastic, ever-changing shape.

The broad cotton clearings lay fallow every other year, giving the islands a pleasant chiaroscuro pattern, living green swatches (golden in high summer when the cotton flowers were in bloom) alternating with fields brown with last year's growth. Even Beaufort (*byoo'fit,* in the soft, slurred local accent), for all its wartime dilapidation, had a faded appeal, especially along the waterfront, where the planters' shuttered town houses loomed behind high oyster shell and mortar walls.

Gentle taunts crept into missionary letters home as the long autumn advanced. "Just think, you poor, freezing wind-pierced mortals! *We* have summer weather," Towne wrote her sisters around the time of the Honey Hill battle. "The fields are gay with white, purple and yellow flowers, and with the red leaves of sumach and other shrubs. Our woods are always green. *You* can't see a leaf. Chill November! I pity you." Looking ahead to her third winter on Saint Helena, she exulted in the consciousness of full health and strength: "I eat like a horse," she wrote, "sleep like a top, do any amount of work, and read nothing!"[38]

The pace of the teachers' lives quickened during the cool months. With the cotton gathered in, groundnuts collected for mash and meal, and yams stored away for the winter, the denizens of the black settlements sought to learn what the Yankee books could teach. By the end of 1864, twenty-five hundred former slaves were enrolled in thirty Sea Island schools.

Lizzie Botume taught letters, counting, and sewing in a new wooden schoolhouse with a piazza, glazed windows, an airtight cast-iron stove, pine benches for the scholars, and, for her, a high desk with a countinghouse stool. The Gullahs called this Yankee wonder the "Hooper Bell School," after the philanthropist friend of Lizzie's who had donated the bell. She insisted on its proper name: the

Whitney School, after the abolitionist family from Belmont, Massachusetts, that helped finance it.

Towne and Murray conducted their school in the Brick Church just off the Saint Helena high road. Towne doubled as consulting physician for the island. When smallpox broke out not long after she arrived at the Oaks, she drew on her half-forgotten homeopathic training to bring such relief as she could to the settlements. Within a few weeks she had the rounds of five plantations. "I have had good luck with my patients," she reported with pride, "and my fame is tremendous."[39] The school flourished, too. By the autumn of 1864 more than two hundred students were enrolled.

She and Ellen introduced the mysteries of the alphabet to islanders of all sizes, sorts, and ages at the Brick Church, a sturdy building,* but crowded and subject to pedagogical gridlock: one group misbehaving riotously while another shouted the lessons and a third puzzled out the hieroglyphics in a tattered book. The teachers, meantime, alternately bawled reproofs and corrected mistakes.

As 1864 drew in, Towne packed for a move to a new schoolhouse, partly for larger quarters, and partly, too, to escape the Brick Church Baptists, who found her cool Unitarianism too rational for their taste. The building would have been finished long ago but for the incompetence (if not ill-will) of the Treasury. The government paymaster was six months in arrears, obliging Towne's contractor to send his workmen away to "literally fish for themselves" in the tidal pools and creeks until the greenback supply began to flow again.

Towne planned to open the new school on the first day of 1865. She managed, just at the last, to cajole a couple of the handier of the missionary men into knocking together a belfry to surmount it. In the Sea Islands, a bell was no mere affectation. The Gullahs cared little for Yankee notions of clockwork time. They measured the day by the position of the sun, the state of the tide, or some other regular natural occurrence, such as "frog peep." Towne counted on the regular tolling of the bell to teach the islanders the lesson of punctuality.[40]

In December 1864, though, the islanders, white and black, were listening for a deeper note on the southwesterly breeze—the trum-

---

*It still stands, sturdy as ever, in a grove of live oaks off U.S. 24.

peting of the guns. "Deserters say Sherman is coming," Harriet Ware whispered on December 4. And a week later: "Savannah is in Sherman's hands. We hope and trust this is no South Carolina rumor."[41]

THE COAST DIVISION KEPT UP a steady pressure on the Charleston & Savannah. Colonel Potter's brigade pushed up the narrow peninsula between Tullifinny Creek and the Coosawhatchie River to within a thousand yards of the railroad. Firing 30-pounder Parrott rifled cannon from a slashing in the pinewoods, Potter's gunners sought to interrupt the running of the trains.

"Our guns now play upon the road and day before yesterday smashed a locomotive which was attempting to pass," reported John Gray, a staff officer with General Foster's headquarters who had accompanied Potter to the front. A young Boston lawyer with limited field experience, Gray doubtless exaggerated the shattering effect of the cannonade. And in fact the disabled locomotive, one shot-up boxcar, and two or three lengths of broken rail were the sum of the damage. Even with fairly constant shelling, traffic continued to pass in both directions.[42]

The Coast Division did, however, cause an anxious several hours for C & S passenger Louis Manigault, who set out from Charleston on December 4 for the family's rice plantation, Gowrie, on Argyle Island in the Savannah River. The panting locomotive dragged the shabby cars southward through the glittering Low Country swamps, past the war-zone hamlets of Pocotaligo and Grahamville, and over the Savannah seven miles below Gowrie.

The Manigaults of Charleston, Huguenot by ancestry, rich, widely traveled, and politically aloof, lived off a comfortable fortune (at least half a million dollars in 1861) built on trade and slaves. Charles Izard Manigault, the patriarch, had married well: Elizabeth Heyward, a daughter of one of the two or three largest slaveholders in America. A hard and canny capitalist, he acquired Gowrie in 1833 and added the adjoining plantation, East Hermitage, in 1849. Other holdings included Marshlands near Charleston (with views of Fort Sumter and the Atlantic beyond), the Silk Hope plantation on the headwaters of the Cooper River, the tall, elegant Parker-Drayton House on Gibbes Street in Charleston, and several rent-producing commercial properties in the city.[43]

Louis Manigault, Charles and Elizabeth's second son, grew up swathed in privilege, with servants to attend him and humor his whims, private tutors, long stretches living, traveling, and studying in France, and two years at Yale. Quitting New Haven in 1849, he set out on a grand tour, following in the track of his father, whose merchant travels in the 1820s had carried him entirely around the world, with extended stops in China, the Philippines, and Chile. Returning home in 1853, Louis took up what he assumed would be his life's work, managing the family's rice holdings on Argyle Island.

A hundred slaves worked the Savannah River plantations. Slave mechanics and carpenters built and operated Gowrie's elaborate system of dikes, ditches, and floodgates. Slave field hands turned over the earth and set the rice plants into the ground. Parties of slave women and children patrolled the fields to drive off the bobolinks (rice birds, the planters called them) that flew over in sky-darkening flocks in the spring and fall. Slave gateminders flooded the fields at intervals to drown grass and weeds and, as the rice plants matured, to keep the top-heavy stalks from falling over. Laboring in the watery, stupefying heat of late summer, slave gangs reaped by hand, using sickles or rice hooks; they stacked the sheaves for threshing; and they ran the steam thresher in Gowrie's handsome three-story millhouse, the largest on the river.[44]

Louis Manigault, thirty-six years old in 1864, was bland of feature, of average height and sturdily built, with thinning hair and a closely trimmed beard; and in a wartime photograph he wears the crabbed, resentful expression of an indulgent man too long denied his accustomed pleasures. He had seen no active service in the war. So far as he was concerned, his younger brothers Gabriel and Alfred, both long-service cavalrymen, had fulfilled the family obligation to the Confederacy.

Alfred, twenty-four, was in Charleston on convalescent leave. Racked with recurrent malaria, he awaited word on his application for a permanent posting there. Gabriel, thirty-one, a subaltern in the Fourth South Carolina Cavalry, had been taken captive at Trevilian Station, Virginia, in June. He reported tolerable conditions at the island prison of Fort Delaware below New Castle, Delaware. Louis had volunteered some months ago for duty as private secretary to Dr. Joseph Jones, a senior Confederate medical officer. Jones set out

The South Carolina planter Louis Manigault, shown in Samuel Stillman Osgood's 1855 portrait. Former slaves broke into the family home and disfigured several Manigault portraits after the war. With squatters taking over his Savannah River plantation in the winter of 1865, Manigault regretted the loss of what he recalled as "that former mutual & pleasing feeling of Master towards slave and vice versa" of antebellum times. (Gibbes Museum of Art/Carolina Art Association)

in September on an inspection tour of military hospitals and prison camps in central Georgia, taking Manigault along as companion and transcriber.

He had seen slaves whipped and shackled and studied the fever-season death lists for Gowrie settlement. He had passed through a north China village in the grip of a cholera epidemic and toured a

Shanghai prison. But nothing in the Savannah bottomlands or the dungeons of the Middle Kingdom had prepared him for his first view of the hospital sheds at Andersonville.

"One can only compare it to a Hades on earth," Manigault wrote his wife, Fannie. The noisome wards of the "so-called hospital" (his phrase), housed in four long lean-to sheds, presented as harrowing a scene as the American Civil War could show. The camp, opened in February 1864, was designed for 10,000 men. With thousands of fresh prisoners taken in Sherman's Atlanta campaign, the population had climbed through 32,000 by late summer. In August alone, 2,992 Federal prisoners died at Andersonville.

"I supposed they would show us where to camp, but nothing of the kind," Samuel Miller, a Pennsylvania-born Indiana cavalryman captured during General George Stoneman's raid to Macon, recalled of his arrival at Andersonville's North Gate. "We walked around that afternoon, looking for some place to squat but found none. So for the first night we slept on the ground in one of the narrow streets, no supper and no breakfast."[45]

Miller finally found something to eat: moldy corn bread, beans infested with black bugs, a strip of ancient bacon—standard Andersonville fare. Scurvy was endemic. Men's gums would swell, their teeth loosen, and their toes rot off. Fecal debris poisoned the main water supply, a shallow, sluggish stream that dried to a trickle in late summer. Prisoners burrowed into the ground like animals for shelter from cold, rain, and blistering sun. Gangs of stronger prisoners preyed on the weak. Thievery, extortion, even murder were common. A man risked death merely for extending an arm across Andersonville's notorious Dead Line.

"Some starving every day," Ohioan Asbery Stephen, a hospital orderly who kept records of the sick, wounded, dead, and dying, noted in August. "From the 1st to the 15th their was 1700 men died in the prison. Myself not so well."[46]

In September, after the fall of Atlanta, the Confederates shipped out several thousand Yankees, some to Millen in north Georgia, others to Savannah and Charleston. Even with the culling, one in every four or five prisoners lay dangerously ill; on average in mid-September a hundred men died every day of disease, malnutrition, and neglect. The overpowering odor of death floated permanently over the camp. Boiling clouds of green flies tormented the living and feasted off the dead. There were, according to Manigault, 9,266 Federal graves in the Andersonville cemetery.[47]

"I am hungry."

The words were a refrain and a lament in the pocket diary of the Indiana soldier Henry Sparks, taken with eleven others near Richmond in January 1864. In late March, the guards marched his party out of Richmond's Belle Isle Prison, bound—so Sparks persuaded himself—for the exchange queue. Instead, after a long, slow, miserable journey by rail, he passed through the North Gate at Andersonville. On August 9, 1864, trooper John Lee died, the seventh of Sparks's arrival group of twelve to perish there.[48]

"Am hungry."

Sparks hoarded his meat ration to barter for life-sustaining vegetables; he once negotiated a trade of a shaving of rancid bacon for a cube of soap. He judged it a fair exchange: a day without nourishment for a chance to wash away the pine smoke that stained his skin black. After a few weeks in camp, Sparks contrived to obtain a coveted appointment as a hospital orderly. He gave it up after a couple of days. "I can't bear to see so much misary here as there is among the sick," he wrote in his diary. Work in the wards robbed him of all appetite for the increased rations that came with the job.[49]

The sheds held two thousand of the weakest cases, "miserable, complaining, dejected living skeletons," Dr. Jones said of them, "crying for medical aid and food."[50] A single medical officer attended the entire camp. A researcher mainly, Jones spent most of his time in the Dead House, performing autopsies, picking apart bowels, brains, and hearts, work that might have saved lives in some theoretical future, but brought no relief to Andersonville's still-breathing corpses.

Prisoners pegged out at such a rate that a volunteer Roman Catholic priest could not meet the demand for the sacrament of the dying. He only managed to get through his day's work by severely editing down the service. Trusties carried out 67 bodies on April 4; 114 on August 14. Surveying the hospital records, Dr. Jones observed that in only a few months the record keepers listed 500 deaths under the heading of *morbi vani*.

"In other words," he explained, "the men died without having received sufficient medical attention for the determination of even the names of the diseases causing death."[51]

On September 17, 1864, while Jones worked up the notes of his inspection tour and Louis Manigault classified and copied them out, 130 prisoners died at Andersonville, a record for one day. "At almost every step Death is busily engaged selecting his victims," Manigault wrote his wife. "Some poor unfortunate is either breathing quietly his last in his wretched tent; or a corpse scantily covered with the Yankee blue-shirt is stretched across your walk, his mouth open, his eyes gazing wildly, hands clinched, and body drawn up." Somebody would turn up eventually to pin an identifying scrap of paper to the victim's vomit-stained shirt. Then a cart would come along and a trusty would jump down, collect the withered body, trundle it through the South Gate, and dump it into a ditch, close-packed with the rest of the day's dead.[52]

"Saw some dreadful scenes and got some raw beef," Asbery Stephen recorded one August evening.

And a month later: "Dreamed of home and baked goose—All vanity."[53]

Were the Confederates criminal, heartless—or merely incompetent and overwhelmed? Civilians in the neighborhood made some effort on the inmates' behalf, though not much. "A good many ladies came to view the prisoners but did not make fun of us," Henry Sparks noted pathetically in his diary. "9 died last night on this side of the camp."[54] Distressing as conditions were, Manigault could hardly fault the Confederacy, still less the camp commandant, Henry Wirz—"the old Captain," the Yankees called him, a dark and frail forty-one-year-old Swiss with a limitless capacity for enduring the suffering of others. It was General Grant, after all, in response to the Confederate refusal to treat Federal black troops as prisoners of war (some were shot on the battlefield; some were returned to their prewar owners; some were put on the auction block and sold into slavery), who suspended the regular exchange cartel.

Grant's policy kept his brother marooned in the Delaware River, Louis reminded himself. As for Gabriel, his views moderated with each passing week. "We are all very much interested in the subject of exchange, & I think that many officers here favor a yielding of the negro question on our part which prevents it," he wrote from prison in September. Richmond refused to compromise. For his part, Louis retreated in the evenings to his tent in the pinewoods upwind of the Dead House and hardened his heart, remembering that, collectively, the Yankees had "clad every one of our families in mourning."[55]

Andersonville delivered the first sharp jolt to Manigault's planter-class equanimity, but only the first. Absent in Macon, Charleston, or Augusta for most of the war, he had left an overseer in charge at Gowrie—William Capers, a distant cousin of his father's. Competent, trustworthy and quick with the whip, Capers managed the rice enterprise profitably and kept Louis, Fannie, and their children *petit* Louis and Josephine supplied with vegetables and pork when hunger began to gnaw at the Confederacy. In Augusta, meantime, wartime shortages and the boundless unreliability of slaves meant drudgery and hot work for Miss Fannie: she baked bread; she made soap; and she took up the mending, too.

Capers supervised a volatile community at Gowrie. Slaves there felt the pull of freedom from Port Royal; talk of escape and even of insurrection agitated the settlements. As early as 1862, in fear of an outbreak, Manigault had driven a coffle of two dozen of the more unruly hands upcountry to Silk Hope, out of range of the Yankee contagion.

Manigault and Capers suspected a carpenter named Jack Savage of stirring up most of the trouble. Illiterate but quick-witted and sly, Savage built and maintained the wooden floodgates and trunks essential to rice farming. Manigault thought so well of his work that he used to show it off to visiting planters. For all his artisan skill, Capers regarded him as lazy, insolent, and incorrigible. Savage lit out for the swamps in February 1862. With other fugitives, he subsisted in that decaying amphibian world for eighteen months before returning of his own accord, half-wild and in rags, but defiant still.[56]

Capers disliked Savage and meant to dominate him; Manigault positively feared him. "He was the only Negro ever in our possession who I considered capable of Murdering me, or burning my dwelling at night," he wrote in the Gowrie plantation book. In the short run, Capers won the battle of wills with Savage. At his insistence, Manigault sold him for $1,800 at auction in Savannah in September 1863.[57]

The overseer did not live to enjoy his triumph for long. Fever laid him low during the summer of 1864 and in October he died. (If he heard of it, Savage surely regarded Capers's end as just, for none of his own four children had survived Gowrie's deadly summers to live to adulthood.) So Manigault was on his way down to Argyle Island early in December to install Capers's successor.

He reached Gowrie without incident, though the army held up the cars at Grahamville for a couple of hours so troops could be rushed up the line to meet another Yankee lunge at the Charleston & Savannah. He knew of Sherman's approach; his Savannah acquaintances could talk of little else when he passed through late on Sunday the fourth. All the same, he went about his business at Gowrie as if nothing would ever change on the place.

"The Negroes all looked well, and seemed pleased to see me," Manigault wrote serenely in the plantation journal. The 1863 and 1864 rice harvests had been good in the circumstances—around ten thousand bushels each year. With a little luck, things might turn out favorably yet for 1865. Manigault struck an agreement with a new overseer, J. W. Bandy. He brought the journal up to date. And he supervised the unpacking of his private library, shipped downriver from Augusta for safekeeping at Gowrie.[58]

Then, all of a sudden, as though they had dropped out of the hazy late autumn sky, Sherman's vedettes appeared in the neighborhood. On the sixth, leading elements of the Federal Fourteenth Corps reached Sister's Ferry on the Savannah. Within a day or so Manigault could distinctly hear picket firing away to the north.

He boarded the cars for the return to Charleston on December 8. The army again halted the train near Grahamville. The Confederates were dropping back to the railroad under enemy pressure; Manigault here saw infantry in line of battle for the first time. "Minié Rifle balls were falling on the track, & the enemy only 3/4 of a mile from us," he wrote. "We were for a time in great danger of being captured. Wounded men, fresh from the battle field, were brought to the Pocotaligo Depot, whilst we took on the Cars the Bodies of several who had been killed."[59] Shaken but untouched, he reached Charleston that night and continued on early the next morning to Marshlands, the family country seat seven miles out of town.

"At breakfast," he noted complacently, "my Father & Alfred thought it very wise in my having returned before being cut off & congratulated me on my escape."[60]

WHILE POTTER'S FIELD FORCE HARASSED the fare-paying passengers of the Charleston & Savannah, the Fifty-fifth Massachusetts marked time in the rearward defenses at Boyd's Neck. Word reached Charley Fox there on December 9 that one of his officers, Lieutenant Edwin Hill, on temporary loan to Potter, had been killed in the skirmishing south of the railroad: yet another casualty for the Fifty-fifth on this ill-omened expedition.

Honey Hill had come to obsess Fox. Something had gone obscurely wrong for him there. "This is a warm, pleasant, beautiful day, like a day in New England in early June, all around being apparently cheerful and happy," he mused in a letter to Mary at home in Dorchester. "One would scarcely imagine the fearful scenes of Wednesday were possible, or that the men would be ready to re-enact them."[61] Fox had never given anyone cause to doubt his steadiness under fire—until now, for Major William Nutt had begun to wonder aloud where the colonel had strayed the afternoon of November 30, and for what purpose.

Fox could barely bring himself to put the insinuation into words. Nutt accused him of skulking; that was how he interpreted Fox's truant stroll into the pines with the leading companies of the Fifty-fifth. Fox had missed the charge up the causeway in consequence. As for Nutt, he'd handled himself well in the battle, as Colonel Hartwell acknowledged—he even had shot a horse out from under him.

Nutt spoke openly and mockingly of the incident, but made no move to file a formal charge. In denying Fox a venue for a defense and judgment he intensified his discomfort, a lurking embarrassment he could not always hide behind the dark coil of his flowing beard. Fox tried, not very convincingly, to make light of it.

"I don't pretend to any great degree of courage, but certainly after the battles of Virginia I should not be apt to run away from Honey Hill," he wrote Mary.[62]

Not a popular officer, Fox was yet a conscientious one, famous for his punctilio. He banned gambling in camp on Sundays. He enforced a no-fires-on-picket order to the letter on quiet Folly Island, prohibiting even tent candles. He made "such a pow-wow," one of his officers complained, "that one would really think we held an entrenched camp in the midst of the rebels and that they were intent on devouring us."[63] In fairness, Fox asked no more of others than of himself. At Boyd's Landing he slept with the troops under canvas in a rain-sodden field when he might easily have claimed a few feet of dry floor in an abandoned house nearby; nor would his conscience allow him to accept the navy's standing offer of a hot bath—one of the manifold advantages of steam—aboard one of the gunboats.

Fox's relations with James Trotter and the other black petty officers were no easier. Trotter had made his way from Cincinnati to Boston early in 1863 to enlist in the Fifty-fifth Massachusetts. Articulate and astute (he taught school in Ohio before the war), with a highly developed grasp of social circumstance, Trotter acted as a mentor to the junior noncommissioned officers. He pushed them to master drill, to carry out routine military tasks to perfection, to attend the regimental evening school sessions that taught reading and writing— to *force* the officers to advance them. Many of the men who came into the Fifty-fifth had barely been able to make their mark. Alonzo Boon had been one such.

"I spoke to him of the importance of learning, telling him that I would gladly help him, and that when he could read I would recommend him for Sergt.," Trotter wrote after Boon's death in action at Morris Island. "Right manfully he took hold, and before he died he had acted as orderly Sergt., and could make out all the papers and [had] written three letters home."[64]

Alfred Hartwell, Charley Fox's predecessor in command of the Fifty-fifth, had promoted Trotter to acting lieutenant and recommended him for the permanent rank. Governor Andrew drafted commissioning papers for Trotter and two other sergeants. When Hartwell moved up to command the brigade, Trotter expected Fox to follow through on the matter. He did not. Fox's views were equivocal, and the NCOs knew it.

Scouting Andrew's wishes, General Foster, the department commander, refused to discharge the sergeants so they could return as second lieutenants. Foster claimed that no law authorized the commissioning of black officers. "This is a model way to promote military discipline and efficiency," Trotter wrote acidly. "They differ with Napoleon. He always secured the perfect good behavior of his soldiers by promoting the deserving."[65] Fox made no effort to argue Foster around. Trotter and the others had been resentful ever since.

"An officer told me that it was 'too soon,' that time should be granted white officers to *get rid of their prejudices*," Trotter wrote Edward Kinsley in Boston. "So that a white Lieutenant would not refuse to sleep in a tent with a colored one. Of course he *supposed* that an objection of this kind would be made always by the white Lieut., and that educated decent colored officers would never object to sleeping with the former whatever might be his character. Yes, there is really more turning up the noise on account of the commissions *in our very midst* than elsewhere; *and no other reason is given except Color*."[66]

Fox's tactless handling of the issue added fuel to the petty officers' grievance. When a newly commissioned white officer turned up at the Fifty-fifth's camp, Fox went out of his way to send for Trotter and explain that he had known nothing about the appointment. He failed to persuade him.

"How else could it have been done? *Col. Fox dissented with Col. Hartwell when he recommended colored men for commissions*."[67]

There matters stood. As it happened, Foster eventually agreed to approve commissions for men of "ability, manners & education" on application from a regimental commander *if* the other regimental officers endorsed the arrangement.[68] Fox did not request the appointment of Trotter or anyone else. Even if he had, most of the white officers of the Fifty-fifth would have objected; several would have resigned on the spot.

Fox knew that the sergeants viewed him as an obstacle. He regretted that. All the same, he took pride in his record. He had, for example, once ordered a white soldier in arrest for addressing one of his men as "nigger," an insult so common many officers would simply have let it pass. Fox emphasized the point by sending the offender to the provost under an armed escort of blacks. The African Americans of the Fifty-fifth saluted him for it. "A few cases like this will teach these fellows to attend to their own business," Sergeant Richard White thought—naively, as time would show.[69]

Moody, saturnine, and intermittently depressed, Fox cut a forlorn figure even in palmy times. Honey Hill had multiplied his troubles.

Had he funked it there? Nutt's sneering charge left him uneasy in his skin. As it happened, though, events were soon to chase away his private phantoms.

The roll of cannon fire could be heard from the direction of Savannah all through the morning of December 11—Sherman's guns, Fox reckoned. A day later, one of Sherman's scouts made contact with Union warships in Ossabaw Sound. The navy obligingly ferried the ranger around to Hilton Head. Reliable witnesses reported actually sighting him there: incontestable evidence that the western army had materialized out of the Georgia barrens at last.[70]

# 2

# The Laws of War

SHERMAN'S COLUMNS WERE SUBSISTING on rice now. The fat Georgia country lay in the army's blackened wake, and these first days of December were the leanest of the march. But with gnawing hunger came a heady anticipation of victory, plunder, resupply, and mail as the van pushed up to Savannah and an opening to the world beyond the pinewoods and blackwater swamps.

"All right so far," Captain John Fox of the Second Massachusetts wrote home. "The overland campaign has been a success. I am well though rough and dirty. No casualties in the 'Old Second.' We can hear the bells ring in the city."[1]

The veteran Second Massachusetts, Second Brigade, First Division, Twentieth Corps of the Army of Georgia, had cleared Atlanta on the morning of November 16, 1864, just as the fires that consumed the city's core were dying out. The last warehouses and foundries had been battered down the day before, railroad depots and roundhouses wrecked, lines torn up, tinder ignited. Fox and the others sat up late watching the spectacle from the roof of their billet. The glare lit up the country for miles around; great gouts of flame shot high into the air and buildings collapsed with a hiss, sending red, orange, and yellow sparks skyward in pulsing clouds. In a bizarre touch—"like fiddling over the burning of Rome," thought the regiment's second in command, Lieutenant Colonel Charles Morse—the band of the Thirty-third Massachusetts (said to be the army's best, and Sherman's favorite) struck up outside headquarters, diverting the commanding general with selections from *Il Trovatore*.

It had been an astonishing March to the Sea, unrolling without mishap or delay. Advancing in two wings, the Twentieth and Fourteenth corps under Major General Henry Slocum on the left, the Seventeenth and Fifteenth corps under Major General Oliver Otis Howard on the right, Sherman's army met scant resistance and suffered few casualties. The Confederate commander, Lieutenant General William Hardee, showed himself a paltry opponent. "In all our marching through Georgia he has not forced me to use anything but a skirmish line," Sherman reported—a "puerile" effort in his view.[2]

The Second Massachusetts guarded the Fourteenth Corps trains for the first week of the march, then caught up to its own corps near Milledgeville, the Georgia capital. Food and drink were abundant in the early stages. Morse, twenty-five years old and a veteran of Cedar Mountain, Antietam, and Gettysburg, celebrated Thanksgiving fifteen miles out of Milledgeville with "fat turkeys, sweet potatoes, honey and various other luxuries, and drank to the memory of the day in some old applejack of the country." With fresh fowl and pork available from every wayside farm, the men affected to despise the usual campaign staple—tough, flayed fresh beef from the droves that trailed the columns.[3]

From the outset, Sherman suspended the ordinary rules of campaigning. "This is probably the most gigantic pleasure excursion ever planned," reckoned Captain Charles Wills of the 103rd Illinois of Howard's wing. "It already beats anything I ever saw soldiering, and promises to prove much richer yet."[4] Foragers despoiled the local people, stealing anything they could lay hands on: food, clothing, livestock, house pets, musical instruments, furnishings, silver plate, jewelry. The main columns broke up miles of railroad track. Outriders torched barns, mills, cotton gins, and, sometimes, dwellings. A charred streak thirty miles wide marked the army's passage.

The bummers' thievish habits and promiscuous use of the lucifer match left some of Sherman's officers queasy. "At least I am glad to remember that I have not only not abused nor insulted a single person," Major Henry Hitchcock told himself, "but have repeatedly stopped the depredations of soldiers." Hitchcock saw at once that no

Lieutenant Colonel Charles Morse, Second Massachusetts Infantry, in a steely mood. The war had
given Morse some of the most powerful friendships
of his life—and then taken them away. But nearly
four years of hard soldiering only left him more
determined to finish the job. "I had rather campaign till I am fifty years old than make any terms
with rebels while they bear arms," he wrote home
at the outset of the Carolinas campaign. (Massachusetts Historical Society)

such scruples governed Sherman. On the contrary, he expressed frank
admiration for the arsonists' work, boasting later that he could scan
the horizon in any direction and see smoke rolling up as from some
great bonfire.[5]

A lawyer by trade and a prewar acquaintance of Sherman's, Hitchcock joined the general's staff around the time of the fall of Atlanta
in early September—a triumph of incalculable importance, coming as
it did after a depressing summer of stalemate in the East, the dubi-
ous high point of which had been the second-line commander Lew

Wallace's stand against the Confederate raider Jubal Early near Washington. A military innocent even by the amateur standards of the Civil War, Hitchcock hardened himself gradually to the casual cruelties to be encountered almost every day of the march. All the same, certain scenes shamed him still: as when, for instance, Sherman ordered rebel prisoners to the front as human shields.

The commanding general evidently held Confederates collectively responsible for the wounding of a cavalry lieutenant in Howard's van. He had trod on a shell Confederate sappers left buried in the road, touching off an explosion that sheared off part of his leg. Coldly furious at what he regarded as an act of barbarism—akin, say, to poisoning a well—Sherman outfitted the prisoners with picks and spades and sent them on ahead of the light forces. "They begged hard," Sherman recalled, "but I reiterated the order, and could hardly help laughing at their stepping so gingerly on the road." Hitchcock approached the wounded cavalryman along the verge, lying pale, silent, and in shock, and covered up to his chin with a thick blanket. A case could be made, he decided tentatively, for Sherman's apparent breach of the laws of war. The prisoner detail unearthed seven buried torpedoes without further accident.[6]

Disturbing in a different way were the streams of refugees that trailed the army, thousands of tattered, half-starved fleeing slaves. Curiosity overcoming fear, groups of women and children collected in front of their shanties as the dusty columns passed, watching in silence.

"Suddenly one, seized with a desire for her freedom, would rush in, bundle up the bedding, clap it on her head and trudge off by our side, leading by the hand some young child toddling along," Lieutenant Samuel Storrow of the Second Massachusetts wrote home. "How they managed to keep up with us I can't imagine, but they did."[7]

If Storrow felt a helpless pity for the refugees, the abandoned prison compound at Millen filled him with sorrow and rage. He met none of the living there; only the broken-down remains of rough shelters leaning into the greasy red clay and unmarked, untended graves, nearly a thousand of them.

Henry Sparks, the Indiana cavalryman transferred to Millen from Andersonville in mid-October, had found the camp spacious by comparison, though rations and other amenities were no more plentiful.

Dosing himself with sweet gum tea, a sovereign remedy for bowel complaints, Sparks reported his health as good in the circumstances. Not so for most of the others.

"Thirteen thousand brave boys want help," he scrawled in his pocket diary a few days before the Twentieth Corps set out from Atlanta, "and many more will die if they are not removed before cold weather."[8]

The Confederates had hastily cleared Millen on Sherman's approach. Poking around the empty huts, Storrow kicked at animal bones so clean they gleamed. He stumbled over two putrefying corpses; with his sword, he scooped out a shallow grave for them. Just twenty-one years old, with the prospect of a bright future should he survive the war, Storrow told himself he'd rather be left to rot on the battlefield than endure a living death in such a place.[9]

Sherman's columns tramped on beyond the fertile country into the flat, sandy, and claustrophobic near-wilderness of the pinelands. Hardee's overmatched corps remained docile. "We have not heard a rebel gun since the 22nd of last month," Charles Wills remarked on December 1. The vanguard reached the swamps girdling Savannah on the tenth and the army went into line of battle that day for the first time during the campaign—a precaution merely, for Sherman had no intention of attacking, not yet, anyway.

"General will not butt his army against breastworks; 'flanking' is better," remarked Hitchcock, still trying out the newly learned jargon of war.[10]

By contrast, calamity simplified General Hardee's task. He concentrated everything on the built-up approaches through the drowned lands. "They really only had to hold the roads, the same in a less degree as in the defense of Boston," Charley Morse observed, thinking of home; "it would only be necessary at first to have batteries on the Milldam, Cambridge &c." Sherman saw that, too. He ordered the columns to close up and invest the city.[11]

The Confederate lines, curving north to south from the Savannah around to the Little Ogeechee River, looked formidable, though in fact they were but lightly held. In any case Sherman felt less urgency to wreck or capture Hardee's little army of nine thousand and get possession of Savannah than to establish contact with the navy and open a seaborne supply line for his sixty thousand men, very hungry now, and starved for news of home.

Hardee, too, faced famine during these first days of December. Along with the troops, there were twenty thousand civilians in Savannah to victual. The Second Massachusetts struck the Charleston & Savannah north of the city, tore up track, and burned the long wooden trestle striding over the swamps, severing Hardee's only all-weather supply line and, incidentally, completing General Hatch's fumbled assignment of two weeks before. Only a single route remained open to the Confederates, an old wagon road winding northward from the Carolina bank. Hardee detailed slave labor gangs to build a makeshift pontoon bridge so he could bring up rations and, when the time came, withdraw from the city. His orders, peremptory ones from the department commander, General P. G. T. Beauregard, were to save the garrison at all hazards.[12]

Railroad wrecking stoked the appetite. The Second Massachusetts foragers shook grain out of stacked rice straw and raided plantation storehouses for threshed and polished rice. "We are hoping in time to get some oysters," John Fox wrote wistfully to his sister Fairy. Sam Storrow, still little more than a boy and with the appetite of a starveling wolf, dreamed of meals from a sumptuous past. "We had nothing for breakfast and were in a fair way to have it cold for dinner and minced for supper," he wrote home in his neat, precise, copybook hand. By now the army's detestable cask beef, so encrusted with salt it scalded the tongue, seemed like a luxury to him.[13]

This was Storrow's second tour as a soldier. The youngest son of the renowned engineer Charles Storer Storrow, the builder of the new industrial city of Lawrence, Massachusetts,* he had dropped out of Harvard in September 1862 to follow his older brother into the nine-month Forty-fourth Massachusetts. With John Pope's army routed along Bull Run and Robert E. Lee across the Potomac in Maryland, Storrow acted on impulse and against his family's wishes.

He had only just reached home from Fayal in the Azores, where he had gone in the spring to recover from a bout of eye trouble. The affliction kept him from his college work, but not from the newspapers. Storrow left Fayal in August full of news of the Seven Days' battles and expected to hear of the fall of Richmond when he landed in

---

*The elder Storrow designed the famous Merrimack River Dam, textile mills, and boardinghouses—and became Lawrence's first mayor, in 1853.

Boston. Instead, the harbor pilot reported a calamity: rebels threatening Washington, thousands of young men rushing to its defense. He went back to Harvard as his father wished, though not for long.

"What is the worth of this man's life or that man's education, if this great and glorious fabric of our Union is to be shattered to pieces?" he wrote his father.[14]

So Charles Storrow came home from an engineering commission in Europe in October to find his son on the way to New Bern, North Carolina, with the Forty-fourth. It proved a dull post, its chief amusement a camp boy who could sing and whistle at the same time. Storrow felt no regret when the regiment passed out of existence in June 1863. Returning to Harvard, he was restless as before, though determined this time to skip a repeat experience of the "drudgery and servility" of private soldiering.

Several acquaintances from the defunct Forty-fourth had moved into the new black regiments, but Storrow passed up the offer of a lieutenancy in the Fifty-fourth Massachusetts. Edward Bartlett, who had served in the ranks with him, accepted a second lieutenant's commission in the Fifth Massachusetts Cavalry. In the infantry regiments, advancement could be swift. Alfred Hartwell, only twenty-eight years old, rose from beginnings as a lieutenant in the Forty-fourth to captain in the Fifty-fourth to major, lieutenant colonel, and colonel in the Fifty-fifth. Yet Storrow hesitated. The chance of a posting to the Second Massachusetts came his way during the summer of 1864. He accepted at once.[15]

Storrow and John Fox, with shoals of Boston and Cambridge connections in common, were friends from the start. "Storrow (our new lieutenant) promises well," Fox noted a few days after the new officer's arrival. Storrow appreciated the "gentlemanly" air and unhurried competence of Fox and the others. "Everything is done in regular army style," he saw, in contrast to the slipshod Forty-fourth. Taking charge of Company D, Storrow adapted easily to the ways of Sherman's army: before leaving Atlanta, he assigned the company's most incorrigible thieves to the foraging detail.[16]

Away to the south, Howard's Army of the Tennessee advanced along the right bank of the Ogeechee River toward a rendezvous with the navy. Major Thomas Osborn, Howard's chief of artillery, sent up rockets and high-angled shells through the long December nights to alert the inshore squadron. When the bluejackets failed to respond,

Howard sent his best scout downriver in a dugout canoe to seek them out. Meantime, he completed preparations for a December 13 assault on the vulnerable landward side of Fort McAllister at the broad mouth of the Ogeechee, the capture of which would open the river to the transports.

A thirty-four-year-old evangelical Maine Yankee, a West Pointer with a high-pitched voice and a curious set of nervous, twitchy mannerisms, Howard had prospered after an accident-prone early war career. He lost his right arm at Fair Oaks on the Virginia Peninsula in 1862.* A year later, he experienced two mortifying failures commanding the Eleventh Corps of the Army of the Potomac: at Chancellorsville, where Stonewall Jackson's famous flank attack shattered his corps, and at Gettysburg, where troops under Jackson's successor, Richard Ewell, drove it helter-skelter through the town. Taking the Eleventh Corps west in the autumn of 1863, Howard revived his career under Sherman, who in due course rewarded him with promotion to command of the Army of the Tennessee.

"Howard is a Christian, elegant gentleman, and conscientious soldier," Sherman wrote. "In him I made no mistake."[17] He was known in the army as "Christian" Howard, or alternately as America's Havelock, after Sir Henry Havelock, the ferociously fundamentalist British hero of the Indian Mutiny of 1857. "Whatever a man's professional calling, he ought to aim evangelically at doing good," Havelock had said. America's Havelock shared the aim.

Nobody ever accused Sherman of making a fetish of elegance. He was tall and lean, wheezy with asthma and too many cigars, subject to depressive fits, badly shaved, slovenly in his dusty field coat, mildewed collars, and mud-encrusted trousers. His parched features were in constant motion. He talked incessantly, and seemed to know everything. Ordinary soldiers regarded him as virtually infallible. ("They think I know every road and bypath in Georgia," he once said.) When a long streamer of Spanish moss hanging from a mulberry

---

*In a rare flash of wit, Howard once suggested to General Philip Kearny, who had lost his left arm in the Mexican War, that they buy gloves together in the future. But Kearny was killed in action in September 1862.

Union Major General Oliver Otis Howard, the steady, capable commander of Sherman's right wing in the March to the Sea and the Carolinas campaign. A deeply religious nature and genuine humanitarian impulses made "Christian" Howard something of an oddity for a professional soldier. "I expect during my life to have a good deal to do with the negroes," he wrote his wife in April 1865. A few weeks later, War Secretary Edwin Stanton appointed him commissioner of the Freedmen's Bureau. (Library of Congress)

tree caught Henry Hitchcock's eye, he remarked offhand that he'd always associated it exclusively with live oaks. Sherman launched into a dissertation on *Tillandsia usneoides*, that bromeliad relative of the pineapple also known as long-beard.

"General says it is found on all kinds of trees in low and swampy districts," Hitchcock recorded in his diary, only too willing to accept correction.[18]

Sherman and Howard watched the Fort McAllister attack develop from the roof of a rice mill. Howard studied the blue figures maneuvering in the distance, fidgety himself but a picture of composure next to Sherman. The commanding general paced back and forth, smoking compulsively, spilling ash all down his subfusc front, absently rubbing his unruly tangle of russet hair so that it stood up like the crest of some exotic swamp bird. His choler mounted as the abbreviated afternoon of December 13 drew in. Howard tried to distract him by showing off the powerful telescope the signalers were using to scan to seaward for the navy. This soothed his ragged nerves for the moment. Sherman's cruel streak ran deep, as the Confederate prisoners on the Savannah road could testify, but he did not throw away soldiers' lives. He dreaded this frontal assault.

The attacking troops, a Fifteenth Corps division under William B. Hazen, fell behind schedule, delayed in the bogs. When Hazen turned up at last, the sun only a handsbreadth above the horizon, he used up most of the remaining daylight reconnoitering, throwing out skirmishers, sending parties forward to disarm torpedoes sown in the approaches, and carrying out other tactical evolutions he evidently regarded as important in the circumstances. The Confederates had cleared the timber from the environs of the fort and the works— abatis, ditch, and gun muzzles glinting in the hard, raking light of the sinking sun—were visible from the mill roof in all their intimidating detail. Just as Hazen signaled the advance, Howard caught sight of the stack of a steamer in the offing. Presently it stood in close enough for an exchange.

"Who are you?" the navy queried.

"General Sherman."

"Is Fort McAllister taken?"

"Not yet, but it will be in a minute."[19]

Hazen's 1,500 infantry stormed McAllister at dusk, advancing in a single line thinned out to reduce casualties. The first wave touched off a half-dozen torpedoes, powerful detonations that rained dabs of bloody flesh on the sedge. The advance swept on, over the abatis, down into the ditch, and up the steep far side. The leading troops vaulted the parapets. "They were blue with our men," Sherman remembered, "and shouted so that we actually heard them, or thought that we did." Hazen's losses added up to around 130 killed and wounded, most of them from torpedoes.[20]

Sherman fairly vibrated with excitement. Wrote Hitchcock, "General says he never wants anything done better!"[21] The little steamer identified herself as the naval tender *Dandelion*. Sherman commandeered a skiff and a crew to row him over to the captured fort, then detailed fresh oarsmen to pull him down the moonlit Ogeechee to the tender. He wrote steadily until midnight in *Dandelion*'s close cabin, announcing in a dispatch to Henry Halleck, the army chief of staff in Washington, his advent in the Low Country, Hazen's capture of Fort McAllister, and his preparations for the siege of Savannah.

"The army is in splendid order, and equal to anything," Sherman wound up. "I regard Savannah as already gained."[22]

The news flashed out to an anxious North. "We were very happy to see your name in the papers of Thursday last," Lizzie Howard wrote her husband from Maine. It was her first word of him since Atlanta. She had decided to shut down the Augusta house and winter over with his mother in Leeds, she went on; she was well and the children, Grace, Guy, Charlie, and Jamie, were flourishing, though diphtheria had broken out in a neighboring town, cause for high alarm. Grace was a great help around the house. Even little Jamie had learned to make himself useful. He set out the napkins and cutlery at mealtimes.

"You will come and see us all before spring, won't you?" Lizzie asked him.[23]

Renewal of contacts restored the army's sense of solidity. "Try to imagine how entirely cut off we have been," Hitchcock wrote his wife the night of the Fort McAllister assault. "It was the oddest feeling in the world to see the New York papers again," he went on a couple of days later; "one felt as if he had been buried alive and resurrected. I had a real fellow feeling for Rip Van Winkle." Sherman scanned the papers, too, and discovered that his infant son Charley, six months old, had died in South Bend, Indiana, on December 4. Sherman had never seen him.[24]

The Second Massachusetts awaited the opening of the cracker line in camp on Argyle Island. The regiment crossed in flatboats on December 15 to guard the rice mill at Gowrie plantation there. The swift current swept the unwieldy boats along, carrying Charley Morse's downstream from the landing where it grounded uncomfortably within range of a Confederate battery on the South Carolina bank. Drawing picket duty, Sam Storrow followed later, after a night fog came drifting up the valley. It was ten o'clock before he reached camp, soaked to the skin and bone-tired.

Details of the Third Wisconsin ran the Gowrie mill, enlisting Louis Manigault's slaves—freedmen now, for the time being anyhow—to process rice for the army. When J. W. Bandy, Cousin Capers's successor as overseer, protested, the Wisconsin soldiers sent him into the mill to pound rice alongside the former slaves. The rebel battery opened fire during the forenoon of Friday the sixteenth, interrupting the threshing operation, scattering troops and laborers, and setting one of the storehouses alight. A gunboat opened up from the lower end of Argyle Island, catching Gowrie in a cross fire. Storrow led a party of skirmishers down to the river's edge. Dropping down into the mud, they began peppering away at the enemy gunners on the far bank.

In his first experience of combat, a skirmish in North Carolina in '62, he had felt none of the shriveling of the cods the veterans had warned him to expect. He lay with the others in a pine brake just off the road, looking up toward the shredded tops of the trees. A Confederate battery kept up a steady fire. There was a lot of falling wreckage from the pines. A shell sailed past with the sound of tearing cloth. Someone shouted an order and he rushed forward. He tripped a few yards along and fell over a crumpled, still-warm form. The ball had entered the boy's left eye and exited the back of the skull. As he regained his feet a powerful urge to bolt swept over him. But he found himself rooted to the spot, paralyzed. After a moment the feeling returned to his legs. By then, though, the impulse to run had passed.[25]

Stalking the rebel battery on the Savannah Back River was hot, damp, dangerous work. Alligators loitered in the shallows. Venomous snakes slithered in the undergrowth. Storrow stripped off his coat, then his waistcoat. Fire from the battery slackened, picked up again. "Down, down!" he called, teeth flashing white in his sunburned face.

A shell skimmed through the mud and sliced the top off the head of one of his skirmishers, killing him instantly.

The enemy gunners let up in midafternoon and the threshing resumed. The rest of the brigade crossed to Argyle Island Friday evening. The first of the mails arrived the next day, the seventeenth. They brought John Fox word of the grave illness of his uncle William. The report affected him strangely, even set against all the bitter experience of loss crowded into these last three of his thirty years: Harvard classmates; men known briefly, then buried; his brother Tom. At first it had seemed a small thing: a ball in the foot. "You're a devilish lucky dog," he wrote Tom a couple of weeks after Gettysburg. "You've no idea what you have escaped in the way of work since the fight." News of Tom's death reached him at the end of July. Weakened from a winter camp bout with malaria, Tom had simply refused to heal.

"War is almost the only thing that interests me now," John wrote their father fiercely.[26]

The impact of this distant crisis briefly unlocked his war-numbed emotions. "Death in all forms has been a matter of everyday occurrence with me in the Army," he reflected in a letter home, "and yet I have had a constant feeling that those left in peace were exempt from danger and that the end of this war would find at least the old *home* circle unchanged except, perhaps, by the addition of a few young lives and a few gray hairs." Now it looked as though the familiar circle would soon be broken.[27]

The full brigade rafted over from Argyle Island to the South Carolina bank at dawn on Monday the nineteenth, sloshing through the rice swamps toward the Confederate battery. The main column deployed on a series of mounds each rising a few feet above the bog. Thin lines of skirmishers strung out along the dikes connected one mound with the next.

The opposing forces glared at each other across the rice stubble for the next thirty-six hours, exchanging volleys and rounds of cannon fire to no great effect. Charley Morse looked for more Twentieth Corps infantry to cross and join troops from Foster's command moving down from Port Royal to cut off Hardee's line of retreat. He learned early on the twenty-first that Savannah had fallen without a fight. Twenty-four hours later the Second Massachusetts lay in a comfortable camp on the river two miles above the city, on sandy ground in a grove of live oaks.

As at Millen, the liberating Federals arrived a few days too late for war prisoner Henry Sparks. This time, though, luck was with him. Shipped to Savannah ahead of Sherman, he coughed his way onto a sick list and, with a $10 bribe of a guard, into an exchange of invalid prisoners.

"Joy to tell," he wrote in his diary, "I am paroled and on my way to Yankee Land."[28]

A brass band greeted repatriated prisoners on the quay at Annapolis. They were "little livid brown, ash-streak'd, monkey looking dwarfs," thought the poet/newspaper correspondent Walt Whitman, "with a horrible look in their eyes and skinny lips." Indiana congressman George Julian examined a group of returning POWs there for the Joint Committee on the Conduct of the War. "I never before had been so touched by any spectacle of human suffering," Julian wrote in retrospect. "They were in the last stages of life, and could only answer our questions in whispers." They were, he saw with a shudder, hardly more than living skeletons.[29]

The War Department gave Sergeant Sparks two months' back pay, $48, and a furlough home to the Ohio River village of Rising Sun, Indiana. News of Savannah's capture reached him there just before Christmas.

HARDEE WENT AWAY IN THE NIGHT, over the slave-built bridge with a thick layer of straw on the deck to muffle the sound of his retreat. The first units pulled out at dusk just as the fog rolled in. The wind rose later to a noisy near-gale, shredding the fog but deafening Sherman's pickets. Around midnight, though, they detected movement across the pontoons. Skirmishers probed the outworks, found them deserted, and pushed on toward the city. The mayor of Savannah met John Geary, one of Sherman's division commanders, on the outskirts at half past four and surrendered the place. By sunrise the national colors were floating over the Cotton Exchange and the Custom House.

"Savannah is ours, and fairly won," Sherman wired President Lincoln.[30]

So ended the March to the Sea and the Siege of Savannah. Did Sherman let Hardee go? Some of his officers thought so. "Gen. Sherman left open one way of escape," Otis Howard's brother Charles, who served on his staff, wrote home. "We are sorry he did so but still it is all for the best. Probably it saved life in as much as he would have assaulted the city in a day or two." Perhaps; though what if the army should meet Hardee's corps elsewhere, later?[31]

Not a few veterans wondered whether an ungrateful North would sell Sherman's achievement short, so effortless had it seemed. "I hope you people have not begun to grumble because we have not taken Macon and Augusta and have not captured all Hardee's army at Savannah," Charley Morse wrote his brother Robert in Boston.[32] In a month, he reminded him, the army had marched three hundred miles through the rebel heartland, wrecked two hundred miles of railroad, consumed or destroyed essential stores and industrial capacity, and knocked the Confederacy's richest state out of the war.

Rations were soon arriving in quantity. The army set about the ritual of refitting for the next campaign. Morse wrote Robert for a parcel of paper collars; notepaper, envelopes, and stamps; a pair of good top boots; "a box of something good to eat adding a dozen bottles of nice liquor and a gallon or two of good sherry wine"; two hundred cigars; a hairbrush and a couple of toothbrushes; and a dozen pairs of white gloves. He asked, too, for a detailed map of Spain, so he could follow Wellington's movements as narrated in his current reading, Napier's *History of the War in the Peninsula*.[33]

Morse judged Savannah with its fine houses, ornamental gardens (mostly gone by, except for late roses and red-blooming japonica), and stately files of live oak a "very pretty old fashioned city." Most of the staff officers were quartered in the Pulaski House, a famous hostelry gone to seed after four years of war. Coverlets were frayed, bed linens stained, dishes chipped, forks missing—none of it replaceable with Savannah's port blocked up. The proprietor, a one-legged Vermonter, avidly sought the army's custom at first; his interest cooled when Sherman explained that his officers were not in the habit of paying board. The Pulaski lost most of the local trade, for the city's leading citizens sheered off the hotel bar out of a disinclination to drink with the Yankees there. "They regard us just as the Romans did the Goths and the parallel is not unjust," Sherman remarked. Morse found the inhabitants to be "intensely rebel" behind their outward mask of resigned acceptance.[34]

Naturalized Northerners were no more reconciled than the natives. Captain Daniel Oakey of the Second Massachusetts called on two uncles, an aunt, and several cousins in Savannah, all Boston-born.

"He found them the bitterest kind of Secesh," Morse reported. To the retreating Confederates, though, Savannahians seemed only too eager to truckle to the invaders. "A gentleman who came from Sav'h. the night after the evacuation tells us the streets were filled with Yankee flags," one of Hardee's division commanders, Major General Lafayette McLaws, wrote his wife Emily, herself hard on the run from Sherman. "What do you think of the submission meeting in Savannah," Emma Manigault asked her brother Louis, wondering whether any of the numerous Manigault connections there had attended, or whether long lines were forming outside the provost office where contrite ex-rebels could swear the loyalty oath.[35]

The first Northern jobbers turned up in Savannah within a few days of the surrender. Working their army connections, if they had any, they schemed to get their hands on the twenty-five thousand bales of cotton stored in Savannah's riverfront warehouses. A merchant from Hallowell, Maine, approached Howard about business opportunities, reminding him that they had been boys at school together. Another Maine acquaintance wrote on behalf of his brother, a New York merchant, patriotic, loyal, and withal "a professed follower of our Lord and Savior Jesus Christ"—the strongest possible recommendation in Howard's view. He was incorruptible even so.[36]

For the most part, victor and vanquished behaved with propriety. Regimental officers dropped the easygoing ways of the march and ran taut camps. "This living on the country and burning and pillaging gets troops in a bad way," John Fox wrote his sister Fairy, "and makes a great deal of work to bring back the old discipline." Savannah fell quiet after evacuation night, when civilian mobs broke into stores and warehouses for grain and other goods. "There are some misdeeds committed," Howard conceded, "but probably as few if not fewer than in the days of the dirk and the bowie knife."[37] In one of his first acts, Sherman ordered the distribution of army rations to the needy. Northern benevolent societies floated aid schemes for Savannahians black and white. No less a personage than Edward Everett, who had preceded Lincoln at the Gettysburg cemetery dedication with a two-hour oration thirteen months before, appealed to a gathering at Faneuil Hall in Boston to gin up for war-blighted Southerners returning to the Union.*

---

*One of his last appearances; he died on January 15, 1865.

Sherman advised the local people to take the oath and return to work. Schools, shops, and churches reopened within a day or two of the surrender. The city gave off a rather spurious air of normality, at least until Savannah whites began to realize they might soon face the most dreaded of all predicaments: the arrival, hoof and horns, of black occupation troops. McLaws's sources reported that the Yankees intended to garrison the city with African American regiments. "They say however that these troops are under more strict discipline than the whites," he wrote gloomily to his wife, who reached Augusta safely with their children a few days after Savannah's fall.[38]

To McLaws, the uncertainties of a refugee existence for his family were preferable to life under Federal rule. "When I think of the chance of your being in want and dependent on the kindness and even charity of the Yankee officials, I feel grateful that you are away," he wrote Emily. Few rebels were so fastidious as McLaws. Those with military or government connections flooded Union officers with appeals. Honey Hill victor Gustavus Smith's wife, "a native of New London, Connecticut, and very handsome," according to Sherman, turned up to complain about the roistering young staff officers quartered on her landlady. In tribute to her looks, Sherman investigated the matter himself.[39]

The Reverend Cameron McRae, rector of Saint John's Episcopal Church opposite Sherman's headquarters in Madison Square, sought out Christian Howard for protection. He volunteered to omit the customary Sunday prayer for Jefferson Davis in return for the posting of a Yankee guard in front of the church. By way of reply, Howard attended services at Saint John's on Sunday the twenty-fifth, Christmas Day.[40]

The troops were becoming restive in their camps on the city's outskirts. Charley Morse dreaded the poisonous exhalations of the swamps. John Fox wrote dejectedly that he had fared better in the field than in his riverfront bivouac. "I suppose if we hadn't anticipated so much in the way of comfortable living we shouldn't feel so blue about it," he wrote Fairy. "As it is we live wretchedly. You can't forage here." Tom Osborn, Howard's artillery chief, consigned himself to God and General Sherman. "Tonight, the close of the year 1864, finds me in Savannah, Ga.," he wrote his brother on New Year's Eve. "The close of 1863 I was in Bridgeport, Ala., the close of 1862, in Falmouth, Va., the close of 1861, in Washington, the close of 1860 in Watertown, N.Y., as a law student and the close of 1859 as a college student in Hamilton, N.Y. What next?"[41]

What, indeed? The army held it as an article of faith that the coming campaign would end the war. No less an authority than Sherman himself had pronounced the rebellion a shell. Storrow and his messmates speculated endlessly on the next stage of the journey that had carried the Second Massachusetts from its mustering-in camp at Brook Farm in 1861 to the Shenandoah Valley, Bull Run, Antietam Creek, Chancellorsville, Gettysburg, north Georgia, Atlanta, Savannah, and, now, the marches of South Carolina.

"Seriously, it would not surprise me to be in at the death and witness the fall of Richmond," he wrote home. "In that case, the Second will have boxed the compass indeed, and to some purpose."[42]

Storrow, for one, fantasized about the fall of wicked Charleston. "Think of Massachusetts regiments marching through the streets of Charleston and being quartered in the building where the vile serpent of rebellion first reared its head," he mused. "It would be the romance of the war."[43] A perfect ending, he regarded it: abolitionist Massachusetts striking down slavocrat South Carolina in her pride.

Augusta, Columbia, even Wilmington in North Carolina were other potential targets. Senior Confederates were guessing along with everyone else. McLaws, with orders to defend the line of the Combahee River above Pocotaligo, heard from his Savannah agents that Sherman aimed for Charleston, though he assumed that the Yankees themselves had planted the information. In any case, he wrote Emily, Sherman could go wherever he chose. General Beauregard had asked McLaws with his eight thousand ill-equipped troops not only to slow Sherman, but to oversee the evacuation of slaves, livestock, and supplies in his path. "I am afraid he cannot be prevented from injuring us very much," McLaws went on. "There is great alarm all through the country, and a strong disposition to give up." For his part, he sounded only too willing to negotiate a separate peace. He sent Emily a good thick piece of gray cloth from which she could make up a winter cloak, figuring it would never serve its original purpose and become a new Confederate major general's uniform.[44]

For a while, Charley Morse also believed Charleston would be the army's next stop. "This will be an easy job if the troops under Foster *don't attempt to aid us any*," he jibed. "The idea of their failing to cut the Charleston & Savannah Road!" This was by way of a fling at his friend John Gray, who handled the legal business for General Foster's command. Charley's brother and Gray had been young lawyers together in Boston. Now Robert Morse was making lots of money while Gray rusticated at Hilton Head. They met at the New Year when Gray came down to Savannah with dispatches, traveling in company with a courier from General Grant's City Point, Virginia, headquarters.[45]

In the messenger's pouch lay a letter from the general-in-chief endorsing Sherman's "Project for January," the Carolinas march. Grant had intended to transfer Sherman's army to Virginia by sea for the last campaign against Lee. Sherman fought hard for his own scheme. With sea transport in heavy demand, he estimated an over-water move would use up six to eight weeks. He could *march* to Virginia in eight weeks, he assured Grant, and knock the Carolinas out of the war at the same time. Sherman roughed out an advance that would threaten Augusta, Charleston, and Columbia all at once, paralyzing such forces as a reeling, disoriented enemy could throw against him. He promised to turn up in Southside Virginia by the end of March. The combined forces could then move on Lee. Grant thought it over and agreed to fall in with Sherman's plan.

The Carolinas preoccupied Sherman all through a boisterous New Year's dinner with his claque at Thomas Green's house in Madison Square. He regarded the operation as considerably more difficult— and more important—than the March to the Sea. The decanters circulated, bumpers were drunk, and gusts of conviviality rattled the windows and rustled the dusty leaves of the banana trees growing in tubs in Green's wide hall. Finally Sherman rose and, with a short, clipped speech about the work yet to be done, restored a measure of decorum to the party. He then motioned Howard aside and, stabbing with a tobacco-stained forefinger at a map of the South Carolina coast, instructed him to shift his two-corps wing to Beaufort on Port Royal Island, march inland to Pocotaligo, and cut the Charleston & Savannah—and do it all by January 15.

Howard went conscientiously to work, calling that same evening on the commander of his Seventeenth Corps, Major General Francis Blair. He broke in on a New Year's jollification in full cry. "My coming seemed to surprise the party," Howard, a famous teetotaler, remarked slyly; "suddenly all rose before me in a stiff and dignified style, as cadets at command in a mess hall after a meal." After a private word with Blair, he backed out of the room with a killjoy bow. Blair cleared the wine fumes from his head and drafted orders that put the first of Sherman's troops in motion for Beaufort.[46]

The flatlanders of the 103rd Illinois were ferried over to Port Royal Island in the steamer *Crescent*. "Just before dark we saw a school of porpoises which looked just like a drove of hogs in the water," Charles Wills wrote in his diary. "Some of the men wanted to go foraging when they saw them."[47]

CONDITIONS WERE ANARCHIC in the Savannah hinterland. Sherman's detachments plundered without restraint, and clouds of hungry and demoralized Confederates stripped the countryside as they withdrew beyond reach of the Federals. Planter families were exposed and defenseless: in fear of the Yankees, of undisciplined rebels, of their own slaves. The familiar world of comfort, order, and security was breaking down before their eyes.

"I suppose you know about the Yankees on Argyle Island," Emma Manigault wrote her brother Louis from Charleston on December 21. "No doubt they have ruined everything by now." Miss Emma anticipated the sacking of Gowrie by three days. On Christmas Eve Union troops burned the main house, the kitchen building, the servants' house, and the brick threshing mill, exempting only the eleven brick double-houses of the slave settlements. The Yankees carried off ten thousand bushels of rice and rustled every mule on the place. They felled Gowrie's towering water oaks for firewood. To add insult, they destroyed most of the widow Capers's clothes.[48]

The spinster sisters Manigault, Emma and Harriet, prepared to ride out the Sherman hurricane in Charleston. "We are just waiting to see what will be the next thing," Emma wrote. Events had stunned her septuagenarian father into an uncharacteristic passivity, anyway for the moment. "I don't believe Papa intends to trouble himself about moving negroes or anything of the kind," she went on. He seemed to have resigned himself, and his property, to the lottery of fate.[49]

True, there was a randomness to the Federals' demolition work. It was as though a tornado had come ripping through the Savannah

River rice lands. Gowrie was a ruin. Yankee detachments ransacked the neighboring Potter place, stealing impartially from James Potter and from his better-off slaves: soldiers killed two of Mary Jess's fat beef cattle and a number of hogs; they expropriated her kitchen furniture, her stone jars of lard, and her modest stocks of sugar, tobacco, and wine; they scooped the honey syrup out of all her hives.[50] But the King, Anthony, and Barclay plantations were untouched, as were the Heyward and Chisolm places on the South Carolina bank. Even Daniel Heyward's fine brick thresher survived the Sherman visitation.

South of Savannah, from their camps around Midway, Judson Kilpatrick's cavalry raided the rich Liberty County long-staple cotton country, terrorizing the whites, carrying word of emancipation to the slave settlements, stampeding cattle, emptying storehouses, burning gins and mills. As elsewhere, the Federals showed a casual disregard of color, stealing without prejudice from blacks as well as whites.

A party of forty troopers, probably a detachment of the Fifth Kentucky Cavalry, turned up at Samuel Elliott's place at Laurel View near Sunbury, announced that Elliott and his family were henceforward and forever free, and then confiscated without apology or recompense 800 pounds of bacon, 15 hogs, 7 cattle, 30 ducks, 210 pounds of clean rice, and a wagon and harness. The troopers also relieved Elliott of $65 in old bank bills he had managed to accumulate over the years.[51]

"I would not have felt so bad if they had not took my money, but that was the last thing I had in the world," Elliott lamented. "They took my pants & coat & all. They did not leave me a thing."[52]

At nearby Halifax plantation, the widow Jane Harden, her daughters Annie and Ada, and her niece Sallie LeConte retreated into the shuttered gloom of the great house to await the bluecoats. She had managed to get off a distress signal to Sallie's father, Joseph LeConte, in Columbia, South Carolina, a few weeks before Savannah's fall. As Sherman closed in, LeConte prepared to push south to Liberty County to attempt a daring rescue.

Joe LeConte had taught chemistry and geology at South Carolina College in Columbia until the war drained off all his students. He worked for a while as a chemist mixing chloroform for the Confederate medical department, then joined his older brother John as a researcher in the Columbia laboratory of the government's Niter and Mining Bureau, which manufactured gunpowder for the army.

The LeConte brothers were scientists by vocation, members of the Georgia planter class by birth and upbringing. With infinite toil, most of it the involuntary contribution of slaves, their LeConte grandfather had hacked Woodmanston plantation out of the Liberty County wilderness in the closing years of the eighteenth century. By 1823, the year of Joe's birth, Woodmanston was a profitable rice and long-staple cotton enterprise of thirty-three hundred acres and two hundred slaves.

Their mother died during Joe's third year. He carried with him no distinct memory of her, "either of her face or any event in her life," except for one: he vividly recalled the bowl filled with her drawn blood that stood on the bureau in her bedroom on her deathday.[53] Their father tried, with fair success, to fill both roles. He handed his passion for the natural world down to Joe, passing many instructive hours with him in the garden with its stand of tall and lush camellias, and in the wilderness of Bulltown Swamp along the edge of Woodmanston. The two were much together: partial compensation, perhaps, for the loss of a mother and a haphazard early education that saw the boy run through nine tutors in as many years.

His father soon enough allowed him to explore on his own. Joe wandered deep into Bulltown Swamp, collecting specimens, observing swamp exotica, and writing up elaborately detailed field notes. Strong, healthy, and athletic, he learned to perform gymnastic feats of amazing dexterity; and even in later life he sometimes found swimming easier than walking.

When LeConte went off to Franklin College of the University of Georgia in Athens in 1838, he had never ventured farther from home than Midway eight miles distant, and then only to visit his mother's grave. He journeyed north to medical school in 1843 and took a degree from the College of Physicians and Surgeons in New York City two years later. Returning to Georgia, he married Bessie Nisbet in 1847 and settled into medical practice in small-town Macon.

But neither a planter's life—he inherited Syfax plantation in Liberty County, with forty slaves—nor medicine could hold LeConte's attention. A reliable income from Syfax enabled him to walk away from the Macon practice in the summer of 1850 and go to Cambridge, Massachusetts, to study at Harvard with Louis Agassiz, the Swiss-born natural historian then at the peak of his fame.

Slaveholders among abolitionists, the LeContes—the pregnant Bessie* and their daughter Emma, born in 1847—boarded in the same house with lawyer, novelist, and Free-Soiler Richard Henry Dana. They caught occasional glimpses of Ralph Waldo Emerson. LeConte idolized Agassiz, whose *Études sur les glaciers* (1840) and *Système glaciaire* (1847) demonstrated the existence of a recent geological ice age. With an ambition to become a teacher/discoverer in the Agassiz mold, LeConte accepted a faculty position at South Carolina College in 1857. John LeConte followed him to Columbia later that year.

Then the war came. Full of doubt about secession at first, LeConte accepted the accomplished fact. "It was in the atmosphere," he wrote later; "we breathed it in the air."[54] The Confederate government requisitioned some of the college buildings for a soldiers' hospital, but allowed the LeContes to stay on in their campus house, a large, comfortable dwelling[†] on the south side of the green near the main gate opening onto Sumter Street.

War, blockade, and the uninspiring routine of the Niter and Mining Bureau left LeConte out of the scientific mainstream. He had read his idol Agassiz's attacks on Darwin's *Origin of Species*, published in 1859; with the severing of outside contacts he doubtless missed some of the Darwinian rebuttals. He lost touch with his Harvard connections. Books and journals were difficult to obtain. As the war ground on, the daily struggle for food, firewood, and other essentials absorbed most of his energy. He would have years of catching up to do when the fighting ended.

If it ever ended: war weariness had descended upon the LeContes by the end of 1864. Burdened with a sickly infant (Caroline, born in 1863), Bessie LeConte found even routine domestic tasks beyond her ability. "I can't at all understand how so simple an affair as knitting a stocking should appear an insoluble problem," her clever, snappish daughter Emma complained. "Mother can't conquer the mystery of 'turning the heel'—there it is again—'Emma, how many times did you say I must knit plain?' I think I shall put my pen down and run away."[55]

---

*Sallie LeConte arrived in November 1850.
[†]Now Lieber College at the University of South Carolina.

Joseph LeConte, Confederate government scientist,
teacher, planter, slaveholder. The war cost LeConte
everything but his energy and sunny disposition. On his
first postwar visit to his boyhood home, Woodmanston
plantation in Liberty County, Georgia, he found a
wilderness: "cotton houses, corn houses and negro cabins
decaying and tumbling down, the gardens all gone to
ruins." LeConte abandoned the suffering South for a
new start in California. (Georgia Historical Society)

For Miss Emma, the severities of war compounded the ordinary
burdens and contradictory moods of adolescence. She now wore
uncomfortable homespun underclothes "such as we used to give to
the negroes." In her echoing wardrobe hung two calico dresses and a
black-and-white plaid homespun frock, tattered survivors of prewar
days. "We have a couple of old silks," she noted mumpishly, "care-

fully preserved for great occasions and which do not look shabby for the simple reason that all the other old silks that still survive the war are in the same state of decay." Emma followed news of the war attentively; the Confederate cause could fire her imagination still. A lot of the time, though, she wished it would just go away.[56]

"Truly we girls, whose lot it is to grow up in these times, are unfortunate," Emma lamented. "It commenced when I was thirteen, and I am now seventeen and no prospect of it yet ending. No pleasure, no enjoyment—nothing but rigid economy and hard work— nothing but the stern realities of life." She envied her cousins Julian LeConte and John Harden their heroic life in the army. For herself, she anticipated the worst: "Now that everything is lost, perhaps we will all have to work for a living before long."[57]

Joe LeConte's rescue errand to Liberty County meant a joyless Christmas in Columbia. Sherman had seemed an abstraction ten weeks ago when fourteen-year-old Sallie went down to Halifax for a visit with her aunt and cousins. Now the Vandal King was about to arrive in the neighborhood. "Sherman is swooping down through Georgia from mountains to coast," LeConte wrote, "scattering frightened women and children in his path, like a swooping eagle among a flock of doves." He hoped to beat the Yankees to Liberty County, collect Sallie and the Hardens, and carry them away to the safe haven of interior South Carolina.[58]

Sherman's army outmarched him. On December 11, on the Charleston & Savannah south of Grahamville, LeConte discovered that the Yankees had seized the Savannah River bridge. Within forty-five miles of his destination, he had to turn about, double back to Columbia, and follow a detour of eight hundred miles over the ramshackle Confederate railroads. Reaching Macon on December 20, he heard that Kilpatrick's cavalry had already passed through Liberty County. The Yankees were encamped south of the Ogeechee within easy distance of Halifax.

LeConte's train rattled past the Andersonville stockade on the twenty-first. He hardly noticed it at the time. ("I never heard of any harshness, much less cruelty, practiced there," he remarked later.) The next stop, Thomasville, was packed with refugees from Liberty County. In Doctortown, twenty-five miles southwest of Halifax on Christmas Day, a bright, mild Sunday, he heard that the bluecoats had killed all the livestock on the LeConte and Harden plantations, and taken away most of the corn.

A Confederate scout slipped through the lines a day or so after Christmas with a letter from Sister Jane. Yankees were still swarming in Liberty County. They had returned to Halifax and smashed up the furniture there. If he could get through at all it would have to be on foot, Jane went on, for the enemy had killed or confiscated virtually every horse, farm jack, and wheeled vehicle in the county. A day or two later, when another scout reported the Yankees gone, at least for the moment, he resolved to try to push on through.

LeConte struck out for Halifax at noon on New Year's Day 1865—Bessie's birthday, he reminded himself. The road rose to a hill, then ran through pine brakes, familiar country evoking memories of a boyhood lived mostly out of doors: the warmth of the pale sun, the abrupt trumpeting of the cranes, the fetor of the rotted swamps. Once he saw, or imagined he saw, three tall figures, dark, motionless, and evidently studying him. Yankee troopers resting their horses? As he approached they remained immovable: three upright planks of a burned trestle, they turned out to be.

He reached Walthourville, ten miles from Halifax, just before dark. Yankee raiders had burned the depot and several houses. Le-Conte tapped at the barred, double-locked door of an undamaged dwelling. His coat might once have been Confederate gray, a passport hereabouts: the stranger invited him in, fed him the local news and a meager supper at a cold hearthside, and offered him a bed.

LeConte regained the road at daybreak. "Oh, Papa," Sallie cried as he crossed the threshold at Halifax, "did they let you come?" Then she dissolved in tears. She was in health, Sister and his nieces, too, but the house was a shambles: broken trunks, splintered bureaus, overturned wardrobes. The Yankees, Miss Jane told him, had come calling every day for two weeks.

He walked over to Syfax in the afternoon. For some reason, probably lack of transport, the enemy had left all the rice and cotton. The overseer, J. R. Calder, told him the slaves—former slaves, now, Le-Conte supposed—were in a state of general insubordination. One of the hands let slip that vengeful Yankees were on the prowl for neighbor Sam Varnedoe, one of his tutors from Woodmanston days and, briefly, a commissary officer at Andersonville. Grossly fat, Varnedoe had been an anomaly among the starving scarecrows of the prison stockade. When they found him, the bluecoats swore, they meant to "grease their boots with his lard."

The fugitives marched for Doctortown at first light on January 3: LeConte, Sallie on a spavined horse with a carpetbag strapped behind her, and the manservant Joshua. LeConte walked; Joshua led the flatulent horse. Not long after sunrise a light breeze carried the sound of gunfire their way—Yankee foragers, LeConte guessed, beginning their morning's work of shooting every hog, cow, duck, turkey, or chicken in sight. They hid in the pines until nightfall, then retreated to Halifax.

A Confederate militia commander turned up under a flag of truce on January 7 with an offer to lead the women through the lines. Sallie and her cousins left with the wagon train. Encumbered with such of her life's possessions as Kilpatrick's raiders had spared or overlooked, Sister stayed behind. LeConte promised to return for her. In a week of tedious travel, he saw Sallie and the Harden girls safely to Thomasville, where they boarded the cars for Macon. Then he doubled back for Jane.

It was an epic of danger and discomfort. Federal patrols combed the area. The militia colonel had gone off somewhere and LeConte decided against waiting for him to return and fix another truce. Heavy rains had swollen the water maze between Doctortown and Walthourville to double its normal size. He could no longer pick his way across on drift timber, dry-shod, as he had been able to do a week ago. Struggling through waist-deep water and a swift current, he cleared the morass with difficulty, raising Walthourville just before sunset. He pushed on to Halifax at first light the next day.

He left Miss Jane to finish the packing and paid a farewell call at Syfax. Calder summoned the people. LeConte invited them to return with him to Columbia; they preferred staying on at Syfax. All right, LeConte told them, but they would have to work. They said they would, though not for Calder. "They seemed to think their day of deliverance from overseers was come," LeConte gathered. After further negotiations, the hands agreed to put in a crop for 1865 under the loose supervision of William Jones, an elderly kinsman of LeConte's who farmed in the neighborhood.

LeConte, Jane Harden, three other Liberty County ladies, Jane's maid and her baby, and the driver Simon moved off from Halifax late in the afternoon of January 16 in two farm carts laden with thirteen heavy trunks. One of the animals, a broken-winded old dray horse, nearly foundered in the thick bluish mud of the causeway over the first of the swamps. The hames snapped under the strain; then the traces parted. When they finally cleared the causeway the horse broke down entirely, bringing the caravan to an early halt for the day.

The refugees were nearly two weeks on the road to the railhead at Albany. Racking his bones, LeConte ferried Sister's belongings, close to a thousand pounds' worth, in nine canoeloads over the still-rising swamps. The dispirited horse collapsed and sank to the bottom; LeConte and a servant cut the traces and dragged him to the bank. Out of the fens, across the surging Altamaha River and beyond reach of the Yankees at last, the little convoy pushed on southwest from Doctortown in a cold rain over roads shin-deep in mud. It froze at night, only to be churned into glue during the next day's stage.

Then, from one day to the next, life became bearable again. The sun appeared in a torn sky and dried the roads. The caravan traversed fertile country untouched by war. On the cars out of Macon an important-looking officer confided to LeConte that John Bell Hood's Army of Tennessee, reported destroyed in front of Nashville only a month ago, had in fact survived and would turn up any minute now to take up the defense of South Carolina. The LeConte party halted for a night just east of Augusta at the plantation of Professor Holmes, a Niter Bureau colleague. After weeks of dodging Yankees and rigging pine bough shelters in the woods, LeConte warmed to Holmes's absent-minded, inefficient, but well-meant hospitality.

"Always late breakfast at Prof. Holmes'," LeConte noted in the morning. "The family is so large it takes a long time to get up. The breakfast is so large it takes a long time to cook. Then after breakfast the plantation is so large that Prof. Holmes has many little things to look after. Then finally there are so many to take affectionate leave of, and the ladies have so many last words to say."

It was nearly noon before they got off. By then sleet was clattering against the leather window flaps of the carriage Holmes had loaned them. Even so, they were almost home and—or so LeConte thought—with a comfortable lead on the Yankees.[59]

WITH THE ARMY ON THE GO, Sherman tapped the Department of the South for troops to garrison the Savannah forts. General Foster sent Charley Fox's Fifty-fifth Massachusetts. The regiment landed at Fort

Thunderbolt the night of January 13 and made its first acquaintance with the western army the next day. Like their general, most of Sherman's veterans had no use for African Americans in arms, whether freeborn or lately enslaved; there were taunts and bold, insulting stares, though no serious incidents.

To Fox's relief, the novelty soon wore off. "Since they have seen our Guard mounting and Dress Parade, and found out that we have seen some hard fighting, they are disposed to be quite friendly," he wrote Mary at home. Savannah whites were appalled. "Of course, we create much sensation among the Georgians," James Trotter remarked cheerfully. "They have great fear of colored troops and are trembling because of our proximity and the expectation of our coming to town." Some of Sherman's officers voiced the hope that the Fifty-fifth would draw provost duty in the city, to further vex and mortify rebel Savannah.[60]

The brothers Fox met at last, at Charley's quarters on January 14. Face to face for the first time since Charley had mustered out of the Army of the Potomac nearly two years ago, they exchanged family news and reviewed their service lives, which had taken such different courses. And they mourned Tom. Charley had been rocking in a schooner off Folly Island Bar waiting for the wind to shift when an officer brought aboard a Boston newspaper with the report of Tom's death. The shock had sucked the breath out of him and buckled his knees. He leaned against the rail while his vision cleared. To seaward, the blue immensity stretched away forever. He willed himself to put the matter aside. He would grieve later. John's reaction, he now learned, had been identical. The war was a sort of insulator, the brothers agreed, cushioning the immediate impact of loss.

"I didn't expect to see Tom again in the army," John had written after his death. "I thought, too, that I might be killed—death is very common with us. If I live I shall feel his absence more at home and years hence than I can now. Perhaps this is a wise provision of Providence to enable me to do my present work better."[61]

They moved on to safer topics, trading complaints about shortages of food and forage, and about Savannah itself. Filthy beyond description, with hundreds of dead horses and mules rotting in the alleys and vacant squares, the city looked a "mongrel" place, Charley thought, "half New England and half southern, and in many respects the worst of each." John offered felicitations for Charley's thirty-second birthday, only three days away. And Charley led him on a tour of the Fifty-fifth's camp.[62]

The hard-shelled Sherman veteran judged his brother's establishment a shade amateurish. "His command looked well," John wrote their father. "A little too much of the 'town meeting' style among the officers and rather too much 'bobolition' talk for a military organization." John knew one of the Fifty-fifth's officers of old, the froward Major Nutt. But he and Charley steered clear of Honey Hill.

John had learned most of the details from their father, who in turn queried him about Nutt, a onetime petty officer in the Second Massachusetts. Ambitious and excitable, he could be insubordinate if not properly snubbed. "It may be merely an impression, but I think if Charley were a little more distant, reserved and on his dignity and allowed less palaver in his command, he would be less likely to have difficulty with inferior officers," John suggested, perhaps expecting Parson Fox to pass along the advice as his own, as more acceptable coming from a father than a younger brother. "A regimental commander should be an absolute despot—his will and word law—not the presiding officer of a debating club."[63]

The calumny itself? Dismiss it, and put Nutt in arrest if he kept up the chatter. John Fox had witnessed the full range of responses to the shock of combat, and he spoke with authority. "As for Charley's courage, I shouldn't think he would bother himself about it at all," he wrote. "Courage is a thing that can't bear argument or discussion. If his officers blackguard him in such a way, he must court martial them or force them to resign. If it is only common talk such as one hears, it is best to treat it with dignified silence and wait for another fight to prove it false."[64]

Charley lapsed into another prolonged spell of brooding reflection. The experience of four years of army life cast a harsh light on much that had once been obscure. "These war times have made one at least to know that errors in a measure excusable before are now without excuse," he wrote Mary in a more than usually severe mood, "omissions for which one might have been held nearly blameless are now radical faults."[65]

# 3

# The Sherman Lands

JOHN GRAY RETURNED TO HILTON HEAD in early January in company with Charley Morse. Gray catechized Morse about the Atlanta and Savannah campaigns, partly to satisfy his own curiosity, but also to gather material for a semi-invalid friend in Boston, future war-chronicler John Ropes. Morse retailed his experiences at leisure in Gray's quarters, a picture of comfort after the rigors of the March to the Sea. "Plenty of luxuries and a fine view of the ocean," he wrote home, postcard style. "It did me good to see him eat," Gray remarked of the gaunt, leathery Morse. And Morse found most of what he'd sent to his brother Robert for in the well-stocked sutlers' shops along Robbers' Row, even the map of Spain.[1]

With the steady beat of the Atlantic surf as a backdrop, Gray and Morse talked of the war, their work, home connections. Morse showed interest in the Port Royal Experiment. A onetime Second Massachusetts tentmate of abolitionist Robert Shaw, he sympathized with the work of the Sea Island missionaries. Like his chief, General Foster, Gray disliked the meddlesome Gideonites. They made him feel, as he put it, "anti-anti-slavery." They were in complete agreement, though, about Sherman.

Gray had caught his first glimpse of the Great Man just a couple of weeks before, with Foster aboard the packet *Nemala* in Wassaw

Sound. Flush with the McAllister success and with a new audience to dazzle, Sherman performed at his voluble best that day. He meant, he said, to turn north with the sun and instruct South Carolina in the realities of the war it had so thoughtlessly unleashed. "His campaign," Gray wrote in paraphrase, "would be one of the most horrible things in the history of the world; the devil himself could not restrain his men." It was a vintage Sherman monologue—brilliant, intemperate, indiscreet.[2]

"He has his notions," Henry Hitchcock once remarked of Sherman, "but he always means less than he says." Recovered from his fit of hero worship, Gray, too, saw beyond the general's reckless hyperbolic riffs. "His bragging reminded me almost of the *New York Herald;* however, I believe him a very prudent man and far from rash," he advised Ropes. Charley Morse shared Gray's enthusiasm. "I doubt you people appreciate what a great genius Sherman is," he wrote home. "About himself he seems to care nothing either what people think of him or what position he holds. How few generals would have resisted the temptation after the capture of Atlanta or Savannah of coming to Washington and having their greatness acknowledged."[3]

In the event, Washington came to Sherman in the person of the most powerful of Lincoln's cabinet officers, the dyspeptic, excitable, and shrewd secretary of war, Edwin McMasters Stanton. The secretary, it turned out, wanted to interrogate Sherman about the army's treatment of the thousands of former slaves who followed the columns to Savannah—specifically, an incident in which Jefferson C. Davis, commanding the Fourteenth Corps, drew up his pontoons and left a mass of refugees to choose between the swift current of Ebenezer Creek and Joseph Wheeler's Confederate cavalry. Many drowned, dozens at the least. And reports persisted that Wheeler's troopers had set about the panicked crowd, slashing away with homicidal effect.

Stanton stood near the emancipationist wing of the Republican Party, partly for political reasons, partly out of detestation for the rebel planter class, and partly perhaps out of real feeling for the cause. Sherman's attitudes were baldly racist, though doubtless no more so than other men of his background, particularly in the army. He expressed himself on racial matters with his characteristic lack of tact.

Union Major General William Tecumseh Sherman. With the capture of Savannah in December 1864 he pronounced the rebellion a shell. His troops placed absolute confidence in Sherman and resented the slightest criticism directed his way. "I doubt you people appreciate what a great genius Sherman is," Charles Morse wrote home to his family in Boston. (Library of Congress)

"My first duty will be to clear the army of surplus negroes, mules and horses," he wrote the war secretary in mid-December; just the sort of conjunction, equating human beings with animals and regarding both as impedimenta, that seemed to confirm his callousness—in Stanton's view, anyway.

Sherman put up a vigorous defense. "Of course that cock and bull story of my turning back negroes that Wheeler might kill them is all humbug," he assured Henry Halleck, who had tipped him to the underlying purpose of Stanton's New Year's junket. "I turned nobody back. Jeff. C. Davis did at Ebenezer Creek forbid certain plantation slaves—old men, women and children—to follow his column; but they would come along and he took up his pontoon bridge, not because he wanted to leave them, but because he wanted his bridge."[4]

In Sherman's view, the freed people were an encumbrance and a danger to the fighting columns. The refugees certainly were a distraction, at least in a strictly military sense. But this was a political war and, whether the politically witless Sherman recognized it or not, a war for freedom. He noticed, of course, that African Americans hailed him as a deliverer. He enjoyed the adulation. "They flock to me, old and young," he wrote his wife, "they pray and shout and mix up my name with Moses."[5] He considered them a nuisance all the same. Still, whatever may be said of Sherman's reflexive racism, whatever his motives, he would soon show himself capable of acting decisively in the freed people's interest.

Stanton reached Savannah on January 9. Sherman showed him around the camps; the troops impressed the war secretary with their improvisations out of tent canvas and scavenged clapboard. Stanton particularly admired the craftsmanship of one soldier with light fingers and rococo tastes who had converted the rich gilt frame of a plundered mirror into a tent door. Turning to business, he questioned Sherman closely on the Ebenezer Creek episode, on the refugee problem generally, and on allegations that government recruiters were dragooning freed slaves into the army and pocketing the bounty cash. And, to Sherman's unconcealed annoyance, he asked for a meeting with Savannah's black leaders.

The general arranged it for the evening of January 12 at his headquarters in Madison Square. He had already received several delegations of freedmen there, treating each with a courtesy revolting to

Savannah's "refined Southern gentlemen," as Hitchcock noted with approval.[6] In fact, Sherman's civil manner toward individual African Americans contrasted with the habitual vulgarity of his pronouncements to Halleck, Stanton, and others. In the all-male group of twenty he summoned to meet Stanton were newly freed slaves, former slaves who had purchased their freedom, and several freeborn blacks.

Sherman stood near the fireplace, an elbow resting on the mantlepiece. Members of the delegation disposed themselves informally about the room. They chose Garrison Frazier, an elderly Baptist preacher who had bought himself out of slavery before the war, as their spokesman. Frazier answered without hesitation when Stanton asked how the newly freed population could sustain itself.

"The way we can best take care of ourselves is to have land, and turn in and till it by our own labor," he said.

Parson Frazier here planted the seed of Sherman's plan to resettle freed slaves on the abandoned plantations of coastal Georgia and South Carolina. So far, so good; but then Stanton, with a basilisk stare, ordered Sherman out of the room so he could, as he put it, inquire candidly into "the feeling of the colored people" about the general.[7]

Stung into a fury by this curt dismissal from his own headquarters, Sherman at least had little cause for apprehension about the meeting itself. He had handpicked the delegation, after all. "Some of us called upon [Sherman] immediately upon his arrival, and it is probable that he did not meet you with more courtesy than he met us," Frazier told Stanton. "His conduct and deportment toward us characterized him as a friend and a gentleman."[8] After the session, Sherman checked his resentment long enough to collaborate with Stanton on a coherent refugee policy. Together they initiated a resettlement program of potentially revolutionary impact.

It grew out of Sherman's Special Field Orders Number 15, issued on January 16, 1865. At the outset, anyway, the project sought to make homesteaders of former slaves. Here the conservative soldier found himself in temporary alliance with two of the most radical of Republicans in Congress, Charles Sumner in the Senate and George Julian in the House. Both politicians were strong supporters of black homesteading, especially when it involved the breakup of large plantation holdings. Julian's Committee on Public Lands sought to extend the 1862 Homestead Act to forfeited rebel lands, which would be parceled out to the Southern poor, white and black. Sherman's orders covered the coastwise region from Charleston south to the Saint Johns River in Florida. These lands, to be distributed in forty-acre plots, were to be set aside exclusively for black colonization. Sherman gave Rufus Saxton, whose radical convictions were certainly known to him, full charge of the settlement program.[9]

His mission achieved, Stanton moved on to Hilton Head and Beaufort, where he expected to meet with Saxton, now styled inspector of settlements and plantations, and take a firsthand look at the Port Royal Experiment. Sherman turned back to purely military matters. By mid-January, Howard's two corps were in cantonments around Beaufort, ready to advance on the Charleston & Savannah at Pocotaligo. To the north, Slocum's wing prepared to jump off from Sister's Ferry on the Georgia bank of the Savannah River and strike from there into the South Carolina heartland.

RAIN FELL IN GRAY STREAKS throughout the day, a dull and comfortless Christmas on Saint Helena Island. Laura Towne and Ellen Murray passed the morning (and fended off a holiday-induced depression of spirits) wrapping presents for their scholars: a workbox with needle book, pincushion, thread, buttons, and scissors for the girls, a comb and a knife for the boys. Towne checked and restocked her pharmacopoeia, for with the onset of winter and the arrival of the first of the Sherman refugees sickness had broken out in the settlements. Seven hundred Georgians reached Beaufort Christmas night, all of them weak from hunger and exposure, many of them desperately ill.

Only too aware of the limits of her few months' course in homeopathic medicine, Towne sought a consultation with an ancient sorceress known as Katie, "who remembers worshiping her own gods in Africa, but who has been nearly a century in this country."[10] Blind, afflicted with pains in her eyes, she was a fortune-teller, a hierophant, a preparer of philters, and a goofer doctor besides. Towne hoped to make an ally of her with offerings of medicines for her aching eyes. Possibly blind Katie could recommend folk remedies to supplement the True System—and hint, too, munching her jaws, at what the future might hold for the refugees. Towne sent over packets of tea and sugar and a warm shawl as Christmas tokens. Katie returned her best thanks with a dozen large yams in a sweetgrass basket and two quarts of groundnuts.

The war news held mostly good, though naturally the army's intentions were unreadable. Sherman and Foster had met at Hilton Head, Towne knew; reports were circulating that the Great Man's manner had been glacial. Sherman certainly held a low opinion of Foster's abilities as a soldier. As for the Gideonites, they detested him. Foster obstructed the land distribution efforts of Rufus Saxton, their favorite general, and his agents violated Saxton's pledges by carrying off Gullah men to Hilton Head for impressment in the army—boys as young as fourteen or fifteen, mature men with large families to support.

Sherman received Saxton "with flattering honor," or so Towne had heard. Saxton guessed at once that Sherman intended to drop the problem of the "surplus negroes" on him. He told Sherman bluntly that he lacked the means to look after thousands of desperate Georgians. His islands were thickly settled already, thousands of Gullahs and mainland refugees living in hugger-mugger, every cabin packed to the rooftrees. For the plan to work, General Foster would have to find troops to garrison the outlying Sea Islands, from Edisto below Charleston to Saint Simons in Georgia, as well as the hundred-mile-long coastal strip Special Orders Number 15 would open to settlement.[11]

Saxton had fought a three-year battle against the encroachments of the Department of the South. Foster's predecessor, David Hunter, was sympathetic to emancipation but heavy-handed, particularly in the matter of recruiting; Hunter had carried out what amounted to the shotgun enlistment of Sea Island freedmen. Foster was actively, malignantly hostile, and by the end of 1864 he had knocked most of the fight out of Saxton. Just as Sherman began to show him signs of favor, Saxton indited a long letter of complaint and justification to Stanton, and concluded it with his resignation.

Senior officers of the department opposed him at every turn, Saxton complained, challenging his authority, demanding elaborate amplifications of his official acts, even annulling his orders. The issues were usually petty. In Hunter's day, Saxton approached the department's second in command, an Indiana brigadier named John Brannan, for a consignment of shelter tents stored in a Hilton Head warehouse

Union Major General Rufus Saxton, inspector of settlements and plantations in the Sea Islands, striking a soldierly pose. A true believer in emancipation, Saxton promoted self-sufficiency for former slaves through homesteading. "It is delightful to hear a military man express so strong a confidence in Absolute Truth," one of the Gideonite volunteers said of him. (Library of Congress)

under yellow fever quarantine. Brannan refused to unlock the building. "Now it is notorious that whenever one of General Brannan's men wants anything from the same warehouse, he gives a special order and it is opened for him, but not for General Saxton, the *Abolitionist*," one of the Gideonites observed.[12] Brannan even refused Saxton the use of a government boiler to power the Beaufort gins, delaying the processing of the all-important cotton crop.

Foster's soldiers abused and debauched the Gullahs, cheated them shamelessly, confiscated or trampled their crops, tore down their fences for firewood, and rustled their livestock. The refugees were even more vulnerable, universally regarded as fair game for sport and plunder.

Rice hand Jack Flowers ran from his home plantation on the main late in 1861, a few weeks after the Yankees took Port Royal. He traveled by night and stood all day in swamp water up to his chin to confuse the bloodhounds. Drifting down a tidal creek to the Coosaw River in a basketboat on a moonless night, he paddled over to Port Royal Island and the promise of freedom. A Federal picket's challenge alerted the rebels, who called out a query. The Yankee said he'd taken a contraband. What should he do with him?

"Cut him up for fishbait," came the reply.[13]

Leading a jenny mule, William Drayton walked away from his master's place on the Combahee, slipped through the Federal lines at night, and made for Beaufort, where he enlisted in the Thirty-fourth U.S. Colored Troops. The post quartermaster relieved him of the jenny, for which he'd paid $200, three-quarters of it in hard-won silver and gold. Drayton caught occasional glimpses of the animal in service with a government team, but never saw a penny's compensation from the quartermaster.[14]

Flowers and Drayton were fortunate. Sea Islanders reported Yankee shootings, beatings, and rapes as well as property crimes. Soldiers preyed licentiously on the Gullah women, to whom bitter experience taught the consequences of resisting a white man's sexual advances. "The morals of the old plantation life seemed revived in the army of occupation," Saxton noted with disgust. Such outrages, he wrote Stanton, only confirmed the freed people's inbred distrust of whites, and of the new Northern regime.[15]

Saxton seemed powerless to punish offenders. Foster's provost officers ignored him. The missionaries had long ago ceased to doubt Saxton's heart; now they questioned his toughness. He gave in too easily to Foster's bullying. "I have always felt that Gen. Saxton ought to have absolute authority and that his word should be law," Edward Pierce, one of the original Port Royal volunteers, wrote Laura Towne.

"This would be better even if he did make mistakes. But he does not seem to hold his ground as he should."[16] Possibly Saxton, bred to the military's hierarchical ways, felt he could go only so far in challenging a superior. Whatever the reason, he rarely showed backbone enough to satisfy the Gideonites.

He never wavered, though, in his support for black homesteading. He incited the Gullahs to claim squatter sovereignty over the sixty thousand confiscated or abandoned Sea Island acres the Treasury controlled. "I hope that all your people will make haste to select and stake out their lots," he wrote the former slave Prince Rivers, an NCO in the African American First South Carolina and one of the first to file a land claim.[17] He detailed army carpenters to build model cabins on family-size plots, to be sold to homesteaders at bargain rates. To confound Northern speculators, he threatened to use army cotton funds to drive up bids at the land auctions.

The Treasury Department pursued various contradictory policies, most of which favored the speculators. Reports of the fabulous wealth to be stripped out of the island cotton mines seemed almost to madden these tycoons. ("There are Yankees who believe that the almighty dollar is the only living and true God, and it is said some of them would wade into the mouth of Hell after a bale of cotton," Congressman Julian would remark.) Saxton found an ally in his campaign for preemptive land sales to former slaves in Mansfield French, an itinerant Ohio evangelist, editor of the periodical the *Beauty of Holiness*, and (more to the point) friend of Treasury Secretary Salmon P. Chase. Between them, Saxton and French persuaded Chase to reserve nearly all the government lands for the freed people at the homestead rate of $1.25 per acre.[18]

Impassioned, hortatory, and driven, Saxton promoted the program tirelessly, touring sunstruck island churches and advising the overflow crowds to put in their claims at first opportunity. French usually came along to sermonize. Sometimes Rivers, a native of Edgefield, South Carolina, who had stolen his master's horse to reach the Yankee lines and had become the most aggressive army recruiter in the islands, would rise to deliver an inspirational pitch for enlistment, ending with a reminder of the government's liberal land-purchase terms for veterans.

Saxton envisioned an industrious Jeffersonian self-sufficiency for the Gullahs. To say he had millennial expectations for the land scheme is to understate the case. Applied throughout the South, it would guarantee the future and inaugurate "such a measure of prosperity as the world has never seen." The stakes were tremendous. The framework of emancipation would collapse if the government failed, here and now, to help build an independent class of black smallholders.[19]

He could not, however, convert the Treasury's direct tax commissioners in Beaufort. They refused to recognize the freed people's claim tickets; they denied them squatters' rights; and Secretary Chase eventually reversed himself, suspending the preemption sales and offering government lands to the highest bidder. Treasury agents reported an average sale price of $11 an acre—at nine times the homestead rate, far beyond the means of most former slaves.

Saxton pressed Stanton and Senator Sumner to lobby Chase. He told Sumner of a former slave who had bid $2,000 for a parcel, an enormous sum, accumulated with God knew what pains, only to see a speculator snatch it out of his grasp for $2,500. The family had toiled as slaves on that very soil for generations.

"They are now homeless, except at his mercy, and God help them when they are in the power of a man who could do them such a wrong," Saxton wrote the senator. "And this will be the fate of many of these poor people, unless our good president interposes his authority."[20]

Lincoln declined to intervene. Within a few months, Edward Philbrick amassed for himself and his Boston investors eight thousand acres of prime Saint Helena cotton land. He and his associate Arthur Sumner, a volunteer teacher who had taken on a plantation superintendency, dismissed Saxton's efforts as strength-sapping charity. The task, it seemed to them, lay beyond reach of benevolence alone.

"No petting & negro-worshiping will be possible on a large scale," Arthur Sumner thought, "and therefore the great national principles of industry, labor, economy must decide the fate of the black."

"There is far more danger of being unjust to the negro than of petting him—whatever that may mean," Saxton shot back.[21]

Laura Towne saw in the free market argument only the means to new forms of coercion. "They *force* men to prove they are fit to be free by holding a tyrant's power over them," she said of Philbrick and his cotton allies.[22] She knew, too, that without a bit of capital (land, in this case), prosperity was an unattainable dream. The poorer a man was, the poorer he would likely remain.

The land issue exposed the rivalries, jealousies, and differing aims among the Yankee volunteers. Money, power, the island air: something worked a change in New Englanders who came south to do antislavery work and stayed to raise cotton. "He is now a landed proprietor, or a planter, as he calls himself," Towne said of the amiable Arthur Sumner, whom she otherwise greatly liked, "and he takes a planter's view of all things."[23] Philbrick metamorphosed in easy stages from Brookline abolitionism into an avatar of the planter class, a prosperous, self-assured gentleman in white linen spanking along from plantation to plantation in a fast-moving sulky.

Philbrick came to regard his laborers in traditional patriarchal style as "simple, childlike people, almost ignorant of malice, patient and easily influenced by an appeal to their feelings." Like many Bostonians of his background, he compared them favorably to the feckless Irish. Elizabeth Botume believed, with Sherman, that the ex-slaves were destined to form a perpetual peasantry. Soap, needles, and thread, she thought, would be of greater use to them than book knowledge. Few Northerners followed Laura Towne's lead in simply accepting that the races were different, in their virtues and in their vices, too.[24]

Well-meaning and, after his own fashion, devoted to the cause, Arthur Sumner expressed some of the deepest of the Yankee contradictions. In his harsher moods he found the Gullahs repellent. "The negroes of these Sea-islands are the most degraded slaves south of Dixie's line," he wrote a friend. "I hope so for the sake of their race; for a meaner, more ungrateful and unhandsome lot than those of our district I pray that I shall never see." At other times he attributed what he regarded as their failings to circumstance.

"These people are what slavery made them," he once said. "I don't blame them; but there they are."[25]

Philbrick ran up substantial cotton profits for himself and his partners—all for the best, for in his view the richer he grew, the better off his workers would be. He did say, according to Towne, that he intended to sell his holdings to the freed people at cost "as soon as he finds it for their interest," though he gave no hint of when such a time might come.[26] The 1864 harvest was down—shortages of manure during the early months, and later on the army worm loose among the bolls—but even so Philbrick, acting as agent, sold and shipped north the cotton of nearly two hundred independent black smallholders. This meant cash for the farmers and custom for the Yankee traders; in Philbrick's laissez-faire world, benefits all around.

All the same, Philbrick at the New Year of 1865 wore the aggrieved expression of a prophet scorned. It was contract time. The hands saw him not as E. Philbrick, philanthropist, but as whitefolks, and therefore a man to be approached with caution. A Gullah delegation called on him on January 6 with a demand for higher wages for the next twelvemonth. The men stared in blank silence as Philbrick explained that most of his ready money would go into preparations for the new crop. "They had evidently been listening to any amount of talk about the wealth I had acquired at their expense," he thought. The discussion went on in a cold downpour. Finally, one of the men alleged that the "big iron cage" in his office was stuffed full of greenbacks.

"A dollar a task! A dollar a task!" the delegation began to chant.[27]

The cry spread to the other plantations. A Pine Grove woman called May's Comba turned up at Philbrick's door and invited him out onto the piazza. She and her friends complained of Yankee thimbleriggers putting up the price of cloth and watering down the molasses. The few bales each family on her place produced in 1864 had hardly been worth the effort. If Philbrick wanted cotton, she said, he could pay a fair wage for it. He listened, then made his best offer.

"If any one wants to work on this plantation I will give them so and so (naming terms)," he wrote a friend, quoting himself, "but if anyone don't like my wages they may go and find better, but they can't use my land to plant their corn and 'tater' on. That's my rule."[28]

May's Comba and her friends shuffled off toward the settlements, chewing over this lesson in hard Yankee economics. The Gullahs at least could count on a meager wage to supplement their winter diet of sweet potatoes and hominy. The Sherman refugees were arriving from interior Georgia with nothing but their wretched lives. The plantation superintendents saw the displaced people collecting on the Beaufort wharf as labor competition that would keep wages down. The missionary teachers saw only misery there.

Joining General Saxton for a New Year's Day tour of the refugee camps, Lizzie Botume found more than a hundred Georgians quartered on the Beaufort jetty, exposed to a bitter east wind, some covered with old blankets or bits of carpeting fastened with thorns or sharp sticks, a fortunate few wearing cast-off soldiers' coats or crocus skirts of coarse bagging cinched at the waist with twine. The better-dressed women wore headkerchiefs fashioned from pieces of worn sailcloth.

"How are you?" Botume called out to a crowd of new arrivals shivering along the edge of the wharf.

"Us ain't no wusser than us been," someone shouted back.

The government threw open several plantation houses for refugee shelters, eight or ten people to a room. Botume visited a resettled woman to whom she'd given a needle and some thread. She had crammed her entire family of seven into a little room and she sat on the edge of a rough bedstead, "trying to sew the dress she ought, in decency, to have had on." Botume itemized the refugees' entire stock of possessions, all they were able to carry away: Spanish moss and a few rags for bedding; a hominy pot; two earthenware plates; and a broken-backed chair.[29]

Northern benevolence could be a powerful thing, but it was slow-acting and unsystematic. The missionaries had mostly sympathy to offer; the Sherman refugees needed warm clothes, shelter, food, and medical attention. Government rations were sparse, government doctors indifferent. One medico sent out to the settlements handed Botume a packet of Dover's powders and quinine and withdrew to the whites-only hospital in Beaufort without examining a single patient. "I never felt so helpless," said a subdued Towne. Arthur Sumner, who deftly maintained good relations with both Northern camps, cotton and charitable, dispatched an urgent request to the New England Freedmen's Aid Society in Boston for old clothes and blankets. The society's members were willing, but collecting, packing, and shipping the goods took time. Meanwhile, typhoid, pneumonia, malnutrition, and exposure were killing off dozens every week.[30]

Towne did what she could, though she complained of the refugees' baffling reluctance to follow her medical directions. "Nearly all who are ill take the dropsy as they get better and so go walking about as usual, till their lungs fill, and then they take the floor and die in a day or so," she wrote.[31] She had nothing that would cure the dropsy, nor yet an incantation that would cause firewood, warm clothes, and blankets to appear.

She found sanctuary in the new schoolhouse. There she could forget, for a moment, the insistent needs of the human wrack washing up on the islands every day. The school opened on January 6, everything in place except the bell, for which she expected once again to draw on Northern philanthropy. Harriet Ware's rang sweetly, but it weighed just 25 pounds and could be heard for only a mile or so. Hers must be larger, "for she calls only one plantation, and we five or six to school." She calculated that a 50-pounder, with a range of three miles, should be adequate for the job.[32]

Towne's Penn School became, with Lizzie Botume's, a showpiece of the Port Royal Experiment. Delegations of distinguished northerners were arriving along with the fighting troops Sherman and Howard were packing into the islands. Many came with absurdly unrealistic expectations. When one officer asked Botume how her students were progressing, she shot him a questioning glance. He blundered on:

"I mean how far along have they got? Are any of them able to take up book-keeping, for instance?"

She explained calmly that only a handful of her students could count to one hundred, or tell right from left. At least the fellow had the good manners to look abashed. Many of the visitors trooped through the schools with an infuriatingly proprietorial air, pocketing books, kicking at the furniture, speaking of the students as though they lacked all power of hearing, speech, and sight.

"If they could have seen those children at recess, when their visit was over, repeating their words, mimicking their tones and gestures, they would have been undeceived," thought Botume.[33]

General Howard struck the teachers as an outsider of the better kind, certainly for a soldier—especially one of Sherman's. He felt a genuine sympathy for the emancipated people. With his brother Charles, he had taken a lively interest in the personal fortunes of one former slave, a Georgian named Washington Kemp.

Leaving a wife and two daughters behind in interior Georgia, Wash Kemp followed the army to Savannah and somehow managed to attach himself to the Howards. Talking it over, they decided as an exercise in practical humanitarianism to offer Kemp a passage north and a place with their widowed mother on her farm in Leeds. He would learn farming Maine-style, and perhaps someday buy the place for himself. When Charles Howard left for Washington and Maine on New Year's Day carrying dispatches from Sherman, he traveled in company with Kemp.

Rufus Saxton at once recognized General Howard as an ally. He took him around to Miss Botume's school on January 12 and the general gave a little speech there, exhorting the children to work hard at all they tried. They promised him earnestly that they would. Lizzie Botume's pupils charmed the homesick soldier. He loved their singing: marching songs, the Yankee battle anthem "John Brown," the islanders' own hymns:

> My sister, you want to git religion,
>   Go down in de Lonesome Valley;
> My brudder, you want to git religion,
>   Go down in de Lonesome Valley.
>
> Go down in de Lonesome Valley,
> Go down in de Lonesome Valley, my Lord,
> Go down in de Lonesome Valley
>   To meet my Jesus dere.[34]

Howard visited the Penn School on January 18. The children positively sparkled with intelligence, he wrote home to Lizzie. "The school bears the look of our best New England village schools," he went on. "The order, reading, the arithmetic & the singing strike you with wonder. You can't help saying, that this is not the stuff to make slaves of."[35] Towne's students were impressed, too; not just with the general's shoulder straps and golden sash but with his mysteriously empty right sleeve, neatly folded over and pinned to his coat front.

Howard fit his sightseeing around preparations for the opening phase of the campaign. With twenty steamers a day arriving from Savannah, Blair's Seventeenth Corps and a division of John Logan's Fifteenth Corps—troops, artillery, wagons, animals—were in bivouac on Port Royal Island by January 10. Blair set his advance units to work repairing the shell road as far as the Port Royal Ferry landing on the Coosaw River, the crossing point for the move on the railroad.[36]

Gideonite schoolteachers gather in the shade of live oaks in front of a broad-porched house near Beaufort. Two boys lean against the tree at left, unsure whether they're invited into the photograph. Through the exertions of Northern volunteers, thousands of freed men, women, and children learned to read and write. By 1865, though, a malaise had set in—what Gideonite veterans called the "plantation bitters," a manifest exasperation with former slaves and their troubles. In any case, with war's end most volunteers regarded their work as done. (Western Reserve Historical Society)

Almost overnight, the teeming Sea Islands became a cockpit of conflict. Three years of close association had taught the Beaufort garrison, the missionaries, and the Gullahs a lesson in coexistence. Now the fighting soldiers tipped the balance, taking their cue from Sherman. The Great Man signally failed to charm the Gideonites, not that he made much of an effort during his stopover in Beaufort.

"The ladies pronounce Gen. S. 'horrid looking;' he is not at all handsome, & has no great humanitarian feelings," Willard Saxton remarked. "He is in strong contrast to Gen. Howard."[37]

Few of Howard's officers shared his interest in the Sea Islands experiment. They were more likely to agree with Foster's people (and with Sherman, too) that the abolitionists were spoiling the former slaves. "Nigger's Heaven," they dubbed the islands, though not in range of Howard's hearing.

The officers' messes and drinking resorts were noisy with indignation over the latest do-gooder outrage: Colonel Thomas Wentworth Higginson's "Leaves from an Officer's Journal" in the January number of the *Atlantic*. Higginson, a Boston soldier/abolitionist who commanded the First South Carolina, rhapsodized about Prince Rivers—onetime slave coachman, serving U.S. soldier, Beaufort landowner, and, for the moment, Northern magazine celebrity.

Rivers cut a striking figure. In Higginson's portrait he was six feet tall, with an athletic build, the grace of a panther, and a natural air of command. "No antislavery novel has described a man of such marked ability," Higginson wrote. "If his education reached a higher point, I see no reason why he should not command the Army of the Potomac." Sherman's officers patronized the eastern army and its generals, but even they drew the line at this admittedly extravagant conclusion. Henry Hitchcock predicted that all the attention would make Rivers "conceited." The Treasury men agreed, and anyway they resented Rivers for his effrontery in buying up prime Beaufort town lots, properties that might otherwise have gone to favored Northern associates.[38]

The missionaries, Foster's officers, and the T-men drew together in their fear and dislike of the ragged, longhaired, swaggering westerners. "Strange, rough-looking, unshaven, and badly dressed, they seemed like a gang of coal-heavers, when compared to the trim and smug fellows here," thought Arthur Sumner. Besides, they consumed everything for miles around, food, drink, and firewood, reducing the missionaries to a spare diet of hominy and sweet potatoes fried in tallow. The army monopolized sea transport, delaying supplies, causing a coal shortage, and interrupting the mails. Troops swarmed over the Beaufort shops and swept the shelves clean, buying everything from "a jews harp to Worcester's Unabridged," according to Sumner. Yet they brought scant profit, for they almost never paid in cash, inviting the counterjumpers instead to show up on the next battlefield to collect their debts.[39]

Otis Howard found the Saxtons—Rufus and Matilda, Willard, Mary, and their infant son Eddie—thoroughly domesticated in their pied-à-terre on Bay Street in Beaufort. The brigadier with his lustrous sidewhiskers and the statuesque Tillie certainly made a handsome couple. Howard warmed, too, to the toddler. He "petted him & received his familiarities as if it reminded him of home scenes," Willard Saxton could not help noticing.[40]

Glimpses of the Saxton ménage only deepened Howard's yearning for his family. He had appealed to Sherman at the New Year for a short leave—"Now let me off," he begged, "I don't ask but for two days at home"—but the Great Man abruptly refused him. He thought of sending to icebound Leeds for Lizzie and one or two of the children. "These old trees, green and luxuriant—how very much you would enjoy it here," he wrote her. He let go of the notion reluctantly, deciding in the end that he would certainly be deep into South Carolina long before Lizzie could reach Beaufort.[41]

Howard intended no irony when he described to her the impact of his army on the isolated, self-contained, and—to many Sherman veterans—intolerably comfortable Yankee province of the Sea Islands.

"It seems almost like sacrilege to allow my rough soldiers to disturb their quiet and order," he wrote in his wobbly slanting left hand. His orders against thievery and vandalism were no more effective here in Union territory than they had been in rebel Georgia two months before. The spirit of the army remained lawless. "It is almost impossible to keep the soldiers from seizing every horse and mule and appropriating sundry other things that don't belong to them," he went on. They rustled government animals and sold them to unsuspecting Gullahs. Provost troops collared the local men for buying stolen livestock; the soldiers went unpunished. Saxton convened a court-martial, but convictions were virtually impossible to obtain. For their own protection, he finally declared Beaufort off-limits to blacks.[42]

In individual cases, Foster's and even Sherman's men often showed kindness and consideration to former slaves. John Gray thought soldiers had no business being mixed up with "bobolition"— Saxton "commands two regiments and a lot of schoolmarms in a town as peaceful as Cambridgeport," he once remarked acidly. Still, he took a lively interest in his housekeeper's daughter, a ten-year-old fast

Laborers, some half-buried in bolls, prepare cotton for ginning in Beaufort. Profit-seeking Northern investors pressured former slaves to work on cotton plantations as wage earners. They resisted, preferring to tend their own subsistence plots of yams and corn. "The negroes can see plainly enough that the proceeds of the cotton will never get into their black pockets," remarked Laura Towne. (Library of Congress)

learning to read. He asked his mother to make up a packet of books for her, titles meant to entertain rather than instruct.

"I do not wish any good or useful works of which she seems to have some of a most doleful and stupid sort," he wrote, doubtless with the schoolmarms in mind, "but some easy fairy books, particularly the history of Hop-o-my-Thumb, of whom I found she had never heard."[43]

Hitchcock's lawyerly eye caught nuances the well-intentioned Howard either failed to see or preferred to ignore. Saxton acquired his "fine, airy, large-windowed, many porched" Bay Street town house at a tax sale for $2,000—nothing illegal or even sharp about it, but it rang false all the same, Hitchcock thought, in light of the brigadier's fervid speechmaking in favor of land for the freed people.

"Saxton is not popular with our officers generally," Hitchcock observed, "many of whom—justly or unjustly—think or say they think he took up the 'nigger business' in order to get advancement." Weighing the evidence, he went on judiciously:

> *Per contra*, Gen. Howard is said to think very highly of [Saxton] as a sincere and conscientious man; Gen. Sherman evidently does not hold that opinion. Either is likely to be prejudiced, one for and the other against him—Howard's kind disposition and truly Christian charity, and Sherman's quick way of judging men, with his dislike of theorists and 'abolitionists,' etc., and his special appreciation of men of action, perhaps disqualifying either.[44]

To the skeptics' disgust, Edwin Stanton backed Saxton during his Sea Islands stopover in mid-January. The war secretary thoroughly deranged Foster's headquarters at Hilton Head during his brief call. "He has been very bearish and boorish, as is his nature," Gray remarked.[45] The visit to Saxton in Beaufort ran a good deal smoother.

The Twenty-sixth USCT paraded along Bay Street in honor of Stanton. Saxton laid on a formal dinner for him at the Bay Street house. He and Tillie surrendered their bedroom to Stanton: a slight inconvenience, as Willard Saxton presently learned, in comparison to the reward.

"A memorable day in our family, & the dawn of a new era in the history of this work for the instruction & elevation of the freedmen," Willard recorded in his journal entry for January 15. "The General gets up a plain Brigadier, & retires at night a Brevet-Major General; I get up, as usual, plain Captain Saxton, & lay my head on my pillow at night, by the side of a happy wife, a Brevet-Major."[46]

The Saxtons served the Stanton entourage a celebratory breakfast of beefsteak, mutton, and turkey, then embarked upon the obligatory school tour. Stanton complained to Lizzie Botume about his health (a griping of the bowels; no wonder, after that morning meal) and declined her invitation to lunch, saying duty called.

"Public office is like a treadmill," he told her with a weary shrug; "when one steps on he must move on, and there is no halt or rest after that."[47]

The rumor raced through the islands: Stanton had sacked Foster, replaced him with Howard, and promoted Saxton. Anyway, the last part was true. Saxton won new powers and responsibilities, too, along with the brevet.

"He has entire control of all the colored people now in, or who may hereafter come into the Dep't.," Willard exulted. "All this in black & white, & his authority cannot be controverted or interfered with, by Foster or anyone else."[48]

Refugees continued to pour in from Georgia and the South Carolina main, hundreds every week. While Saxton celebrated his promotion with a new round of visits to the island churches, Foster launched a counterstroke. Saxton and Parson French were stirring up the blacks beyond endurance, he wrote Sherman, filling their heads with all manner of unrealistic notions. Worse yet, Saxton abused his new powers by threatening "to have the head cut off" of any officer who tried to thwart him.[49] With Stanton's endorsement and a second star, Saxton meant to ride roughshod over his old nemesis. The missionaries urged him on. Without consulting Foster, he threw open outlying Edisto to black colonization and drew on Foster for troops to garrison the island.

Meantime, the Army of the Tennessee moved on the Charleston & Savannah. Blair's corps set off at midnight on January 14 for Port Royal Ferry. When Howard turned up around sunrise the light forces were on the mainland and had scattered or captured the Confederate pickets. The sounds of singing floated over from a group of slaves' cabins—mainlanders celebrating the Jubilee, someone told him.

The leading troops, a brigade drawn from Logan's corps, pushed on through the damp and shaggy Low Country wilderness, skirmishing with Confederate rear guards under Lafayette McLaws, whose infantry were dug in along the railroad at Pocotaligo. The skirmishers approached the main Confederate works late in the afternoon. "You'd better get out; we are the Fifteenth Corps!" they called out. Cannon fire, loud, even startling, like thunder, sounded intermittently through the night. With bluecoats lapping his flanks, McLaws withdrew without a fight to a new line beyond the Salkehatchie River.

"All done in one day what the army in this Dep't have been trying three years to do, & in the failure of which so many lives have been sacrificed," Willard Saxton observed.[50] Confederates charged that the dour, trouble-prone McLaws had been drunk during the retreat. He had crossed James Longstreet at Knoxville in eastern Tennessee in 1863 and ended up before a court-martial in consequence.* Now South Carolina cavalrymen reported having seen him doubled over along the side of the Salkehatchie River road, spewing into a ditch while the Federals were brushing past the Pocotaligo defenses.

Whatever the case, Howard pried McLaws out of his works on Saturday and on the Sabbath he bestrode the iron of the railroad, on Sherman's schedule and at a cost of only a dozen casualties. Captured Confederate documents contrasted Howard's precision and economy of effort with John Hatch's elephantine approach to Honey Hill six weeks ago, a tribute to Howard's generalship that pleased him almost as much as a show of appreciation from the Great Man himself.[51]

A FEW SOUTH CAROLINIANS were hopeful still. They accepted the comforting fiction of Hood's amazing recovery after the Nashville debacle. They trusted Lee to perform a conjurer's trick and produce the troops and weapons that would deliver them from the Yankees. At Oak Lawn Plantation on the Edisto River south of Charleston, Ann Elliott waited stoically upon events, even as the assurance of inherited privilege that had sustained her for all her sixty-one years began to slip irrecoverably away.

William Elliott had left her a widow in February 1863. Now his death seemed to have foreshadowed the cataclysm: Gettysburg and Vicksburg; Spotsylvania, Petersburg, and the Richmond siege; the fall of Atlanta and Sherman's sudden appearance in the Low Country. In public life William Elliott had been a moderate Whig Unionist. Beginning with the Nullification episode of thirty years back, John Calhoun and his fire-eater successors had driven him from practical politics, though he kept his hand in as a gentleman theorist, evangelizing for the industrialization of the poor, backward, agrarian South. He remained an ardent defender of slavery—a divinely ordered institution, in his view, not to mention the foundation of Elliott prosperity and power.

---

*Longstreet accused him of failing to prepare adequately for the assault on Fort Sanders, Knoxville, in November 1863. The military court vindicated McLaws.

Political affairs were a duty. William Elliott's heart beat highest when from the gallery at Oak Lawn he could follow streamers of waterfowl drifting across the winter sky, or hear the baying of the pack tearing along the creek bottoms. His *Carolina Sports by Land and Water*, a collection of lighthearted sketches of Low Country outdoor life, was a modest hit in the 1850s. Large hunting and fishing parties used to gather at Oak Lawn then, overfed, hard-drinking men doing their best to drive all the game out of the country. They and their black gillies, bearers, and beaters pursued the devilfish (a large ray, with hornlike pectoral fins) on the water and bear, wildcat, and fox in the pine brakes. Elliott once claimed, miraculously, to have destroyed two bears with a single gun blast, and thirty ducks with one load of bird shot. In a typical passage from one of the sketches, he apostrophized the supreme instant at which the dogs pick up the scent and bound off in full cry:

> Huntsmen, is it not charming? Does it not make your pulse quicken? Is there not a thrill of pleasure shooting through your frame? Have you a wife? a child? *Have you a neck?* If you can, at such a moment, answer questions such as these, you do not feel your position and are but half a sportsman![52]

The Elliott sons, Thomas Rhett, William, and Ralph, attended Harvard or the University of Virginia. The Elliott daughters, Ann, Mary, Emily, and Harriet, studied French and the piano at finishing school in Charleston. Master William and his wife presided over great balls at Oak Lawn, the younger Elliotts and their beaux and belles whirling around the ballroom till dawn in the buttery glow of the Argand lamps. Miss Hattie married a handsome, romantic Cuban revolutionary exile, Ambrosio Gonzales, known in the family as "Gonsie." Miss Mary accepted a more conventional suitor, the solid, humdrum Georgetown rice planter Andrew Johnstone.

William Elliott's calls for economic experiments that would break the South's dependence on rice and cotton grew more urgent as the sectional crisis deepened. In *The Letters of Agricola*, published in 1852, he repeated his argument for the indispensability of slavery as an economic and social system, whatever those officious, interfering Northern abolitionists might say. Even so, Elliott opposed secession in 1861, though he accepted the result, became a loyal Confederate, and saw his three sons into the rebel army.

By January 1865, events had pulped the Agricola letters into so much wastepaper. Elliott lands on Hilton Head and Port Royal islands—Myrtle Bank, Ellis, Shell Point, The Grove, and Bay Point plantations—were in Yankee hands or overrun by squatter contrabands. Mainland slaves were restive and hard to control. Ralph Elliott ordered several recaptured Oak Lawn runaways whipped, and sold off two others at auction in Charleston. Now Sherman's shadow fell across the mainland holdings—five large plantations in the Edisto and Ashepoo districts.

War had scattered the younger Elliotts. Thomas served on the staffs of a succession of second-line generals, backwater postings that left him free to manage the surviving family holdings. Ralph commanded a company in a South Carolina cavalry regiment on picket duty along Pamlico Sound. William Jr., though tubercular and intermittently feverish, handled recruiting and conscription assignments in interior South Carolina—light duty, though potentially dangerous, as his sister Mary Johnstone had nightmarishly discovered.

Her husband, a conscription-enforcer, invited three deserters into their home at Flat Rock, North Carolina, in 1863 for dinner and a discussion of the mechanics of amnesty and a return to the army. The renegados murdered Andrew Johnstone in cold blood for his trouble. Now Mary struggled to raise their six children on her own. Lonely, homesick, overworked, chronically hard up, she looked to the future with dread, and prayed that the hard hand of war would spare her fifteen-year-old son.

Hattie Gonzales lived in besieged, blockaded Charleston with her husband, a staff officer with good army connections and the brashness to exploit them shamelessly. Ann and Emily Elliott, spinsters both (and likely to remain so, given the war's grievous toll on the males of their generation), lived with their mother at Oak Lawn. From his camp on Pamlico Sound, Ralph fretted over whether he should try for a leave and go down to his mother's place before Sherman could get there. For all he knew, the high command had matters well in hand. Yet nobody had been able to stop Sherman up to now.

"I trust that, with Beauregard on the C&S RR & Hardee in Sherman's front you may still be spared the necessity of fleeing from your dear and beautiful home," he wrote his mother. "What a mortification it is to be here idle whilst *old men, boys & Georgians* are battling for our own dear homes & firesides."[53]

In fact, Confederates had beaten the Yankees to Oak Lawn, partly for their own resupply, partly to deny provender to the enemy. Commissary officers paying in all but worthless scrip had assessed Ann Elliott for nineteen hundred pounds of fresh beef in November. They were due to return for bacon any day. South Carolina militia recruiters were threatening to conscript her overseer, whose Confederate War Department exemption carried little weight with state military authorities these days.

Like the rebel generals, Ann Elliott was paralyzed with indecision. Hattie urged her to abandon Oak Lawn and withdraw to Charleston. Gonsie, a famous string puller, offered to divert a boxcar to Adams Run to collect her valuables. She had heard fearful stories of the Charleston bombardment, though, and the idea of falling in with the refugee columns appalled her. But she didn't dare linger at home.

"The truth, the melancholy truth, is that we have no troops to crush Sherman, that we have heard not one word of help from Virginia & that the whole state is at the mercy of Sherman," Hattie admitted.[54]

William minor, on the other hand, believed the Yankees could still be stopped. Lee ordered reinforcements to Sherman's front in late January, a cavalry corps under Lieutenant General Wade Hampton, a famous South Carolinian and a commander with a good fighting reputation. William passed along the news to his mother.

"Hampton's men are eager to fight him. *They* have no doubt as to the success of our cause," he wrote her.[55]

The Federal columns, meantime, were on the march.

"I can hear firing in the direction of White Point," Miss Emily reported from Oak Lawn on January 29, "but they sound like our guns."[56]

HOWARD'S CAVALRY PATROLS FANNED OUT in search of the floodbound left wing. Heavy rains and the overflowing Savannah River worked to his advantage, leaving him plenty of time to fill his victualing and ammunition wagons and, incidentally, to take in more of the Port Royal Experiment. He addressed Lizzie Botume's Sabbath school, commending the virtues of hard work and self-reliance in his high, piping voice. "His earnest, simple manners made a deep impression," thought Willard Saxton, who, with little Eddie in tow, helped out Lizzie most Sundays.[57]

Howard's farewell contained a hint of apology for his unruly soldiery. "I trust the memory of us may be pleasant after the smart of roughness shall be forgotten," he wrote Rufus Saxton. "Stick to your sturdy integrity and your unflinching faith in a righteous God and he will make you prevail in every good work."[58] If Saxton appreciated Howard's blessing, he showed no regret at the departure of his ill-mannered army.

On the Savannah, the Second Massachusetts struck tents on January 17, crossed to the Carolina bank, and slogged through Hardeeville to the half-drowned hamlet of Purysburg. Charley Morse had succeeded Colonel William Cogswell in command of the regiment just a few days before, and the order to march caught him unprepared. "I have not a decent coat except my dress one and I have been obliged to buy good trousers and boots," he complained. A sheathing of india rubber would have served Morse better. Rain fell incessantly from the nineteenth to the twenty-third. Water stood two feet deep in the road, trapping most of General Slocum's wing on the Georgia side. "The country is navigable for vessels of the largest draught," Sam Storrow joked, making light of miserable circumstances. Pickets rowed to their posts in rafts, skiffs, and scows. The surging current swept away the corduroying, broke up the pontoons, and cut off part of the Twentieth Corps' train.[59]

Morse faced manpower problems as well. He would march short one capable company officer, for Sam Storrow had accepted Cogswell's invitation to follow him to his new command, a brigade in the Third Division. The ranks were so thin that Morse felt obliged to apply for a draft of conscripts, something no commander liked to do. "I shall expect to receive at the end of this campaign at least 800 good men all of the best moral character warranted not to desert for at least three days after assignment," he quipped. He knew better, of course. In an 1864 draft, more than half the Second's allotment of conscripts, a hard set of parricides, graverobbers, cardsharps, and drunks, melted away on the long trip from Boston to Atlanta.[60]

In ancient days, the thousand-strong Second Massachusetts won admiration for its perfect turnout: shoes and belts blacked and polished bright, brass all ablaze, muskets safe for the whitest glove. The officers were earnest, hardworking, gentlemanly, and aloof—hard to distinguish from West Pointers, though most in fact were Harvard men. "We have earned the name of the 'stuck up' Massachusetts regiment," Morse wrote then. Now, four months short of four years in the field, the Second marched into South Carolina with patched trousers, sun-bleached blouses, flapping brogans, and a complement of fewer than two hundred officers and men.[61]

Morse faulted the politicians. With a political will, veteran units could be kept up to strength—witness the Third Wisconsin of his own brigade, another 1861 regiment. "Batches of recruits 200 at a time come from their state without a guard and without a single loss by desertion," Morse observed. While the old units were starved for men, Governor Andrew called new regiments into existence with a sweep of his pen. Cavalry and heavy artillery units might be trumpery and irrelevant (infantry veterans swore they were), but they gave the governor lots of officer's commissions to bestow. Cynics attributed Andrew's enthusiasm for African American enlistment to a bookkeeping anomaly: blacks recruited for Massachusetts regiments in other states counted toward the Commonwealth's draft quota. The governor expected young white male voters (and their textile manufacturer employers) to show their appreciation at election time.[62]

Sherman's autumn victories were only a partial tonic for a war-weary North. Grant's army lay immobile in the Petersburg lines and the memory of the terrible cost of his 1864 campaign remained vivid. "Everything is changed in the Army of the Potomac," a former aide wrote Howard. "Most of the old officers are dead or out of the service." President Lincoln had already called for a new 300,000-man levy for 1865. "Nothing much short of a miracle can save me from a draft this time," Howard's brother Rowland wrote mournfully. Governor Andrew could hardly be blamed for seeking recruits in unlikely places. He had even sent state agents abroad, into the German states, and in the ranks of the Second Massachusetts in January 1865 were a number of men who understood no more than a few words of English.[63]

Morse grieved over the slow disintegration of the Second Massachusetts. Fiercely loyal to the regiment, he swore he would never leave it, not for promotion nor yet for a staff appointment; and in fact, not long after Gettysburg, he had refused the offer, a flattering one, of a colonelcy in one of the new black units. Now he commanded a skeleton, the tired, ill-clad bones of the "Old Second."

Only a couple of years out of Harvard when the regiment marched away from Brook Farm on July 8, 1861, Charley Morse had drifted with the wartime current, taking the experience as it came. Boston, Cambridge, and the Morse home on Jamaica Pond had bounded his prewar world. In the army he glimpsed something of what lay beyond. Harpers Ferry, Virginia, with its dark, narrow streets and leaning stone buildings, reminded the cosmopolitan Bob Shaw of a Rhenish town. The views from the Shenandoah eminences were as romantic as any in the Swiss cantons or Tuscany, or anyway so Shaw insisted.

Such a freight of terrible experience packed into a few years, scenes that would remain as vivid as though they had happened yesterday no matter how long he lived: a raw Virginia afternoon in March 1862, and a row of corpses in front of the courthouse at Strasburg, twenty of them laid out for burial, their faces covered by the capes of their overcoats. Morse stepped over the bodies and entered the building. A boy of sixteen or so sat with his back to a wall, arms drawn across his abdomen, eyes closed, face drained of color. The wound meant the end of him, Morse knew. He would die here, and he would die alone.

At Cedar Mountain in August of that year, a meeting engagement with Stonewall Jackson and a hecatomb for the Second Massachusetts: 40 dead, 93 wounded, 40 missing. Only 7 of 23 officers survived unhurt. Falling back, the regiment abandoned some of its wounded on the battlefield, among them Major James Savage, Morse's particular friend. The enemy surgeons cut away Savage's shredded leg and prepared to take off an arm, Morse heard later; but on October 22 he died of complications in a rebel hospital in Charlottesville.

At Antietam in September, confused fighting along the edge of an orchard, the men lying low and firing at gray figures moving through a field of ripening corn: Jackson's corps again, and one man in every four in the Second Massachusetts killed, wounded, or missing. A spent musket ball struck Morse in the temple, knocked him down, and raised a monstrous blue welt above his eye. He and Shaw lay in their shelter tent that night, the dead all around giving off the odor of herring left too long in the sun. They talked quietly of home—the Morses in Jamaica Plain, Charley's mother dying of cancer that summer, his sister Ellen, pretty, lame, and housebound, their neighbor Francis Parkman, the historian, a kinsman of the Shaws, and Shaw's

Brahmin parents, high-minded, demanding, prepared to sacrifice a son to right the world's wrongs.

A letter arrived two days after the battle for Thomas Dillon, a private in Morse's company, Irish-born, a soldier for six weeks, now a corpse. The letter found its way to Morse, along with the rest of Dillon's belongings. "One of the most affecting things I ever read," Morse thought, "yet it is only one instance among thousands." Hundreds were buried where they fell; and row upon row of metallic coffins with bodies packed in charcoal awaited shipment home.[64]

At Culp's Hill in July of 1863, in the cool of the early morning of the third day of Gettysburg, an ill-judged order to advance. The Second Massachusetts and the Twenty-seventh Indiana crept forward in line of battle through a meadow toward a copse thick with enemy infantry—Jackson's again, only Richard Ewell commanded now with Jackson two months in his grave. The Indiana troops drifted away. The Second fought on until a messenger turned up with belated permission to withdraw. The stretcher-bearers carried off another forty-four men killed and eighty-four wounded.

So the endless war had exacted a tribute of the most powerful friendships of Morse's young life: Jim Savage, "nearer to being a perfect man than anyone I ever knew," dead in a Virginia hospital; Tom Robeson, shot down in the meadow at Gettysburg; genial Tom Fox, smiling through the pain as he hobbled back from the edge of the woods below Culp's Hill, dead at home before the month was out; Bob Shaw, killed at Fort Wagner, his body dumped into a common grave.

"I find my feeling for old classmates is weak compared to the friendships formed in the 2nd—like yours & mine," Shaw had written Morse not long before his death.[65]

Luck held for a few of the originals, Cogswell, James Grafton, Morse himself. And John Fox: "I have been in every action of the regiment without being touched even in my clothes," he had written home after Gettysburg. "Verily they will have to try a silver bullet on me. I don't brag about this and you needn't either."[66] Grafton, too, seemed to lead a charmed life; shot in the head at Cedar Mountain and in the leg at Chancellorsville, he mended each time and returned to service, though he still walked with a pronounced limp.

Surely the end could not be far off now. In tearing high spirits, Fox anticipated new fields for forage. "If I ever come home I will shoulder my crutch and show, if not how fields were won, how sweet potatoes, pigs and rice were procured to any extent," he wrote Fairy.[67] Downpours made the going slow, at least at the start. Weighed down with his new responsibilities, Morse foretold difficult days ahead—a test for overconfident troops accustomed to easy success and fallen out of the habit of mourning.

"The first hard fight will take this army by surprise," he predicted, "but I believe there is good stock enough in it to hold its own after it recovers from the first shock."[68]

For now, the only battles were with the slanting rain, the mud, and the spindly pines that retreating Confederates dropped across the roads. The Second Massachusetts bogged northward through deserted country beyond Purysburg to firmer ground around Robertville. The dwelling places hereabouts were more substantial than those in Georgia, if still, Morse thought, no better than second- or even third-class at home. Most of the valuables had been carted off, but in one house he found good furniture, a piano, and a library of several hundred richly bound volumes, including a complete set of the works of Thomas Carlyle.

The inhabitants had vanished as though swept away in the freshet, except for a few yokel whites and the occasional furtive slave. Skirmishers caught glimpses of Joseph Wheeler's cavalry vedettes flitting through the damp woods. The Georgia experience had hardened Morse, drawn down the last stocks of sentiment that survived the battles of 1862 and 1863. Putting the torch to a home, watching a man's livelihood, his dreams, and his future melt in the heat of the flames—such scenes, reenacted day after day, had lost their power to stir him. He wanted to come to grips with the enemy and throttle him and, unlike those at home, he hardly cared how long it took.

"I had rather campaign till I am fifty years old than make any terms with rebels while they bear arms; we *can* conquer a peace, and it is our duty to do it," he wrote his father from abandoned Robertville.[69]

By January 29 most of the Twentieth Corps lay concentrated near the hangdog town. Sherman's columns menaced Augusta, Columbia, and Charleston all at once. "I hope the rebels know as little as we do which one is in the most immediate danger of a visit," Morse remarked. Nor were the officers of Howard's wing any better informed. "General Sherman says it is to be the greatest campaign yet undertaken," artillerist Tom Osborn noted. "So General Hooker said before Chancellorsville and he was correct"—though not in the sense he intended. But it was different this time. For all Sherman's gasconade, the army believed that he would deliver the goods.[70]

General Howard fretted not so much about where the army would go as about which laws of God and man it would breach along the way. The troops ignored his orders against plundering, figuring, rightly, that they ran slight risk of punishment. Like Morse, though for other reasons, Howard, too, anticipated a test—and he wondered whether the bold, arrogant Sherman was riding for a fall.

"You have done one new thing under the sun," Howard's friend E. B. Webb had written at the close of the March to the Sea; "don't be too sure you can repeat it. Don't think me a croaker. I have the most infinite confidence in Gen'l Sherman and Gen'l Howard, but there are some things that cannot be done. History shows that they have not been done."[71]

A superstitious dread crept up on Howard, the notion that the army would be required somehow to atone for its sins. "Next Monday we shall probably swing off again and trust to a kind Providence," he wrote Lizzie from Pocotaligo. "We do so many things that are wrong in this living off the country in the way we do that I do not like it and I am afraid of retribution."[72]

# Part Two

# The End of the War

*February–April 1865*

It was winter soon and already soldiers
were beginning to come back—
the stragglers, not all of them
tramps, ruffians, but men who
had risked and lost everything,
suffered beyond endurance and had returned
now to a ruined land, not the same men
who had marched away but transformed.

William Faulkner
*Absalom, Absalom!*

# 4

# The Smoky March

SHERMAN'S ARMY EMBRACED THE ROLE of scourge. "Our mission was not to fight," Captain Daniel Oakey of the Second Massachusetts wrote in retrospect, "but to consume and destroy." Hardly anyone felt the least compassion for South Carolina, that cess of rebellion. "She richly deserves the worst that war can do," thought Sam Storrow. The Carolinas assignment harmonized perfectly with Charles Morse's savage mood. He had threatened to arrest the good-natured, unoffending Oakey for overstaying a leave; and he regarded the "chivalry," as the army mockingly dubbed all white South Carolinians of the propertied classes, with cold-blooded ferocity.[1]

"Pity for these inhabitants I have none," Morse wrote home as the van of the Twentieth Corps struck north from ruined Robertville on the first stage of the Campaign of the Carolinas. "They are rebels and I am almost prepared to agree with Sherman that a rebel has no rights, not even the right to live except by our permission."[2]

Sherman marched with 60,000 healthy, campaign-toughened men, 68 guns, and 2,500 wagons carrying seven days' forage and rations for three weeks. General P. G. T. Beauregard, a South Carolina favorite, the hero of Fort Sumter, Shiloh, Charleston, and Petersburg, drew the task of stopping him with such scattered resources as he had on hand: demoralized regulars, reluctant militia, and half-feral cavalry totaling fewer than 25,000 men.

Beauregard threw Wheeler's cavalry and the depleted infantry divisions of Lafayette McLaws and Ambrose R. Wright in Sherman's immediate front. A division of South Carolina militia garrisoned Charleston. Moving slowly eastward from Tupelo, Mississippi, were the remnants of the Army of Tennessee, retaining their designations as corps—S. D. Lee's, Stewart's, Cheatham's—but mere phantoms in fact. Robert Lee put Matthew C. Butler's cavalry division in motion for South Carolina toward the end of January, the only troops he could spare from the hard-pressed Army of Northern Virginia penned up in the Richmond-Petersburg lines.

In the classic formulation, Sherman had Beauregard on the horns of a dilemma. His left wing, Slocum's Fourteenth and Twentieth corps, threatened Augusta from the southeast. His right, Howard's Fifteenth and Seventeenth corps, menaced Charleston from Beaufort. A third potential objective, the rail junction of Branchville, South Carolina, lay between the two horns. Uncertain of Sherman's intentions, Beauregard elected to defend all three places. In the event, Sherman aimed for Columbia, and thence for Goldsboro, North Carolina, four hundred miles distant from his start lines.

The feints froze Beauregard. He lacked the energy, or perhaps the imagination, to concentrate his forces for a challenge to one or the other of the Federal wings. He decided instead to await developments. By the time Sherman's schemes matured, it would be too late for Confederate forces in Charleston and Augusta to combine to check him.

Even so, Beauregard possessed one advantage of his handicaps, in theory anyhow: With Sherman's approach, his forces would recoil onto their bases, growing stronger as they fell back. Arms and ammunition were stockpiled in Columbia. Beauregard counted, too, on the winter freshets—the January-February rains would be the heaviest in twenty years—and the "impassable" barrier of the Salkehatchie swamps to delay the Federals, perhaps stop them altogether.

For his part, Sherman anticipated a collision at some point, though as usual he felt no great urgency about bringing off a battle. ("Of course I must fight when the time comes," he once remarked, "but whenever a result can be accomplished without Battle I prefer it."[3]) Sherman sought a moral effect above all. He meant to show the civilians in his path, all of them—planters and plantation mistresses, the lesser gentry, drivers of slaves, sandhill farmers, tavern keepers, turpentine distillers, millers, cotton factors, and gin operatives—that the collapsing Confederacy could no longer protect their property, nor yet shield them from misery, want, and famine.

The campaign opened formally with the advance of Howard's wing north from Pocotaligo on Wednesday, February 1, 1865. The Fifteenth and the Seventeenth corps pushed up the narrow neck separating the Coosawhatchie and Salkehatchie Rivers, dark country, spongy underfoot, thickly grown with cypress, eerily empty, quiet, not far removed from a state of wilderness. Sherman, his quick eye darting over the landscape, suggested that the *Harper's Weekly* artists traveling with the army execute a single pen-and-ink sketch to represent all of South Carolina: "one big pine tree, one log cabin, and one nigger."[4] In places in Whippy Swamp, the first of innumerable boggy obstacles, the water stood twelve feet deep. The roads were reserved for wheeled vehicles. The troops filed along the grassy verges, now showing the first spring green in patches, or in cold, ankle-deep slime along the edges of the swamps.

These were poor, dilapidated precincts, a region of tumbledown dwellings, knock-ribbed mules, and milkless cows. Most of the inhabitants were white women, noted Tom Osborn, with lots of dirty, halfnaked children hanging onto their skirts. When Osborn asked a drabbletail group gathered in front of a stick-chimney shanty to account for their husbands, two or three acknowledged the men were away soldiering; another claimed to be an old maid. "I hain't never had no husband," one amiable slattern told him with a sly grin.[5]

Wheeler's cavalry capered in Howard's front, burning bridges, felling trees, and plundering industriously. "We didn't expect that of our own people," a Low Country farm woman told Henry Hitchcock bitterly. The Yankees, however, met and even exceeded expectations of rapaciousness. Logan's Fifteenth Corps showed a special aptitude for scientific thievery. "This is Sherman's old corps & has the reputation of understanding the phrase 'living on the enemy' better than any other in the army," Sam Storrow remarked, with a touch of envy. Bummer details robbed the occupied farms of such forage and provisions as had escaped rebel notice. They burned the abandoned ones.[6]

Orderly Port Royal, with its early blooming snowdrops and jonquils, seemed a world away from the chaotic mainland. The live oaks, so appealing to Otis Howard in the islands, here lost their charm. "It makes you feel sad to go through a long avenue of these trees & moss—so much like a cemetery style," he wrote Lizzie. And every morning those impious bummers ranged far ahead and out on the flanks of the army, sweeping over the land like a pestilence. "There were houses," he added somberly, "but now *chimneys* mostly." He could not shake the conviction that the freebooters were courting disaster for everyone. "God is my tenet," he said, "yet anything is possible."[7]

Carrying dispatches from Foster's headquarters at Hilton Head, John Gray caught up to Howard's columns on the second day of the march, slowly overtaking the Fifteenth Corps train, more than five hundred wagons stretching the full twenty miles from Pocotaligo to Hickory Hill. The wagons churned the road into mire; in some places standing water reached the horses' bellies. Wherever the columns had passed, the destruction was nearly total.

"With one or two exceptions all the buildings and fences on the road were burned," Gray wrote home, "and it was a curious sight to see how the fires gradually died out, from the bright red flames pouring forth from the house and cotton gin in the immediate rear of the army to the utter blackness near Pocotaligo where the army had passed a couple of days ago."[8]

The Carolinas campaign, he could see already, would fail his friend Ropes's test of generalship. For all the western army's success at Atlanta and on the March to the Sea, Ropes remained a skeptic, unwilling to accept Gray's impetuous judgment of Sherman as "the greatest military genius of the country."[9] Beginning with the battles around Atlanta, Sherman had faced second-string commanders—Hood, Hardee—and, from Atlanta to the sea, second-line troops.

"It is necessary to Sherman's military reputation that he should be matched against a first-class man, and that he, like McClellan, Meade and Grant, should know what it is to have plans broken up by a wary, skilful and bold, and active, and strong foe—that he should have his experience of an Antietam or Gettysburg or Wilderness or Spotsylvania," Ropes had written. "Since he has commanded an army, it has all been pretty plain sailing."[10]

Judicious among his law books in Boston, Ropes might have thought twice before airily wishing another heroic nightmare of Gettysburg on the country.* As for Sherman, riding with the Fifteenth Corps headquarters, "plain sailing" could hardly have been a less happy choice of metaphor.

The Great Man had been uncharacteristically taciturn. Now, with the return of the rains and Slocum still trapped on the wrong side of the Savannah, he sought release in spasms of ill-humor. "No one can approach Sherman without being snubbed," Osborn noted. "His high nervous temperament and sarcasm are now at their highest pitch."[11] At one halt, he vented his frustration on a young woman who had ventured out of doors, baby on her hip, to seek his protection from foragers. Still grieving, perhaps, over the death of his own infant son, he berated her for exposing the child to the bitter east wind and looked the other way while his troops emptied the storehouse of wax candles and soap—ill-gotten gains, or so he charged, of her husband's criminal dealings with blockade runners.

Howard's success in the overflowing swamps of the Salkehatchie on February 3 tranquilized Sherman—for the time being, anyway. The Seventeenth Corps van had driven the rebel cavalry across the river at Broxton's Bridge the day before; Wheeler's troopers fired the bridge and lay on the far bank in entrenchments. Howard bypassed the strongpoint, pushing on another five miles to Rivers' Bridge.

The Salkehatchie here spilled out into a densely wooded marsh more than a mile wide, fed by many small streams. A causeway carried the road over the swamp. Confederate rear guards had burned some of the causeway bridges and cut away others. From a bluff on the far bank, Lafayette McLaws covered the approach to the main channel with infantry and artillery. A Seventeenth Corps division under Joseph Mower failed in a frontal assault on McLaws's position late on the second. Mower, aptly nicknamed the Swamp Lizard, put his troops to work at once hacking two flank approaches through the ooze. Pioneer troops repaired the lagoon bridges, recycling half-charred stringers or hewing fresh ones out of the cypress woods and using boards from a dismantled country church as planking.

---

*Ropes's younger brother was killed at Gettysburg with the Twentieth Massachusetts.

Mower's infantry crossed at Rivers' Bridge in a rush on the cold, gray afternoon of February 3. His losses over the two days were around a hundred killed and wounded. Osborn, the artillery expert, was scathing about McLaws's use of the guns. "They have only directed their fire down the straight section of the road while if they had swept an arc of ten or fifteen degrees they would have done us great damage," he wrote.[12] With both flanks imperiled, McLaws pulled out before the Swamp Lizard could snap him up. Upstream, at Buford's Bridge, the Fifteenth Corps crossed the Salkehatchie unopposed.

The notion that a skilled commander could use guile and maneuver to attain his ends continued to strike Hitchcock with wonder. "These rebs, though they cannot tell how or when W. T. intends to 'flink 'em,' are always alive to the *fact* and its consequences the moment it is done, and act—and evacuate—accordingly," he observed.[13] And it was true. On the fourth, the Confederates were gone from Howard's front. That day, too, the right wing emerged at last from the Low Country quagmire.

Howard paused for a couple of days to let Slocum catch up. Kilpatrick's cavalry and the Fourteenth Corps had begun crossing the swollen Savannah on February 3, days behind schedule, and were rushing to pull up level with the Twentieth Corps. The roads were submerged beneath broad sheets of water. Corduroy sank under the weight of the trains. Off into the woods the axmen waded, felling and trimming the pines and arranging new layers of logs in the muck. To clear the Coosawhatchie drowned lands Slocum's pioneers, working through the night, knocked together a 300-foot corduroy causeway and sank it in 3 feet of water, pinning the log sections together to keep them from bobbing to the surface.[14]

Nothing detained the foragers. They reached the Midway whistle-stop on the Charleston & Augusta Railroad—the army's first objective—in a rainstorm on the morning of February 7 and offered to hold it until the skirmishers could come up. By mid-afternoon Howard had infantry upon the tracks—the Seventeenth Corps at Midway, the Fifteenth Corps a few miles down the line at Bamberg. Far from putting up the sharp fight that Sherman here expected, the Confederates offered Howard no resistance at all.

On the seventh, too, Howard's vedettes reported contact with Slocum—two divisions of the Twentieth Corps were across the upper

Salkehatchie and squelching north toward the Charleston & Augusta. Next day, Seventeenth Corps details began breaking up the railroad west from the Edisto toward Bamberg while Charles Morse's Second Massachusetts, in the Twentieth Corps van, joined in the work of destruction west of Blackville, spoiling three miles of track before nightfall.[15]

By Henry Slocum's estimate, a thousand men could abolish five miles of road in a day. Negligible Confederate resistance allowed Sherman to employ the optimum force, which Slocum defined as three sections of a thousand men each: one to overturn the rails and pry loose the wooden ties; a second to stack the ties and lay the rails atop the stacks; a third to light off the ties and heat and bend the rails. Slocum recommended the use of Poe's railroad hooks for the latter job. They gave a clever double twist to a red-hot rail, making it impossible to straighten except in a rolling mill.[16]

Morse explained the process in a letter to his brother:

> The reg'ts are scattered along for a mile—arms are stacked and the men "fall in" on one side of the track—At a given signal they take hold of the rail-tie, or whatever is in front of them; the order "Yo-heave" is then given which means lift and lift together; at this the whole length of the railroad begins to move and the movement is kept up until the whole thing goes over with a smash.[17]

Here was joyful vandalism with a strategic purpose. The wrecking of buildings for their boards, sheathing, posts, and beams had a military rationale, too. Fifteenth Corps fatigues disassembled an entire hamlet at Buford's Bridge. "There was a town of 20 or 25 houses here, but we have used it up in building bridges," Charles Wills of the 103rd Illinois noted laconically. Much of the damage was wanton, though. Seventeenth Corps troops swarmed over Woodlands, the estate of William Gilmore Simms, man of letters, romance novelist ("the Southern Cooper," admirers called him), South Carolina patriot, and slavery apologist. "He has a fine library," Tom Osborn wrote. "I think it will be saved. I should have no objection to seeing it burned. His influence has been very great in carrying on this war." Bummers set fire to thick stands of spectacularly combustible pitch pine. Smoke from the burning forests blotted out the sun. Wind-whipped flames singed the hair and clothes of men in the infantry columns and panicked the draft animals in the trains.[18]

General Howard's van crosses the North Edisto River near Orangeburg, South Carolina, in this William Waud sketch. Sherman's troops, adept at improvising temporary crossings, will quickly finish this one, appropriating whatever materials are at hand. "There was a town of 20 or 25 houses here," Charles Wills of the 103rd Illinois wrote home from a wrecked hamlet on the Salkehatchie River, "but we have used it up in building bridges." (Library of Congress)

The reunited wings pushed north for Columbia. Howard's skirmishers occupied Orangeburg, an important rail junction with lines leading to Charleston and Augusta, on the morning of February 12. By noon the engineers had completed a difficult bridging of the North Edisto, here a swiftly flowing stream forty yards wide. Fire raced through the town's business district as the first troops of the main body crossed. Sherman and others claimed an ill-natured Orangeburg merchant had lit off his own store before running away, touching off a general conflagration. Bummers were more likely responsible. The infantry turned to and fought the fires. The refugee orphanage was saved, and Sherman himself paid a call on the little waifs there.[19] All the same, by sunset half of Orangeburg lay in ashes.

Beauregard, who had reached Columbia on February 10, passed up a chance to strike Howard's head of column at Orangeburg. The right wing concentrated at Sandy Run, a dozen miles below Columbia, on the fourteenth. Slocum's wing, delayed by bad roads and burned bridges, approached Lexington, twenty miles west of the capital. Judging the Congaree River too turbulent for bridging, Sherman sent Howard with the Fifteenth Corps on to the Saluda River north and west of the city. He ordered Howard to cross the Saluda and then the Broad, which meet at Columbia to form the Congaree, enter the capital, and destroy the public buildings, railroad property, the state arsenal, gunpowder, woolen, and cotton mills, and the Palmetto Iron Works, which manufactured explosive shells, solid shot, minié balls, and cannon. Libraries, asylums, and private dwellings, Sherman said, were to be left alone.[20]

The Fifteenth Corps crossed the Saluda on pontoons on Thursday, February 16, and moved up to the Broad. The city on its sandhills lay in plain view: the unfinished granite statehouse, the town hall market with its tall clock tower that rang in secession in December 1860, wide avenues lined with magnolia, oak, and mimosa. "From our position it looks much like Peoria from the left bank of the river," thought the Illinoisan Charles Wills. Looters, white and black, could be seen carrying off bags of grain and meal. Confederate cavalry cantered about in the streets. Osborn ordered one of his battery commanders to unlimber his 20-pounder Parrotts and fire into the city.[21]

BEAUREGARD, HARDEE, AND McLAWS were helpless before Sherman. Along with other miscalculations, Beauregard seriously underestimated the speed of the Federal advance. By February 14, when he peremptorily ordered Hardee to evacuate Charleston, Howard's wing stood between Hardee's corps and the capital. Nor could the vestigial Army of Tennessee reach Columbia except by a wide and time-consuming detour to the north.

"Our forces, more or less demoralized, occupy a circumference of about 240 miles from Charleston to Augusta," Beauregard wrote Lee in Virginia. "The enemy, well organized and disciplined and flush with success, numbering nearly double our force, is concentrated upon one point (Columbia) of that circumference. The result cannot be long doubtful."[22]

Under pressure from Howard, McLaws backpedaled north to Branchville, then sidled forty miles to the east toward Hardee on the coast. In effect, he marched his division out of the battle. As for the charge of drunkenness, he sidestepped that, too. McLaws conducted a nimble defense of himself after the nighttime withdrawal from

Pocotaligo, preferring countercharges, collecting affidavits, and sending memos flying up and down the chain of command. He was more effective in this role than in opposing Howard, who advanced unhindered. He won the paper skirmish, anyway; Hardee unequivocally cleared him.[23]

A private agony gnawed at McLaws. He had heard nothing of Emily and the children for weeks. "How are you situated? What are you doing? How is your health? What are the children occupied at? How is their health? What do they talk about? Do they think of me often?" Beside himself with worry, the tough, hard-hitting infantry commander of Marye's Heights and the Peach Orchard now confessed himself ready to quit.

"I am tempted to run away, leaving all other considerations behind me, all to be sacrificed to the gratification I would experience in clasping my wife once again in my arms," he wrote Emily.[24]

The cavalryman Matthew Calbraith Butler put up a stiffer fight, skirmishing energetically on Howard's front. A native South Carolinian, the eleventh of sixteen children, Butler had gone to war with the South Carolina magnifico Wade Hampton in 1861. He recovered from a severe wound at Brandy Station in 1863 (it cost him his right foot) in time to see hard fighting around Richmond in the summer and autumn of 1864. Lee's troops were drifting home to their farms in their thousands early in 1865, but the Confederacy could still field rows of generals. Lee sent Butler and Hampton to Columbia together, to defend the Palmetto State with whatever force they could gather.

With fifteen hundred cavalry and a few companies of infantry, Butler halted on the south bank of Congaree Creek below Columbia on February 15, entrenched, and awaited the Fifteenth Corps van. His troopers covered a long causeway that led over flooded bottomlands to the crossing. Advancing through ribbons of cold fog, the leading Federals, Charles Woods's First Division, fanned out on either side of the causeway to lever Butler out of the works. The rebels fired several ragged volleys, then withdrew across the creek, the rear guards burning the bridge behind them.

This inconsequential encounter used up the last of Alfred Manigault's strength. Febrile, gaunt, barely able to mount a horse, he had dutifully rejoined the Fourth South Carolina Cavalry in late January. Falling back from Congaree Creek, he caught a violent chill and fell into a coma.[25] The brigade surgeon loaded Manigault into an ambulance that jolted him, insensible and still in his soaking clothes, out of the threatened capital north toward a makeshift hospital in Winnsboro.

The roar of Howard's guns and the steady rumbling of the ambulances along Main Street brought Columbia's four-year Confederate fantasy life abruptly to an end. Only a few weeks before, fantasy and reality had commingled in the grand event of the winter season, the Great Bazaar for the Confederate wounded at the new capitol building. The marbled halls were hung with festoons of aromatic evergreen and upholstered in rich damask. Ladies served up real coffee. Mrs. General Joe Johnston contributed an embroidered crepe shawl as a raffle prize. There were toys and baubles from Europe. Trestle tables buckled under the weight of luxuries unsampled for years.

"Everything to eat can be had if one can pay the price," Emma LeConte remarked. "A small slice of cake is two dollars—a spoonful of Charlotte Russe five dollars, and other things in proportion." Mrs. Annie Snowden raffled off her famous flaxen-haired wax doll baby, whose adventurous career had commenced with a run from her Liverpool birthplace through the Yankee blockade. She raised $2,000. "One could buy a live negro baby for that," Emma's Uncle John pointed out.[26]

The convalescents—raw, shocking reminders of war borne on litters from the Texas booth in the Hall of the House to the Georgia booth in the senate chamber, hobbling gamely under the evergreens on crutches, or trundled down the polished corridors in wheelchairs—were the stars of the bazaar. Grace Elmore caught sight of an attendant matter-of-factly feeding a man with both arms shot away. A moment later her glance fell on an acquaintance, a bravo of her prewar circle named Walker Adams.

"I would not have recognized him," she wrote that night, still in a state of shock, "looks like an old man, is paralyzed, and tho' his brain which oozed from the broken skull was replaced, his mind has never been right since; and how bright and agreeable he used to be."[27]

A crowded, dim-lit, chilled, and hungry city awaited Sherman. The LeConte families, pooling resources, subsisted on two meals a day: corn bread for breakfast, a small cube of beef, a few potatoes, and hominy for dinner. There were the Georgians to feed, too: Jane Harden and her daughter Ada were refugeeing with John and Josephine LeConte. Wood sold for a hundred dollars a load when it could be obtained at all, and Joe LeConte kept just one fire burning in the house. The gas popped on and off at whim, so that sometimes there were only smoky tallow candles, at two dollars apiece, to read or sew by.

The Elmores—Harriet, relict of Franklin Harper Elmore, banker, railroad developer, and political protégé of John C. Calhoun*; her daughters Grace and Sally; and a shifting population of maiden aunts, she-cousins and itinerant widows—lived nowadays by binge and fast. "Every time there is a rumor of Yankees," wrote twenty-six-year-old Grace, "we have a spread to prevent their getting our good things. Then we economize closely when the rumor proves to be false." Coffee and sugar were unobtainable, but the Elmores were well-supplied with poultry, sausage, and sorghum from the family plantation on the Congaree twelve miles below Columbia, though for how much longer nobody could say.[28]

Rumors flew and anxieties mounted with Sherman's approach. The peace conference at Hampton Roads, Virginia, in early February yielded agreement on a sixty-day armistice. England and France were prepared to recognize the Confederacy on March 4—the date, so it happened, of Abraham Lincoln's second inaugural. Judson Kilpatrick, the Yankee cavalry raider, would ride into town any minute now.

The fire bell so unnerved Aunt Sally Rhett that she spent a night fully dressed rather than risk having to receive Kilpatrick in her nightgown. That was a false alarm. Sally Elmore roused Grace in the middle of the night to say the Yankees were within a dozen miles of Columbia. In the morning, Wade Hampton himself sent word denying the report.[29]

The LeContes in cloister at South Carolina College packed up the books of the family library for safekeeping. Miss Emma prepared for the Yankees by culling her private correspondence. "I have destroyed most of my papers, but have a lot of letters still that I do not wish to burn, and yet I do not care to have them share the fate of Aunt Jane's and Cousin Ada's in Liberty County, which were read and scattered along the roads," she wrote in her diary. She found a safe

---

*He succeeded Calhoun in the Senate in 1850, but died only a few weeks and one speech after taking office.

place for them, secreted them where no oafish, blundering Yankee would ever think of looking.[30]

Joseph LeConte's Georgia odyssey had ended with his return home on February 7. He made preparations to take flight again almost at once. Orders arrived from Richmond on the tenth to pack up the Niter Bureau labs and move them out of Sherman's path. Word reached Columbia on the thirteenth that the Yankees were in Orangeburg.

With nonstop effort, LeConte saw the government crates into the cars at the Charlotte depot. He found panic and a cosmic disorder there. Jostling crowds of women, many with children, begged for places in the train. The gunpowder labs took priority, and LeConte ignored their entreaties. "It is difficult to see the surging, pleading mass and remain unmoved, it is difficult to resist the strong tide of human sympathy; still I try to remain calm," he wrote. "The authorities say there is no danger." Even as the Orangeburg report raced through the city, General Hampton continued to assure Columbians that Sherman would not come.[31]

Emma sewed deep pockets onto the inside of her hoopskirt, on the assumption that not even Sherman's vandals would be so unmannerly as to search for valuables there. She heard cannon fire for the first time on February 15, a dark, cold, mizzling Wednesday. Trains were pulling out of Columbia every hour, wagons rattling through the streets all day and all night. Her father left by the Winnsboro road early on the sixteenth at the head of a convoy of two wagons, two carts, and a buggy, with an escort of three whites and twenty-two blacks, most of the latter slaves hired out to the Niter Bureau. One of the carts contained as much of the family's wealth as LeConte had been able to gather up on short notice: linen, blankets, clothing, silver sugar bowls and cups, family pictures, jewelry, and wine. The Yankee great guns opened fire in the forenoon. A stray shell penetrated the college compound, whirring past the LeConte piazza and exploding not far off. The cannonade continued intermittently until dinnertime.[32]

Beauregard wired Lee early in the evening that he intended to evacuate Columbia, and a few hours later he was gone. Hampton stayed overnight to supervise the final withdrawal. Howard, on the Broad, ferried over Colonel George Stone's brigade of Woods's division to cover the pontoniers throwing across the bridge that would

Emma LeConte, shown here at age seventeen, in a photograph made in Columbia, South Carolina. She had grown weary of the war, and fretted it would go on forever. "No pleasure, no enjoyment—nothing but rigid economy and hard work—nothing but the stern realities of life," she recorded in her diary. (South Caroliniana Library, University of South Carolina)

carry the Fifteenth Corps to the gates of the capital. Straggling cavalry from Wheeler's command looted shops and storehouses in the darkened city. The army had tumbled hundreds of bales of cotton into the streets for burning, a routine practice on the approach of Yankees. Wheeler's troopers cut open bales and set fire to loose cotton as they pulled out.[33]

Mobs raided the state commissary for rice, bacon, and salt. One of the LeConte servants, Henry, returned from uptown to report corn, flour, and sugar covering the ground like snow. He brought back quantities of meat, rice, and sugar for the LeConte larder. A tremendous detonation just before dawn practically lifted Emma out of her bed. A looter, it turned out, had accidentally touched off a store of gunpowder at the South Carolina Railroad depot, blowing himself and twenty others to kingdom come. The blast shattered Bessie Le-

Conte's nerves. In her nightdress, her long hair loose, she wandered aimlessly from room to room, dazed, milk-white, close to hysterics.

Hampton issued orders early on Friday the seventeenth prohibiting the burning of cotton in the streets. They came too late. The stuff smoldered in long rows and burning tufts shot about on a hard, gusty northwesterly wind, touching off new fires. Butler's troopers, the last organized Confederates to leave, withdrew through the east end of the city between nine and ten o'clock in the morning.

Grace Elmore watched them pass from her front gate. "I had one little bottle of wine and a wine glass which I gave as long as it lasted," she wrote in her journal. "We gave all the blankets we could possibly spare, for many of the men had no coats. Some of the men had breadths of carpet wrapped around their shoulders." On the other side of town, Colonel Stone's Iowa troops accepted the formal surrender of Columbia from Mayor Thomas Goodwyn.[34]

Stone's lead regiment swung down Main Street from the north and halted in the market square. Large crowds were gathered there—a few sullen whites, escaped Federal prisoners, convicts from the city lockup, and hundreds of jubilant blacks. One or two U.S. flags were unfurled. The freed slaves were generous with whiskey, and many of Stone's Iowans were presently drunk. Sherman saw some of these men clumsily turning a fire engine onto a row of burning cotton bales. Other witnesses reported troops disabling the fire apparatus by slashing the hoses with their bayonets.[35]

Columbia was awash in spirits. Government warehouses stocked quantities of medicinal liquor. Casks of wine were packed into the cellars of downtown stores. There were enormous private stores: whiskey and wine, like cotton, were convertible assets in a disintegrating economy. In the days leading up to the evacuation a great deal found its way into the hands of the "servants" (the Elmores reported several demijohns of whiskey missing from the storeroom) and thence into the bloodstreams of the occupying troops, who only too plainly liked their liquor hard.[36]

With Stone's brigade detailed for provost work, Howard ordered the Fifteenth Corps to pass through Columbia and encamp east of the city. The 103rd Illinois paused long enough to sample the refreshments available in quantity along the route. Courteous freedmen proffered scuppernong claret, hock, champagne, and whiskey in glasses, tin cups, bottles, buckets, decanters, and gourds. "The boys loaded themselves with whatever they wanted, whiskey and wine flowed like water, and the whole division is now drunk," Charles Wills observed. The men talked as though Columbia would be destroyed as a matter of course.

"I think the city should be burned," Wills decided, "but would like to see it done decently."[37]

Reports of the Yankee arrival reached the LeContes late in the morning. Emma rushed upstairs to her bedroom window and looked out to see the Stars and Stripes floating over the new statehouse. After a while the first bluecoats appeared on campus and set up a guard detail. The rising wind whipped the sentinels' hats from their heads and tore at the yellow hospital flag the Confederate medical staff had run up in hopes of preserving the college compound.

The entire Fifteenth Corps marched past the college gates. The LeContes watched in meek silence. Aunt Josephine found the Yankees deeply impressive, drunk or sober. "I hardly ever saw a more hardy rigorous set of men, well clothed & fine equipments in all respects," she wrote her son Julian, wondering how the boy's amateurish Chatham Artillery, with its threadbare men, crowbait horses, and honeycombed cannon, could possibly stand up to this virile, bristling military machine.[38]

A party of Yankees foraging to Columbia's eastern verges turned up at the Elmores', breaking into Mrs. Elmore's wardrobe and pulling her clothes from the drawers and presses, pounding away discordantly on the piano, and scrawling graffiti on the billiard table. They cleared out the storeroom. Soldiers carrying long, metal-tipped pine rods poked around in the garden in search of buried silver and gold. A team of Yankee humorists hitched themselves to the Elmore pony carriage and drew it about the yard, shouting and laughing. In the carriage, as passengers, rode a half-dozen of the Elmore turkey cocks.

"They cleared the yard of all the poultry but one old rooster and one old drake that crept under the house and stayed there," Grace recorded.[39]

Her mother set off in high dudgeon in search of responsible authority. Stepping over or sweeping past drunks and pushing to the middle of Main Street, she intercepted a group of important-looking officers on horseback, one of whom she took to be Sherman himself.

"I spoke to him twice and he paid no attention," she told Grace later. "Then I tapped him on his boot sharply with my parasol."

The officer turned and glared down at her from atop his charger.

"Your men are robbing my house and I want a guard," Harriet Elmore called out.

"This is not the place to get one," he snapped.

She gave him a hard stare and he relented a bit, gesturing vaguely toward Hunt's Hotel. She managed to speak to someone in a blue uniform there. A guard turned up at the Elmore place toward evening.[40]

The fired cotton had burned itself out by late afternoon. Around dusk, the winter sunset a pale yellow streak beyond the Congaree, fresh fires broke out in Cotton Town in northwest Columbia, in a row of wooden whorehouses on Gervais Street, and along the riverfront. From the LeContes' back third-floor piazza, Miss Emma could see the circling Yankee campfires and, on the eastern horizon, the Hampton country place aglow. Henry, back from another expedition uptown, told her wind-assisted fires were roaring down Main Street from Cotton Town all the way to the capitol.

Drunken soldiers crowded the streets, singing, blaspheming, shouting incoherent threats; Emma saw, or thought she saw, staggering bluecoats with turpentine-soaked cotton firebrands spreading the blaze to windward. A burning house lit Sumter Street beyond the high campus wall as bright as day; sparks showered down on the LeConte roof and the dry, rushing wind carried the flames so close Emma could feel the heat on her cheeks. It was, she thought, like a medieval picture of hell.[41]

She slept for an hour or two. At four o'clock she arose and looked out the front windows to see the capitol engulfed, the entire city wrapped in flames, columns of black smoke rolling across a copper-colored sky. Groups of refugees huddled in the streets around trunks, sticks of furniture, and other belongings pulled from their burning homes.

Two or three of the college buildings were smoldering. Emma could see shadowy figures moving crabwise along the rooftops, beating out embers glowing in the shingles. Across the green, someone leaned out of an attic window of Uncle John's and brushed sparks off the roof. Burned-out women and children collected inside the campus's main gate. Bessie LeConte, trembling, near tears, the baby Carrie in her arms, stood poised at the front door, ready to skip onto the green the instant the house exploded into flame.

Howard and his staff were in the streets all night trying to control the infuriated soldiery. Troops drifted in from the outlying camps and joined in the riot. Renegade Yankees committed innumerable crimes: looting, arson, scattered assaults on townspeople. There were reports of vicious rapes of black women, and at least one rape and murder. Howard finally ordered Stone's besotted troops out of the city. As the night wore on, he summoned two of Woods's brigades and all three brigades of William B. Hazen's division to fight the fires and quell the mobs.

Hazen's troops gradually cleared the streets, arresting around 400 soldiers and civilians. Resisters were shot—more than thirty altogether, two fatally. Several insensate soldiers were trapped in the inferno and incinerated. The burned district covered at least 36 blocks—some 450 buildings—from Cotton Town to the capitol. The business district, Hunt's Hotel, an Ursuline nunnery, and some of the city's finest dwellings were a smoking desolation.[42]

The wind shifted to the east toward dawn, then dropped. The sun rose dim and red through the murk. Emma felt dull and listless, in a state between dreaming and waking. For the third successive night she had hardly slept. She washed the soot from her face and felt a little better. The fires were dying out.

"When they are gone," Miss Emma wrote from her overcharged heart, "I will walk out of the campus and see it all—yet how I dread it."[43]

Tom Osborn rode among the ruins early Saturday morning. "There remains only a forest of chimneys," he wrote, awestruck. The tall magnolias and oaks along the avenues and the shrubberies and gardens that lapped the mansions were seared and soot-blackened. The homeless squatted in the streets and in Sidney Park with their meager salvaged belongings. There were no religious services on Sunday, even though the Roman Catholic, Trinity Episcopal, and Presbyterian churches had survived the fire. The bells of the city, sacred and secular, were silent.[44]

Howard, that famous abstainer, had presided over the most notorious drunken rampage of the war. His whiskey-fueled troops, tur-

The ravaged cityscape of Columbia, South Carolina, in the winter of 1865, viewed from the new state capitol. "There remains only a forest of chimneys," an awe-struck Thomas Osborn reported after a ride among the ruins on February 18, 1865, the day after the fire. Wind-fanned flames consumed 36 blocks, around 450 build-ings, from Cotton Town to the capitol. Neat piles of rubble along the edge of the avenue show the cleanup has already begun. (Library of Congress)

pentine and cotton, and boisterous winds finished, emphatically, what delinquent Confederates had started. As Henry Slocum observed, "A drunken soldier with a musket in one hand and a match in the other is not a pleasant visitor to have about the house on a dark, windy night." Sherman himself accepted no responsibility for the firestorm, then or afterward. For policy purposes he blamed the destruction of Columbia on Wade Hampton, that terrific grandee, a great slave-holder, and, in Sherman's view, a braggart, a windjammer, and the self-appointed "special champion" of South Carolina.[45]

The widow Elmore trudged once again into the city center. As she told the story, she found Sherman presiding over a levee of some kind. Admitted to the room, she witnessed a testy exchange between the general and an ancient, now homeless lady of Columbia.

"Gen. Hampton set the fires going," Sherman told her.

"No, my house was set on fire long after Hampton left."

"Then your negroes did it."

"No."

"Well, my troops did not do it."

"They cut the hose of the engine that came to put out the fire, for I saw them do it."

"Well, if they did," answered Sherman in a tone that closed the matter, "such is the fortune of war."[46]

Fifteenth Corps details dumped ammunition stocks into the Congaree, blew up factories and powder mills, twisted rails, wrecked locomotives and rolling stock, and disabled the gasworks. When the rear guard marched out on Monday, February 20, it left Columbia isolated, cut off from the world, as though, in Emma LeConte's words, the city and its environs were "suddenly smitten with some appalling curse."[47] Not a rail lay straight upon a roadbed within twenty miles of Columbia. Stocks of food and medicine were dangerously low. There were no mails, no telegraph, and no news: only silence, the acrid aroma of wet, charred wood, and blackened stone.

"Yes, I have seen it all," Emma wrote five days after the fire. "It is even worse than I thought." Along the entire length of Sumter Street only one house stood: the Mordecais', a brick dwelling. "Bedell's lovely little house is in ruins," she went on, "while, as if in mockery, the shrubbery is not even scorched."[48]

With famine in prospect, Mayor Goodwyn appealed to Sherman. "Go to Howard," the commanding general told him crisply. "He runs the religion of this army." Howard suggested that Goodwyn follow the Federal example and send out forage parties to scour the countryside for provisions. He also left behind five hundred head of cattle for the city's fifteen thousand citizens, with salt for preserving the beeves as they were butchered, wire to haul a ferry back and forth across the Congaree, a stock of medicine, and a hundred muskets to arm a home guard.[49]

At the LeContes, it looked as though Henry, his wife Mary Ann, and Maria and her children would go off with the Yankee refugee train. "They are free," Emma understood, "and we ask as little as possible of them." If the chambermaid Jane offered to clean her room, very well. Otherwise she did it herself.

"This afternoon I washed the dinner things and put the room to rights. This is my first experience in work of this kind and I find it is better than doing nothing."[50]

FROM ALL QUARTERS, individual destiny and total war clashed in unequal struggle. Joseph LeConte played light-foot with Kilpatrick's cavalry in another picaresque tramp through the winter swamps and woods. Alfred Manigault lay comatose in the Winnsboro hospital. The elder Manigaults awaited the arrival of Union occupation troops in Charleston. From Monck's Corner on the Northeastern Railroad, Lafayette McLaws, lonely, defeated, and wanly sober, tried to puzzle out the enemy's intentions and wondered where his refugee family had been cast up.* The Elliotts of Oak Lawn took to the roads and dispersed, leaving the place to Sherman's bummers.

The brothers LeConte wandered about lost for a day or so, then fell in with the refugee stream on the Allston road, meeting one of the Rhetts "with an immense train of wagons," as Joe LeConte put it, "his manservant and his maidservant, his ox and his ass and everything that was his," including a drove of forty hogs, a flock of fifty turkeys, and a large contingent of relations. With enemy cavalry everywhere, the LeContes hid in the woods at night. A Yankee patrol discovered their caravan early in the morning of February 19, the third day out.[51]

LeConte watched from a thicket as the troopers rifled through his manuscript papers, railroad bonds, the family silver. They drank off as much champagne as they could hold at so early an hour and filled their saddlebags with the rest. Then they piled the broken boxes and trunks atop the wagons and set the lot on fire.

Smoke curled up into the overcast. Presently the cavalrymen moved off, tipsy, in high spirits, a good deal richer. An enemy patrol picked up John and his son, Joe learned later from the blacks in their party, who had a knack for moving easily back and forth between rebels and Yankees. He and Allen Green, a gunpowder lab colleague, turned back for home after dark. A crescent moon had risen in a clearing sky. It was bitterly cold now and their footfalls rang on the iron surface of the road. They waded the Little River; the remains of the bridge, burned earlier in the day, still smoldered. Green, laboring with a damaged lung, gave out at first light. He sat down on a stack of rails, laid his head on his knees, and refused to go on.

---

*Emily McLaws and the children were safe in Washington, Georgia, as it happened.

The fugitives hid in the woods by day and billeted themselves on friendly farm folk at night. More than once, LeConte experienced the curious auditory phenomenon of imaginary voices, sinister and beckoning by turns. But nobody shot at them, and the country people generously shared out their dwindling stocks of food. On the twenty-third, a Thursday, they encountered a party of three refugees who reported the Union troops had gone from Columbia. The refugees said, too, that most of the city had been destroyed.

Fragments of storm cloud tore across a leaden sky and the rains returned. Green lurched along in painful jerks, the picture of misery in a sodden blanket cape and a cowled hood, until he collapsed again, this time for good. LeConte left him at a house on the Columbia road and pressed on, covering the last leg into Cotton Town in a sprint.

No refugee account, however lurid, could have prepared him for the extent of the devastation. "Not a house remaining," he saw. "Only the tall chimneys standing gaunt and spectral, and empty brick walls with vacant windows like death heads with eyeless sockets. Met not a living soul."[52] The streets were silent except for the ragged barking of dogs. He hurried past the capitol and through the Sumter Street gate. Everyone was safe and well, he discovered to his inexpressible relief: Emma flushed with joy; Bessie calmer now; baby Caroline quiet; Henry still in residence after all, splitting firewood, standing guard over the women, and foraging for daily rations of meal and salt junk. As for LeConte, he was practically bursting with energy and, strange to say, high spirits.

"My life in the woods agreed with me astonishingly," he confessed. "I was never healthier in my life."[53]

LeConte escorted Miss Emma to church on Sunday the twenty-sixth, his forty-second birthday. The reading, from the first chapter of Lamentations, more closely matched his daughter's grieving spirit than his own buoyant mood:

> How doth the city sit solitary, that was full of people! how is she become as a widow! she that was great among nations, and princess among the provinces, how is she become tributary. . . . The ways of Zion do mourn, because none come to the solemn feasts: all her gates are desolate: her priests sigh, her virgins are afflicted, and she is in bitterness.

Columbia in ruins, and away to the southeast all the Low Country in motion: a black flow toward the Federal liberators, a white ebb moving away from the Federal conquerors. Union troops of the Department of the South dodged here and there along the defenseless seaboard, raising alarms and, especially when the raiders were African American, igniting triumphal celebrations in the slave settlements.

The Yankee approach put Ann Elliott out of doors. She had left Oak Lawn for Charleston around February 1, taking only personal effects and leaving the boxcar her son-in-law Gonzales had sent empty on the siding at Adams Run. Miss Ann sold off her carriage horses and weighed the risk of shipping stored cotton from the Edisto estates north to Cheraw, South Carolina—unaware, of course, that Cheraw lay on the line of Sherman's march.

The Yankee warships standing off Sumter raddled her nerves, and she gave up the notion of stopping with Hattie in Charleston. "I realized today how good for nothing I am when hearing some shells fired at the City as I supposed—'twas a blockade runner wh. had run aground," she admitted.[54] Gonsie again intervened, fixing her up with a plantation refuge near Darlington, on the Northeastern Railroad, thirty miles below Cheraw. The place sounded almost too good to be true.

"There are 200 negroes on it & everything," she wrote. "We can carry our stock & poultry & be all to ourselves. The negroes are well clothed & well fed & under discipline. We will have plenty of wood & lumber to build with & there is plenty of accommodation for our Servants."[55]

While Ann Elliott allowed herself to dream that corners of the Confederacy survived where the old life might yet be lived, Oak Lawn lay abandoned and open to plunder. Sometime after February 10, with Sherman's army on the Edisto, the mansion went up in flames. Bummers packed up what they could carry away and smashed the rest. Then they put the torch to the place. Fire gutted the main house and parched the ornamental laurels and wild oranges. Treasure hunters—Yankees and probably freedmen, too—dug up the lawns, scattering shards of delicate bohemian glass and the blue-and-gold dessert set in the spoil.

The enemy has toppled roof and gable,
And torn the paneling from ancient rooms;
What generations of old men had known
Like their own hands, and children wondered at,
Has boiled a trooper's porridge.*

Ann Elliott, with her daughters Ann and Emily, left Charleston just ahead of the Federals. Lafayette McLaws reported the successful evacuation of the city during the night of February 17. The first Union troops marched in the next morning. On the twentieth, the day before the Twentieth Corps passed through Winnsboro, Alfred Manigault died in the hospital there. His nurse abstracted $50 from his pockets to pay for his burial in the Episcopal churchyard in the village. He suffered a lot toward the last, she told the family later, veering in and out of consciousness, coughing up blood, and muttering enigmatically in French.[56]

Cannon fire from Morris Island harried the retreating rebels, but McLaws managed to pull away with slight damage and most of the garrison's paraphernalia. Pyrotechnics lit the night sky: muzzle flashes of the Federal great guns from the island batteries and the warships; warehouses ablaze along the waterfront; Confederate ironclads burning in the river. Exploding ammunition stocks shot red, orange, and yellow columns of fire and embers hundreds of feet into the air.[57]

Charles Manigault witnessed the fireworks from the family mansion on Gibbes Street. He had reclaimed the place, abandoned during the worst of the bombardment, only a day or two before the first Yankees entered Charleston. Manigault possessed abundant energy still in his seventieth year, especially in service of the family's fortune. He had commuted into town nearly every day during his exile, climbing high upon a stool in one of his countinghouses, a Dickensian figure, short of sight and hooked of nose, to tot up losses and make projections for the future.

He had long ago lost all his illusions about the Confederacy. The great thing now was to salvage as much as possible from the wreck. Charleston's wharves and commercial streets were silent, forsaken.

---

*William Butler Yeats (born 1865), *The Dreaming of the Bones*, on another, earlier civil war.

Still, for all its flash and roar, the cannonade had done surprisingly little damage, though in 1863 a shell sailed through Louis's bedroom, entering by one window and exiting by another. But it had failed to detonate, and "only smashed those two blinds and sashes," according to Charles. The Manigault city properties showed signs of neglect, but were otherwise intact.[58]

Inland, along the upper reaches of the Cooper River, the Federals came with axes and firebrands. The Manigaults' "numerous faithful ancestral family negroes" at Silk Hope plantation led Union troops straight to the silver and other treasures, and to the carefully packed family portraits and boxes of bric-a-brac, objets d'art, and souvenirs from Manigault travels.[59] The raiders carried off the silver and one large box of valuables. They left the portraits behind, as too unwieldy to transport.

By his own reckoning, Manigault had treated the people at Silk Hope well. He let them plant a little for themselves and keep poultry and even a hog or two. He learned, later, that the slaves—not the Yankees—had broken into and vandalized the family portraits. He recognized belatedly what had led them to it—"hatred of their former master & of all his family." Some of the Manigault likenesses were discarded and left to wilt in the rain. Others were nailed to the walls of cabins in the former slave quarters. The most severely damaged portrait was Charles Manigault's own.[60]

At Marshlands, Yankee raiders and the freed people carried off sixty cases of old Madeira, tables and chairs, bedsteads, and farm equipment. Manigault, never too defiantly rebel to solicit favors, managed with Federal help to cart away most of what remained: clothing, pictures, two fine clocks, some furniture. An obliging Yankee gave him a pass through the lines. Another escorted him to and from Marshlands, helped him load the carriage, and afterward politely declined the offer of a dozen bottles of wine as a douceur.

Manigault's former slaves claimed Marshlands under the leadership of the quondam driver Frederick. "He encouraged all the negroes to believe that the farm, and everything on it, belonged solely to them, & that their former owners had now no rights or control there whatever," Manigault wrote in a tone of astonished outrage.[61] The new order baffled him. The former slaves were transformed. Their assertive, demanding new character bewildered and frightened him.

"The little Negroes who used to watch for my coming, to open the gates & climb on the sulky to take a little ride, were now taught to shun me & never call me master again," Manigault wrote bitterly. "2 or 3 of the negro men on the farm had provided themselves with guns & Moses (one of the principal hands) stated loudly that if I ever threatened to move *him* off the place he would shoot me on the spot."[62]

Conditions were more tolerable in Charleston, despite the presence of thousands of Low Country black refugees. One could batten down in Gibbes Street, avoiding Yankee and freedman alike. Manigault imported a subsistence from Marshlands, a hundred bushels of corn and all the hay on the place. When the servants walked out, he hired a white woman to cook, wash, and milk the cow. His daughter Emma assumed responsibility for the housekeeping.

Family contacts were gradually restored. Word of Alfred's death threw Gibbes Street into mourning. But Louis reported from Augusta that he, Fannie, and the children were safe, though living close to the knuckle. ("No more children now, until the War is ended, more than likely never again," Louis vowed.)[63] Gabriel had won his parole finally and was assumed to be working his way cautiously from Fort Delaware through the lines toward home.

All the while, conqueror and conquered were storing up stocks of gall that would last for a generation—and poison the lives of African Americans for a century and more. While Charleston whites barricaded themselves at home, their former servants danced in the streets. Whites mourned their Confederate dead. They lamented the loss of their property and perquisites. Blacks celebrated Jubilee, and waited impatiently for the promised forty acres and a mule.

The invaders had grievances, too. Charles Fox investigated reports that the enemy had left the black dead of the Fifty-fifth Massachusetts to molder on the battlefield after the fighting on James Island in July of 1864. Walking the abandoned lines, Fox confirmed the charge—to his rage and disgust.

"The bones of one of our best sergeants lay where he died," he wrote bitterly to his wife Mary. "I do not wish to pursue this subject, it is too disgraceful to humanity. I shall have the remains collected tomorrow and buried with proper service. So help me God, if I had my way, the procession, escorted by the whole regiment, should pass through the main street of Charleston and the relics be placed in a conspicuous place in the principal cemetery."[64]

Fox had come ashore with Alfred Hartwell's brigade at Bull's Bay and marched into Mount Pleasant on the east bank of the Cooper around noon on February 17, the day of Charleston's fall. Cheering former slaves lined both sides of the sandy track that led into the village. On the near shore, masked and half-buried in sand, lay the batteries that had tormented the besieging Yankees those last eighteen months. The Stars and Stripes now fluttered over forts Moultrie and Johnson. Fox was briefly in tears.

"If I were to live to the extreme of the usual age of men, the memory of this day would remain bright and distinct to the end," he wrote home. "Even now I can hardly realize that the birth place of the rebellion is in our hands. May the cradle be also the grave of the child of sin."[65]

On February 21, 1865, Fox led the Fifty-fifth Massachusetts Infantry (Colored) in formal parade through the streets of occupied Charleston. The troops sang "John Brown," "Babylon Is Falling," and "Kingdom Coming." The symbolism of this bravura performance— former slaves in a citadel of the South, the potent anthems, ecstatic freed men and women aswarm in the streets—intoxicated him.

"Those who were there," Fox wrote Mary in a state of exaltation, "will remember it in after years as the greatest of the events of their lives."[66]

MARCHING WITH HARTWELL'S BRIGADE, the Fifty-fifth Massachusetts trailed the Elliotts and McLaws's retreating Confederates up the line of the Northeastern Railroad. The expedition pushed on at a respectable pace, given the condition of the roads, but failed to overtake the rebel column.

Charley Fox here experienced for himself some of his brother John's characteristic style of campaigning. In a fair imitation of Sherman, Hartwell's column marched light, living on the country and, for a few days, anyway, out of touch with its base. The lawlessness, the lack of restraint, troubled Fox, and he wondered what would become of the inhabitants of these drab bottomlands and sand flats, caught in the whirlpool of the Federals' swift and brutal passage. In his view Sherman's campaign was a stunt, little more.

"To march through a country, drive away its white population, carry off all stores and provisions, destroy its crops and mills, and leave the slaves, simply telling them they are free, is in my opinion worse than nothing toward the end," he wrote Mary. "But a march of 200 miles through South Carolina sounds well."[67]

As it happened, Sherman's army found disappointingly little to steal or burn in the bleak late-winter landscape beyond Columbia: the sandhill country looked "too barren," thought Tom Osborn, "for the meanest weeds."[68] To keep up the feign, the left wing marched east by north, as though aiming for Charlotte and Salisbury, North Carolina. The right wing advanced along parallel roads to the south, toward a crossing of the Wateree River west of Camden.

The Columbia riot had forced Sherman to rethink his light-hearted approach to march discipline. The practice of stripping the country bare ("leaving not a meal for a single person where there are a dozen to feed, nor a shinplaster to buy with," as Osborn put it) only lengthened the refugee tail that streamed for miles behind the columns.

Howard blamed organized Yankee banditti for the worst of the excess, blue-clad gangs preying upon the helpless, black and white. Sherman issued orders to tighten the foraging rules and punish the more blatant thieves. "This army has done some awful stealing," admitted Charles Wills. "Inspectors pounce down on the trains every day or two now and search them. Everything imaginable is found in the wagons." One inspection team returned to the main column with two exotic kine in tow. Known locally as African swamp oxen, they were wildebeests in fact, and alleged to belong to Wade Hampton.[69]

Bummer marauding touched off a brief season of execution and reprisal. Slocum's infantry discovered eighteen of Kilpatrick's troopers dead along the wayside, their throats slit from ear to ear. Two Federal soldiers were murdered near the Wateree and left along the verges with notes pinned to the corpses vowing "death to all foragers." Union officers accused Hampton's cavalry of the crime. For his part, Sherman let it be known that he would permit no Confederate drumhead court to condemn his troops, however viciously they behaved. "If any of your foragers are murdered, take life for life, leaving a record in each case," he told Howard. J. E. Smith, one of Howard's division commanders, ordered the execution of two Confederates captured in Federal uniform. They were shot "on the spot," Smith reported.[70]

The skies opened again on February 23 and rain fell steadily for sixty hours. Current-driven driftwood wrecked the pontoons over the Catawba River at Rocky Mount, stranding the left wing's Fourteenth Corps on the south bank for three days. The luckless Slocum once again felt the steel edge of Sherman's temper. The flood also caught Howard this time, trapping the right wing along Lynch's Creek, a mile over its banks and swimming deep.

With the delays, the army drew down the last of its stocks of hard bread and coffee. "Sherman has been heard to say that this army can live on fresh meat alone for 30 days," wrote Wills. "I'd like to see it tried on him." Nobody had a good word to say about the local bread-stuffs, which army bakers produced from confiscated corn ground just before the arson details fired the mills along the line of march. Wills, for one, detested these oven-bread substitutes, calling them "death balls."[71]

So the foragers ranged far afield. Civilians in the army's path put their silver, jewelry, and china underground, hid away stocks of lard and molasses, and sent the boys and old men off into the woods. But experienced bummers were rarely outwitted. A Second Massachusetts foraging party disinterred cotton and corn buried in a family graveyard along the Cheraw road. The corn, most of it anyway, ended up in the men's haversacks.

The Charlestonian Emma Holmes, rusticated near Camden, prepared for the arrival of the yahoos, as she called Sherman's troops, by stuffing her watch and money into her bosom and packing handkerchiefs, stockings, and a new pair of shoes into a mailbag that she fitted under the hoop of her skirt.

War circumstances had led Miss Emma, twenty-six years old, the well-educated daughter of a gentleman planter/physician, to accept a $100 a month position tutoring the oldest eight of the eleven children of John B. Mickle and wife. Mrs. Mickle was harried, overworked, and hopelessly uncultured; that is to say, she had never read Sir Walter Scott's Waverley novels. The children struck Emma as backward and dull—clodpates who had never heard of *Gulliver's Travels*, "Jack in the Beanstalk," or the Trojan War.

The Mickles's gaucheries appalled her. "Hogs jowls are brought on table, grinning ghastly with every tooth still projecting," she complained. "Dogs and cats eat under the table, & the kids often join them. To crown the whole, Mrs. M nurses her new baby before me & any man, white or black, that happens to pass by."[72] Mrs. Mickles's grammar left a lot to be desired, too, and her children talked like sandhillers.

Miss Emma was sitting with an account of Livingston's *African Travels* open in her lap when the first of the yahoos turned up, two soldiers from the Fifteenth Corps. They only stopped at the gate. Five bluecoats materialized the next morning, demanding breakfast and making free of the place while it was being cooked. The Yankees spilled Emma's ink on her bedroom floor, requisitioned her empty purse, and pocketed her toothbrush and toilette combs. In turn, she taunted them mercilessly. They made war on women and children. They were fainthearts who tricked the gallant Confederates out of their works; true soldiers would attack head-on. She harangued a Pennsylvanian in Logan's corps for full three-quarters of an hour before he managed to escape.

"In fact," Emma boasted, "I hurled so many keen sarcasms, such home thrusts, that the Pennsylvanian said I was the best rebel he had met, and that it was such women as I who kept up this war by urging on our brothers and friends."[73]

Yankee details burned the cotton gin, eighty bales of cotton, and two hundred bushels of corn; they removed quantities of wheat flour and most of the preserved meats from the Mickles's larder. In Camden, Emma heard, they set fire to the square from the commissary to the Bain Brothers' store, leaving the pharmacy, the jail, and the depot in ashes.

Then they were gone. The Federals moved on to Cheraw, forty miles to the northeast, an old settlement of broad streets and handsome dwellings that still showed mildewed traces of prewar white paint. Sherman paused there from the third to the fifth of March for rest, revictualing, and drying out. A few torn copies of recent newspapers circulated, allowing the army to catch up with events—the Federal occupation of Wilmington, North Carolina, and Charleston, and Joseph E. Johnston's return to command the rebel army in their front. By reliable report, a captured dispatch from Hampton to Butler read, "Do not attempt to delay Sherman's march by destroying bridges, or any other means. For God's sake, let him get out of the country as quickly as possible." The troops celebrated the Lincoln inaugural on March 4 with a "gunpowder jollification" and toasts to the president's health in stolen wine.[74]

The army cleared Cheraw on Monday the sixth, leaving a burned-out business district behind, and crossed the 500-foot-wide Pee Dee River on pontoons. On the eighth, in wild showers of rain, the Federal columns passed out of South Carolina. Osborn, for one, felt glad to be quit of it. "I must insist that it is the meanest patch of country in America," he wrote. "The people are a cringing sycophantic race, who have always been led and gulled by a dozen ambitious blockheads." To Wills, the Old North State—allegedly only halfheartedly secessionist and Confederate—looked vaguely like home. The small farms were prosperous to all appearances, with neat plain houses, tidy outbuildings, and well-tended cornfields.[75]

The days were stretching a bit now, but still the rains came down. Floodwaters spread for a mile beyond either bank of the Lumber River. Engineers poled out to the main channel in small boats to survey for the pontoons. Axmen felled pines, thousands of them, for a double-laid wooden causeway over the lake bed.

The Second Massachusetts, detailed as rear guard for the crossing, saw the last wagon over to the east bank after midnight on March 11. The column bogged toward the night halt over a road that sometimes gave way without warning, like rotten ice on a pond at home. Forest fires cast an orange glow on the ragged edges of drifting clouds: the army's barnburners, with North Carolina's farms off-limits, ignited resin pits and the sap notches of pines instead. Thick columns of smoke rose high into the sky and spread, forming the pillars and roof of a vast fanciful temple.[76]

Howard's van entered Fayetteville, North Carolina, on the Cape Fear River, in the forenoon of March 11. The army tug *Davidson*, announcing itself with the blast of a steam whistle and trailing a plume of soot, glided up to quayside there twenty-four hours later. She brought dispatches, telegrams, and news. "I see by the papers that a Major Osborn has been wounded and captured on the North Carolina coast," Tom Osborn mused. "I am not that man and I do not know who he is." Word reached Charley Morse, camped with the Second Massachusetts on the edge of Fayetteville, that mail would leave Twentieth Corps headquarters for the steamboat at four o'clock. He could hardly have been more astonished had his own mother peeled back the tent flap, ducked inside, and invited him home to Jamaica Pond for Sunday dinner.[77]

Morse struck off a letter to his brother Robert, reporting only a single skirmish since the brigade left Savannah, but a never-ending battle with rain, wind, cold, mud, rivers, and swamps. "When I tell you that since the 8th day of February I have not drawn from the commissary a single govt. ration you can understand how entirely we have lived off the country," he wrote. "There have been times of terrible anxiety when it seemed as if the country could yield nothing."[78] Something usually turned up: bacon, hominy, a little rice. But unlike Georgia, this had been no picnic.

John Fox reported in a hurried note to his sister that Sherman's columns had left South Carolina a howling wilderness, that the troops had marched the soles off their shoes, that Carolina damp had rotted away their clothes. "My horse, Tom, has given out with rheumatism after standing service so long," he wrote Fairy. "I have to pull him along on the march. I had hoped he might last as long as his master." He asked her for the latest news, for he had lived like a hermit these last six weeks, out of touch entirely.

"I understand General Sherman's army is captured. I am so sorry. Is there any other news of note?"[79]

For all their bravado, Fox and his comrades anticipated a renewal of the fighting—one more great battle at least. "I think now is the best time, and they better take advantage of it," Osborn remarked. Sherman ordered the straggling columns to close up for the advance on Goldsboro, and told Howard and Slocum to march light, with four divisions at the head of each column stripped down for swiftness of response should Johnston strike. He passed the word, too, for the refugees to be gathered up and led down to the coast.

In later years, Sherman's veterans ridiculed the extraordinary refugee cavalcade, dwelling usually—as Slocum did—on the droll details, such as "the best way of transporting pickaninnies."[80] By contrast, Howard saw the refugees for what they were: a driven, courageous, and enduring mass of humanity, determined to keep the last wagon in Sherman's train in sight at all hazard.

Howard's heart went out to them. "Bundles on their heads, children in arms, men on mules, women in old wagons & many with little to eat," he wrote Lizzie at home in Maine. "They will do anything, suffer anything for freedom." Estimates of refugee numbers ranged upward to thirty thousand. At a minimum, Howard figured, forty-five hundred men, women, and children trailed the right wing to Fayetteville. Sherman sent a few hundred fortunate ones, white and black, down the Cape Fear aboard a flotilla of captured steamers. Everyone else made the journey on foot, under a light military escort.[81]

Contact with the North Carolina coastal garrisons gave Sherman's army the first hint of Northern reaction to the Carolinas campaign. Tom Osborn overheard a staff officer just up from Wilmington arraign Sherman for premeditated, wanton, and barbaric violations of the laws of civilized warfare. "He will be more surprised than he is now when he has campaigned with him awhile," Osborn observed dryly. True to form, Sherman issued orders to destroy the Fayetteville arsenal brick by brick, wreck machine shops, cotton mills, warehouses, and tanneries, and burn every gristmill in the town except one.[82]

The Federals crossed the Cape Fear on pontoons on March 15 and leaned to the northeast. Johnston, meantime, massed his army on Slocum's front and prepared to throw Hardee's corps onto the Yankee head of column near Smithfield, midway between Raleigh and Goldsboro. Kilpatrick's cavalry bumped into an aggressive rebel skirmish line on the afternoon of the fifteenth near the hamlet of Averasboro in the narrow, boggy neck separating the Cape Fear and the Black Rivers. Kilpatrick's troopers drove the skirmishers back to a line of crude defensive works, threw up barricades of their own, and sent for a brigade of Twentieth Corps infantry to clear the obstacle.

Hardee's eleven thousand infantry held a low ridge commanding the Fayetteville-Raleigh wagon road. His orders were to delay Sherman, and also to smoke out his destination—Raleigh, the state capital, to the west, or Goldsboro, where two railroad lines ran down to the coast, to the east. The Federals would have to knock him out of the way before they could push on to either place.

The Second Brigade of the First Division, with the Second Massachusetts, came up during the night, marching by the yellow light of burning pine knots, blaze and smoke swirling upward in the saturated air. The men slept in line of battle in the mud. When the first scattered firing broke out in the rainy dawn, Captain James Grafton, the often-wounded, seemingly indestructible veteran of Cedar Mountain, Antietam, Chancellorsville, and Gettysburg, led a detachment of around twenty men to the support of the brigade skirmishers in the woods to Kilpatrick's front.

Grafton expected to meet lightly armed rebel cavalry. Instead, he drew a heavy volley from a strong force of entrenched infantry. Within a few minutes he sent word that he had been shot in the leg, but that he could carry on. From behind the stacked brush of the barricades, Morse, Fox, and the others stared intently into the gloom. The firing swelled to a roar. A few moments later a figure came reeling out of the thicket, bareheaded, his face buried in his hands. It was Grafton, blinded and trailing blood.[83]

Hardee's infantry came on at a trot. Ankle-deep in swamp water, the 141 men of the Second Massachusetts stood and slogged it out in the downpour. Slocum fed fresh Twentieth Corps infantry into the line. Sherman himself turned up for a look. At his suggestion, Slocum sent a brigade around by the left to feel for the Confederate flank. A volley from this unexpected quarter chased the rebels back to their second line. McLaws's veterans, dug in there, held on through the gray dissolving afternoon, then withdrew toward Smithfield.

The battle of Averasboro, Thursday, March 16, 1865, little more than a skirmish but even so the sharpest fight of the campaign up to then, cost the Federals 682 killed, wounded, and missing. Hardee reported around 800 casualties. The Second Massachusetts lost Jim Grafton and 5 others killed and 16 wounded. John Fox, charmed still, escaped unharmed. Among those hit were Charley Morse, shot in the shoulder in the swamps, and Samuel Storrow, hit in an arm and a leg as he ran messages for Colonel Cogswell.

Morse examined his wound and saw with relief that it would send him down to the coast in the ambulance train and thence home to Jamaica Pond to convalesce. Word of Storrow's wounding reached him in the field hospital that evening. He had last seen him around three o'clock. Storrow was flushed, breathing hard, his heart hammering, either from excitement or exertion. They spoke briefly, then Storrow moved off on horseback toward the Raleigh road, a thin, bent figure with a dispatch case pressed tight to his side.

The fusillade rang out a few minutes before four. One ball hit Storrow in the padded part of the calf; the second passed through the fleshy part of the arm a few inches above the elbow. The brigade surgeon, J. W. Hastings of the Thirty-third Massachusetts, treated both as flesh wounds. Fully conscious, his wits still about him, Storrow sent word to Cogswell that he had delivered the messages. A few minutes later he died.[84]

Hastings, disbelieving, felt for a pulse, administered a stimulant, tried artificial respiration. "His loss of blood was not great, and—as I have said—no bones were broken, and it must have been the shock that killed him, as well as the fatigue of the day's work," Cogswell wrote Storrow's father.[85] Death, so it seemed, was upon him. Storrow's fragile heart had evidently beaten itself to pieces, like a startled, frightened bird's.

Cogswell drew up a precise description of the grave site for Charles Storrow in case, after the armies moved on, he should choose to come and collect his son's remains:

> He was buried in his uniform, in a coffin: thirty-three (33) paces south, ten (10) paces west of a double one-story house, painted white, with chimneys outside each end of the house, grave running east to west, an old pine stump east end at foot of grave, buried north side of Capt. Grafton twenty (20) miles from Fayetteville on the Raleigh road, one mile east of the mouth of the Lower Little River.[86]

General Slocum fought another, greater battle three days later. Turning east from Averasboro, the Fourteenth Corps uncoiled to a lead of several miles over the Twentieth Corps. Judging the danger to Slocum past, Sherman shifted over to Howard's column nearly a day's march to the south. Circumstance here offered Johnston a chance to damage, perhaps destroy, Slocum before Howard could come up to help. He deployed his army in line of battle astride the Goldsboro road near the village of Bentonville, in swampy country thickly grown with blackjack oak and scraggly pine.

The leading Fourteenth Corps brigade touched off the battle early on the mild, cloudless morning of Sunday, March 19. Slocum recognized at once that heavy forces were concentrated in his front. He ordered the Fourteenth Corps into defensive positions and summoned the two light divisions of the Twentieth Corps. Successive Confederate assaults drove the Fourteenth Corps back three-quarters of a mile onto the leading Twentieth Corps infantry. There the line held. From three o'clock until dark, Slocum's troops repulsed four separate Confederate attacks. With nightfall, the firing gradually died away.

Howard's Fifteenth Corps, closest to Slocum, marched overnight for Bentonville, arriving on Johnston's left rear during the morning of the twentieth. This forced Johnston to suspend the attacks and extend his lines. He held on against three to one odds for another forty-eight hours to cover the removal of the wounded and the withdrawal of the trains. Sherman waited impatiently for Johnston to leave. "I cannot see why he remains," he complained to Slocum. The impetuous Joseph Mower swung out on a flank march on the twenty-first that briefly threatened Johnston's line of retreat across Mill Creek. Sherman peremptorily recalled the Swamp Lizard. The Confederates withdrew unmolested toward Raleigh that night.[87]

Critics assailed Sherman down the years for failing to destroy Johnston's army at Bentonville. Sherman himself conceded afterward that he had erred in suppressing Mower. Johnston was still a dangerous adversary in March of 1865. The possibility remained that Lee could duck out of the Richmond lines, march on Johnston in North Carolina, and join with him to defeat Sherman. The combined armies could then turn back and confront Grant, with a reasonable prospect of success.

So the theory ran. But Sherman seemed to *know* the rebels were beaten beyond recovery. All his instincts told him so. A general action would have achieved nothing but the addition of a few thousand more Sam Storrows and Willie Hardees (the Confederate general's sixteen-year-old son was mortally wounded at Bentonville, his first battle) to the long lists of the dead.[88]

The Great Man ticked off half a dozen reasons for letting Johnston go. He wanted to push on as rapidly as possible for Goldsboro and the junction with generals John Schofield and Alfred Terry, whose corps would boost the army's strength to close to ninety thousand men. Using Goldsboro's rail links, Sherman could establish new lines of supply to refit and revictual his shabby columns for the move on Richmond. And he could ship the seventeen hundred wounded now in his ambulances out of the battle zone, greatly improving their chances of recovery.[89]

At the time, Howard chafed at Mower's recall. Later, though, he puzzled out Sherman's true reason for holding back at Bentonville: most ungeneral-like, the commanding general had decided that "there had been enough bloodshed already." In hindsight, Howard fully endorsed Sherman's course. "Events were already ripening which very soon made me glad that this last battle had not been pushed to an extremity," he wrote.[90]

On the other side, Bentonville filled the Confederates with elation. "It is said we had the whole of Sherman's army to contend against, but every assault was beaten off with but slight loss to ourselves," a reinvigorated McLaws wrote his wife, ignoring the fact that the battle had changed nothing, and that Johnston's casualty totals of more than 2,300 killed, wounded, and missing actually exceeded Sherman's.[91]

McLaws, in fact, sounded positively giddy. He had thrown off the gloom of Pocotaligo, Branchville, and Charleston days. "We are fast concentrating our resources in men and material and if we can gain three weeks I believe Genl. Sherman will be chased out of the state," he wrote Emily. Johnston knew better. He wired Lee a day or two after Bentonville that he could do no more than hinder and annoy Sherman, if even that. He had no chance of stopping him.[92]

With the army's entry into Goldsboro on March 23, Sherman declared the Carolinas campaign at an end—"one of the longest and most important marches ever made by an organized army in a civilized country," he modestly judged it.[93] Prodded by a flurry of sharp directives, the railroad department worked double and triple shifts to put the Wilmington and New Bern lines back into service. The first train chuffed up from New Bern on the twenty-fifth. Soon supplies of all kinds were piling up in the Goldsboro warehouses—and mail, too.

"Will it offend you if we take the liberty of naming our second son after his somewhat distinguished uncle?" Rowland Howard had written his brother in mid-February, as the right wing closed on Columbia.[94] The letter caught up to Howard in Goldsboro, along with a later one from Rowland—admonitory this time. Rowland had taken the burning of Columbia hard.

"We struggled with your brave soldiers thro the swamps of SC and blushed with every decent man in your army over the scenes at Columbia," he wrote. "I trust the Lord Jesus has been with you 'sticking closer than a brother.' The unconscious influence of your campaigns & of the scenes thro which you are passing *must* have a deleterious effect on your faith."[95]

The scolding achieved, Rowland went on to complain of the trials and dangers of the mud season in Farmington, Maine, where, with the frost heaving out of the roads, "no carriage can move with any safety to life or limb."[96]

# 5

## The Shell of Rebellion

ORDERS TO PREPARE FOR THE BURNING of tobacco cached in Richmond reached Richard S. Ewell toward the end of February. A small matter, tobacco, so it seemed to him, with a death sentence pending for the Army of Northern Virginia. But Robert Lee wished it so. Powerless to stop the leakage of men from the Richmond-Petersburg lines or to adequately provision the army, Lee could, however, see to the destruction of a few million dollars' worth of trade goods the Richmond merchants were unable to carry away.

A forty-eight-year-old Virginian, worn to a shadow by wounds and illness, Ewell commanded the Department of Richmond—an impressive posting by the sound of it, but in fact a mere convenient billet for an invalid lieutenant general who refused to admit defeat and go home. Lee's field army manned the capital's main defenses, a long, thin crust of fortifications and entrenchments that curved thirty-seven miles from White Oak Swamp east of Richmond to Hatcher's Run southwest of Petersburg. Only a couple of brigades of local defense troops—boys, old men, convalescents—and a few battalions of Virginia reservists came under Ewell's direct control.

He could stand only so much hopping about on his ill-fitting wooden leg, only so many hours riding strapped into the saddle. His stomach troubled him chronically—loose bowels, an ulcer. He complained of headaches and insomnia. All the same, he carried out his duties faithfully. On February 26, the day after Lee's order reached him, he inspected the four main leaf tobacco warehouses in Richmond and reported that they could be fired without delay and with slight risk of a general conflagration. He instructed the provost marshal to attend to the details. And he summoned Mayor Joseph Mayo and a citizens committee to his headquarters at Seventh and Franklin for a frank discussion of security issues.

Stray troops, Chimborazo hospital malingerers, Yankee prisoners, and vagrant slaves were packed into the city, Ewell reminded Mayo and his colleagues, and they would swarm the hour the army pulled out. He suggested that the committee raise a volunteer force, and offered to arm it. Without much enthusiasm, the mayor agreed to try. The returns came in a few days later.

"I regret to say but one man volunteered," Ewell informed the War Department.[1]

So Richmond, cold, miserable, and hungry in this fourth winter of a war without end, passively awaited its fate. Jefferson Davis buried himself in minutiae, drafting long memos, for one example, about conscription in the western Carolinas, where men vanished into the hickory woods at the first sign of the press gang. Ewell, meantime, virtually had to beg for volunteers to police the dying capital.

Lee had warned the War Department three months before that the depleted, overmatched Army of Northern Virginia could collapse at any time. The military outlook had only worsened since. The troops might stand hunger, illness, and exposure a little longer. Shut up in static defenses, they could not survive the loss of hope.

"Our men are deserting quite freely," Charles Blackford, a cavalry captain on detached duty in the War Department, wrote his refugee wife in Charlottesville. "It looks very blue to them, and the fact that Sherman marched from Atlanta to Savannah without seeing an armed Confederate soldier is well calculated to make them despondent."[2]

The Confederacy's postal services were falling to pieces along with the telegraph and transportation systems. Authentic news of Sherman's firebrand progress spread through the ranks anyway. Desertions rose to critical levels in the new year. During a two-week stretch in February, five hundred men walked away from Henry Heth's and

Confederate Lieutenant General Richard S. Ewell, a famous eccentric in a service abundantly supplied with unconventional personalities. When he conscientiously carried out Robert E. Lee's orders to burn Richmond's tobacco warehouses, the spreading fires destroyed much of the city's core. The Federals held Ewell prisoner at Fort Warren in Boston Harbor for several months after his surrender at Sayler's Creek on April 6, 1865. (Library of Congress)

C. M. Wilcox's divisions south of the James River. Altogether, from February 15 to March 18, at least three thousand men traveled— 6 percent of Lee's strength. Officer applications for sick leave approached record numbers. Blackford estimated that Lee could muster fewer than thirty thousand men fit for duty in mid-February.[3]

This dispirited legion guarded a Richmond civil population nearing the end of its endurance. Firewood sold for $150 a cord in late January. The canals froze over during a severe cold spell through the first week of February, halting fuel shipments and driving prices higher still. Early cabbage seed traded for $10 an ounce. Only human beings were losing their value: by mid-February, the price of slaves at the capital's auction houses had slumped to a tenth of prewar levels.[4]

Charles Blackford staked nearly all his $250 monthly salary for December 1864 on a Christmas turkey. Lee's frontline troops subsisted on a daily ration of cornmeal and a little bacon. Underfed draft animals were too weak to haul the trains or the great guns. Rains washed out sections of the Piedmont Railroad, a vital supply line, drawing down the army's food reserves at one critical point to two days' short rations. Farmers were shy of bringing goods to market in Richmond for fear the army would seize their horses. They resisted selling anything—livestock, food, or fuel—for depreciated Confederate currency.

Butter, tea, sugar, and molasses were rarely available at any price. Even the well-to-do lived mostly off flour, meal, and fat-middling bacon, with an occasional potato or cabbage. The War Department doled out a monthly ration for soldiers on duty in Richmond of 31 pounds of meal and 21 pounds of salt beef. An enfeebled government could not otherwise do more than publish hollow-sounding proclamations.

"This is Friday, and the fast-day ordained by the President," Blackford wrote his wife. "To name one day as a fast day is most amusing since almost any given day is a fast-day for all, whether civilian or soldier."[5]

Richmond was sullen under a gray nimbus of wood and coal smoke. The Irish traveler Thomas Conolly found the city magnificent on its hills above the beer-colored James, but wretched up close. The shops were empty, staple goods rare as luxuries and almost as expensive, streets muddy, paint chipped and peeling, brick and mortar crumbling, late winter weather cold, wet, and blustery.

Skipping past the Federal blockade in the Bermuda-based fast paddle wheeler *Owl*, Conolly had landed on the North Carolina coast south of Wilmington on February 26, passed through Fayetteville ten days ahead of Sherman, and reached Richmond in a slanting rain on March 8. He checked into the Spotswood Hotel, arranged for a steady flow of liquor, hired a black servant, Henry, who could mix a proper cocktail and would turn out to serve it before breakfast, and made contact with the hotel pimp. Conolly found the Spotswood, opened just before the war, as slovenly as its older competitors. He saw butternut everywhere, a demoralizing absence of color. Even the carpets had been taken up in the long hallways, to be cut up into army blankets.

Richmond crowds struck Conolly as wolfish and half-savage, as woebegone as the tenantry at home in Donegal. He gave a wide berth to the "knots of rowdies, pickets of mud-stained, slough-hatted rawboned cavalry" ever-present in the streets.[6] Conolly himself—landlord, member of the parliament at Westminster, toff—had begun to look anything but suave after a few weeks in the Confederacy. He sat down to his first dinner at the Spotswood wearing red breeches, sea boots, and a thick flannel shirt.

Conolly's purposes were strictly private. The Confederacy had stirred his imagination, and he had come for an experience of it. He expected, too, as part-owner of a Nassau-bound cargo to be traded for fabulously profitable rebel cotton, to make money out of the blockade. But it was Conolly's MP status that dazzled Richmond. Prominent Confederates persuaded themselves that this self-indulgent Irish squire could advance their long-running, now desperate campaign to draw the British into the cause.

Conolly effortlessly obtained introductions to the Confederate first family, other high government officials, General Lee. He admired Jefferson Davis, but conceived an instant dislike for his wife, Varina: coarse-featured and masculine in figure, he thought her, and with a sharp, sneering tongue "calculated to damage any cause however good."[7] Conolly dined with the commanding general at his headquarters outside Petersburg on March 16. Like everyone else, he spoke in hushed and holy tones of the magnificent Lee. But it was the meal itself that really enchanted him. This was America, after all. Lee's staff served up the largest turkey Conolly had ever seen.

Lee spoke in generalities that day. He said nothing, of course, about plans on foot for an operation designed to break the siege or, failing that, disrupt the opening moves of the enemy's spring campaign. The attack on Fort Stedman near Petersburg went off on schedule before dawn on March 25. But Major General John Gordon's assault troops showed hardly more than a trace of the old Army of Northern Virginia panache. The Federals repulsed them with ease.

"A little rumpus up the line," General Grant commented dismissively.

With the failure at Fort Stedman, Richmond stepped up outbound shipments of war matériel and machinery and government clerks packed away archives and Treasury valuables for transfer west to Danville, Virginia. Davis sent his wife and children away to Charlotte, North Carolina. He gave Varina a little Colt pistol as a parting gift, for use should the Yankees push up too close.

In the most outrageous display yet of Confederate delusion, the government advertised for black recruits, with a vague promise of emancipation after the war. It was the wildest of all rebel notions—

regiments of slave hirelings fighting for their masters. The old dream of British intervention, and fresh fantasies of Sherman sinking into the Carolina swamps or of a war with the French-backed Mexican emperor Maximilian along the Rio Grande, seemed almost reasonable by comparison.

Richard Ewell repeated the warning: when Lee's army withdrew, Richmond could expect mayhem. He estimated the city's black male population at five thousand, a volatile mass that would be certain to cause trouble. Ewell proposed a sweep of all vagabond men, white and black, with a gunpoint choice of enlisting in the army or quitting Richmond for good.[8]

Nobody was listening, and Ewell lacked the authority to act on his own. A jurisdictional overlap with James Longstreet, who commanded Army of Northern Virginia units north of the James, restricted his freedom of action. Then, too, Ewell's powers were in decline, as anyone close to him could testify. Physically he was lath-thin, tallow-faced, anemic, and there were whispers that his mental edge had dulled as well.

By consensus, Ewell had been Stonewall Jackson's best division commander in the Shenandoah Valley and Seven Days' campaigns of 1862. He mended slowly from the severe wound at Groveton in August of '62 that cost him a leg. Ewell succeeded the fallen Jackson in command of the Second Corps in May 1863, but the injury seemed to rob him of much of his old fire. He failed Lee badly on the third day at Gettysburg. A tumble from his horse at Spotsylvania in May 1864 left him unfit for service in the field. Over his protests, Lee finally sent him away after Cold Harbor.

Sick or well, Ewell was an oddity. A Georgetown, D.C., physician's son, an 1840 West Point graduate, and a Mexican War veteran, he was bright-eyed, long-snouted, bald as a round shot. Some likened him to an eagle; others, less impressed, to a woodcock. He spoke in a high voice with an exaggerated lisp, his waxy head cocked to one side. Ewell cut a slapstick figure at times, and his peculiarities were legendary in the Army of Northern Virginia. A late marriage only embellished the legend.

Lizinka Brown had annexed him around the time of Chancellorsville. They were cousins, he a bachelor and middle-rank Confederate hero, she a landowning, slaveholding widow of forty-four, the daughter of a onetime U.S. senator, Treasury secretary, and minister to Russia, a faded beauty named for the famously beautiful wife of a Russian czar. He could hardly believe his good fortune. For a long time afterward he introduced her as "My wife, Mrs. Brown."

The attachment gave a new dimension to the Ewell persona. "She manages everything from the General's affairs down to the courier who carries his dispatches," observed Colonel James Conner, one of Ewell's staffers. He became the guardian of Lizinka's two grown children: Harriot, dark-skinned and dark-eyed ("not pretty, a very large head and a stout, rollabout figure," according to Conner), and Campbell, posted to his staff as an aide. In an extension of the family/military circle, Hattie and Thomas Turner, another of Ewell's aides, were engaged to be married.[9]

Ewell's coddling of Campbell Brown became a standing joke at his headquarters. "Old Ewell told me he had never exposed Campbell but once," said Turner, adding that the general had confessed with a helpless shrug that he could never face Lizinka should anything happen to her boy. "Hang him," Turner went on, "he never thinks of my mother, I suppose, for he pops me around no matter how hot the fire is."[10]

Brown and the others had been perfectly safe in the Richmond military backwater. Now, in the early spring of 1865, Grant converted it into the Confederacy's front line. He opened the last campaign on March 29, sending Major General Philip Sheridan against the extreme Confederate right southwest of Petersburg. Sheridan turned Lee's flank at Five Forks on Saturday, April 1. With the collapse there, Lee summoned Longstreet, with Charles Field's division, to Petersburg. That left Ewell with one veteran division, J. B. Kershaw's, and a division of reserves under Lee's son Custis to cover everything north of the James.

Ewell started the cadet detachments and three battalions of convalescents down the Darbytown Road for Field's lines at nightfall Saturday. He spent the damp, cloudy overnight living rough, riding the lines and resting at intervals in Longstreet's old headquarters. The Yankees just opposite were quiet, but their guns rumbled on all night to the south. The Federal Sixth Corps attacked on the Petersburg front at 4:40 Sunday morning, breaking through at Fort Fisher just as the sun rose into a sky clearing after four days of intermittent rain. Longstreet managed to patch together a thin but serviceable second line. Lee ordered him to hold it until dark, to give the army and the government time to get away, and wired Richmond that the capital would have to be abandoned before daybreak tomorrow.

A courier caught up to Ewell around ten o'clock with orders to return to Richmond and prepare for the evacuation, the movement of Federal captives out of Libby and Castle Thunder prisons, and the destruction of stores. By then Lee's telegram had made its way to President Davis in his pew at Saint Paul's Church. Charles Blackford followed an impassive Davis out of the crowded sanctuary (it was Communion Sunday) and hurried along Franklin Street to his War Department office.

News-starved crowds formed in front of Ewell's headquarters and outside the Spotswood. Refugees with knapsacks and bundles milled in the streets. Soldiers and government functionaries fought for places in the trains, canal boats, and drays leaving the city. Long lines led to the banks, thrown open this extraordinary Sunday so depositors could collect their gold, jewelry, and securities.

Piles of Confederate and Virginia paper currency blazed up in the streets. Provost detachments dumped commissary stores into the canal. Ward patrols broached barrels of spirits and spilled the contents into the gutters. Dark, ragged figures dropped to their knees to scoop the flowing liquor into jars or even to lap it up as though from the trough. The gasworks were shut down. Secretary of War John Breckinridge advised the city council to appoint a surrender delegation that would meet the Yankees on the outskirts in the morning.

A special train waited for Davis, his cabinet, and the Confederate gold reserves at the Danville depot at the foot of Mayo's Bridge. Charles Blackford at the War Department boxed up a sheaf of official papers for the government train as the last of the evening sun streamed through windows streaked with soot. He locked the desk, walked out into the dim corridor, and pulled the door shut behind him for the last time. Returning to his rooms at Grace and Jefferson streets, Blackford packed a valise, collected his horse, and set out in the twilight, with no food and no money, only a little grass for the horse, leaving by the James & Kanawha Canal towpath for the High Bridge over the Appomattox River, where he aimed to join the field army.

As Ewell had foretold, Richmond exploded into anarchy. Looters appeared in the gloom. Mobs ran from building to building, shattering windows, knocking down doors, sweeping up whatever came to hand. Drink fueled the uprising as in Columbia six weeks before. Vandals punched out all the ground floor windows at the Spotswood. Conolly, the Irish MP, emerged from his room around midnight to witness a riot boiling along Main Street, drunks spilling out of the waterside shebeens, goods and broken glass scattered in the streets, the first of the fires breaking out. He recorded the wild pulsing scene in his diary:

> The streets filled with all the ragamuffins chiefly niggers running & hurrying about & then another crash another explosion & all the windows are rent asunder . . . & now the plundering begins men & women grabbing more than they can carry . . . now the mills are on fire & the crowd rush to get the flour & begin rolling out barrels thro' the street & carrying bags & sacks of flour.[11]

Sometime after two o'clock, Ewell's provost troops set fire to tobacco warehouses on Cary Street, at Eighth and Byrd, and across from the Gallego flour mill on Twelfth Street. The mobs were arsonical too, no doubt inspired by official example: they put the torch to several Cary Street buildings and the arsenal and pushed a burning barge under the Fourteenth Street canal bridge. Ewell sent his convalescent troops into the streets, deployed his mounted staff and couriers for a show of force, and sent to General Kershaw for frontline infantry to overawe the crowds.[12]

Kershaw detached two battalions for the job. By sunrise Monday morning the rioters were quiet, cowed by Kershaw's hard men or insensate with drink. Meantime, Kershaw's main body dashed over the burning canal bridge at the double-quick, crossed Mayo's Bridge to Manchester, and struck the Buckingham road for a rendezvous with Lee at Amelia Court House, forty miles to the west.[13]

Wind-fanned fires burned out of control in the commercial district between the capitol and the James. Ewell passed over to Manchester at the head of his convalescents around seven o'clock. From a rise, with Richmond sharp against the bright east, he watched flames burst through the roof of the Gallego mill across the street from the Shockoe tobacco warehouse. The arsenal blazed furiously a few blocks away.

The fires were jumping from building to building, carried along on a fresh southeast breeze.[14]

Only a weak rear guard remained. South Carolinian Martin Gary pulled his much-reduced cavalry brigade out of the line after moonset, around two o'clock, halting at the intersection of the Charles City and New Kent roads. There the troops rested, awaiting the dismounted pickets left behind to feed the campfires and discourage the enemy from following too closely. Around four o'clock a series of tremendous detonations turned night into day—and roused every sleeping Yankee for thirty miles around.

Gary refused to leave without his pickets and the men lay dozing in the deserted intermediate lines as the sun heaved up. The stragglers finally showed themselves at the top of a rise, comic figures afoot, clumsy in their high cavalry boots. The brigade mounted, sped through the riverside suburb of Rocketts Landing, and entered the smoking city at a trot.

A solid wall of flame blocked Gary's route to the James. The troopers swung away from the hot breath of the fire, plunged through an opening on Franklin Street, crossed the canal single file along a stone conduit, and sprinted over Mayo's Bridge, the Seventh South Carolina Cavalry bringing up the rear. Several men dismounted, packed tinder into the bridge supports, lit it off, climbed back into the saddle, and wound wearily on up the hill to Manchester.

From the high ground, the fire appeared to be general. Black smoke boiled up over Richmond's spires and overspread the stricken city. The arsenal glowed red, to a steady accompaniment of bursting shells. A flotilla of gunboats and small steamers burned at their moorings off the Navy Yard. Edward Boykin of the 7th South Carolina watched a detachment of Federal cavalry canter easily up Main Street. "They were too late to secure the bridge, if that had been their object," he decided.[15] A few minutes later the Stars and Stripes and two small, triangular cavalry guidons rose over the Confederate capitol.

"EARLY LAST NIGHT THE GREAT FIGHT commenced in front of Petersburg," Lieutenant Edward Bartlett of the Fifth Massachusetts Cavalry (Colored) had written home to Concord on March 30. "We could hear the cannonading plainly and see the flashes of the guns."[16]

Rain began falling around midnight, muffling the racket of the opening phase, which saw Sheridan bogging for Five Forks, southwest of Petersburg. Quiet descended on the Fifth Massachusetts camp at Chaffin's Farm, six miles below Richmond, though sleep eluded Ned Bartlett there. He lay warm and dry in the comfortable winter quarters of the departed First New York Mounted Rifles; it was his racing imagination that kept him awake. With luck, he would be part of the army's concluding triumph, the greatest of them all, the capture of the rebel capital.

"There is no doubt but that we shall have some work to do soon," he wrote his sister Martha. "You know that is why I came."[17]

The Bartletts were a prominent Concord family. Josiah Bartlett settled there in 1820 to practice medicine. He and his wife Martha (a descendant of Governor William Bradford of the Plymouth Colony) raised nine children in the famous little town, from Martha, forty-one years old in 1865, to Lieutenant Ned, rising twenty-three. The old doctor had treated nearly everyone in Concord. He made his voice heard, too, on the issues of his time. Nobody attacked the rum sellers with more passion than Josiah Bartlett.

The Alcotts were occasional callers at the Bartletts' high-shouldered brick house on the Lowell road a few steps north of the Common. Ralph Waldo Emerson was a familiar figure, a neighbor, a patient of the doctor's. Bartlett treated the sage's old mother when she fell out of bed and broke her hip. Henry Thoreau taught Martha at the Concord Academy. Ned and his friend Eddie Emerson used to collect birds' eggs for the eccentric naturalist; they called him "Dave," though probably not to his face. Ned's brother Ripley once sought Thoreau's help in finding a publisher for his sentimental poem on the Concord battle of 1775. Thoreau obligingly wrote Rip an introduction to the Boston house of Ticknor & Fields, publisher of *Walden*. Privately, he advised him to keep the verses to himself.

The Bartlett girls attended Nathaniel Hawthorne's funeral at the First Parish Church in May 1864, a grotesque event, according to Annie Bartlett, with overtones of gothic comedy that might have appealed to the defunct novelist himself. Hawthorne's literary friends insisted, against his widow Sophia's wishes, on opening the casket.

"Twas so dreadful to have all the people looking at him when the family were not willing to see him," Annie wrote Ned. "All the poets were there, Holmes, Agassiz, Lowell, Longfellow, Whipple and all the others and 'last and least' Franklin Pierce."* [18]

Dr. Bartlett could be indifferent to his fees, especially with poorer patients. Spinster daughters might live at home, as did Martha, head of the household after her mother's death and a surrogate parent to Ned. Bartlett sons were expected to make their own way in the world. James emigrated west to Detroit to become superintendent of a locomotive works; Ripley followed him to Michigan in 1863. Ned finished up at the Town School in 1860 and went to work for a dry goods wholesaler in Boston. He made $50 his first year and $100 his second—roughly his pay as a $13-a-month enlistee in the Forty-fourth Massachusetts, Company F, Captain Charles Storrow (Sam Storrow's brother) commanding.

Bartlett had seen no action with the Forty-fourth, only the shattered aftermath of it: cotton and corn burning in the streets of a ramshackle North Carolina town; an astonishingly cut-up woods; the wounded, the dying, and the dead. But he had registered a fair amount of miscellaneous wartime experience after mustering out in 1863: recruiting in Boston for Shaw's Fifty-fourth Massachusetts, enlisting freed slaves in Tennessee, and nursing the wounded for the Sanitary Commission in Fredericksburg during Grant's move south from the Rapidan.

The Virginia fighting of May 1864 seemed familiar enough to Bartlett at first, an intensification of the brief, painful North Carolina experience. Passing out lemonade and crackers, he found the lightly wounded first arrivals grateful and full of hope. He heard from a soldier in the Thirty-second Massachusetts that the regiment's Concord men had survived the first two days unscathed. (Later, when he knew the details of the Wilderness battle, that struck him as miraculous.) The wounded believed, too, that their suffering would count for something for once.

"They all praise Grant," Bartlett wrote Martha, "and say that he'll end it this time." [19]

---

*Pierce and Hawthorne were college classmates. Hawthorne wrote the former president's campaign biography in 1852.

The battle ground on. The wounded flooded the temporary hospitals in battered Fredericksburg houses and spilled out of doors onto the grass and under the trees. Long lines of ambulances wound along the dusty roads from Spotsylvania Court House. "I saw a man named Adams from Stow who knew father," Bartlett wrote home. "He is in the 34th Massachusetts and his left arm was shot off."[20] By the middle of May, wounded men were arriving at the aid stations in batches of hundreds at a time.

An exhausted army surgeon gave Bartlett a hurried lesson in wound dressing and complimented him on his quick mastery of technique. ("I told him I inherited it," Bartlett said.) Walt Whitman, obscure still, though Emerson had written a send-off review of *Leaves of Grass* a few years before, created "The Wound-Dresser" out of hospital experiences like Bartlett's:

> From the stump of the arm, the amputated hand,
> I undo the clotted lint, remove the slough, wash off the
>     matter and blood,
> Back on his pillow the soldier bends with curv'd neck and
>     side-falling head,
> His eyes are closed, his face is pale, he dares not look
>     on the bloody stump,
> And has not yet look'd on it.

Bartlett cleaned and wrapped a New Hampshire soldier's splintered arm. He swabbed the stomach wound of an Irish volunteer. He had turned away from the wounded in North Carolina, his gorge rising. Now he forced himself to look upon the shredded limbs, lacerated chests, and smashed skulls; to stay calm, and to be as gentle as he could with sponge, wipe, and lint bandage.

"How are they going to fill the quota of Concord?" he wondered. "Will they have the draft?"[21]

The town had been engaged from the start, from the first sharp skirmishes over slavery extension in the 1840s. South Carolina expelled touring Concord abolitionist Samuel Hoar for antislavery activity. Doctor Bartlett treated fugitive slaves in Concord attics. Wendell Phillips delivered abolitionist harangues at the Lyceum. The incendiary John Brown passed through after the Kansas troubles, stopping for lunch with the Thoreaus. A company of Concord volunteers left for Washington on April 19, 1861, Patriot's Day, a high festal occasion, and fought in the first battle of Bull Run. Louisa May Alcott worked twelve-hour shifts as a nurse in Washington's Union Hotel Hospital.* She fell ill with typhoid and pneumonia and returned home near death. Josiah Bartlett oversaw her slow and painful recovery at Orchard House.

The events of May and June 1864 led Ned Bartlett back to the army. Emerson himself wrote Governor Andrew recommending his young fellow townsman for an officer's commission. Bartlett joined the newly raised Fifth Massachusetts Cavalry in early October at Point Lookout, Maryland, the wind-flayed promontory where the Potomac flows into Chesapeake Bay.

Gales, rain, blowing sand, the eternal seethe of the surf—Point Lookout was a bleak and primitive post. With winter coming on Bartlett built a hearth of beach pebbles in his hut and laid a carpet of oat sacks on the sandy floor. The regiment supplied guard details for the ten thousand Confederate prisoners of war in the Point Lookout stockade. Otherwise, drill and the stableboy grind of tending the horses filled out the days.

Bartlett approached his work conscientiously. He took a regular twenty-four-hour turn in command of the two-hundred-strong camp guard—one musket-carrying cavalryman for every fifty or so prisoners. The rebels were docile enough. So far as he could tell they were decently fed; anyhow, they looked tough and fit. The huts were dry. Water supplies were adequate. Steady breezes carried away the gamy scent of thousands of close-packed men.

Even so, illness periodically swept the camp. The long wooden hospital buildings, equipped with stoves and iron beds with mattresses, coarse white sheets, and two blankets, held as many as two thousand men at any given time; there were a steady two or three deaths a day. The commandant kept eighty or so ready-made coffins stacked near the camp entrance—doubtless, thought Charles Adams, now the Fifth Massachusetts Cavalry's lieutenant colonel, "with a view to encourage the newcomers." Bartlett grew used to the coffins before long, and to the thicket of frail wooden crosses that sprang up in the camp graveyard.[22]

---

*Alcott's *Hospital Sketches* (1863) recounts the experience.

After a while he no longer noticed the rank smell of massed horses or the ammonia reek of the stables. The days were at once crowded and lacking in event, an unvarying routine of morning stable call, water call at noon, mounted drill in the afternoon, evening stable call. One of Bartlett's boyhood chores had been to look after his father's cross-grained mare. But he had no particular gift with horses and was certainly no natural in the saddle; his legs were too short, too thick. Now, finally, he learned to dominate a horse, to ride cavalry-style, steering by touch of the reins and pressure of the rider's legs.

"If you want to turn to the right, instead of pulling the right rein, and turning the horse by the bit, you should just carry your hand to the right," he explained in a letter to Martha. "This brings the left rein acrost the horse's neck, you at the same time pressing your leg, not heel or spur, against the horse, behind the girth. This turns him to the right."[23]

Bartlett learned his new trade under the aloof and glacial Adams, to whom the colonel, Henry Russell, had delegated the task of drill-master. "Col. Adams makes everyone feel uncomfortable by his method of catechizing us as if we were a parcell of schoolboys," complained Bartlett, who along with the rest of the younger officers idolized Harry Russell. The colonel's resignation in early February cast a pall over the mess.

"Now I suppose Lt. Col. Adams will be made colonel and command us," Bartlett fretted.[24]

Adams had come into the regiment in the autumn of '64 after a hard summer of skirmishing, scouting, and flank guard duty with the headquarters cavalry of the Army of the Potomac. Three years in the field—Antietam, Chancellorsville, Gettysburg, two bitter winters of outpost work, the Virginia campaign—robbed him of much of his youthful vigor. Malarial attacks and slow poisoning from a changeless diet of hardtack, beef fried in pork fat, and black coffee left him feeling dull and weak most of the time. And he had lost a lot of hair.

He had only just begun to settle into the job as Russell's understudy when Andrew Humphreys, commanding the Second Corps, offered him a prize place on the corps staff. He had no special aptitude for regimental soldiering, he told himself; such military talents as he possessed were best adapted to staff duties. On the other hand, he had done nothing to merit the gift of a staff posting. And he hated to let Harry Russell down. With Russell leaving the regiment, he felt bound to decline the appointment.

"The army is a great place to learn philosophy," Adams once said; "you get but indifferent as to what disposition is made of you."[25]

Even so, Adams had more control over his fate than most soldiers. He might feel pledged to the Fifth Massachusetts Cavalry, but he could see no reason why the regiment should sit out the end of the war at Point Lookout. So he worked his connections—considerable, through his father, the minister to Britain—to engineer a move to the Richmond front.

Horses fit for frontline service were in short supply in the winter of 1865. Yet Grant obliged Adams with a letter to War Secretary Stanton; and Stanton saw to it that mounts, weapons, and transport were made available. Orders for Richmond reached him around March 20. He left at once for Washington to draw carbines and pistols for the troopers and to reserve shipping. He picked up the latest intelligence too: the Army of Northern Virginia was disintegrating. "Lee hasn't got one week's fight" left in him, he had written his father as long ago as December. "Victory or defeat alike would be ruinous."[26] Lee was three months closer to ruin now. Adams predicted that Richmond would be taken without a fight.

The regiment reached Deep Bottom, eight miles below the Confederate capital, by steamer the night of March 28. "It seems very quiet on the line," Ned Bartlett wrote his brother Ripley the next day, "no muskets but now and then artillery."[27] Colonel Adams took command of all the cavalry north of the James, around two thousand troopers, only half of them mounted.

The Fifth pushed up to the front in a cold, driving nor'easter. The roads were liquid mud. Rain streamed off the troopers' capes and a chill vapor rose from the horses' flanks. The column cleared several lines of disused works before reaching the New Yorkers' comfortable camp in a pine woods. The rifle pits, thought Bartlett, looked like newly made graves.

"Where are you now?" Martha sent anxiously. "Do write as often as possible, and always date the letters."[28]

Bartlett led a dismounted party up to the picket line the night of April 1–2, creeping forward in the iron dark. There were scattered shots, but he saw no rebels. Relief arrived around noon Sunday, and he trudged back to camp. Corps headquarters alerted Adams at nightfall to be prepared to descend on Richmond with the cavalry at a moment's notice.

A blue mist settled into the valley of the James. Officers lay with an ear to the ground, listening for the rumble of iron on paving stones. Rumor tore through the cantonment: "Col. Adams says that the 25th Corps are going into Richmond and that the 5th Cavy are to take the lead," Bartlett heard.[29] Nobody slept much. After midnight a bright glow appeared on the horizon. Presently the order came to mount. Troopers detailed as stretcher-bearers made their way over to a line of ambulances forming up in the half-light. Adams ripped open a message from the pickets: the rebels were gone from his front. Godfrey Weitzel, the Twenty-fifth Corps commander, ordered the cavalry onto the Darbytown Road. A thousand troopers and a battery were in motion by seven o'clock.

Small arms fire sounded ahead. Adams motioned for the regiment to wheel into line. The battery unlimbered and fired a couple of rounds into the trees. The line advanced fifty yards or so, the horses picking their way cautiously through the underwood, then halted. Bartlett with Company E waited in a narrow lane, thick woods crowding either verge; a dangerous place, it seemed to him, his feet rattling in the stirrups. The order to resume the advance echoed along the line. Bartlett started down the Darbytown Road at a gallop. Clear of the woods now, he could see the enemy works, spiky chevaux-de-frise in front. Little flags marked torpedoes buried in the torn earth. The rebel picket fires were still smoldering.[30]

Several heavy explosions set the ground dancing underfoot and thick black smoke rose in plumes over the capital. Bartlett's battalion veered to the right at a crossroads. "We were alone, a sort of independent army on our own hook," he realized.[31] Not for long; after a while the regiment struck the Charles City Road. A signboard there read "Richmond, two miles." The James up ahead appeared to be on fire. Deserted camps stretched away on either side of the road. The tents were still standing, as though the army had only gone out for the day and meant to return in the evening.

The Fifth Massachusetts Cavalry swept down Main Street at a swinging trot. There were friendly infantry in the city by now—

Vermonter Edward Ripley's brigade of the Twenty-fourth Corps, marching with three bands at the head of column. The roar of the flames, the crashing of walls, and the exploding magazines of the Confederate river fleet drowned out the blare of "Yankee Doodle." Bartlett's troopers began to shout, cheer, and sing. Crowds materialized out of the flames. Freed slaves pushed up close, straining to touch the withers and flanks of the steaming horses and the seamed boots of the troopers. Clusters of hungry women and children, white and black, approached the men to beg for hardtack.

General Weitzel accepted the formal surrender from Mayor Mayo at City Hall. "We took Richmond at 8:15 this morning," he wired Grant.[32] In his first act as conqueror, Weitzel appointed Ripley military governor and assigned him to put out the fires. Ripley's regiments went to work at once. It was slow going. Rioters or retreating Confederates had disabled the municipal fire engines and slashed the hose, leaving Ripley little choice but to attack the fire by blowing up buildings in its path. Only a midafternoon wind shift enabled his troops to bring the flames under control.

The city center lay scorched and blasted, as though a thunderbolt had shattered it. Broken glass and blackened brick were ankle-deep in the streets. All the banks and two principal hotels were destroyed, together with the *Examiner,* the *Dispatch,* and the *Enquirer* press offices, Mayo's Bridge, the two railroad bridges, and the Petersburg and Danville depots. The Spotswood, the custom house, and the post office survived. A special postal agent turned up Monday afternoon, taking charge even before the embers had cooled. "I find a large quantity of U.S. property," he reported, "pouches, locks, safes &c."[33] Ripley's fire fighting and the accident of the wind shift had spared the residential neighborhoods.

"We came near being burned out," Lizzie Ewell wrote her uncle the general a few days later. "This house caught & was on fire in six places at once. If it hadn't been for the exertions of the Yankees the city would have been all gone."[34]

Adams's troopers rested in Capitol Square for a few hours, then withdrew to a camp on the outskirts of Richmond. To spare rebel sensibilities, the accommodating Weitzel agreed to garrison the city with Ripley's white troops only. The slight rubbed off none of the luster of the victory for Ned Bartlett.

"We entered Richmond just on the heels of the retreating army," he wrote triumphantly that night. "Now Martha aren't you glad that I am in the army and at the front? It is glory enough for one family to have one of them with the first in Richmond."[35]

Even the morose, self-doubting Charles Adams acknowledged the transcendence of the experience.

"I am still confounded at the good fortune which brought me there," he wrote his father in London. "To have led my regiment into Richmond at the moment of its capture is the one event which I should have desired as the culmination of my life in the army. That honor has been mine and now I feel as if my record in this war was rounded and completely filled out."[36]

NODDING IN THE SADDLE, DRAINED OF VITALITY, his wits astray from pain and sleeplessness, Richard Ewell plodded westward toward Amelia Court House. The column—Kershaw's division, Custis Lee's reserves, the convalescents, a brigade of gunboat sailors, clerks from shut-down government offices in Richmond—moved at a pace adapted to the slowest of Custis's men, converted heavy gunners unaccustomed to long marches. Artillery and supply wagons became entangled, causing endless delays. Hungry, footsore, and demoralized men were dropping out of the ranks, at first by ones and twos, soon by the dozens.

"Everything seemed to go to pieces at once," a veteran of the retreat recalled. "The best disciplinarians in the army relaxed their reins. The best troops became disorganized, and hardly any command marched in a body."[37]

Sheridan's cavalry snapped at the flanks of the column. Shots rang out from the ranks, riflemen firing promiscuously (and without rebuke from their officers) at straying chickens and geese. An officer in Custis Lee's command plucked a bloody kidney out of a slaughtered sheep and tucked it away in a pocket, to be cooked and eaten later. Not everyone could wait for a halt, a smoky greenwood fire, and a handful of parched corn: Ewell saw men devouring raw fresh meat on the march.

Ewell's corps crossed the Appomattox River by the Richmond & Danville Railroad bridge, haphazardly floored for the passage of troops, horses, and vehicles. The men moved by twos and kept to the middle, for fear of tipping the unsecured planks and tumbling into the abyss. Ewell caught up to Lee's main body near Amelia Court House on the overcast afternoon of Wednesday, April 5. Rations were supposed to have been stored there, but for some reason the commissary had failed the Army of Northern Virginia and the troops went hungry. Ewell had fewer mouths to feed now, anyway: straggling and desertion reduced his command by half, to around three thousand men.

The rearguard Seventh South Carolina Cavalry moved out from Manchester after a short halt early Monday and fell in with the traffic stream from Petersburg. Traveling at a slow walk to allow the column to close up, the Carolinians halted for the night on the Burkeville road only eleven miles out of Richmond. They pressed on for the Appomattox after a late start Tuesday, passing a wrack of guns, caissons, and wagons abandoned along the roadside. The trains claimed the right of way, forcing the cavalrymen and their jaded horses to the rough ground on either side of the road.

The Seventh South Carolina crossed the Appomattox at the rail bridge after nightfall and bivouacked with some of Longstreet's infantry a few miles short of Amelia Court House. Yankees were aprowl in the neighborhood. Ned Boykin caught a glimpse of their pickets, and the music of their bands floated over to the rebel camps in the evening stillness.

The pursuing Federals practiced a strict economy of effort. From what Boykin could see, they marched in perfect order during the day and wasted no strength on profitless attacks in the night. "General Grant's large force seemed to be kept perfectly in hand," he wrote, "massed with great care to strike with effect at any given point on our line of march."[38] The chance of a decisive blow presented itself on the afternoon of Thursday the sixth. Sheridan recognized it at once and struck with all the force he could assemble.

The order of march for the day placed Ewell's command between Richard Anderson's corps ahead and the wagon trains behind, with John Gordon's corps bringing up the rear. Sheridan's cavalry darted and lunged at the lightly protected trains all through the showery morning. Ewell turned down a rough road into the marshy valley of the two forks of Sayler's Creek a little before noon and halted there to allow part of the train to pass to the head of the column, for relief from the clawing enemy cavalry. He diverted the balance onto a minor road that led away to the Appomattox. Ewell neglected for some reason to inform Gordon of the change of route. When Gordon fell in behind the trailing wagons, a gap opened between his and Ewell's commands.

Meantime, Ewell learned that Anderson, bedeviled too by the enemy cavalry, had lost contact with Longstreet just ahead on the line of march. Sheridan threw George Armstrong Custer's cavalry division into the gap athwart Anderson's road, and he sent word to Horatio Wright's oncoming Sixth Corps infantry to rush up and close on Ewell, now Lee's rear guard. As Ewell moved off to confer with Anderson, two Sixth Corps divisions were massing in his rear, where Gordon should have been. Anderson and Ewell were cut off from Lee's main body and trapped in the narrow bottom of Sayler's Creek.

Anderson proposed a head-on attack to clear the road to Rice Station. Ewell offered to occupy the Sixth Corps infantry while Anderson launched the breakout try. Rejoining his command, Ewell found the two weakened divisions settled into line of battle on a ridge overlooking the valley facing east, with Kershaw's veterans on the right, Custis Lee's converted artillerymen on the left. Beyond Little Sayler's Creek a cleared field sloped uphill. Federal artillery appeared before long near the farmhouse on the summit.

Ewell, Custis Lee, and their aides watched in silence as two Yankee guns unlimbered. Ewell had no artillery of his own, so the enemy gunners had a free field. Shells were soon dropping uncomfortably close. After a while Ewell began to speak in his ordinary voice, shrill and lisping.

"Tomatoes are very good," he said. "I wish I had some."[39]

With amazing self-restraint, the anxious young men around Ewell managed to choke off their laughter. Possibly Ewell had thrown out what he regarded as a lighthearted remark as a way of easing the tension. Possibly he really did experience a sudden craving for tomatoes. With Ewell it was impossible to say. He turned back toward Anderson, leaving the remark, scriptural to say the least, hanging in the damp air.

Wright's assault troops splashed across the swale, cleared a belt of low brush pine, and charged up the rough slope. The Confederate line delivered a strong first volley, temporarily checking the Federal center. But on Anderson's front Sheridan's cavalry stopped the breakout attempt almost before it got under way. By the time Ewell arrived, the Yankees were lapping both his flanks.

Front, flank, and rear, the bluecoats kept coming. When enemy cavalry suddenly exploded onto Kershaw from behind, Ewell's line collapsed. Kershaw and all but two hundred of his men were taken prisoner. One Yankee regiment alone, the Thirty-seventh Massachusetts, captured nearly four hundred men of Lee's division, including Custis himself. Turning in the saddle as he approached his shattered front, Ewell saw enemy skirmishers about to overtake him. He reined in at the approach of a Yankee cavalryman and handed over his sword. Campbell Brown, safe and sound, surrendered with him.

Scattered pockets of Confederates held out for a while yet along the rough edge of the battle, firing sporadically as the sun sank below the horizon. At his captors' suggestion, Ewell dictated a short message to Brown, for delivery under a truce flag:

"General Anderson's attack has failed. General Ewell and all his staff are prisoners. You are surrounded. Being a prisoner, General Ewell gives you no orders, but advises a surrender, as further effusion of blood is useless."[40]

Sheridan closed his dispatch to Grant with the famous line, "If the thing is pressed I think that Lee will surrender." Ewell reported losses of 150 killed and wounded and 2,800 captured, virtually his entire command. Only a skeleton brigade of Anderson's corps fought free of Sheridan and continued on west to Farmville. Gordon survived an afternoon-long hammering from Humphreys' Second Corps and reached the High Bridge after nightfall, but he left 1,700 casualties in the woods and fields and along the road. Lee lost as many as 8,000 men at Sayler's Creek, a third of what remained of the army.[41]

A party of the Fifth Wisconsin delivered Ewell to General Wright's field headquarters Thursday night. The damaged general was reported as cringing and desperate to make friends with his captors. "He was thoroughly whipped and seemed to be dreadfully demoralized," another Confederate prisoner recalled.[42] One of the Yankee officers found Ewell sitting on the ground, hugging his one knee, his wan face buried in his arms.

"Our cause is lost," he murmured. "Lee should surrender before more lives are wasted."[43]

Cousin Thomas Gantt tried to put a favorable gloss on the Sayler's Creek disaster in a letter to Lizinka Ewell a few days later.

"I regard it as a great relief that Richard is captured," Gantt wrote her from Saint Louis, where he held a colonel's commission in the Union army. "He is now safe from the casualties of the contest and all but madmen must see (I think) that Lee's last battle was an unnecessary carnage. It will add nothing to his reputation."[44]

PICKETS OF THE FIFTH MASSACHUSETTS CAVALRY patrolled the environs of Richmond, collecting armed stragglers. "The object," Ned Bartlett explained, "is to keep all the citizens out or in—& to arrest deserters and rebel soldiers."[45] Combing the woods, pushing through blooming dogwood that flashed white against the gray-brown ranks of budding trees, his company brought in thirty ragged Confederates during the bright, mild morning of Tuesday, April 4. As a reward, Bartlett got the afternoon off and permission to visit the city.

Smoke drifted over the burned district. The shops were shut, the streets quiet. At Libby Prison, a prewar tobacco warehouse, Bartlett tore a small tin "L. Libby" sign from the countingroom door for a war curio. He wandered through the seared commercial quarter and up to Jeff Davis's mansion. He caught a glimpse, too, of Abraham Lincoln, the commander in chief himself, a tall black hat bobbing above an adoring escort, mostly black, that crowded him close as he walked, leading his son Tad by the hand, the two miles from Rocketts Landing to the capitol.

Lincoln's insistence on a pedestrian tour of Richmond pushed his sailor guard detail to the edge of mutiny. The stroll was risky, sure, even though Weitzel and Ripley had established a degree of order overnight that would have amazed Dick Ewell. All the same, Lincoln's presence put the occupation forces on high nervous alert. With cause, too—for Ripley had hardly settled into his office at City Hall when a Confederate soldier approached him with warning of a plot against the president.

His name was Snyder, and he had served in a shadowy Richmond-based unit known as Rains's Torpedo Bureau. The bureau handled routine operations such as the sowing of explosives in the James. Its agents also carried out behind-the-lines sabotage. Snyder spoke vaguely of a mission aimed at leading U.S. government officials. He

*iew taken from south side of Canal Basin, Richmond, Va., — April, 1865. showing Capitol, Custom House &c.*

A lone Yankee petty officer stands sentry along the Canal Basin against a backdrop of gutted Richmond in April 1865. Fires deliberately set by the retreating Confederates spread from the tobacco warehouses and left much of the city center a smoking desolation. But Thomas Jefferson's capitol, top center, survived to soar grandly above the ruins. (Library of Congress)

could supply no names or facts, he said; just a caution that Lincoln and others might be in danger.[46] Ripley went at once to the president, now safely stowed away aboard the gunboat *Malvern* moored in the James. "I will not be dying all the while," Lincoln had remarked when a friend admonished him about his solitary walks and unescorted carriage rides around Washington. He heard Ripley out, but refused to act on the alarm.[47]

Meantime, Weitzel ordered the city's poor to be fed from captured stores. Ripley set a curfew, rounded up vandals and other doubtful characters, prepared surviving newspapers "for issue under loyal management," and authorized R. D'Arcy Ogden's *corps dramatique* to open with *Hamlet* at the New Richmond Theater. On request, he assigned guards to the houses of terrified Richmond white ladies, and assured them that black soldiers would not be allowed into the city to disturb their slumbers.[48]

The display kept Richmond subdued. The streets were silent and deserted when the Fifth Massachusetts Cavalry passed through the night of April 6 in transit for Petersburg. Colonel Adams saw no one but a lone sentry pacing his beat.

"For the first time I see the spirit of the Virginians broken; the whole people are cowed—whipped out," Adams wrote his father. "By the first of June you will not be able in these parts to find any Confederates."[49]

Some high-ranking rebels had already managed to put some distance between themselves and the Last Ditch. Former U.S. Supreme Court justice John A. Campbell, a Confederate assistant secretary of war* who stayed on after the evacuation, met with Lincoln on April 5 to propose calling the secessionist Virginia legislature into session for the purpose of pulling the state out of the war.

Campbell and his associates weren't asking for much, or so it seemed to Charles Dana, the War Department assistant who ran down to Richmond two days after the surrender to take a look around for Secretary Stanton: a general amnesty in return for a resolution recalling Virginia troops from the Confederate Army. "The president did not promise the amnesty," Dana wired Stanton, "but told them he had the pardoning power, and would save any repentant sinner from hanging." Dana added that the talks with Campbell sounded in keeping with Lincoln's intention, as he had expressed it to Weitzel, to "let the people down easy."[50]

Word of these discussions enraged Lincoln's critics. The president and the Radical Republicans in Congress were drawing near to an irreparable break on postwar restoration policy. Even Stanton, a Lincoln loyalist, went into a frenzy over the Campbell initiative—a backstairs deal, as he saw it, with the very men who had drawn Virginia out of the Union. Hence the Dana mission: Stanton would try to reel in the president, if he showed signs of going too far.

Lincoln so far had pursued a strikingly liberal Reconstruction policy for the errant states—liberal for rebel whites, at least. In partly reconstructed Louisiana, Union authorities appeased whites by deny-

---

*And one of the Confederate peace conferees at Hampton Roads, along with Alexander Stephens and Robert M. T. Hunter.

ing African Americans the vote, though, as the president rightly noted, Union-held Louisiana already guaranteed more to blacks than his own Illinois did: equal access to public schools and the courts, for example. He evidently favored a similar plan for Virginia. Besides, what harm could there be in a legislative resolution extracting Virginia from the Confederacy? As Lincoln knew by the night of April 6, when word of the Sayler's Creek battle reached him, the question would be moot before long, anyway.

"The President told me this morning that Sheridan seemed to be getting the Virginia soldiers out of the war faster than this legislature could think," Dana wrote Stanton the next day.[51]

The formal end came on Palm Sunday, April 9, at Appomattox Court House. "General Lee surrendered this afternoon upon terms proposed by myself," Grant wired Stanton with dramatic understatement.[52] Washington exploded in celebration. Gun salutes rattled the capital. Candles burned through the night in thousands of windows, public and private. Government buildings were hastily fitted with gas jets that flashed "Union" and "Grant" in letters of fire.

News of the surrender reached Richmond on Monday. The Federals celebrated in the rain with cannon salutes, blasts of steam whistles, and massed bands endlessly recycling "Yankee Doodle," "The Battle Hymn of the Republic," and "The Star-Spangled Banner." Ogden's *Hamlet* opened that night before a largely Northern audience.

Journalists and politicians descended upon the fallen capital. Dana encountered the square-built, florid figure of the vice president himself in the faded lobby of the Spotswood, alone in a corner of the hotel's broad, bare hall. Motioning Dana over and seizing him by the elbow, Andrew Johnson delivered a close-range lecture on restoration policy. Rebels, he said, should be allowed back conditionally, and with some penalty. "He insisted," Dana wrote later, "that their sins had been enormous." Dana himself passed along one capital charge: "Ewell set city on fire," he reported to Stanton. Powerful voices, not only Johnson's, were demanding punishment for such crimes.[53]

Freeing himself from the vice president's grip, Dana suggested that he take up the question with Lincoln. Johnson answered evasively. As Dana surely knew, the president and his cabinet had all but ignored him since the inauguration five weeks ago when the veep, all too obviously in liquor, had blurted out a long, maudlin oration before swearing the oath of office. ("It seemed as if he would *never* stop," remarked Susan Wallace, the wife of General Lew Wallace, hero of the Monocacy. "The senators hung their heads, the supreme judges looked like they would sink and altogether it was the most mortifying thing it is possible to imagine.")[54] This solecism—and perhaps other shortcomings, too—made Johnson an untouchable. He evidently hoped Dana would forward his views to Stanton, with whom he otherwise had slight contact.

With Lee's collapse, political questions rose to the top of the national agenda. Among the early visitors to vanquished Richmond, arriving on April 11, were three members of Congress's powerful Joint Committee on the Conduct of the War: Senators Benjamin Wade of Ohio and Zachariah Chandler of Michigan, and Representative George Julian of Indiana.

All three were Radical nemeses of the President, Ben Wade especially. He and Marylander Henry Davis had pushed a punitive Reconstruction measure through Congress in the summer of 1864; when Lincoln pocket-vetoed it, they counterpunched with a savage attack on his policies. The so-called Wade-Davis Manifesto also asserted the right of Congress to the leading role in reconstruction. The president's views were evolving still. On the night of the Radical party's arrival in Richmond, he delivered a speech to a big crowd on the White House lawn that promised a soft peace, but also suggested, however tentatively, that some African Americans—Union army veterans and "intelligent" freedmen, perhaps—might be granted the vote.

Party and political contingencies animated Wade and Chandler. George Julian stood a little apart from them. Principled and doctrinaire, an early and consistent critic of the president, Julian pressed for unconditional black suffrage, treason trials for rebel leaders, and confiscation of planter property for parceling out among the freed people.

His manners were more polished than the brawling, profane Wade's, his language less strident. He still held out hope that Lincoln might yet bend the Radicals' way. His friend Lydia Maria Child, the longtime abolitionist, shared his Jacobin views but clung to an instinctive faith in the president. She cautioned Julian against expecting too much, too soon on the suffrage question—one that stirred "the strongest feelings of pride and prejudice," as she put it. And she reminded him of how far Lincoln had traveled from his backwoods beginnings.

"I think we have reason to thank God for Abraham Lincoln," she went on. "With all his deficiencies, it must be admitted that he has grown continually, and considering how slavery had weakened and perverted the moral sense of the whole country, it was great good luck to have the people elect a man who was *willing* to grow."[55]

George Washington Julian, forty-eight years old in 1865, had come out of a background not unlike the president's. He, too, had been born in an authentic log cabin, the self-taught, self-made son of Quaker settlers in the Whitewater Valley of eastern Indiana. With only a common-school education in the Wayne County village of Centreville, Julian took his moral and intellectual bearings from a small, heterodox collection of books and authors: the Bible; Rousseau, Locke, and Hume; Oliver Goldsmith; William Ellery Channing.

Nothing came easily to him. He mastered Blackstone, but needed three years to work up the nerve to deliver his first address in open court—this in spite of long hours of practice at the Dark Lyceum in Centreville, so named because self-conscious young debaters there practiced their declamations in the protective gloom. Tall, well-formed, and athletic, he tired easily, suffered recurrent attacks of lumbago, and complained of cold feet all through the mild Potomac winter. ("He has to tug a great brick down to table every time we eat and has a dreadful time," his wife lamented.)[56] Famously handsome, with molded features, dark hair swept back from a high forehead, and a neatly barbered, gray-flecked beard, he moved shyly around Washington's drawing rooms—until a dram or two loosened him up, anyhow—and he never properly learned to dance.

Julian had the virtues (incorruptibility, moral vision) as well as the vices (rigidity, self-righteousness) of a secular saint. He possessed little or no conventional political ambition. He remained always the critic, the outsider. It was the great issue itself that fired him, the affront of slavery.

He sought election to the House in 1848 as a Free-Soiler. Campaigning tirelessly for the top of the Free-Soil ticket, Martin Van Buren and Charles Francis Adams, he spoke three or four times a day, traveling from town to town on the back of a seventeen-hand-high horse he dubbed Old Whitey, after slaveholding Whig candidate Zachary Taylor's charger of Mexican War fame.

Amazingly, Julian won that election. But his radicalism played poorly with mainstream voters, even in Quaker-leavened eastern Indiana, known as the Burnt District for its religious and moral fervor. His political enemies hurled the most damaging epithets their limited imaginations could devise. He was a racial amalgamationist and an apostle of disunion. He carried a lock of Frederick Douglass's hair in his pocket.

"They declared that my audiences consisted of 'eleven men, three boys and a negro,'" he wrote later, "and sometimes I could not deny that this inventory was not very far from the truth."[57]

Turned out after a single term, Julian kept up his contacts with the leading abolitionists. He and William Lloyd Garrison became friends. He dined with Adams in Quincy. He fell under the spell of the peculiarly musical voice of Charles Sumner. "He seemed surprised when I told him how many admirers he had in Indiana," Julian recalled of their first encounter, "and I found that others shared his unflattering impressions respecting the general intelligence of the West."[58] Julian ran for vice president as a Free-Soiler in 1852. He moved four years later into the new Republican Party, then rising on the wreck of Whiggery, Free-Soilism and the Know-Nothing movement.

"Laws grind the poor," Julian had learned from Oliver Goldsmith, "and rich men rule the law." Julian believed, though, that a poor man might win a place in the nation's councils and change the law. He regained his old congressional seat in 1860, politicking morning to midnight, trudging from township to township, orating himself hoarse at country crossroads, in barns, porkhouses, and sawmills, and in the churches, town halls and lyceums of Richmond, Centreville, and Cambridge City.

He returned to Washington alone, for he had buried his tubercular wife Anne only a few days after his election triumph. Lonely and bereft, he sought out a Spiritualist medium and tried to restore contact with her. The medium failed him, but Washington had other consolations for a good-looking widower. He remarried in 1863—Laura Giddings, half his age, a daughter of his political mentor, the Western Reserve champion Joshua Giddings. With his father-in-law's backing, he won appointment to two powerhouse committees: public lands and the joint war committee.

The surpassing hour of Julian's political life struck on January 31, 1865, when the House passed the constitutional amendment abolishing slavery. "I thanked God for the blessed opportunity of recording my name where it will be honored as those of the signers of the Declaration of Independence," he wrote the next day. "I have felt ever since the vote as if I were in a new country. I seem to breathe better, and feel comforted and refreshed." With the end of the war, slavery was everywhere doomed—the event of the century, in Julian's view.[59]

War committee membership carried certain privileges, among them the opportunity to celebrate on the South's own defeated ground. Julian, Wade, and Chandler left Washington on Monday, April 10, for Fortress Monroe, where they were to meet the steamer *Alabama* for the onward journey to Charleston and the flag-raising ceremony at Fort Sumter. A Senate sergeant at arms fitted Julian out with a Spencer carbine and a Colt revolver, just in case.

"See now how your Quaker husband will shine & how *fierce* he will look when he gets home with all these weapons & trappings of war," he wrote Laura. "And why *shouldn't* a member of the war committee have arms?"[60]

The party decided at Admiral Porter's suggestion to ascend the James for a visit to Richmond while the *Alabama* coaled. Dodging torpedoes and other obstructions, the river steamer touched safely at Rocketts Landing at ten o'clock Tuesday night. Julian set out in the morning on a horseback reconnaissance, with an army orderly as his guide.

He toured the prisons, the Davis mansion, the inner fortifications. He dismissed Jefferson's capitol, modeled on the Roman Maison Carrée at Nîmes in France, as "an ancient building, not to be compared with our best modern state capitols in size or style of architecture."[61] All the same, the experience of Richmond, so long impregnable, moved him deeply.

"You can't *imagine* how queer I feel in beginning a letter to you from this place," he wrote his wife. "I can hardly believe I am here."[62]

Political reality soon intruded. Julian reported crowds of unruly rebels swirling about the capitol waiting to swear the loyalty oath, doubtless with a wink and fingers crossed. General Weitzel seemed ready to forgive them all. That morning's Richmond *Whig* carried a report, under the headline "Address to the People of Virginia," of the easygoing Weitzel's overture to the state legislature.

"We were all thunderstruck," Julian wrote in his journal, "and I never before saw such force and fitness in Ben Wade's swearing."[63]

He had no occasion to reach for the carbine, though the steamer did strike a torpedo as it dropped downstream to Fortress Monroe. The detonation sent a waterspout skyward and a shiver along the vessel's spine, but caused no damage or injury. He had hardly stopped shaking when he heard the disappointing news that Wade, still in a towering rage over the item in the *Whig*, had canceled the Charleston trip and decided to return at once to Washington.

As it happened, President Lincoln had quietly withdrawn permission for the Virginia legislators to meet. Still aching from the horseback excursion, Julian reached his lodgings at 76 Indiana Avenue on the evening of April 14, Good Friday, around the time the stagehands at Ford's Theater were raising the curtain for *Our American Cousin*.

EVENT CROWDED UPON EVENT. "We are just mourning over the loss of Grafton and Storrow," Bostonian John Ropes wrote his soldier friend John Gray in South Carolina, adding that Charley Morse, recovering from his wound at home, had made the rounds with the sad particulars.[64] Soon, though, there were grounds for celebration: Richmond's fall and, only six days later, the most stunning development yet, the surrender of the Army of Northern Virginia.

"Grant had a fight with Lee & was successful, Confederacy collapsing, gold 151, 7-20 loan selling fast, everything looks splendid, & people look for a speedy peace," Willard Saxton wrote jubilantly. "Where is the last ditch, & where is the Confederacy?"[65]

Charley Fox heard the Appomattox report lying in the camp of the Fifty-fifth Massachusetts in the old Confederate defense lines outside Charleston. An orderly roused him at midnight with word of Lee's surrender.

"I started up in my shirt and drawers, pulled on my boots, threw a blanket over me and turned out the band," he wrote jubilantly home to Mary in Dorchester.[66]

The news capped a triumphant winter in the Low Country. The abolition amendment had cleared Congress in January. Quincy Gillmore relieved John Foster in February as commanding general of the Department of the South, a decisive victory for Rufus Saxton in their long, bitter war. Willard Saxton traveled to *occupied* Charleston at the end of the month in ex-slave Robert Smalls's famous hijacked steamer, a thoroughly satisfying voyage: "Twas worth something to go up on the 'Planter,' with a black captain."[67] Little Eddie Saxton cut two more teeth over the winter, for a total of ten.

Out in the islands, though, cold and hunger dampened the celebrations. Times were terribly hard for the resettled refugees. Laura Towne had distributed the last of the stocks of donated clothing early in the new year. Her appeals for new shipments were unmet so far.

"The people come to our yard and stand mute in their misery, not annoying me with questions but just watching me to see if I have any news of the coming clothing," she wrote her sisters at Oakshade, the family place in Pennsylvania. "There some of them stand nearly every morning when I go to school and there they are when we come home."[68]

Famine threatened in some localities. Most Sea Islanders who queued up outside the government stores for rations were turned away. "No one who can show a finger to pick with and reports an oyster to pick is allowed to come on the Government for support," the Gideonite William Gannett noted.[69] The oyster beds were depleted, though, and wage work hard to find in winter. Towne and Ellen Murray helped out where they could, paying generously for forage and bundles of firewood the Gullahs offered for sale. But the teachers were in low water, too.

"They have found out that we will buy moss from the trees for our cow who, stupid beast, will not eat hay," she wrote home. "You can count every rib on every animal we have got."[70]

Saxton met with continued resistance in his colonization efforts, even after Foster's departure. His scheme to resettle mainland refugees on abandoned plantations on outlying Edisto Island progressed slowly, in part because of the transport shortage. "First, no steamer! Then, no coal! And when one can be had, the other can't," Gannett complained.[71] General Gillmore turned out to be a negligible improvement on Foster, and just as apt to invoke "military necessity" to deny Saxton the resources he needed.

The long evenings passed pleasantly enough for Willard and Mary Saxton, cozy in their half of the Bay Street house. Charles Howard, awaiting appointment to a regimental command, joined them in the parlor most nights for games of whist, Boston, or backgammon. When they were alone Mary read or took up her fancywork; Willard brought his journal up to date.

Entries for the last half of March recorded squally relations between the brothers Saxton. The general could be brusque and authoritarian, just as his "anti-antislavery" critics charged. The conquest of Foster made him more imperious than ever and Willard chafed under the bullying. When Rufus went down to Savannah with the boat crew and *all* the Bay Street servants—every one, not even a cook's helper left behind for Mary—he touched off a shattering row.

"As I pay *half* the servants, I considered I had a right to be consulted about it, but I get insulted, spoken to in a very ungentlemanly manner, to say nothing about its being unbrotherly & selfish," Willard complained. "He is so overbearing & tyrannical he loses all gentlemanly feelings. If I venture a word of remonstrance, I am treated as a driver treats his nigger."[72]

Matilda Saxton tried to heal the rift, or anyway paper it over. Willard made an effort, too, after a few days. "I tried to be natural, as if no word had passed," he wrote in his journal, "& he grew reasonably cordial."[73] Rufus unbent finally, and confirmed the reconciliation by inviting Willard to accompany him to the memorial service at Fort Sumter.

Edwin Stanton had set the event in motion well before the April upheavals. Now, with Richmond occupied and the Army of Northern Virginia abolished, the Sumter memorial carried a tremendous weight of symbolism. The identical frayed color Major Robert Anderson had hauled down in 1861 would rise again in its original place, marking the end of the War of the Rebellion just at the spot where it began, and on the same date.

General Saxton distributed passes to all the missionary teachers and a large party of Gideonites boarded the steamer *Arago* at Hilton Head for the trip to Charleston. Laura Towne fell horribly seasick on the way, but her spirits lifted with a first view of the pulverized fort—and soared higher still when a harbor pilot bawled out a confirmation of Lee's surrender. A lighter ferried sightseers from the ship to the Battery. Towne set out alone, wandering the old city's disheveled streets.

She ended up opposite the slave workhouse. Repelled and fasci-
nated at the same time, she ventured indoors. The stone and iron
struck chill after the warmth of the cobbled street. The Manigaults
had once sentenced the incorrigible Jack Savage to a term of confinement there. "The whipping room was made with double walls
filled in with sand," Towne noticed, "so that the cries could not be
heard in the street." Shaken, close to tears, she backed out into the
dazzling April sunlight.

Charlestonians were unreconciled to defeat, she discovered, especially the women. They shrank away from the Yankees passing in the
street, muttering curses and casting spells. "I wish I had their winding sheets to make when the yellow fever comes," Towne overheard
one woman say.[74] She thought the Secesh would happily have filled
the workhouse with Yankees, shackled them, whipped them, too, had
it been in their power.

The Gideonites were ferried over to Sumter in the mild, blustery
forenoon of Good Friday. They followed a dusty track into the fort,
clambered onto the scaffolding, and took their seats among the crowd,
around four thousand people altogether: Union soldiers and sailors,
leading Republican politicians, a sizable delegation of freedmen.
There were a few white Charlestonians, for already the old masters
were circling to reclaim their places. She had heard the name of
Aiken mentioned—William Aiken, a prewar South Carolina governor,
owner of the South's largest rice plantation. "A mean sneak," Towne
thought him, "who curries favor with both sides."[75] She spotted
William Lloyd Garrison, the English radical George Thompson,
Massachusetts senator Henry Wilson, and other leading abolitionists,
and silently saluted them.

Robert Anderson approached the base of the flagstaff a few minutes before noon and took the halyards in his hands. Frail, hatless, he
began to speak in a thick, choked voice. Then, with an effort, he mastered his emotions. "I thank God I have lived to see this day," he said
clearly, for all to hear; and he gave a sharp tug on the halyards.[76] The
flag shot up to the top of the staff and stretched out stiffly in the
wind.

A muffled cheer went up. "Its rising to its old place," thought
Willard Saxton, "said to the nation, the war is over, slavery is dead,
the Union is saved."[77] The crowd rose and sang the first verse of

"The Star-Spangled Banner." A great gun boomed, quite close. At the signal, cannon salutes thundered out from the landward forts and the long line of Federal warships riding to anchor in the outer harbor.

Garrison, tall and straight but nearing sixty and in feeble health, spoke briefly. "I hate slavery as I hate nothing else in the world," he said. "It is not only a crime, but the sum of all criminality." Then he made way for the principal speaker, the Reverend Henry Ward Beecher, the showy Brooklyn abolitionist. His attacks on Confederate villains and traitors drew frequent applause. Laura Towne was unimpressed, though, and annoyed too that Beecher seemed to direct his remarks to the handful of white Charlestonians present. "He spoke very much by note," she remarked, "and quite without fire." The skeptical John Gray, seated with General Gillmore's party, found the speech "tedious and commonplace." But Charles Howard thought well enough of it to urge his brother the general to read the reprint in the newspapers.[78]

The crowds dispersed among the ruins. There were fireworks in the evening. Gillmore hosted a formal dinner at the Charleston Hotel for Anderson and other high dignitaries. The after-dinner speakers toasted Lincoln, Grant, and Sherman. Joseph Holt, head of the War Department's Bureau of Military Justice, rose to denounce the rebel leaders as "the Iscariots of the human race." Garrison put in a word. He surely marveled at his sudden, unlooked-for respectability—many of these men had regarded him as little better than a dangerous lunatic not long since. Events had swept him into the patriotic mainstream, or perhaps diverted the channel his way. He read out South Carolina's epitaph.

"She has been brought down from her pride of place. The chalice was put to her lips, and she drank to the dregs."[79]

So the official ceremonies came to an end. Dissatisfaction surfaced in some quarters. The Fifty-fifth Massachusetts, with two years' hard service in the Charleston siege, had not been invited, and Charley Fox resented the snub. Still, any lingering disappointment melted away the next day, Saturday the fifteenth, in the warmth of what turned out to be a kind of alternative to the Sumter memorial, as emblematic in its way as the raising of the old flag over the disfigured fort.

Hundreds of former slaves packed into the Zion Presbyterian Church. A hush fell over the eager crowd as the principal speakers settled into their places. A young freedman walked down the aisle leading two little girls by the hand, approached the pulpit, and addressed William Lloyd Garrison. In a short, eloquent speech, he thanked the old abolitionist for a lifetime's labor (the first number of the *Liberator* had appeared on January 1, 1831), then presented the girls. They offered Garrison a wreath of spring flowers and two elegant bouquets.

Adjusting his spectacles and smiling benignly, Garrison promised the little girls, born into bondage, a brighter future. "The Government has its hold upon the monster Slavery," he assured them, "and is strangling the life out of it." Other speakers followed. Storms of applause met every mention of Lincoln's name. "I never saw anything to equal it," Charles Howard said. After the meeting, the celebrants spilled out into Citadel Square and massed, hundreds strong, to escort Garrison back to the Charleston Hotel.[80]

"The procession passed in review before us," Willard Saxton wrote that night, "singing 'We'll hang Jeff Davis from a sour apple tree.'"[81]

# 6

# Booth and His Crime

A HOUSE CLERK ROUSED GEORGE JULIAN from a deep sleep late in the evening of April 14. The President had been shot, W. L. Woods told him in a low voice, and Secretary Seward assaulted in his sickbed at home, slashed about with a long knife. Assassins were on the prowl, the capital open to Confederate attack.

"I was still half asleep," Julian wrote in his journal next day, "and in my fright grew suddenly cold, heartsick and helpless."[1]

He rallied, dressed quickly and went out into the raw, misty night. Word of the crimes had spread and the streets were packed with excited crowds murmuring of conspiracy: not just Lincoln and Seward, but the vice president, General Grant, and other high officials were said to have been killed. Julian drifted with the turbulent stream toward Ford's Theater on Tenth Street. The president lay in a squalid room in the William Petersen house across from Ford's, unconscious, breathing heavily, doomed.

Edwin Stanton's agents in Petersen's frowsty parlor were taking down depositions of witnesses: theatergoers, scene shifters, players. By midnight Stanton had learned the identity of the assassin. It was John Wilkes Booth, a young Maryland actor. Booth had the run of Ford's, day and night. He had played the house only a few weeks before, a supporting role in *The Apostate*. The stagehands and stock players knew him well.

Stanton had just locked up his house in Franklin Square and gone upstairs for the night when a messenger arrived with word of the attacks. His wife called up the stairwell with the news. Stanton disbelieved it at first; he had just come from Seward's. Still, he sent for his factotum Charles Dana to meet him at the theater. Stanton stopped briefly at Seward's place in Lafayette Square, where a soldier at the door confirmed the report, then piloted his carriage through the thickening crowds to Tenth Street between E and F.

Dana arrived to find Stanton in charge and Lincoln laid out awkwardly on a narrow bed in a small room off Petersen's back parlor. A frayed Turkish carpet, once red, covered the drab floorboards. Weak gaslight threw flickering shadows on the biscuit-colored walls. The surgeons said there was no hope, none. All the cabinet, and Chief Justice Chase, were gathered there in a stunned, silent, uncertain group. Stanton motioned for Dana.

"Sit down here. I want you."

The secretary dictated a stream of telegrams. He had already sent a file of soldiers to collect Vice President Johnson and posted guards at the homes of senior government officials. Now, through Dana, he turned out the Washington garrison, directed area commanders to block roads and bridges leading out of the city, and alerted the naval station at Saint Inigoes, Maryland, near the mouth of the Potomac. He dispatched agents to search Booth's room at the National Hotel. He wired the New York City police chief for "three or four of your best detectives" to assist with the investigation. He drafted a statement on the assassination for wire transmission to New York and release to the newspapers.[2]

The Washington military command moved to seal off the capital. A handwritten order reached Captain George Dutton, a Veteran Reserve Corps officer commanding at the Aqueduct Bridge in Georgetown, before midnight: "Allow no one to cross without being a recognized messenger from these Head Qtrs. or War Dept." Dutton interpreted this literally. By dawn a long line of officers, men, and vehicles, many bound for the alerted forts on the Virginia side, had backed up at the bridge.[3]

Word went out for Booth's arrest in the early hours of Saturday the fifteenth. "Twenty-five years old, five feet eight inches high, dark hair and moustache," ran the description. "He took the direction from

Washington toward St. Mary's and Calvert counties." Bill posters and pasteboard photographs of Booth were distributed. George Dutton tacked his to the guardroom wall. Investigators raised the alarm for a second suspect, "a smooth-faced man, quite stout,"[4] athletic and powerful, wanted in the Seward assault—Lewis Paine, a pseudonym for Lewis Thornton Powell, son of a Florida Baptist minister and an ex-Confederate soldier.

"That's enough," Stanton nodded to Dana at around three o'clock. "Now you may go home."

The secretary overlooked nothing, according to Dana. He did, however, jump to what would prove to be an unwarranted conclusion, though natural enough in the circumstances. Stanton decided almost at once that the attacks were part of a broad Confederate conspiracy, planned in Richmond before its fall, designed to destroy the central control of the U.S. government.

A letter found in a trunk in Booth's room at the National seemed to confirm the suspicion. "It appears that the murder was planned before the 4th of March, but fell through because the accomplice backed out until 'Richmond could be heard from,'" Stanton wired General John Dix, commanding in New York City. Later Saturday, in a dispatch to U.S. minister Charles Francis Adams in London, the secretary claimed to have evidence of "a conspiracy deliberately planned and set on foot by rebels, under pretence of avenging the South and aiding the rebel cause." Stanton's orders on April 14–15, issued with what he regarded as more than probable cause, led to the roundup of scores of the usual suspects, perhaps as many as three hundred—innocents nearly all, as it turned out, at least of the crime in question.[5]

"Arrest every person found moving within your district who cannot account for himself," General Christopher C. Augur, commanding the Washington military district, wired the garrison commander at Point Lookout.

"Arrest all suspicious persons," Eighth Corps headquarters in Baltimore ordered the officer commanding at Annapolis. "Suppress any outbreak."[6]

The Petersen house filled up as the night wore on. Prominent congressmen crowded into the back parlor for the death watch. Charles Sumner wept openly through the final scenes. Laura Keene, the star of *Our American Cousin*, attended the president's stricken wife. She unconditionally identified Booth as the athlete who had leapt, dagger in hand, from the president's box onto the painted stage. Abraham Lincoln died at 7:22 Saturday morning. One of the surgeons reached down a moment later to place two silver half-dollars over his eyes.

A faint cold rain fell outside. A detail of officers, bareheaded in the rain, carried the coffin from Tenth Street to the White House. Tired, overwrought, wet, and chilled, George Julian returned to his Indiana Avenue boardinghouse, folded his long frame into a horse-hide chair, rested his icy feet on a warm brick, and started a letter to Laura at home in Centreville. Memory of the crowds, the blaze of their rage, remained vividly with him.

"Poor Mr. Lincoln has just breathed his last. The bells are tolling the event," he wrote her. "I fear we are on the verge of a new and more terrible war than ever. Is it not strange that the assassins made their attack upon Seward & Lincoln—the men of all others who were seeking to restore the rebel leaders to their rights & make the sacrifices of this war in vain?"[7]

The full cabinet turned out in the forenoon for Andrew Johnson's swearing in at the Kirkwood House Hotel. The War Committee—Benjamin Wade, Julian, the others—caucused after lunch. The conversation was heated and blunt. "I like the radicalism of the members," Julian wrote in his journal, "but have not in a long time heard so much profanity."[8] Some of Radicals predicted that they would be able to lead Johnson on Reconstruction policy. Julian doubted that. Lincoln's acceptance of the Tennessee Unionist, prewar Democrat, and onetime slaveholder as his running mate in 1864 had deeply disappointed him.

"He was, at heart, as decided a hater of the negro, and of everything savoring of abolitionism, as the rebels from whom he had separated," Julian observed.[9]

Still, some common ground might be found. Johnson was on record as favoring harsh treatment of rebels, even if he had shown scant sympathy for black emancipation. The War Committee called on him on Sunday at the Treasury building, where he had established temporary quarters while Mary Lincoln cleared out of the White House. Benjamin Wade pressed him for his views.

Congressman George Washington Julian of Indiana. A doctrinaire Radical, he faulted Abraham Lincoln for his reluctance to convert the war into a crusade for emancipation of the South's 4 million slaves. Julian regarded the January 1865 House passage of the constitutional amendment abolishing slavery as the supreme moment of his life. "I have felt ever since the vote as if I were in a new country. I seem to breathe better, and feel comforted and refreshed," he wrote. (Indiana State Library)

"I can only say you can judge of my policy by the past," the accidental president answered. "Robbery is a crime; rape is a crime; murder is a crime; *treason* is a crime, and crime must be punished. Treason must be made infamous and traitors must be impoverished."[10]

This seemed to satisfy Wade. "Johnson, we have faith in you," he told him. "By the gods, there will be no trouble now in running the government." The committee pressed Johnson to radicalize the cabinet, recommending that he replace the physically shattered, politically unsteady Seward ("I fear Seward will neither die nor resign,"

Julian remarked coldbloodedly)[11] with the Massachusetts Radical Benjamin F. Butler.

Lincoln's body lay in state upon a catafalque in the East Room of the White House. Julian turned out Tuesday evening for the viewing, taking his place in the long, seemingly endless queue. He declined an invitation to join the escort that would carry the president's remains to Illinois for burial. With a new administration taking control, he did not care to be away.

"No one can tell what a day might bring; our radical influence is just now all-important," he wrote Laura.[12]

Minute guns sounded from Washington's encircling ring of forts early on the bright, clear morning of April 19. Crowds lined both sides of Pennsylvania Avenue from the White House to the Capitol for the funeral procession: columns of infantry, a battery of light artillery, generals on horseback, the 14-foot-long funeral car drawn by six black-plumed grays, the carriages of Lincoln's family, the new president, congressmen, diplomats. A mass of freed people formed the rear guard.

The intensity of the mood impressed and rather surprised Julian. Lincoln had been a minority president after all, a target of opposition from the left and the right. Radicals—Julian a leader among them—accused him of squandering the victory and betraying the promise of emancipation. The more ferocious of the Radicals believed that, with Johnson steadied on the proper course, real political good might flow from Lincoln's death. Yet, from all quarters, Radical and otherwise, the expressions of anguish were genuine.

"It is wonderful what a hold the president had on the whole country," he wrote Laura. "The sorrow seems to be profound and almost universal, even with those who differed most with his policy & who regard his death as a providential means of saving the country."[13]

Meanwhile, the search for Lincoln's killers went on. Hysteria built all through the week, fueled in equal parts by Stanton's excesses—for a day or two, he saw conspiracy everywhere—and by an outpouring of immeasurable grief for the martyred president.

"I would not be surprised if all the Secesh have to leave for safety," Julian remarked. Reports surfaced of vigilante justice, meted out more often for words than deeds: in Washington, a man badly beaten and shown the gibbet for saying "I'm glad it happened"; in

Maryland, a copperhead editor killed for expressing a similar sentiment. Former Confederates were well advised to turn their coats, or
anyhow dye the butternut cloth black.[14]

Joseph Holt, just returned from the Sumter ceremony, took charge
of the assassination investigation. War Department detectives had
suspected since March that John Wilkes Booth was at the center of a
plot to abduct Lincoln. Landlady Mary Surratt and all the tenants of
her boardinghouse at 541 H Street fell under immediate suspicion.
Though slowed by a broken leg (he landed awkwardly in his leap
from Lincoln's box), Booth had managed to mount a horse and slip
out of the capital over the Anacostia Bridge. He reached the farm of
Dr. Samuel Mudd in Saint Charles County, Maryland, before dawn.
Lewis Paine hid in the woods after his attempt on Seward before
eventually making his way back to Mrs. Surratt's.

Then there were the loose fish that swam around the two assassins: George Atzerodt, who had made no attempt to carry out his
assignment to kill the vice president; Mrs. Surratt's son John, who had
helped Booth plan the kidnap scheme along with Samuel Arnold and
Michael O'Laughlin; Booth sidekick David Herold; Dr. Mudd, who
harbored Booth and set his broken leg; and Edward Spangler, a Ford's
Theater stage carpenter.

Mary Surratt and Paine were arrested late on April 17 at the H
Street house. Detectives had picked up Arnold at Fortress Monroe
and O'Laughlin in Baltimore earlier in the day. Atzerodt, Spangler,
and Mudd were laid by the heels over the next several days. Stanton
ordered the men held in irons aboard two monitors anchored in the
Potomac off the Washington Navy Yard. Mrs. Surratt was taken to a
heavily guarded cell in the Old Penitentiary on the Washington Arsenal grounds. Her son John remained at large. Booth and Davy Herold
hid themselves away in Zacchia Swamp in lower Maryland, a few
miles from the Potomac.

Joseph Holt reviewed the evidence, such as it was, and concluded
that the highest levels of the Confederate state, civil and military,
were directly responsible for the assassination. "This Department has
information that the President's murder was organized in Canada and
approved in Richmond," Holt reported to Stanton. Between them,
they cast suspicion on virtually every senior Richmond Confederate.[15]

Richard Ewell had already been accused of arson—informally,
anyway. Surely the Yankees did not suspect him of having a hand in

the assassination conspiracy? He had a perfect alibi for April 14—he spent the night in a cell at the Old Capitol Prison on his way to Fort Warren in Boston Harbor. Even so, Ewell found himself not merely a prisoner of war, honorably taken at Sayler's Creek, but a political captive, too. He decided to start making his case right away. In a letter to General Grant, an old army acquaintance, he explicitly condemned the Lincoln killing.

"No language can adequately express the shock produced upon myself by the occurrence of this appalling crime & by the seeming tendency in the public mind to connect the South & Southern men with it," he wrote Grant. "Need we say we are not assassins, not the allies of assassins, be they from the North or from the South? We would be ashamed of our own people were we not assured that they will universally repudiate this crime."[16]

In a brief meeting during the Washington stopover with Montgomery Blair, a powerful Missouri Unionist* with good Southern contacts, Ewell denied responsibility for the Richmond fire, blaming it on the capital's own unruly citizens. The charge—that he had deliberately set fire to the city to deny the enemy a million or two dollars' worth of cotton and tobacco—sounded more credible with each repetition. Stretching the truth, Ewell insisted that he had advised against burning the warehouses.

"If I could have had my way, it would never have been done," he said.[17]

Ewell went on to offer an apology of sorts for having given battle at Sayler's Creek. Had he known how powerful a force Sheridan had ranged against him he would never have fought, he said; and as Wright's infantry advanced he had scrawled a dispatch to Lee recommending immediate surrender. Ewell's claims found their way into the newspapers, no doubt through Blair's agency.[18]

The swift Confederate collapse caught Lizinka Ewell unprepared. She could do nothing for her husband from Nashville, where she had gone to reclaim her disputed Tennessee holdings. In the first days after Sayler's Creek Lizinka determined to collect him and retire abroad. She, the general, and her children could live quietly for a time

---

*And a brother of Frank Blair, commander of Howard's Seventeenth Corps.

in Canada or Europe. Lincoln's murder changed everything. All measures of clemency were suspended. At least Ewell would be safe as a captive, protected from the mobs out to avenge the president.

"I regard Fort Warren as the best possible prison," Hattie Brown declared. "The sea air will be of great service to Cousin Dick."[19]

Conditions were tolerable there, Ewell found, the salt air keen, rations of better quality and more plentiful than he had seen for a long time. He and Campbell Brown enjoyed tea and toast with butter for breakfast, beef or ham, potatoes, and onions for dinner. One could supplement the jailers' fare with purchases from the Fort Warren sutler.

Still, despite the inspiriting sea breeze and the sweeping views west beyond the Harbor Islands to Boston, south to Hull and northeast to the open Atlantic, Fort Warren was a prison, not a watering place. The days were interminable. Brown lacked even the anodyne of his prayer book—Sheridan's troopers had stolen it. He and his stepfather were kept apart, and the Fort Warren commandant refused all requests for special treatment for the valetudinarian Ewell.

"His comparative helplessness and the fact that all the Genls. confined with him smoke tobacco, which is as bad as poison to him, make his case altogether exceptional," Brown argued.[20]

There were no exceptions. Only the sketchiest details of her husband's circumstances reached Lizinka in Nashville, and she could learn nothing at all about Campbell or Hattie's young man—even whether they were alive. (Tom Turner, as it happened, had been sent to Johnson's Island Prison in Lake Erie.) Blair reported his interview with Ewell to Thomas Gantt in Saint Louis, who sent a copy of the letter along to Lizinka. "I saw the Genl. limping on the wharf," Blair wrote. "He looked like a gamecock."[21] Ewell declined Blair's offer of a loan, saying he had as much money as he needed and had been well treated so far.

Federal authorities in Nashville held out little hope of an early parole, so Lizinka appealed to Andrew Johnson, an old Tennessee acquaintance. She had known him in Nashville before the war, when he was governor and she held sway as the rich widow Mrs. Brown of Cedar Street, Capitol Hill. Johnson lived in her commandeered house from 1862 to 1864 while he served as the state's military governor. It was Johnson who had arranged for Lizinka's pass (prudently, she traveled in the character of "Mrs. Brown") through the Union lines.

Going straight to the Cedar Street house on arrival, she found Johnson's daughter Martha Patterson and her family in residence.

"She walked in here, and inspected things, without observing the common *ceremonies* of *entering a house*, and then asked to see *no one*," Martha wrote her father. "I had a better opinion of her *ladyship*, but then she is a *rebel*, and nothing better could be *expected*."[22]

That was Lizinka's first mistake. A lonely, friendless man with an invalid wife and an alcoholic son, Johnson doted on his daughter. High-hatting Martha—the haughty Lizinka had sent word that she required the use of "1 or 2 rooms in my own house"—infuriated him. "Perhaps Mrs. Brown could find quarters beyond the limits of Tennessee," Johnson wrote Martha's husband.[23]

Her second mistake was to suggest taking her family into exile. Blair thought it had offended Johnson. "Robert Lee does not talk this way," Blair said, perhaps in paraphrase of the president. "He does not intend to leave the country."[24] She should cultivate "national feeling and a love of country," he went on. She answered that she no longer had a country, nor any property, either: not a pennysworth of "rent, hire or profit" from any of her 120 slaves since 1861. Her debts were mounting upwards of $100,000. Strangers lived in her town house and freedmen were encamped on two of her town lots. Yankee cavalry had ransacked her plantation at Spring Hill in Maury County.

"You know that nothing is left but the bare land & shells of houses—not a fence, not a barn nor a whole stable," Lizinka wrote Ewell. "600 of our hogs were shot and eaten by the U.S. troops last winter. If any are left they are perfectly wild. Every cow, horse and mule was taken of course."[25]

The Mrs. Brown appellation failed her as a safeguard. On April 21, Edwin Stanton ordered the arrest of "Mrs. General Ewell" and her removal under guard to Saint Louis. Lizinka, who had circumspectly sworn the amnesty oath in Missouri four weeks before, fired off a protest letter to the president, supposing "the arrest was made without his knowledge or by some mistake."[26]

Johnson did not reply.

STANTON'S WIRE REPORTING the president's murder caught up to Sherman in Raleigh, North Carolina, on the morning of April 17 as he prepared to step aboard a one-car train for a cease-fire conference with Joseph E. Johnston. The depot telegraph operator flagged him just in time; Sherman held the train and waited for the message to be deciphered.

He read it through slowly on the platform. "President Lincoln was murdered about 10 o'clock last night in his private box at Ford's Theater in this city, by an assassin who shot him through the head with a pistol ball. I find evidence," Stanton went on, "that an assassin is also on your track." In a follow-up wire, Henry Halleck warned Sherman to watch out for a desperado named Clark, five feet, nine inches tall and slender, with a low forehead, dark, sunken eyes, a dark brown moustache and long goatee, hair darker than his whiskers. He was a Texan with "a very determined look," Halleck noted, and he wore a wideawake hat.[27]

Sherman's army had entered Raleigh on April 13. Sherman accepted General Johnston's offer of a cease-fire the next day and the question of terms for a Confederate surrender had preoccupied him ever since. His mood turned edgy and sarcastic, as it often did in anxious times. Henry Hitchcock discovered this for perhaps the thousandth time when he idly asked Sherman what the Confederate commander would do now that Grant had beaten Lee.

"Johnston and I are not on speaking terms," Sherman snapped.[28]

Word of the truce and of Lee's collapse in Virginia electrified the camps around Raleigh. "While we were receiving letters from home, getting new clothes, and taking our regular doses of quinine," Daniel Oakey of the Second Massachusetts wrote later, "Lee and Johnston surrendered, and the great conflict came to an end."[29] Johnston had not actually surrendered yet, but nobody expected the campaign to resume. The question now was whether the rebels would disperse and reassemble elsewhere or, worse, melt away to fight in guerrilla bands. Sherman had to consider the possibility, too, that they might simply continue falling back. He reckoned that Johnston's army—smaller, lighter afoot, with little to carry and nothing to lose—could keep just out of his reach indefinitely. He wanted to bring the issue to a close.

"I will accept the same terms as General Grant gave General Lee, and be careful not to complicate any points of civil policy," he wired Stanton and Grant.[30]

Sherman laughed off the warning about the suspected Texas assassin. "He had better be in a hurry," he wrote Halleck, "or he will be too late."[31] The president's murder hit him hard, though. He wondered how the army would respond; unchecked, his vengeful troops could demolish Raleigh overnight. Sherman tucked the flimsy into a coat pocket, swore the telegraph operator to secrecy, and boarded the car for Durham Station, twenty-six miles up the line.

Sherman and his cavalry escort encountered Johnston, Wade Hampton, and their aides five miles out of Durham on the Hillsboro road, halfway between the picket lines of the opposing armies. A farmhouse stood conveniently near. The commanding generals left the others to pace the hard-packed dirt of James Bennett's yard and passed into the house.

Sherman opened the conference by showing Johnston the Stanton telegram. In Sherman's recollection, large drops of sweat formed on Johnston's forehead as he read it. "We talked about the effect of this act on the country at large," Sherman remembered, "and he realized it made my situation extremely delicate."[32] He offered the Appomattox terms: repatriation and a general amnesty. Johnston made a surprising counter. He proposed surrendering not only his army, but all Confederate forces still in the field. Sherman questioned whether he held such broad authority. Johnston assured him he could obtain it. They agreed to meet again at Bennett's house in twenty-four hours.

Sherman returned to Raleigh fired with a vision of peace from the Potomac to the Rio Grande. The president's killing, Seward's wounding, the supposed plots against Grant and the others suggested the opening of a new, more terrible phase of the war. "There is a great danger that the Confederate armies will dissolve and fill the whole land with robbers and assassins," he foresaw.[33] Sherman admired Johnston as an adversary; now that they had met, he found he liked him as a man. If Johnston could act for Richard Taylor in Alabama and Edmund Kirby Smith in the Trans-Mississippi, perhaps the two of them might settle everything now, soldier to soldier, and avert a terrorist war.

Sherman issued a special order on the afternoon of April 17 announcing the assassination of Abraham Lincoln. He confined the troops to their camps and heavily reinforced the provost detachments. There were no outbreaks of retaliatory violence, only shock, grief, and sullen anger.

"I have not the heart to write about it," Illinoisan Charles Wills recorded in his journal.[34]

The news filled the normally poised Otis Howard with gloom and sorrow. "He has sealed his great work with his life," he wrote his wife. "The grief is almost universal and I have seen more than one general officer shed tears in speaking of Mr. Lincoln. But he has his reward."[35] Lincoln's sad, serious, ravaged features haunted him. They had not met often but the president had never forgotten him after their first interview, had always taken an interest in his fortunes and treated him as though they were friends.

At home in Maine, Howard's son Guy put aside his favorite new book, *The Tanner Boy, or the Life of General Grant,* to mourn the slain president. "What a day has come upon our dear country," Lizzie Howard wrote from Leeds. "God has permitted this great calamity is all we can say. He can lift the dark cloud and show us its silver lining. Oh! that he may do so." Newspaper accounts of the larger conspiracy had deeply alarmed her. With Grant, Sherman, and others, her husband could well be a target of this barbarous enemy.[36]

Sherman reviewed Johnston's surrender proposal with Howard, Slocum, Schofield, and the corps commanders on the evening of the seventeenth. "They did not agree, but I believe Johnston's disposition is good and that he will do the best he can," Howard wrote Lizzie. He and the others advised Sherman to concede such terms as were necessary to avoid having to chase down a fleeing, dispersing army—"a march that might carry us back again over the thousand miles we had just accomplished," as Sherman put it. They addressed various contingencies. What if Johnston insisted on assent to the escape of Jeff Davis and his cabinet? Someone, either Logan or Blair, suggested only half jokingly that Sherman offer a fast government steamer (possibly the little *Bat,* a famous flyer) to convey the rebel leaders from Charleston to the Bahamas.[37]

Howard accompanied Sherman to the second session the next day. The Federals reached the Bennett farmhouse punctually at noon. Johnston and Hampton turned up late. After the preliminaries, Johnston announced that he had been empowered to negotiate a comprehensive settlement. He volunteered to produce the Confederate war secretary, John Breckinridge, as confirmation. A staff officer went off to fetch Breckinridge. A courier delivered a thick parcel of papers that included a draft surrender agreement from the pen of Postmaster General John Reagan, traveling with Davis's movable cabinet.

Sherman pushed Reagan's memorandum aside and settled down to compose one of his own. All his good intentions, his promise not to meddle in civil affairs, were forgotten. He recalled Lincoln's desire for a soft peace. The president had told him at their City Point conference in late March that he wanted the rebel soldiers home and at work on their farms as soon as possible, with their full rights as citizens restored. Sherman wholly approved. "To ride people down with persecution and military exaction would be like slashing away at the crew of a sinking ship," he thought.[38] His draft agreement added up to a broad and astonishingly generous political settlement, dictated by himself.

The troops would disband and deposit their arms in the several state capitals. (Armories in southern capitals had outfitted the first rebel units in 1861.)

Federal courts were to be promptly reestablished. The president would recognize existing state governments as soon as their officers swore the loyalty oath. (Most Southern states were ruled by the original secessionists or their political successors.)

All citizens would be guaranteed full political rights, as well as "rights of persons and property" under the Constitution. (With the constitutional amendment abolishing slavery not yet ratified, this clause could be read as endorsing the return of slave property to rebel masters. On reflection, even Sherman saw that. "It may be the lawyers want us to define more minutely what is meant by the guaranty of rights of person and property," he suggested to Johnston.)[39]

Sherman journeyed back to Raleigh well pleased with himself. He claimed afterward that he cared little whether the new president and the cabinet approved or rejected his terms. At the least, he would be the gainer by the several days' delay, for his engineer troops could finish rebuilding the railroad as far as Raleigh. If he had to go after Johnston again, he would march with adequate supplies, anyway. At the time, though, Sherman evidently believed that he and Johnston, man to man, had resolved all pending questions of war, peace and restoration.

"Influence [the president], if possible, not to vary the terms at all, for I have considered everything," he signaled Halleck. Likewise to Grant, "If you will get the president simply to indorse the copy, and commission me to carry out the terms, I will follow them to the conclusion."[40]

Henry Hitchcock left for Washington with the surrender document early on April 20. Grant scanned it the next day and concluded at once that it would not do. On his urgent recommendation, the cabinet met that night. Andrew Johnson and his ministers emphatically rejected the agreement. Coldly furious, manifestly willing to believe Sherman capable of any enormity, Stanton ordered Grant himself to carry the message to Raleigh and assume command of the army for the final drive against Confederate forces in North Carolina.

Meantime, Sherman floated back to earth. Tom Osborn at Howard's headquarters overheard a senior officer remark that the commanding general expected the cabinet to repudiate the agreement as too liberal. "General Sherman said he had given the terms he understood President Lincoln wished given but if they were not satisfactory he would demand such as the President might desire," Osborn wrote home.[41]

Grant and Hitchcock landed at Morehead City, North Carolina, late on April 23 and came up to Raleigh by rail overnight. Still wobbly and weak at the knees (he was seasick for most of the voyage down), Grant informed Sherman of the cabinet's action. He said nothing, however, about supplanting him in command. Sherman accepted the rebuke calmly. He sent word to Johnston that the truce would lapse in forty-eight hours.[42]

Johnston surrendered without further incident on Wednesday the twenty-sixth. "The convention is signed all right," Sherman wired Grant that afternoon. "Will be down in a couple of hours."[43]

For a day or so all seemed right with the world. "There is no more war!" Howard wrote home.[44] Stanton, however, could not leave well enough alone. In a release to the newspapers detailing the initial surrender compact, Stanton accused Sherman of violating Lincoln's express instruction (to Grant, in a memo of March 3) to avoid political entanglements with Confederate commanders. Sherman was a usurper, a military despot. Stanton went on to insinuate that he had connived at Davis's escape, probably in return for a bribe of Confederate gold. As Stanton's charges gathered momentum, so did the backlash against Sherman.

"A shameful capitulation," George Julian styled it at the time. Looking back a few years later, he was scarcely more charitable. "His action seemed a wanton betrayal of the country to its enemies," he wrote. "All the glory of his great achievements seemed to be forgotten in the anathemas which showered upon him."[45]

The press led the charge, no doubt as Stanton had intended. News of the Sherman peace, the *New York Times* remarked, came like a thunderclap out of a blue sky.

"Had Jeff. Davis himself prepared the memorandum, he could not have conceived a more complete wiping out of scores against him and his confederate leaders in rebellion," the *Times* said. "The general surprise and astonishment may be imagined when [Stanton's] war bulletin informed our citizens this morning that instead of Johnston whipping Sherman in battle, he had defeated him in diplomacy, and probably secured safe conduct for Jeff. Davis and his plunder en route to a foreign country."[46]

The first of the newspaper reports reached Sherman within a few days. In an April 25 dispatch to Stanton, he had freely admitted his "folly" in going too far in the Johnston negotiations. Now he learned that Stanton had let loose the dogs of the press on him. The accounts were shot through with misrepresentations: he had never seen Lincoln's March 3 memo (for Stanton had neglected to send him a copy); and he certainly had not called off Stoneman's cavalry so Davis could slip away to the south. Stanton was a common libeler, a liar, and a coward.

"It is true," Sherman wrote Grant sarcastically, "that non-combatants, men who sleep in comfort and security while we watch on the distant lines, are better able to judge than we poor soldiers, who rarely see a newspaper, hardly hear from our families, or stop long enough to draw our pay."[47]

While Sherman harbored his grudge, Howard and Slocum prepared for the final march. Howard's wing pushed off for Richmond on Saturday, April 29, covering twelve miles. The troops were a model of military decorum. "We are on our good behavior this trip, no foraging, and nothing naughty whatever," Charles Wills remarked. "Not a hand laid on a rail, not a motion toward a chicken or smoke-house, not a thing that even a Havelock would object to." As a reward, Christian Howard (he took a dim view of Sunday travel, anyway) gave the troops the next day off.[48]

The soldiers' anger rekindled as the Northern papers made the rounds. Wills saw a Philadelphia sheet of April 25. "It gives us our first intimation of the hue and cry against Sherman," he wrote. " 'Pap' must be careful. If he has blundered here we will feel it more at heart than we ever did the fall of our leaders before. I won't believe he has made a mistake until I know all about it. *It can't be.*" Osborn dismissed much of what he read as "pure hash" and warned his brothers to ignore it. "It seems to me that never in this world was a man dealt with with such treachery," thought Charles Morse, ever the Sherman loyalist.[49] As always, Howard defended his chief.

"I am deeply sorry for the abuse that Sherman is getting at the hands of the press," he wrote Lizzie. "He meant right & the reasons for offering generous terms were not rightly set forth. How easy it is to impute wrong motives."[50]

Doubts crept in all the same.

"We are very much shocked at Sherman's course," Wills conceded. No one he knew endorsed the original terms. "We all had such confidence in Sherman, and thought it almost impossible for him to make a mistake," he went on. "We can't bear to have anybody say a word against Sherman, but he did act very strangely in this thing."[51]

Six days of fast marching carried Howard's wing from Raleigh to Petersburg. The weather held fair and the roads were dry. The troops' docility continued to amaze Wills. "When a man can pass an onion bed without going for the onions, no one need talk to me about total depravity," he noted drily. The columns met with parties of Lee's and Johnston's men heading south. They struck Wills as apathetic, thoroughly beaten. He recorded the curious sight of hundreds of rebel officers, "Lieutenant General John Gordon among them," walking the streets of Petersburg in full uniform.[52]

Howard reached Manchester, opposite Richmond, on May 9 to find a summons to Washington awaiting him. He went on at once to the capital for a meeting with Stanton, who came straight to the point with the offer of the commissionership of the newly established Freedmen's Bureau. The war secretary told Howard that Lincoln himself had tapped him for the job.

Though Howard asked for a day to think it over, he decided on the spot to accept. The proposal did not come as a complete surprise. "There is talk of offering you the bureau at Washington (colored)," his brother Charles had written after the Sumter ceremony. And he had anticipated such a posting, or something very like it. "I expect during my life to have a good deal to do with the negroes," he had written Lizzie only a few weeks before from New Bern. Howard recognized the government's obligation to manage the transition from slavery to freedom. Rufus Saxton in the Sea Islands had shown him how it might be done. Now he would take responsibility for making Lincoln's Emancipation Proclamation and the pending Thirteenth Amendment a reality for 4 million former slaves.[53]

"I presume I am now fixed here in Washington for a few years at least," he wrote home.[54]

So Sherman and Howard parted company. With military loose ends to be tied up in the Carolinas, Sherman would make his way separately to Washington and a reckoning with his tormentor, Stanton. Journalist Whitelaw Reid, traveling with the touring and inspection party of Salmon Chase, now chief justice of the Supreme Court, crossed paths with him at Morehead City. Stanton's insults rankled still.

"I fancied the country wanted peace," the general barked at Reid. "If they don't, let them raise more soldiers."[55]

SHERMAN REACHED HILTON HEAD on April 30, landing with the concussive impact of a 20-pounder shell. He ordered the captured steamer *Jeff Davis* loaded with stores and troops and sent 250 miles up the Savannah River to Confederate Augusta. The soldiers were to seize the city, its arsenal, and its factories and open a line to Union cavalry raider James H. Wilson, whose thirteen thousand horsemen, after an incendiary excursion through Alabama, were refitting in Macon, Georgia. A second steamer would shortly follow, carrying a permanent garrison and a cargo of clothing, sugar, coffee, and bread for Wilson's command.

Hilton Head exploded into activity. General Gillmore put John Gray in charge of the soldier detail—"a very intelligent officer," Sherman would remark of him a few weeks later, "whose name I cannot recall." Fatigue parties knocked rusted locks off government store-

A coaster ties up to the wharf at wind-scoured Hilton Head, South Carolina, as
Union tugs, light craft, transports, and warships ride at anchor in Port Royal Sound.
An important supply and coaling station, Hilton Head served as a staging area for
Federal naval and military operations in the Southeast. The South Carolina planter
Thomas Elliott, on his first postwar visit to Hilton Head, marveled at what the
Yankees had wrought. "I was lost in wonder at the vast buildings; the wharf is
1,400 feet long & cost $300,000," he wrote. Northerners envisioned a prosperous
future for Hilton Head as an international deepwater seaport. (U.S. Army Military
History Institute)

houses and sent drayload after drayload rattling down to the jetty.
The *Jeff Davis* sailed for the mouth of the Savannah next day. The
laden stern-wheeler pushed upriver against the powerful spring current at a steady three or four miles an hour. "Here we were," Gray
wrote home, immensely pleased with himself, "taking possession of
a town filled with the enemy, as it were single-handed." The *Jeff
Davis* anchored at Sand Bar Ferry three miles below Augusta around
midday on May 4. The horses were unloaded, two wagons were
impressed into Federal service, and Gray led the little detachment
into the city.[56]

To his disappointment, he found Colonel Emory Upton, one of
Wilson's brigade commanders, already in possession and busy sign-
ing paroles for returning Confederates in a makeshift office at the
Planters' Hotel. Gray wandered into Broad Street, crowded with officers and men in rebel uniform. "There is great bitterness in the

town," Gray observed, "but the open expression of it is confined to the young women, who elaborately sweep their skirts out of one's way, and the boys who whistle Dixie."[57] Despite the free flow of whiskey, the rebel veterans, though they continued to wear Confederate gray, were quiet, well-behaved, and respectful.

Augusta had suffered comparatively little. The cotton trade was dead, but basic provisions were available for hard cash or barter goods, as Joseph LeConte discovered. Foraging in Augusta, he filled a borrowed Niter Bureau wagon with enough flour and bacon to feed his family into the summer and returned home to Columbia unscathed through the abandoned South Carolina barrens.

The shock had gradually worn off in fire-ravaged Columbia. Home guard patrols kept the darkened streets safe. Farmers ventured into town with last autumn's carefully hoarded surplus for sale or trade. Constable details gathered up clothing, blankets, and other goods the Yankees had strewn into the streets and put them on public display. Columbians waited in long lines to reclaim their belongings.

City authorities doled out rations of meal and stringy beef. The Yankee cattle left behind to feed the city were for the freedmen's stewpots only, Joe LeConte had been told. "We have no meat, but the negroes give us a little every day," his daughter Emma noted in her diary.[58] Common report reduced the size of the herd, actually some five hundred head, to around twenty half-starved animals, three of which were said to have died before they could be butchered.

Merciful spring came on early. There were no frosts after the first week of March. Hyacinths bloomed in Columbia's rubble and buds miraculously opened on the scorched elms. A soft cosmetic green covered the ugliest of the scars. Early peas, asparagus, spring turnips, and strawberries were available within a few weeks to supplement the inevitable cornmeal and salt meat.

Furloughed soldiers, deserters, and country people drifting in from across the Congaree remained the only source of news. Slaves were refusing to go into the fields. In the absence of regular authority, vigilantes patrolled the countryside. "They supposed they were free," Grace Elmore remarked acidly of the plantation blacks, "but are gradually discovering a Yankee army passing thro' and telling them so does not make it a fact."[59] Rumors of desperate battles and astounding Confederate victories passed by word of mouth, though nothing could be confirmed.

Then, in fantastic succession, a series of heart-stopping reports reached Columbia.

Richmond was given up, and Lee badly beaten!

"Why does not the President call out the women if there are not enough men," Emma LeConte wondered. "We would go and *fight*, too."

Black troops were on the march for Columbia!

"Heavens, haven't we suffered enough? The very thought is enough to make one shudder," Miss Emma declared.

Lee had surrendered!

"This is worse than war."

Lincoln was dead, his murder arranged by Andrew Johnson; and Johnson himself shown the lamppost by a Washington mob!

Emma rejoiced at this last. "The first feeling I had was simply gratified revenge," she confessed. "The man we hated has met his proper fate. The next thought was how it would infuriate them against us—and that was pleasant, too."

The French had seized New Orleans; the United States had proposed peace with the restoration of slavery in return for a Confederate alliance against Napoléon III. French warships were standing off Beaufort, off Georgetown, off Hampton Roads.

These last reports were swiftly contradicted. "I will *never* believe another French rumor or any other rumor that means hope to this unhappy land," Emma vowed.

Along with provender, Joe LeConte brought cloth, leather, and tallow for candles back from Augusta. His daughter tried to ignore the six bolts of imported unbleached homespun, but they only loomed larger the longer she left them alone. "It makes me groan in spirit to think of wearing this heavy stuff as underclothing all the hot summer," she wrote. She attacked it finally, working and trying to read (Gibbon still; slow going) at the same time. She tutored Sallie in arithmetic, Latin, natural philosophy, reading, spelling, and composition, and studied German on her own.

Her spirits lifted as the spring advanced. The first of the paroled soldiers reached Columbia. "One meets long-absent, once familiar faces on the streets," Emma remarked; and presently her cousin Julian turned up at home across the College Green, his feet so blistered he could barely walk.[60]

Paroled war prisoner Gabriel Manigault arrived at his brother's house in Augusta after a long odyssey from Fort Delaware. Prison life evidently agreed with him, Louis remarked, for Gabriel appeared in robust contrast to the living skeletons he had observed a few months before at Andersonville. Louis managed to post a letter through the lines to their father in Charleston, the old man's first news of Gabriel since the Yankee advent in mid-February.

"He is in perfect health, looking stouter and better than I have ever seen him," Louis wrote of him. "His prison-life has been a most interesting one & he is full of conversation and pleasing anecdotes."[61]

Charles Manigault wondered how the family would manage to live. Confederate securities and scrip were worthless, except for papering over cracks in bombardment-damaged plaster. Three of the four Charleston banks in which he owned shares had sunk under the weight of loans to the Confederate government, leaving no wreck behind. Freedmen were ascendant at Silk Hope. As for Argyle Island, "I have not heard a word," he wrote Louis. "But conditions must be bad enough, the plantation probably totally sacked and abandoned."[62] He did not expect an 1865 crop from either estate.

"You will have to look out for yourself as I have not one Cent to give you," Charles warned Louis. "Nor one cent of income thus far from any property I possess & no better prospects ahead and even should you wish it, such is our position that we cannot offer any of your family an asylum with us."[63]

The patriarch kept to himself. Broad, Meeting, and King streets were crowded with insolent former slaves. He had not yet gotten over his shock and outrage at the appearance of the black garrison. Charles Fox, in the camp of the Fifty-fifth Massachusetts on the east bank of the Cooper River, had no more use than the waspish old Charlestonian for the run-down, sullen, corrupt secession citadel. Fox avoided the city except when military business required his presence there. He even kept away from church. He felt he owed that much to the men.

"I think I shall be a better Christian to stay away," he wrote Mary one spring Sunday morning. "I can get along very well with the rebel officers and soldiers and some of the citizens, but bad as I may be in some respects myself, I cannot sit and pretend to worship a just God side by side with those who consider my men as brutes and chattels, and would gladly dig their graves."[64]

The occupation authorities in Charleston set aside a formal day of mourning for the murdered president. Camp buildings were dressed in black, memorial services read, gun salutes fired. In public, anyway, former rebels maintained a respectful silence. Fox thought the Charlestonians he met condemned Wilkes Booth's work as thoroughly as he did himself. They were watchful, too, of the effect of the assassination on the Yankees. All the same, close observers were already taking note of a returning confidence, even swagger, in some Southerners, especially the refugee Low Country planters.

"Secesh are coming back quite freely nowadays and looking about as much as they please," a Northern plantation superintendent reported.[65] The emancipated people interpreted rebel manners in the chilling context of the president's death. Lincoln lived in the imaginations of former slaves as the personification of freedom.

"They are inconsolable and won't believe he is dead," Laura Towne wrote. "In the church this morning they prayed for him as wounded but still alive and said that he was their saviour—that Christ saved them from sin and he from Secesh, and as for the vile Judas who had lifted his hand against him, they prayed the Lord the whirlwind would carry him away and that he would melt as wax in the fervent heat and be driven forever from before the Lord."[66]

The Gullahs flooded the Yankees with urgent questions.

"Uncle Sam is dead, isn't he?"

"The government is dead, isn't it?"

"We going to be slaves again?"[67]

The people went about with bits of black cambric attached to their clothes. One man wore his coat inside out, to expose the black lining. Schools, praise houses, and public buildings were draped in black. A few, though, discerned a kind of fitness in Lincoln's martyrdom.

"The churches are all in mourning," a soldier in the Third USCT wrote his friends in the North. "But I shed not a tear for him. He has done the work that was given him, and today sings the song of redeeming love."

Sleeps in Jesus, blessed sleep,
From which none ever wake to weep:
A calm and undisturbed repose,
Unbroken by the last of foes.[68]

Now the last of the foes had been vanquished. With confirmation of Johnston's surrender in North Carolina, the troops around Charleston prepared to stand down. Charley Fox packed up his heavy winter blankets and overcoat for shipment home to Dorchester. Word spread that the Fifty-fifth Massachusetts would be mustered out by July 1. Meantime, Fox readied the command for a move up the Edisto River to Orangeburg. The Fifty-fifth had been detailed for garrison duty there.

Up-country whites lived in dread of the arrival of black occupation troops. A Federal detachment marched into Columbia on May 18, the first Yankees in the city since Sherman's withdrawal three months before. These were troops of the Twenty-fifth Ohio, Colonel Haughton, the white regiment in Alfred Hartwell's Coast Division brigade.

"He seems to be a gentleman," Emma LeConte remarked tentatively of Nathaniel Haughton, "and his men are under strict discipline. They molest no one and are polite."[69]

JUST RETURNED FROM TEXAS, Lew Wallace plunged into the manhunt for John Wilkes Booth. He sent Eighth Corps cavalry here and armed steamers there. He assigned plainclothesmen to the depots and wharves to watch for suspicious characters. He banned the display and sale of Booth portraits in Baltimore shops.

Wallace's dreams were vast, and to an astonishing degree he approached their picaresque fulfillment. At various times, the incomparable drama of the Civil War offered him the role of soldier, secret agent, diplomat, empire builder, avenger of Lincoln. Circumstances, his own shortcomings, kept the grandest of fantasies just beyond his reach. Still, his high romantic imagination refused to let them go.

Wallace had ascended meteorically during the war's early phase. From a lawyer's office in Crawfordsville, Indiana, he rose to become, successively, the state's adjutant general, colonel commanding a volunteer infantry regiment, and major general commanding a division in Grant's Army of the Tennessee. His notorious wrong turn on a Tennessee byroad in April 1862 almost cost Grant the battle of Shiloh, but after a brief hiatus nothing worse befell him than promotion to command of the Middle Division, Eighth Corps, at Baltimore. In July 1864, along the Monocacy River in Maryland, his 5,800 mostly raw

troops held on long enough to allow the Washington defenses to prepare for the arrival of rebel raider Jubal Early. Wallace lost the Monocacy battle, but gained a critical day for the capital. Grant himself put
in a good word for him.

Born in Brookville, Indiana, in 1827, raised by his father, Wallace
was a truant boy, bored with school but obsessively and impression-
ably bookish. He raced through the three lurid volumes of William
Prescott's *History of the Conquest of Mexico* (1843) at age sixteen, a fate-
ful selection. The historian's epic sweep and virtuoso depiction of
tragic heroes and exotic locales entranced him. Prescott led him to the
sea meadows of Point Isabel at the mouth of the Rio Grande with an
Indiana volunteer regiment during the Mexican War. Prescott, the
experience, and his own tentative reworking of the Spanish conquest
in novel form gave him a spirit-saving imaginative outlet through the
dreary, law-bound 1850s.

The coming of the war made anything possible. Grant, even Lincoln, were not just figures one read about in the newspapers, but
familiar and accessible men who could be approached with great
plans and schemes. Wallace went to the president early in 1865 with
a modest proposal to snatch Texas from the collapsing Confederacy
and expel the French from Mexico. War and blockade had transformed the flyblown towns of the lower Rio Grande into the busiest
cotton markets in the world, conduits for war goods not just into
Texas but throughout what survived of the Confederacy. Bold action
there would forward the cause of the Mexican Republicans, knock
Emperor Maximilian off his purloined throne, enforce the Monroe
Doctrine, smother the Matamoros-Brownsville trade, and deny the
beaten eastern rebels a fortress/haven, all at the same time.

A corps of forty thousand French troops kept Maximilian in
power. With General Wilson preparing to launch his Raid to Selma
and General E. R. S. Canby about to advance on Mobile, the War
Department could spare no troops from the Department of the Gulf
for a campaign on the Rio Grande. Besides, Secretary of State Seward
held a veto over any operation with potential for trouble with France.

All the same, Wallace intrigued Lincoln with his talk of supplying the Mexican Republicans with arms, gold, and, before long, perhaps, veteran U.S. troops. "This is the argument of a thief," Wallace
claimed the president told him, "—all right, if you don't get caught."[70]
Lincoln sent him along to Grant. The general in chief met with Wal-

lace privately and authorized him to go to Texas and see what he could stir up.

Grant provided two pretexts for the mission. For public consumption, he ordered Wallace to inspect "the condition of military affairs" on the Rio Grande from the U.S. outpost at Brazos Santiago, the narrow sea-opening through Padre Island to Point Isabel on the mainland. Further, Wallace would investigate claims that Maximilian's police were picking up rebel deserters and exiled Texas Unionists and handing them over to Confederate authorities at Brownsville. Federal sources at Brazos reported that some of the repatriates had been tried by drumhead court and hanged.

Privately, according to Wallace, Grant encouraged him to make contact with the Mexican Republican forces of Benito Juárez and determine whether they were willing to intercept and turn back any organized Confederate military units that crossed the Rio Grande.

Wallace traveled from Baltimore by rail via Indianapolis to Cairo, Illinois, then by steamboat to New Orleans. He was in a tearing hurry. "Everybody is complaining of railroads and steamboats," he wrote his wife Susan, "everybody is mad and impatient."[71] There were compensations: Officers' wives crowded the vessel and a string band sawed away at nightly dances. The fare was first-rate, too. Bushwhackers fired into the side-wheeler below Memphis, causing a temporary panic, interrupting dinner, and costing one unlucky passenger an arm. Wallace worked at a Spanish grammar, and went ashore at Vicksburg for a few hours to tour Grant's battlefields of 1862 and 1863.

Lack of transport—Canby claimed everything that swam—delayed him in New Orleans. The famous Saint Charles Hotel had gone sadly to seed. "The vermin almost devour me," Wallace complained. "Then one imagines all the time that the air he breathes is laden with smallpox."[72] On the other hand, he basked in the role of man of mystery. Even Mrs. General Canby wondered aloud why this politically well-connected major general had come to the Gulf, and what he proposed to do there.

Wallace collated reports from U.S. agents in Brazos Santiago and dreamed of conquest. As many as a hundred ships lay off Bagdad, the Mexican settlement on a sand spit at the mouth of the Rio Grande, off-loading munitions, medicine, clothing, and blankets, and taking on cotton lightered downriver from Matamoros. Wallace estimated

Union Major General Lew Wallace, soldier, secret agent, artist, dreamer. He schemed to arrange a Confederate surrender in the Trans-Mississippi and lead a U.S. army into Maximilian's Mexico. Instead, the hyperactive Wallace found himself confined to Washington military courtrooms for the trials of the Lincoln conspirators and Andersonville jailer Henry Wirz. (Indiana Historical Society)

rebel strength in the region at two thousand troops. With a small army of his own he could occupy Brownsville, shut off the lucrative and strategically important rebel trade, force the surrender of Trans-Mississippi commander Edmund Kirby Smith, and block the retreat of bitter-enders into Mexico.

Wallace petitioned Grant to create a Military Department of Texas, appoint him to the command, and ship a veteran infantry division and a cavalry brigade to the Rio Grande. He requested westerners ("You know how easily southern people affiliate with them"), and specifically for his own former regiment, the Eleventh Indiana, and the Eighth Illinois Cavalry.[73]

The steamer *Clifton* carried him to Brazos in early March. The deserter story turned out to be massively exaggerated. The Mexicans had returned four men to the Confederates, and only two were in jail.

For all Wallace knew, they were scoundrels of the first water. And there was no evidence at all that Unionist Texan exiles had been sent back, let alone hanged.[74]

Wallace's strategic/diplomatic initiative showed promise, however. When the local Confederate commander, Brigadier General James Slaughter, agreed to a parley, Wallace drafted a provisional agreement calling for a cessation of hostilities in all the Trans-Mississippi, with the offer of parole, immunity from prosecution, and civil rights for any soldier who swore the loyalty oath. He proposed to show it to Slaughter, and proceed from there.

They met on the wind-sculpted sands of Point Isabel. Wallace tapped his Secret Service fund and played host. The conferees dined well, drank companionably into the warm evening, and retired together as newfound friends. "If our good people could have seen Gen. Slaughter and myself lie down to sleep upon the same blanket, as quietly as two children in the same little bed, I fear my character for loyalty would be forever lost," he wrote Susan. Slaughter, too, fell under the spell of the Texas stars. A reluctant rebel in the first place, as he confided to Wallace, he was now ready to call it quits. He only wanted a face-saving way out. A joint U.S.–ex-rebel filibustering expedition against the French in Mexico would answer perfectly.[75]

In his dispatch to Grant, Wallace proposed joining forces with Slaughter and his surrendered Confederates to make war on Maximilian.

"It is understood between us that the pacification of Texas is a preliminary step to a crossing of the Rio Grande," he wrote. "Gen'l Slaughter was of the opinion that the best way for officers in his situation to get honorably back into the Union was to cross the river, conquer two or three states from the French and ultimately annex them to the United States. In short, I think they anticipate such a step as the immediate consequence of peace."[76]

Slaughter promised to submit the proposal to Kirby Smith and set off for Brownsville. The semi-independent satrapy of the Rio Grande, Lew Wallace, proprietor, must at that moment have seemed within the dreamer's grasp.

"I have started negotiations with the rebel military authorities in this neighborhood," he wrote Susan grandly. "What I aim at now is bringing Texas, Arkansas and Louisiana back into the Union."[77]

They were two boys playacting. Slaughter's immediate superior, General John Walker, accused him of talking "the blackest treason" with Wallace. Like Mrs. General Canby, Walker wondered what errand had brought Wallace to the Rio Grande. "The fact that an officer of his high rank is found in so remote a corner has in itself something sinister and suspicious," he admonished Slaughter.[78] In a sharp reply to Wallace, Walker treated the proposal as so much waste paper. The Trans-Mississippi would stand or fall with the Confederacy.

So Wallace knew by month's end that there would be no surrender in Texas—not to him, anyhow. He nevertheless accounted the mission a success. He had established contact with the Juárez forces in the Victoria Mountains (where his agent found weapons-starved Juáristas being trained to shoot with bows and arrows) and satisfied himself that the Mexicans would be willing, if properly equipped, to try to disarm retreating Confederates. Wallace's hope of an independent command had vanished for now, but Mexico might yet offer a field for name and fame. The outbound packet from Brazos landed him in New Orleans on April 5.

Wallace learned of the president's death in the train on the return trip to Baltimore. Reaching his headquarters on April 18, he sent out a flurry of orders intensifying the Eighth Corps search for Lincoln's killer. He wired Stanton that he had established "a perfect chain of picket boats" on the Chesapeake between Annapolis and Point Lookout, and assigned armed guards to every steamer plying between Baltimore, Annapolis, and the Eastern Shore.[79]

Booth and David Herold emerged from their swamp thicket and crept down to the Potomac the night of April 21–22. Dr. Mudd had done a slapdash job on the assassin's damaged leg. It had swollen hugely and Booth was in a lot of pain. He bore up well with the wound—his first, for he had promised his doting mother that he would stay out of harm's way and had taken no part in the war until now. Two ornamental details stand out from Booth's Maryland childhood: his actor father allowed no meat at the family board, and his parents were married on May 10, 1851, Wilkes's thirteenth birthday. As for Herold, he was "a pretty little man," in the words of a contemporary, red-cheeked, with long, thin, dark hair; but he was otherwise a nonentity, and not a very bright one at that.

Booth led the horses down to the river, weighted them, towed them out into the stream, slit their throats, and watched them sink.[80] They crossed to the Virginia bank in a skiff and hired a wagon to carry them on to the Rappahannock River. Booth wore a ten-day growth of dark beard, a black soft hat, and dark clothes, and limped along with two crude pasteboard splints fastened to his broken leg.

A freedman named Peyton Washington poled the fugitives across the 300-yard-wide Rappahannock in a scow. They fell in on the far bank with three paroled, homeward-bound Confederate officers of John S. Mosby's command—M. B. Ruggles, A. R. Bainbridge, and William Jett. Herold spoke to them first, out of Booth's hearing. Booth himself approached Ruggles a moment later to solicit his help in pushing on south.

"I suppose you have been told who I am," he said coyly. Then he leaned back on his crutch and drew a revolver.

"Yes," he went on as though he were back on the stage, "I am John Wilkes Booth, the slayer of Abraham Lincoln, and I am worth just $175,000 to the man who captures me."

Ruggles led Booth and Herold to the Richard Garrett farm south of Port Royal, Virginia, and stayed there with them for a night. Booth was talkative. He laid out the conspiracy in detail, Ruggles recalled later. He had intended to capture Lincoln and carry him south, using him as a hostage to bargain for peace. When the abduction scheme fell apart he decided to kill the president, Grant (advertised as accompanying Lincoln to Ford's Theater the evening of April 14), and others. Only he and Lewis Paine, Seward's assailant, were in on the murder plot. Now that the Confederacy was exploded, he meant to escape to "the silver mines of Mexico," a fantasy place where he expected to strike it rich.

The fugitives spent the next night, April 25–26, in a tobacco barn on the Garrett place.While they slept a Federal cavalry detachment sent down from Washington followed a warm trail that led to Willie Jett abed in a Bowling Green boardinghouse. Lieutenant Edward Doherty of the Sixteenth New York Cavalry interrupted Jett in the act of sleep and gave him the choice of candid conversation or a noose. Jett, half-dressed, groggy, and full of alarm, admitted he had left Booth at the Garrett farm the evening before.

Doherty's detachment reached the Garrett place before dawn. The troopers dismounted and surrounded the farmhouse. One of Garrett's sons indicated that Booth and Herold were hidden in the tobacco barn. Doherty's men sealed it off. Then Doherty shouted out a demand for Booth to surrender.

"I am a cripple and alone," Booth called back.

"Come out. If you don't come out, I'll burn the building."[81]

Negotiations went back and forth. Everton Conger, a War Department detective accompanying Doherty, moved around to the back of the barn with matches and straw.

Booth called out, "Oh, captain, there is a man here who wants to surrender awful bad."

Doherty asked for Herold's weapons.

"I own all the arms," Booth shouted, "and intend to use them on you gentlemen."[82]

Doherty approached the barn door and told Herold to put out his hands. Seizing his wrists, Doherty pulled him out of the building. Conger, meantime, lit the tinder he had heaped against the back wall. One of the troopers caught a glimpse of Booth through the leaping flames and squeezed off a shot. Doherty kicked open the door and plunged inside. Booth lay on his back, blood oozing from a wound in his neck. Doherty's men carried him onto Garrett's porch. He died there around seven o'clock. Doherty emptied Booth's pockets of a diary, two pistols, a Bowie knife, a compass, and a draft on a Canadian bank for £60 sterling. He borrowed a darning needle from Mrs. Garrett, sewed Booth's body into a saddle blanket, and struck out for the Potomac.[83]

Doherty's detachment escorted Herold and Booth's corpse up to Washington in the steamer *John S. Ide*. War Department agents transferred prisoner and cadaver to the monitor *Montauk*, where Paine and some of the others were being held in irons below decks. The guard detail fitted Herold with standard conspirator hardware: a ball and chain and handcuffs. Booth was buried in an ammunition box under the stone floor of a storeroom at the Old Penitentiary.

Stanton, meantime, moved swiftly to organize a military commission to try Booth's accomplices. He named General David Hunter to head the court and brought Lew Wallace down from Baltimore as second-ranking officer. Joseph Holt of the Bureau of Military Justice would head the prosecution.

Stanton's haste and his insistence on a military trial—a dragnet affair where the rules of evidence were loose and harsh punishment more likely than in a civilian proceeding—drew criticism from the start. John Ropes, for instance, strongly objected to the court-martial, even before he knew the details of the commission's makeup.

"What I say is, let the law take its course," he wrote John Gray. "I go in for hanging, confiscation and everything generally, only I want to see it done according to law. If a man is to be killed, let it be done *secundem artem.*"[84]

The court convened in a third-floor room of the Old Penitentiary on May 9, three days short of four weeks after Lincoln's mortal wounding. The eight prisoners, hooded, manacled hand and foot, their irons clanking, were led into the long room the next morning to hear the charges read out. The hoods, one of the trial officers thought with a shudder, suggested an inquiry out of the Inquisition. Fidgety, restive, dreaming of Mexico, Wallace took his place on David Hunter's right. With pen, ink, and pad, he began to sketch the scene.

# Part Three

# Something Like Peace

## *May 1865–November 1866*

Pay ransom to the owner
And fill the bag to the brim.
Who is the owner? The slave is the owner.
And ever was. Pay him.

Ralph Waldo Emerson
"Boston Hymn"

# 7

# Exile and Return

SHERMAN'S ARMY PUSHED ON through the ravaged Virginia country-side toward Washington. Charles Wills found the much fought over Rappahannock Valley barren and unattended, with scarcely 20 per-cent of cleared tracts under the plow, fences long since burned for firewood, livestock stolen, driven off, or running feral in the scrub oak thickets. "This certainly does not largely rank the Sahara," Wills remarked.[1] A month back, Robert Lee expressed relief that the parolees of the Army of Northern Virginia would be home in time for spring planting. But the country hardly bloomed yet; nor would it anytime soon.

The government turned to General Howard to restore life to the desert he had helped create in the South. He took formal charge of the Bureau of Refugees, Freedmen, and Abandoned Lands on May 15, 1865, with headquarters at the corner of Nineteenth and I Streets, Washington, in the confiscated house of a former senator who had bolted with his rebellious state in 1861. By week's end he had ap-pointed eight assistant commissioners, including Rufus Saxton, an architect of the Port Royal Experiment, for South Carolina, Georgia, and Florida.

"We are fixed here for the present, I guess," wrote Willard Sax-ton in Beaufort, pleased (and not a little impressed) with his brother's sudden ascent. "There is a great deal to do, & I hope God will give

Rufus wisdom, & the authorities in Washington the power & means of doing, all that has to be done."[2]

Howard confronted an enormous task. War's end had thrown the mass of 4 million former slaves onto the world with virtually nothing: no land, no savings, little or no schooling, no experience of politics, the legal system, or the free economy. Congress expected the bureau to protect the freed people, distribute emergency relief to the destitute, build an equitable free labor system, and establish a system of basic education throughout the South. Whether out of oversight or stinginess, the bill's sponsors neglected to give the bureau a budget. Howard could draw on the army for manpower, transport, and rations. He could solicit northern charitable societies for money, supplies, and volunteers. Otherwise, he would have to proceed on his own, and good luck to him.

"It seems he has just been put in charge of the Freedmen's Bureau," his brother Charles wrote their mother. "He has not had much experience in such matters, but good common sense and the power of attention to business will soon make him master of the situation."[3]

Sherman wished Howard well, even if he did rate his chances of success at slightly better than nil. "Though in the kindness of your heart you would alleviate all the ills of humanity it is not in your power," he wrote him. "Nor is it in your power to fulfill one-tenth of the expectations of those who framed the Bureau."[4] He advised Howard to resist abolitionist pressure to deploy the bureau as a weapon of social revolution. Sherman had heard from Chief Justice Chase that the government would insist on the franchise for former slaves, a notion he found fantastic. Forcing black suffrage on the South, he warned, would almost certainly touch off a new war.

"I am more than unusually sensitive on this point," Sherman wound up, "because I have realized in our Country that one Class of men makes war and leaves another to fight it out. I am tired of fighting and if the theorists of New England impose this new condition I dread the result."[5]

Whatever happened, Sherman's veterans would not be called upon to garrison the tumultuous South. One last march, a short one, lay ahead: the Grand Review of the Armies in Washington. The army cleared its befouled camps around Alexandria, Virginia, late in the afternoon of Tuesday, May 23, and closed up to the Long Bridge. The Fifteenth Corps' First Division crossed in the evening and bivouacked in the streets and vacant lots of the capital. The rest of the Fifteenth Corps, then the Seventeenth, the Twentieth, and the Fourteenth corps, followed during the night and early Wednesday morning. By daybreak the leading formations were massing in the streets around Capitol Hill for the second day of the Grand Review.

Walt Whitman observed the western troops closely—more than 150 of Sherman's 186 infantry regiments came from the Transappalachian states—and contrasted them with what he had seen the day before of the Army of the Potomac. "These western soldiers are more slow in their movements, and in their intellectual quality also; have no extreme alertness," he thought. "They are larger in size, have a more serious physiognomy. They are largely animal, and handsomely so."[6] Sherman's men had cleaned themselves up for the occasion. Most wore new uniforms, their arms were burnished bright, and one division commander fitted out each man in his column with a pair of white gloves.

Sherman and Howard swung their horses into Pennsylvania Avenue at nine o'clock on the mild, sunshot morning of May 24. A light northeast breeze carried a few puffy clouds gently toward the Blue Ridge. Seventy-five thousand people had watched the Potomac army pass in review; if anything today's crowds, packed ten deep in temporary wooden stands that lined both sides of the avenue from the Capitol to the White House, were larger. Colorful flags, banners, and streamers, the silver glint of bayonets, and the dazzling yellow of the generals' sashes flashed out against the somber backdrop of the still-mourning city. The volume of sound swelled to a hurricane roar: brass bands playing medleys of marching anthems, drums, repercussive cheers, the unison tramp of the slow-moving mass, the clop of horses' hooves, the metallic rumble of vehicles on the cobbles.

At the crest of Treasury Hill Sherman turned in the saddle and glanced back toward the Capitol. The Fifteenth Corps marched like the lords of creation, straight and steady with a swinging stride, looking neither right nor left. He had wanted to show the world that he commanded a proper army after all, well organized, drilled, and disciplined. They were model troops today, whatever they had been, however they had behaved, in Georgia and the Carolinas.

"The column was compact," Sherman remembered with pride, "and the glittering muskets looked like a solid mass of steel, moving with the regularity of a pendulum. There was no wonder that it had swept through the South like a tornado."[7]

Sherman and Howard advanced at a walk. The adoring throng pelted them with bouquets; Sherman slipped a sort of lei around his shoulders and laid a floral wreath along the neck of his charger. Otherwise, recalling the newspaper attacks of last month, the public's fickleness, credulity, and susceptibility to manipulation, he hardly acknowledged the cheers, meeting the crowd's uproarious volleys, in one journalist's phrase, with grim composure.

Sherman raised his sword in salute as he approached the reviewing stand in front of the White House. Holding the reins to his side with the stump of his absent arm, Howard saluted with his left hand. They entered the mansion grounds, dismounted, and approached the canopied grandstand. Sherman and Andrew Johnson clasped hands. Stanton, to the president's right, made a slight movement, as though to offer a hand. Sherman, looking grimmer than ever, according to the journalist, who observed the scene through field glasses from across the avenue, declined ostentatiously to accept it.

"The fact was universally noticed," Sherman wrote years afterward, still exulting over the effects of his long-meditated revenge for Stanton's attack.*[8]

The columns came on and on, hour after hour. Black pioneer troops carrying picks and spades led each infantry division. Bringing up the rear, the authentic Georgia and Carolina touch, were ambulances, pontoons, farm jacks loaded with hams, poultry, furniture, and other examples of bummer pelf, and representative former slaves, men wearing cast-off soldier clothes, women in head rags leading children by the hand.

Blair's Seventeenth Corps followed, then the Twentieth Corps. The well-scrubbed Second Massachusetts, John Fox present against odds for this valedictory moment ("I have been in every action of the

---

*Charles Dana disputed Sherman's account. "The Secretary made no motion to offer his hand," he recalled. "As the general passed, Mr. Stanton gave merely a slight forward motion of his head, equivalent, perhaps, to a quarter of a bow."

The Union Twentieth Corps, Army of Georgia, swings down Pennsylvania Avenue in Washington on the bright, warm afternoon of
May 24, 1865. Captain John Fox and fewer than two hundred survivors of the bled-down Second Massachusetts marched with the
corps in the triumphal Grand Review of the Armies. "I have been
in every action of the regiment without being touched even in my
clothes," Fox had written home, and the charm held to the last.
(Library of Congress)

regiment without being touched even in my clothes," he had boasted)
moved off from the Capitol at a few minutes past eleven o'clock.
Cheers pealed out for the Second by name as it swung smartly down
Pennsylvania Avenue. A raucous huzzah went up for Charles Morse
from the stand in front of Willard's Hotel. He peered into the crowd
but recognized no one, and never discovered afterward who had initiated the salute.

The Fourteenth Corps formed the rear guard, clearing the White
House around half past three and following the Twentieth Corps out
of the city to new camps northwest of the capital. The crowds dis-

persed. The dust settled and the last scents of ten thousand blooms drifted away on the stir of evening air. The Second Massachusetts occupied a clean, comfortable bivouac near Bladensburg. Accommodations were luxurious, with hotel-quality board for the officers and fifty pounds of ice a day.

"New times, these, are they not?" Charley Morse wrote home.[9]

Within a week, Sherman had taken leave of the army. "The time has come for us to part," he said in his farewell orders. "Our work is done and armed enemies no longer defy us." Sherman advised the veterans in his last orders to return docilely to their farms, factories, and offices. Their lives of excitement and adventure were over, he told them; they should disperse content with having done their duty, grateful they still possessed their whole skins.[10]

The parading veterans were, of course, the fortunate ones. The final returns had not been tallied, but whatever the ultimate tabulation, the cost of four years of Civil War had been agonizingly high. More than a million men, North and South, were accounted casualties. Northern losses reached 640,000; 475,000 Southerners were dead, wounded, or missing. Of the total, 110,000 Union men and 94,000 Confederates died or were mortally wounded in battle. Disease and accident claimed more soldier and sailor lives than hostile fire: 255,000 Federals, 152,000 Confederates. Altogether, one ablebodied Northerner in every ten was a casualty, compared to a cataclysmic one Southerner in every four.[11]

The survivors looked now to the future. Fully recovered from his Averasboro wound (two clean scars, and the shoulder muscles mending nicely), Charley Morse had rejoined the Second Massachusetts a few days before the Grand Review. He came down from Boston in easy stages, with a stop in New York City to call on Jim Grafton's father and a visit to Bob Shaw's parents at their country place on Staten Island. General Slocum seemed surprised to see him when he turned up at headquarters. After an awkward pause, Slocum handed him a just-received War Department order mustering him out of the army. He had been absent a long time and his "services were no longer required," the order read.[12]

"Did you ever know anything more cruelly unjust—the idea of serving faithfully for more than four years and then being kicked out of the service without being asked whether or not I wanted to go," Morse wrote his brother Robert.[13]

Slocum intervened, and the adjutant general's office rescinded the order. Morse would stay with the regiment to the end. After that, who could say? "I am still eligible to good situations," he advertised in a letter home, "no preference for town or country, salary not less than $2,000, best of references given."[14] Slocum offered to recommend him for a Regular Army commission. If that fell through, he went on, it would be "Ho! for California" to prospect for a postwar life.

"I wouldn't care if it carried me to Kamschatka so long as I could have some responsibility and not be altogether a subordinate," he wrote Robert.[15]

The Twentieth Corps disbanded on June 7. The Third Wisconsin, brigaded with the Second Massachusetts from the start, headed at once for home. "They cheered us and we cheered them but a good many of us felt more like blubbering," Morse confessed. The Second drew provost duty in Washington and shifted camp to an open field near the Capitol. Damp, heavy summer heat settled on the city. Morse longed for a cool, pine-scented respite in the White Mountains.

In the event, he found himself less ready for release than he had anticipated. Morse issued his farewell orders to the Second Massachusetts on July 12 "with more pain than pleasure," he admitted. The regiment entrained for New York on July 15 and proceeded by rail and steamer to Readville, near Boston, where it pitched camp for the last time. By July 26 the regiment had been paid off and discharged.[16] Morse went home to Jamaica Pond to await events, caught, as so many young men were just then, in that painfully intense, sometimes prolonged period of decompression and adjustment to civil life.

"It is most difficult to realize that our war is over," Charles Wills wrote in his diary, speaking for tens of thousands. "I have almost a dread of being a citizen, of trying to be sharp, and trying to make money."[17]

As summer approached, John Gray continued to shuffle papers for General Gillmore in Charleston and Hilton Head. He regarded his immediate future as settled, if not particularly enticing. "I suppose I shall return and open a law office in Boston, because there is nothing else for me to do," he wrote his mother. "After a few weeks it will all seem natural and inevitable enough."[18] He had yet to decide whether to accept John Ropes's invitation to join his promising law practice. It sounded too easy somehow, too safe.

"I should like it only too well," Gray had written his friend. "But I am afraid that if I am to do or make anything I ought to sail on my own bottom."[19]

There was plenty of time to think things over, for so little army business came Gray's way now that he found himself inventing work, drawing out every assignment and deliberating discreetly over petty questions he might have settled in five minutes—busy idleness, in his words. Existence, if numbing, at least was comfortable. His pay had risen to $200 a month; his mess bill ran to only $75; and he and his messmate had acquired a cow that supplied any quantity of milk, cream, and sweet butter.

"A cow is a great economy," Gray wrote home, enchanted with the discovery.[20]

Ned Bartlett marked time in bivouac with the Fifth Massachusetts Cavalry on the broad James opposite Harrison's Landing in Virginia. The new locale graded as an improvement over guard duty along the Southside Railroad ("We wish you did not have to be so near the cars," sister Annie had written, "it must be so dangerous in those narrow cuts"),[21] but not by much: drill, drill, and not even the change of pace of picket work now there was no longer any enemy to be on the alert for.

"The great question is what is to be done with us," he wrote his sister Martha at home in Concord. "Rumors fly around as thick as bees. Some say the corps is to be sent to Texas (that is an idle story), & others that the regiment is to be mustered out soon. What does father think I'd better do—stay in or go out if I have a chance to?"[22]

His sisters kept him up to date on Concord news. Cousin John Goddard had been killed with the Fourth Massachusetts Cavalry in an affray at the High Bridge over the Appomattox three days before Lee's surrender. The First Parish Church held a memorial service for the martyred president. "The drapery was as it was Sunday only a picture of Abraham Lincoln was in front of the pulpit shrouded in black," Annie wrote him, "and the communion table was covered with a black cloth with a basket of white flowers and a wreath of English Violets." Emerson spoke. "Old as history is, and manifold as are its tragedies, I doubt if any death has caused so much pain to mankind as this has caused," he told the gathered mourners. Then the bells tolled, and the minute guns boomed.[23]

A grieving peace descended upon the town. War had changed everything; yet nothing had changed. It had been a fine spring in Concord. "Father said tell you we had asparagus on 19th April, the earliest we've ever had it but once for thirty years," Annie wrote Ned. There were fresh soldier graves in Sleepy Hollow Cemetery. Invalid veterans queued up at the post office for their pension checks. Lieutenant Bartlett still faced perils his sisters could scarcely imagine: the accidental discharge of a weapon, a typhus outbreak, a steamboat explosion. Yet home routines were immemorial. Martha and Annie took their vesper walks as always along the slow-moving Concord, through the fens to the river reach beyond. There were hands of Boston in the parlor. Annie sent her brother a detailed description of a new game, played outdoors on cropped grass. One used multicolored mallets to knock multicolored balls through iron hoops driven into the ground.

"I hope you can understand," she wrote, dissatisfied with her description of croquet. "It is pretty hard to explain anything by writing."[24]

Camp rumors were accurate for a change. Orders for the Rio Grande reached the Fifth Massachusetts Cavalry around May 20. "I only wish we were there—well-mounted and careering over the plains of Texas," Bartlett wrote home.[25] Such a ride would almost certainly have finished off Bartlett's commanding officer, Charles Adams. Bartlett had never much admired the haughty colonel, but he could see that he had suffered.

Dull-eyed, gray unhealthy skin stretched tight over the bones of his face, Adams looked a decade and more older than his 30 years. When he left the regiment for the last time at the end of May his weight had dropped to a skeletal 130 pounds. His nerves were shot and his aching, swollen, malarial joints tormented him at night. Too ill and discouraged to think of the future, he traveled north to Quincy and then on to coastal New Hampshire for a few weeks in the Isles of Shoals, where he hoped to restore his run-down body and shattered, regretful spirit.

"A great experience was over," Adams wrote in retrospect, "and its close was for me a Dead Sea apple. But I intended it well!"[26]

BEATEN, BANKRUPT CONFEDERATE SOLDIERS headed home to an overturned world. Their Confederate banknotes were worthless. They owned little more than the disintegrating clothes on their backs. Kinsmen and friends were dead or maimed. Their homes were ransacked or seized, their fields overgrown, their fences burned, their corncribs and cotton houses emptied, their livelihoods gone. Their leaders were in arrest or discredited. They had nothing to do, no place to go.

Virginian Charles Blackford had failed to overtake Lee's army after he left Richmond the night of the fire—there wasn't time. He met a cavalryman along the road to Appomattox who told him about the surrender. Blackford turned north for Charlottesville, where he picked up official word of the collapse of the Army of Northern Virginia. He and his refugee wife camped for weeks in a single room at the university there.

Blackford set out alone on a "prospecting tour" in mid-June, walking the first forty miles toward his Lynchburg home, for his horse had cast a shoe and he had no money to replace it. He jumped a gravel train at Tye River and rode the rest of the distance home, covered, crown to boots, in fine white mineral dust.

Blackford found his mother well. He reopened his law office and sent back to Charlottesville for his wife. There were no courts in Lynchburg, nor business of any kind. "People on Main Street sat out on the sidewalks gossiping and smoking, and some with tables playing chess, backgammon and cards," he wrote. "As the sun moved they moved from one side of the street to the other to get the shade."[27] A case finally came Blackford's way: a disagreement over a Confederate contract. He hazarded an opinion. Each of the two disputants paid him a half-dollar.

"I was amazed at my wealth, seized it, closed the office and went home to show the spoils to my wife," Blackford remembered. "With part of it we bought our first herring and a slice of cheese."[28]

Ralph Elliott, with the grudging paid help of a few of his former slaves, put a modest crop of corn, cotton, and potatoes into the ground at one of the smaller places along the Edisto River below Charleston. Lacking tools, seed, and capital for wages, he sowed late and uncertainly, and could only wonder whether the effort would sustain the scattered Elliotts through the winter.

Emma Holmes's cousin Willie Guerand, wounded at Bentonville with the Palmetto Guards, turned up at her mother's place in Camden with his arm in a sling. She watched others, hundreds of "home-less, penniless, clothesless" men, stream through the half-burnt South Carolina town. Emma LeConte's Harden cousins, parolees, too, from Johnston's army, rested briefly in Columbia, then struck south, on foot, for Liberty County, Georgia, and whatever remained to sustain life there.[29]

Lafayette McLaws made his way to Augusta, where he expected to rejoin Emily and their children at last. Along with so many other senior Confederate officers, McLaws contemplated a military career abroad. He took the trouble to obtain a recommendation from Ben-jamin Yancey, of the fire-eating South Carolina Yanceys, for a com-mission in the army of Argentina. "He is a graduate of the West Point school—the distinguished military institution of the United States," Yancey wrote, though he made no mention of McLaws's services to the defunct Confederacy.[30]

Union authorities in Augusta informed McLaws that he could no longer appear in public in his uniform; when he protested that he had nothing else to cover himself with they instructed him to strip all badges of rank from his coat and tunic. Even so, the hand of occupa-tion lay surprisingly light. In fairness, McLaws had to admit that. If the Federals objected to his major general's baubles, they yet permitted him to retain a small arsenal: a double-barreled shotgun, a rifle, a car-bine, two Colt pistols, ten pounds of powder, and two bags of shot.

Gabriel Manigault pushed on from Augusta to Silk Hope, near Charleston, his long tramp from Fort Delaware almost at an end. He found the freed people on the place helping themselves to Manigault provisions, sheep, and cattle. War and imprisonment had sharpened Manigault's wits and made him bold. He was a cavalryman, after all; he pushed on to Charleston and laid plans for what he dubbed the "Last Raid" of the war.

Manigault hired two butchers, returned to Silk Hope, rounded up thirty beeves and a hundred sheep, and drove them the forty miles to Charleston. He lost but one cow, a stupid beast that wandered away from his bivouac in the woods during the night. The animals were slaughtered and the meat and hides sold. Manigault cleared $900 on the cattle raid. His father used the money to restore commercial buildings on East Bay damaged in the bombardment of 1863.[31]

Stephen Elliott plodded homeward from Raleigh, where he had surrendered with Johnston. Wounded at Petersburg in 1864 and again at Bentonville, he had lost the use of an arm, he wrote his cousin William Elliott, as well as his home and profession. The army surgeon predicted that he would eventually regain the use of the arm. The Sea Islands plantations were another matter, though Elliott had every intention of fighting for them. What he did not know, could not guess, was how vindictive the Yankees were likely to be, or what precisely they meant when they talked about "freedom" for former slaves.

"The best terms that I can permit myself to expect are something very far short of a general confiscation of landed property, a plausible keeping of the promise of emancipation in such a way as will not destroy our industrial system and will remove some of the—to them—objectionable features of the affair," he wrote Cousin Will from Sandy Hill, South Carolina.[32]

Bleak as his prospects were, simple survival no longer presented itself as a day-to-day issue. For the first time in four years nobody was shooting at him. Everything else would surely fall into place sooner or later. "We have heard from Savannah that organ playing and selling flowers and rice and eggs are the means by which our relatives there earn a livelihood," Elliott wrote his cousin.[33] He had lived through the Wilderness and the earth-shattering explosion of the Petersburg mine. By contrast, peddling rice and eggs counted as no sort of hardship.

JOSEPH LECONTE'S COURAGE failed him for once. He grew despondent, his daughter Emma wrote in her diary, indifferent even to the stagnation of his scientific career. The occupation, with its authoritarian clique of military satraps and Treasury agents, seemed worse to him than the war itself. He wore the cast-off blue of a Federal soldier who had died in the campus hospital. He supplemented handout rations of beef, bacon, and cornmeal with a tierce* of rice he had pilfered from the Niter Bureau. The Yankee colonel Haughton granted him permission to use a derelict flatboat to ferry corn across the Congaree into Columbia. It was a Micawberish existence, as Emma noted.

---

*A cask, between a barrel and a hogshead in size.

"The tithe he gets therefrom will keep our two families for awhile. It is pretty bad but I do not think I will starve. We have been very low several times but something always turns up at the last moment."[34]

LeConte cleared only two hundred bushels of corn out of the few thousand he landed from the unhandy flatboat. He divided them with his brother John and used some of his own in trade for clothing and shoes. With a thin stream of milk from a pair of pinchbelly cows, he calculated that the LeConte clan and the ten servants still on the lot would survive through August, anyway, when he expected a windfall from the sale of what the Yankees had left of the 1864 cotton and rice crops at Syfax. A small garden would presently yield tomatoes, turnips, and cabbages. Bessie LeConte took in a little cash by selling some of the milk to the Federal garrison.

The Honey Hill veteran Alfred Hartwell came up from Charleston to take command of the occupation forces in the Columbia-Orangeburg region, with headquarters in the capital. He called on the LeContes right away. They had a Harvard acquaintance in common, the mathematician Benjamin Pierce, and anyhow General Hartwell counted on the academical brothers to bring their influence to bear for a timely reopening of South Carolina College. Hartwell offered both families a loan of money to see them through the transitional months. They declined, with Emma's fierce approbation, for she detested Hartwell on sight. "A vile, miserable tyrant," she thought him, and a whoremonger besides—rumor held that he and his staff disported nightly with freedwomen of the town. In fact, Hartwell's manners were impeccable and he was generous in his private dealings with rebels. "Courtesy to all is the part of the soldier," he instructed his officers, and he advised them to keep off politics, race, and other sensitive topics in conversation with local whites.[35]

All the same, Hartwell intended to enforce the Emancipation Proclamation. The LeContes found him a disturbing change from the accommodating Nathaniel Haughton. ("The negroes dislike him," Miss Emma remarked of Haughton, "and say he is no Yankee but half a rebel.")[36] Hartwell admonished the Episcopal rector for omitting the prayer for the president. He arrested former Confederate treasury secretary George Trenholm and sent him north to prison. And he laid down the law in a series of blunt manifestos.

To the citizens of Orangeburg, on May 20:

Those capable of reason and properly informed should know that
the Union is and shall be preserved and that slavery is dead. No
expression of disloyalty will be allowed.

To his own officers, on June 9:

The colored people will not be turned off the places on which they
have lived in any case whatever without orders from these headquarters. Whites [will not] throw off those who have been their
slaves. Where the former owners refuse or neglect to make or offer
fair contracts with the colored people, it will be necessary to use
strict measures.

To the freedmen, also on June 9:

The time has come for you all to do your best to show that you are
fit to be free men in this great Republic. Observe sacredly the marriage tie. Learn to read and write. No one must leave his wife, children or aged parents while he can assist them. Be prudent and quiet
and orderly.[37]

Emma LeConte responded to Hartwell's blizzard of letterpress
with a kind of nervous scorn. "I suppose he thought things were
going on too smoothly under Haughton and he was needed to stir
up a fuss and make the people realize their position," she decided.
The diarist Mary Chesnut seized on Hartwell's strictures on marriage.
"If he succeeds he will do more than the Christian Religion & a
million parsons have done for the white race," Chesnut wrote from
Mulberry plantation near Camden, northeast of Columbia. Grace
Elmore felt simple gratitude that she did not live in Orangeburg,
where the Fifty-fifth Massachusetts Infantry (Colored) comprised the
garrison.[38]

War's end everywhere had forced blacks and whites into revolutionary adjustments of their long, complex, interdependent, and tor-
tured relations. "John C.'s people begged they might go on supporting him as they always had done—simple-hearted peasants," Mary
Chesnut wrote. "He yielded gracefully to their persuasions—but
went back next day & hired them for wages."[39] For every account of
faithful retainers staying on as before, though, there were a dozen of
former slaves taking to the roads. Some went in search of sundered

family. Some sought the protection of a Federal garrison. Many streamed from the interior toward the Low Country in response to rumors that land could be had there—Sherman's "40 acres and a mule."

Mary Chesnut expressed a common planter view, accurate so far as it went. Most blacks at Mulberry doubtless were simple-hearted peasants, but they were canny enough to know that their best chance to prosper lay in keeping close to home. It *was* home—something the old masters failed to acknowledge or even recognize when they waxed over how touchingly eager their former slaves were to continue to serve them.

The governess Emma Holmes fled uncouth Mrs. Mickles and her knucklehead offspring with the Yankee arrival and flew to her mother in Camden. As the servants slipped away one by one she learned to make up her bed, dust the furniture, knead the biscuit dough. "Yesterday I made my first butter, of which I felt rather proud," she recorded in her diary. Her brother Alester set up as a dealer in firewood and livestock, though with scant success at first. Her uncle James Gadsden Holmes swore the loyalty oath so he could draw the Yankee ration of sixteen quarts of rice or grist a week. Uncle Octavius Theodosius Gibbes raised $60 repairing watches and clocks and selling fishing line. Poverty forced Miss Emma to ply the needle. "I've always declared I would never take sewing as my means of livelihood, for it would soon kill me or at least make me feel like committing suicide," she wrote gloomily. But she earned fifty cents' worth of sugar and soap for each mended garment.[40]

Grace Elmore added to her burden of petty care a daily reading of his official labor contract to Jack, the Elmores' man of all work. "Every day he makes some demand and when I decline says, 'But Miss Grace, ain't it in the contract?'" Managing Jack, together with the inconvenience of rising at five o'clock every morning to see to her own breakfast, soon began to wear her down.

"I don't like to live among the pots and kettles," she wrote pettishly. "I hate always being beset with small worries."[41]

Jack left no record of his side of the dispute. He may have adjusted his workload to the pittance wages the Elmores were able to pay. Possibly he wanted a vacation, a few weeks off, the first in his life. With the abolition of slavery in the British Empire in the 1830s, a Parliamentary investigating committee soberly defined the condition of emancipated Jamaicans as *otium cum dignitate*—"idle dignity." This entailed working for a few hours a day, a couple of days a week, as the whim bit. The old masters of the South encountered the condition, and complained bitterly and ceaselessly of the congenital laziness of their former slaves. Northerners were somewhat more understanding.

"He will work, if he is treated like a man," journalist Sidney Andrews wrote of the typical freedman. "He is unquestionably sensitive about his freedom—it is the only thing he has that he can call his own."[42]

The Union authorities were caught between two fires. Attempts to take the part of the emancipated people enraged Southern whites. African Americans resented Federal efforts to force them into labor agreements with their former owners. A report reached Hartwell's headquarters of armed blacks in the Barnwell District tearing up labor contracts and dropping the shredded sheets at his soldiers' feet. Hartwell sent out a detachment to arrest the insurgents, but by the time it arrived they were safely across the Savannah River and in hiding somewhere around Augusta.[43]

Reports from the interior suggested that the manners of slavery times—wanton violence, occasional murder, the old abominations of whipping and punishing—persisted still. "Of course slavery is nearly dead," the Gideonite William Gannett wrote, "but the ruling passion is strong in death." Reaching Orangeburg in late May, Sergeant James Trotter of the Fifty-fifth Massachusetts found the system "in full operation as it had always been." The conflicts and ambiguities of occupation duty deeply discouraged Charley Fox, Trotter's commanding officer. South Carolinians were refusing to behave as Fox had imagined they would: whites were insufficiently submissive, blacks insufficiently grateful. "Peace as we now have it, surrounded by the opinions and influences that here exist, is in many respects a change for the worse," he wrote his wife, Mary. For Trotter, born into slavery, the experience was exhilarating. The ancient edifice was tumbling down, and he had a hand in the demolition.[44]

Tremors of revolution rocked the miniature world of the Fifty-fifth's officers' mess. General Hartwell pushed through commissions for Trotter and another NCO, W. H. Dupree. Colonel Fox swore them in as second lieutenants on July 1, 1865. "Our *best* officers do not manifest any 'Colorophobia,'" Trotter wrote his friend Edward Kinsley in Boston. "I do not know how it will all turn out, but Dupree and I will try to do our duty as officers, let prejudice be as great as it may." Hartwell assigned him to the brigade's Commission on Labor, charged with making certain that planters gave the freed people an equivalent for their toil.

"The former slaveholders wince under this new order of things," Trotter wrote. "It seems to hurt them sorely—having to treat as intelligent free men and women, and draw up a written agreement to compensate for labor done those whom they have tyrannized over with impunity, treating them as so many cattle, but they have to do it."

Still, planters and freedmen alike were beginning to adjust, Trotter thought, perhaps naively. Most former slaves were content and to all appearances working faithfully, he reported; most former masters were submitting with reasonably good grace, or anyhow without overt signs of hostility.

"I have several times been out on the plantations," he wrote Kinsley. "I went 22 miles without any guard save a good Colt revolver, which I had no occasion to call on. The Chivalry all treated me with respect and were very skillful in concealing whatever bitterness they may have felt when seeing a 'nigger' with shoulder straps riding along the road to Columbia visiting their plantations in order to see that they were treating the colored people properly."

The Trotter-Dupree swearing in turned out to be one of Charley Fox's last acts as commanding officer of the Fifty-fifth Massachusetts. He headed home to Dorchester in early July. Fox's Honey Hill nemesis William Nutt succeeded him. Trotter, for one, hailed the change. "He is very popular with the Regt and with everybody whose regard is worth anything," he said of Nutt.[45] Fox shared neither Trotter's admiration for the captious major nor his sunny view of the South's future. A gathering of a thousand country blacks for a regimental religious service just before he left for home had given him fresh occasion for gloom. Fox saw nothing but trouble ahead, the inevitable three-cornered clash of unrepentant rebels, exploitative Yankees, and vulnerable freedmen.

"What is to become of them ground between the two millstones of prejudice and self-interest, God only knows," he wrote Mary. "Singing is going on all around the camp, but I can hardly feel as joyful as those engaged in it."[46]

As the summer advanced, reality lay somewhere between Trotter's rose-tinted enthusiasm and Fox's grim vision. There were street rows between whites and blacks in Charleston and Savannah. In at least one instance white troops refused to mount guard with blacks. Many black enlistees resented the speedy demobilization of veteran regiments while their own units remained in service guarding sullen whites and thankless freedmen.* Though they had only just celebrated their second payday in nearly two years, the men of the Fifty-fifth Massachusetts were fretful, on edge. They wanted to go home.

White Southerners were awakening slowly from the bad dream of defeat. With the approach of laying-by time planters could see that crops would be short this year. Occupation realities were sinking in, too. The unpredictable Yankees might tilt one way today, another tomorrow. Whites appreciated Major Nutt's orders to sweep Orangeburg's streets clear of vagrants and prostitutes and his use of garrison troops to force blacks to observe their labor contracts. At the same time, reports of soldiers' rough treatment of field hands prompted General Hartwell to deny enlisted men authority to inflict corporal punishment. He also barred all but specifically designated officers from approving contracts, for many had been tipped so heavily in the planters' favor that deductions for food, clothing, seed, and other necessities would leave the hands with little or nothing of the gathered crop.

Whites croaked ceaselessly about work arrangements. An Orangeburg planter complained to Hartwell that he could no longer drive his laborers. "He said that he gave them plenty to eat and clothing and a smart person could do the task that he gave them in half a day, and all the remainder of the time they could work for themselves," wrote B. J. Butler, a private in the Fifty-fifth Massachusetts who overheard the exchange.[47] Butler was skeptical. He sought an opportunity for a private word with the freedmen on the place.

"The colored people inform me that the majority of them get four quarts of meal or corn for one week, and that their task is one acre of

---

*Regiments were disbanded by seniority. The Fifty-fifth Massachusetts, mustered into service in July 1863, would not ordinarily have been due for release until mid-1866.

ground to work over in one day," he wrote the *Weekly Anglo-African.* "If some of the soldiers did not give them meat to eat they would not get any, and if they kill a hog they are arrested for stealing. If any of them are sick and send for a doctor, he will say let them die or go to work."[48]

The long, hot summer wore on. Columbia whites shut themselves indoors on the Fourth of July while thousands of blacks spilled into the streets to celebrate with the Federals. The parade passed through the campus of South Carolina College and the Yankee officers gave speeches in front of the main hall. "Such horrid degradation!" Emma LeConte wrote in her diary.[49] She refused to watch the fireworks that night, but she could not stop her ears to the clash of arms, the stamp of feet, and the screech of "Yankee Doodle" at the daily dress parade just beyond the campus wall.

Miss Emma enjoyed a respite from one irritant, anyway. There were no mosquitoes that strange summer. "I wonder if it is because there are no railroads to bring them up from the coast," she mused.[50] Emma read Carlyle's essays and contemplated an assault on the Koran. The question of a dress for Mary Palmer's wedding preoccupied her. Mary had asked her to be a bridesmaid and she wanted to look her best. But there was no money and she had no idea what she would wear.

Such news as reached her father from Liberty County sounded discouraging. Uncle William Jones, looking after the LeConte interests there, wrote that Yankee bagmen had swept through the county, buying up as much cotton as the freed people could steal for five to fifteen cents a pound. "The negroes seem crazy about cotton," Jane Harden reported. "Uncle Wm. had Joe's cotton moved into the rice house at Syfax and had the steps knocked away but the negroes got up on the string pieces and took the greater part."[51] Jones suggested selling off the remainder for whatever price he could get.

Expectations for the 1865 crop were low. "I have been doing all I can to make your negroes work, but it has been rather an uphill business," Jones wrote the LeConte brothers. He had managed to plant only thirty acres of corn and sixty acres of rice at Syfax. Blacks were insubordinate. Whites were fearful. Liberty County remained utterly cut off, cast back into the eighteenth century. Nobody credited reports that the east Georgia railroads were to be rebuilt and running again by autumn.[52]

Miss Emma found a dress for Mary's wedding—white muslin. Aunt Josie dressed her hair for the fete and decorated it with a spray of white roses.

TWO NARROW FLIGHTS OF STAIRS led to the third floor courtroom in the U.S. Arsenal complex on the Potomac south of the Capitol. Looking in from the entrance, the Military Commission sat on the right side of the 40-foot-long room at a rectangular table covered with green baize: David Hunter, the president, at the head; Lew Wallace, August Kautz, and the other members according to rank along the sides; Joseph Holt and the prosecution team at the foot opposite Hunter.

The seven men accused of conspiring to murder Abraham Lincoln were seated behind a wooden railing upon a raised platform facing General Hunter. Though their hoods had been removed after the first day, a brief session on May 9, the prisoners were manacled hand and foot. A heavy iron door opened behind them into a corridor that led to the cells of the Old Penitentiary. Witnesses addressed the court from a box in the center of the room. The walls were freshly whitewashed, all the woodwork newly painted white. The high spring sun streamed in through four tall, barred windows.

The eighth conspirator, Mary Surratt, widow, sat apart from the others, near the reporters' table. She wore deep black. A dispatch in the *New York Times* described her, flippantly, as approaching "Falstaff's ideal, fair, fat and forty." (She was forty-two.) Her ankle irons clanked as she entered the room. Quiet, still, passive, Mrs. Surratt kept her face turned to the wall throughout the trial. "She came into the court always wearing a heavy veil, which she raised only once for identification," General Wallace remembered. That, presumably, was when another observer noticed her "feline gray eyes."[53]

Nearest to Mrs. Surratt sat conspirator Davy Herold, small and dark, with a stooped figure, long black hair, and bad teeth. Lewis Paine, Seward's assailant, yellow-haired, six-and-a-half feet tall, "looked like a young giant above all the others," the journalist Noah Brooks thought. Holt entered into the evidence the heavy, horn-handled knife with which Paine had slashed the secretary of state. George Atzerodt, sinewy and sallow, struck Brooks as "the completest personification of a low and cunning scoundrel." He found black-

Lewis Paine, Secretary of State William Seward's assailant, shown here in a Lew Wallace courtroom sketch. Paine displayed no remorse during the trial or afterward, when he, George Atzerodt, David Herold, and Mary Surratt were led to the scaffold. (Indiana Historical Society)

bearded Michael O'Laughlin more sinister still: "A California vigilance committee in 1849 probably would have hanged him 'on general principles.'" Edward Spangler, the stage carpenter, was heavily built and slovenly. Samuel Mudd, red-faced, in shirtsleeves with a white handkerchief knotted about his neck, gave off a self-assured, confident air. Samuel Arnold, the last in the row, looking "as uneasy as a caged whelp," in Brooks's phrase, stared distractedly out one of the grated windows toward the green treetops and a strip of blue sky.[54]

The accused were arraigned on May 10—John Wilkes Booth's birth date, so it happened, and the date, too, of the presidential proclamation that declared the rebellion "virtually at an end." They all entered pleas of not guilty. From the start, challenges were raised about the legality of trying the conspirators by court-martial now the fighting had ceased. At best it lay on "the very extreme verge of the law," John Gray thought, and it seemed plain to him even from distant South Carolina that this court had been organized to convict. His lawyer friend John Ropes concurred.

"Had the prisoners been tried before a respectable Court Martial I might have judged the Government more leniently," he wrote Gray from Boston. "But to try them before Hunter and those other weak and prejudiced men is monstrous."[55]

True, it was anything but an all-star cast. Hunter, an unreliable field commander, spent most of the last phase of the war sitting on one court-martial or another. Like Hunter, Kautz was an old army veteran with experience of military justice only. Thomas M. Harris had practiced medicine before the war; he was something of a military nonentity. An argument could be made for Wallace's theoretical fitness as a jurist. He had, after all, been bred to the law and practiced it for some years. But Mexico entranced him and he did not always give his full attention to the case.

The daydream distracted Wallace from the drone of the prosecution team leading government witnesses to describe conspiracies and lurid side plots: secret ciphers and keys, the burning of steamboats, Booth's speculations in Pennsylvania oil, commissions for rebel raiders, Jacob Thompson's bank account, the City Point explosion, and the starvation and torture of Union prisoners at Belle Isle and Andersonville prisons.

He heard from Kirby Smith finally—regrets they had not managed to meet, a disclaimer that he lacked authority to negotiate the surrender of his thirty-six thousand troops in the Trans-Mississippi, but still hoped to find an honorable way out. (The war's last major clash occurred in Kirby Smithdom on May 12, at Palmito Ranch on the Rio Grande near Brownsville, when a Union brigade pushed inland from Brazos Santiago and attacked a small rebel force encamped there.) Wallace advised Grant that he suspected Kirby Smith of being in secret league with Maximilian. If he could hold out for another few weeks, Wallace warned, Imperial Mexico would move to annex Confederate Texas.[56]

A week into the trial, Wallace passed along news of General Sheridan's departure for the Gulf to General José Carvajal, Benito Juárez's arms agent in the United States. "I infer from that that he will command the invading columns of our army in Texas," he wrote. Wallace urged Carvajal to raise money for a supply depot at Point Isabel and advance posts along the Rio Grande, so Mexican Republican forces could join Sheridan's triumphal advance. As soon as he could, Wallace himself would come down to take command.[57]

"Now is the time for action," he went on. "Give me the means and I will return Matamoros to Juárez in three weeks after Brownsville is in our possession and after that the reduction of the frontier east of the Sierra Madre inevitably follows."[58]

The capture of Jefferson Davis in flight toward Kirby Smithdom removed one variable from Wallace's Texas-Mexico equation. (It also threatened to complicate his schedule. "I expect he will be put on the Jeff Davis court—if Jeff is brought before one," his wife Susan would remark.)[59] President Johnson had charged Davis in a May 2 proclamation with engineering the Lincoln assassination. A War Department circular offered a $100,000 reward in gold for his arrest. Two of James Wilson's cavalry regiments claimed the prize. Federal mounted detachments seized Davis and his entourage near Irwinville, Georgia, on May 10, a few hours before the conspirators were led into the Arsenal courtroom to hear the charges against them.

A fugitive since the evacuation of Richmond, Davis had been reunited with his refugee family on May 7 near Dublin, Georgia. The party—the Davises, ex-postmaster Reagan, equerries, servants, and teamsters—halted late in the afternoon of the ninth for a short rest in a pine brake north of Irwinville. Davis planned to separate again from Varina and the children and push on through the night. But he slept as though drugged, waking only with the outbreak of carbine fire just before dawn. The Yankee cavalry, the Fourth Michigan and the First Wisconsin, had opened on each other in the darkness, leaving two troopers dead and five wounded.

Davis reached for his wife's raincoat, mistaking it for his own in the gloom. Varina draped a shawl over his shoulders. As he emerged from the tent a Union trooper approached on horseback, staring along the barrel of his gun. The Confederate president gave himself up in the cool twilight of the Georgia dawn. He was taken to General Wilson's headquarters in Macon seventy-five miles to the north, then on to Augusta, where the Federals added his estranged vice president, Alexander Stephens, to the captive party.* After the downriver run to Savannah and the sea leg to Hilton Head, Davis and the others were led aboard the steamer *William P. Clyde*, bound for Fortress Monroe.

Wilson broadcast the story of Davis's flight in women's clothes—embellished it, for the Federal cavalry commander clothed the fugitive in one of Varina's hoopskirts. "He Puts on His Wife's Petticoats and Tries to Sneak into the Woods," a headline in the *New York Times* alleged. Garbled versions of the arrest traveled at the speed of ridicule.[60]

"The great head & President of the proud southern Confederacy was caught one morning with his wife's dress on, pail on his arm, going for a bucket of water, & is now on his way to Washington (perhaps to the gallows)," Willard Saxton had heard in Yankee Beaufort.[61]

The low comedy denouement may actually have worked in Davis's favor. Feeling against him ran high in the wake of Andrew Johnson's accusation. Now Northerners could view him more as a figure of derision than a murderous villain. All the same, Stanton ordered him securely held at Fortress Monroe, in fetters if necessary; the prisoner would be given no opportunity to cheat a potential Lew Wallace military court.

Already, though, doubts were building about a grand conspiracy with Davis at the head. The War Department agent Charles Dana interviewed scores of suspects caught in Stanton's dragnet. "In most cases neither the examinations nor arrests led to anything," he conceded later. "The persons had been acquaintances of the known conspirators, or they had been heard to utter disloyal statements and had been reported to the department by zealous Unionists." John Gray found theories of a rebel government conspiracy contemptible. "How ridiculous to put in the evidence of a blind beggar who has heard Confederate officers talk about killing 'Old Abe,'" he remarked. Even so, Stanton wanted Davis brought to trial.[62]

Endless afternoon succeeded drowsy morning in the hot, airless Arsenal courtroom. The Hunter commission sat from ten o'clock until

---

*Union authorities arrested Stephens at his home near Crawfordsville, Georgia, on May 11.

one, recessed for lunch, and returned at two for the afternoon session. Prosecutor Holt called a series of witnesses in an attempt to show that senior Confederates had directed the assassination plot. Holt's star witness, an agent provocateur named Sanford Conover, served up hair-raising details of rebel plots to fall on Chicago, free thousands of Confederate prisoners, and touch off an uprising there; to introduce plague into the loyal states by means of infected clothing; and to poison the water supply of New York City.

Conover testified that he had infiltrated a group of rebel agents planning the assassination in Montreal with the knowledge and approval of the Richmond government. Lincoln, Johnson, Stanton, Seward, Chief Justice Chase, and Grant were all to be killed. Conover claimed that John Surratt arrived in Montreal from Richmond on April 6 or 7 with dispatches for Jacob Thompson, a Confederate envoy in Canada. One was from Judah Benjamin, the Confederate secretary of state; the other, in cipher, from Jefferson Davis himself. Conover said he watched Thompson read through the papers in his room at the Saint Lawrence Hotel.

"Thompson laid his hand on [the dispatches] and said, 'This makes the thing all right,' referring to the assent of the rebel authorities," Conover told the court.[63]

William Browning, Andrew Johnson's private secretary, testified that someone left a card in Johnson's box at Kirkwood House on April 14. "Don't wish to disturb you," it read over the signature of J. Wilkes Booth. "Are you at home?" Barkeep Peter Taltavul said under oath that Booth came into his place next to Ford's Theater around ten o'clock that night, ordered a whiskey, asked for water, drank both off, left a dollar on the bar, and walked out alone. Ten minutes later Taltavul heard a voice cry out that the president had been shot.[64]

Other witnesses established Booth as the gunman and described his flight from Ford's. Sergeant Silas T. Cobb, on guard duty at the Navy Yard Bridge over the Anacostia River, testified that a man approached rapidly on horseback between 10:30 and 11:00 and that he halted when one of the sentries challenged him.

"I asked him, 'Who are you, sir,'" Cobb said.

"'My name is Booth.'"

"I thought he was a proper man to pass, and I passed him," Cobb told the court.[65]

Booth's role was never in doubt. Besides, he was dead. Holt had to work hard to link some of the others to the murder, especially pale, matronly, nearsighted Mary Surratt. It was a sad and shabby sort of conspiracy. "There does not seem to be anyone connected with it but second-rate actors, quack doctors and such people," John Gray decided.[66] Wallace took in the testimony, made notes, conferred with the others on the court, put in an occasional question. But his mind, his emotions, were engaged elsewhere.

"Texas is in a fearful state of anarchy—Walker's division has disbanded & bands of the men are plundering indiscriminately," one of his agents there wrote him. "A large party is reported en route to Mexico—some say to join the Empire, but Col. Ford thinks the instinct of race will eventually put them all on our side in case of a war with the Empire."[67]

Wallace chafed at his confinement in the courtroom, but there were scores of witnesses yet to hear. To compound his anxiety, his business affairs had gone awry all of a sudden: questionable investments, bad guesses, poor management on the part of his associate Aaron Blair.

"By this time, my dear, you have read Aaron's letter and know we are not as well off even as those who have nothing," he wrote Susan. "What do you think of it? Have you enough philosophy to make light of poverty?"[68]

John M. Lloyd and Louis J. Weichmann gave the most damaging testimony in Mary Surratt's prosecution. Both men had been held briefly as suspects; both turned state's evidence. Lloyd kept the Surratt family's tavern in Prince George's County ten miles from Washington. Five or six weeks before the killing, he testified, John Surratt, Herold, and Atzerodt delivered two carbines, ammunition, a length of rope, and a monkey wrench to the tavern. Mrs. Surratt turned up on the Tuesday before the assassination with instructions about the "shooting-irons."

"She told me to get them ready; that they would be wanted soon," Lloyd told the court.[69]

Weichmann drove Mrs. Surratt out to the tavern on the afternoon of April 14. She repeated the order about the carbines, Lloyd said, gave him a pair of field glasses to store with the weapons, and asked him to set aside two bottles of whiskey for later use. Booth and

Herold turned up late that night or early on the fifteenth, he went on, to collect the weapons, gear, and liquor.

Weichmann, a War Department clerk and a boarder at Mrs. Surratt's on H Street, testified that Booth, Lewis Paine, and Atzerodt called frequently at the house, that Booth, Mrs. Surratt, and John Surratt met privately there on occasion, and that Booth dropped in for a short visit on April 14.

Conspirator Paine had presented himself at Mrs. Surratt's in the character of a Baptist clergyman named Wood. It struck Weichmann as droll that a Baptist should board with Mrs. Surratt, an observant Roman Catholic. Then, too, the hard-looking, rough-spoken Paine seemed miscast for a parson's part, even if, as alleged, his father sustained the role at home in Florida. "Mrs. Surratt herself remarked that he was a great looking Baptist preacher," Weichmann told the court. (The accused suppressed a smile at this aside.) Paine once left a medium-sized false moustache, black, on a table at Mary Surratt's. "When I found it I thought it rather queer that a Baptist preacher should use a moustache; I thought no honest person had any reason to wear one," Weichmann said primly. He pocketed the moustache and carried it to his War Department office, where he amused his fellow clerks by trying it on, together with a pair of spectacles.[70]

The Lloyd and Weichmann testimony together made a fairly persuasive circumstantial case against Mrs. Surratt, if they were telling the truth: mysterious dealings with weapons, shady people haunting the H Street house, whispered conversations about subjects unknown. Yet Holt presented no evidence that she had known of Booth's resolve to abandon the abduction plot and attack the president and other leaders instead.

Mrs. Surratt's lawyer, Senator Reverdy Johnson, a Maryland Democrat, led Weichmann on cross-examination to attest to her exemplary character and ladylike demeanor. Weichmann volunteered that she made her religious duty regularly, at least once every two weeks during the five months he had boarded with her. Other witnesses portrayed her as kindly, thoughtful, and so poor-sighted that she could not run a length of thread through a needle's eye, read by candlelight, or recognize an acquaintance passing close in the street.

Mrs. Surratt told Stanton's investigators that she went out to the tavern on the fourteenth on business, to collect money owed her for a land sale. Defense witnesses corroborated this. They testified, too, that they had never heard her express disloyal sentiments or talk of kidnapping, much less killing, the president. True, her daughter Anna kept photographs of Davis, Stephens, Beauregard, and Stonewall Jackson—but she displayed likenesses of Union celebrities, too—McClellan, Hooker, Grant.

As for Lloyd, several witnesses suggested that he had implicated Mary Surratt out of fear for his own neck. "He cried bitterly," testified the detective who came to the Surratt tavern to arrest him, "and hallooed for his prayer book." Besides, according to half a dozen defense witnesses, Lloyd's powers of observation were seriously impaired that day. "He was pretty tight," admitted the tavern tap, Joseph Nott, who had served him off and on all day long.[71]

Questions arose about the adequacy of Mrs. Surratt's representation. Senator Johnson, a leading constitutional lawyer, filed an able brief challenging the military court's jurisdiction. But that was as far as he got. General Harris questioned whether Johnson regarded the loyalty oath required of defense counsel as binding. Johnson answered the insinuation with an angry lecture on loyalty and individual liberty. He also volunteered to swear the oath again. David Hunter took Harris's part. "I hoped the day had passed when freemen from the North were to be bullied and insulted by the humbug chivalry of the South," he spat out.[72] Wallace tried to calm all parties with a proposal to waive the oath, but by then the damage had been done. Johnson left the court in high dudgeon that afternoon and never returned, handing over Mary Surratt's defense to two junior associates.

The case against the Marylander Samuel Mudd sounded less convincing even than the one against Mrs. Surratt. According to the officer who had interrogated him, Dr. Mudd responded to a rap on his door at four o'clock in the morning of April 15 to find two strangers in his yard, one holding two horses, the other on horseback. The mounted man wore heavy whiskers, called himself Tyler, and sought treatment for a broken leg. Mudd said he learned only later that the strangers were Booth and Herold. He had met Booth but once, he testified, the previous November when Booth purchased a horse in his Charles County neighborhood. He had not recognized Booth behind his whiskers, nor did the photo the officer showed him look at all like the shaggy caller with the swollen leg. Only on later reflection did Mudd identify the stranger as the man he had known in Bryantown six months before. He had never met Herold at all.

The prosecution called several of Mudd's former slaves to testify about his political views. He fed and sheltered Confederate soldiers. He threatened to send insubordinate slaves to Richmond to work on rebel fortifications. He knew John Surratt well—Surratt visited Mudd's farm a dozen or more times in 1864 and 1865. He spoke out against the government with mounting violence after the Emancipation Proclamation.

"Last year, about tobacco planting time, I heard Ben Gardiner tell Dr. Samuel Mudd in Beantown, that Abe Lincoln was a God-damned old son of a bitch, and ought to have been dead long ago; and Dr. Mudd said that was much of his mind," former slave Milo Simms, fourteen years old, told the court.[73]

Louis Weichmann returned to the stand to testify that in December or January last he had been present when Mudd introduced Booth to John Surratt. Mudd denied that, swore he had not even been in Washington then. Though Weichmann could not recall the date of the meeting, he stuck to his story—which, if true, would place Mudd near the heart of the conspiracy.

William Evans, a post office clerk and part-time minister, testified that he had passed Mudd riding toward Washington on a lathered horse about March 3 last, the day before Lincoln's second inaugural. Earlier in the winter (he could not say precisely when), he had observed Mudd going into Mrs. Surratt's boardinghouse. Evans was a chatty, discursive witness. Holt must have cringed at some of his testimony. Thomas Ewing Jr.,* representing Mudd, came to his feet after a while to interrupt Evans's flow of otiose detail.

"We do not want your personal history," Ewing advised.

"You seem to be so precise, I want to give you everything connected with it," Evans answered.

"We are not so precise as to your personal history."

"A little of it will not do you any harm."

"I do not think it will do any good in this case."

---

*An Ohio-born lawyer, and William T. Sherman's brother-in-law.

"We are all free and equal men," Evans reminded him, "and can talk as we please."

The court finally quieted Evans, but not before he offered a startling explanation for the exactitude of his account of Samuel Mudd's movements.

"I hold a secret commission under the Government to arrest deserters and disloyalists wherever I find them," he revealed. "I am a detective."[74]

A more levelheaded prosecution witness, a Troy, New York, lawyer named Marcus Norton, produced testimony with far greater potential for damage to the accused. Dr. Mudd—"It was either he or a man exactly like him," said Norton, glancing up toward the dock— had burst into his room at the National Hotel on March 3. He seemed agitated and in a hurry, and said he was looking for John Wilkes Booth. Norton directed him to the floor above.[75]

More testimony: Mudd in Washington in December 1864, his whereabouts from March 1 through 5. "The everlasting commission is just out," Wallace wrote his wife after one interminable session. "I feel like a boy out of school."[76] Still more: news of the assassination reaching Bryantown the afternoon of April 15, Mudd hearing it then; the case of Michael O'Laughlin; the case of Samuel Arnold.

The trial began to wind down during the last week of June. Wallace duly noted that 361 witnesses had generated 4,300 pages of testimony, "making a solid pile of MS somewhat over 26 inches high." Restless, impatient, Mexico-obsessed, he assured himself that the ordeal couldn't possibly last beyond another few days. He also hazarded a prediction of the outcome.

"I have passed a few words with my associate members, and think we can agree in a couple of hours at farthest," he wrote Susan on June 26. "Three, if not four, of the eight will be acquitted—that is, they would be if we voted today."[77]

JOURNALIST WHITELAW REID found the Sea Island colonies well established when he passed through with Chief Justice Chase's inspection party in the spring of 1865. Rufus Saxton had settled ten thousand mainland refugees on Edisto by the end of May, pushing the working, landholding freed population of the islands well above thirty thousand. If not flourishing, the Gullahs and the newcomers alike were mostly better off than before, and they were largely self-sufficient, too. "They have erected their own cabins," Reid noted, "secured whatever cheap furniture they contain, and clothed themselves far better than their masters ever clothed them." Saxton, he discovered, stood "in the light of a patron saint" to the islanders, who sang a new version of a venerable spiritual in praise of him:[78]

Gen-e-ul Sa-a-axby a sittin' on de tree ob life,
Roll, Jordan, roll,
Gen-e-ul Sa-a-axby a sittin' on de tree ob life,
Roll, Jordan, roll,
Gen-e-ul Sa-a-axby a sittin' on de tree ob life,
Roll, Jordan, roll,
Roll, Jordan, roll,
Ro-o-oll, Jordan, ro-o-oll![79]

Saxton left no doubt about his policy when he spoke at a mass meeting of blacks at the Zion Church in Charleston in mid-May. "I wish every colored man, every head of family, to acquire a freehold, a little home he can call his own," he told the crowd. Much remained to be done. After three years of Yankee volunteer effort, Reid estimated that barely one black in every twenty on Saint Helena could read and write. As many as twelve thousand refugees remained unprovided for, and subsisted precariously on occasional earnings and such government rations as were available. Northern merchants scandalously cheated the emancipated people out of what little they possessed—though, as Reid observed, the army regulated the swindle now and "in most cases, they do not now probably pay over two prices for what they buy."[80]

Merchants, traders, boosters, speculators, sharps: by whatever name, Northerners viewed the South Carolina Sea Islands as ripe for exploitation. As a deepwater harbor, Port Royal outclassed Charleston or Savannah. Island soil still produced the world's best cotton—and would turn out a lot more of it now with voluntary labor. Gullahs with mules, seed, and tools to buy, cabins and byres to keep up, children to feed, clothe, and educate, would stimulate such a trade as the Low Country had never known before.

"It is very clear that you can treble and quadruple and quintuple your money here in two or three years—if you don't lose it all by investing in the wrong place," Reid told his Northern audience.[81]

An African American regiment on dress parade in Beaufort. The regimental
sergeant major, a commanding presence, stands just off to the right of the first line.
Along with drill, officers such as Colonel Charles Howard supervised literacy and
citizenship classes for enlistees. "I have to teach them how to stand erect and call
no man master," Howard wrote, "and at the same time . . . obey [military] rules
and laws." Later in 1865 he urged his brother, Freedmen's Bureau commissioner
Oliver Otis Howard, to authorize his troops to enforce bureau orders that rebellious
whites routinely flouted. (Library of Congress)

Charles Howard, the newly appointed colonel of the 128th U.S.
Colored Troops, busied himself with regimental duties, supervising
literacy classes for his soldiers. In his off-hours, he pursued a promising courtship of Elizabeth Botume's niece, Fanny Langton. She
helped out at the school near Beaufort and Howard, in the teaching
line himself now and a friend of Lizzie's in any case, needed no
excuse to call. Miss Lizzie would invite him to take the nooning with
them, or sometimes tea in the shade of a thick stand of blooming ole-
ander. The pomegranates were in flower, too, a vivid scarlet, Charles
wrote home, charmed and already half in love.[82]

The end of the war had taken Howard emotionally unawares.
The world had moved along while he was frozen in a state of wartime
suspension. "I am growing old I think rapidly," he wrote his brother

Rowland. "Wish I might not lose my youthful glow of feelings but think I am fast doing so." Then, almost before it began, the affair with Fanny Langton lapsed, mostly on account of his own irresolution. ("He don't know his own heart yet," Willard Saxton thought.) General Saxton was lobbying hard for four Low Country black regiments, including the 128th USCT, to be taken into the Regular Army as a brigade, with himself in command. Charles awaited the outcome of Saxton's intriguing with indifference.

"If [the 128th] is mustered out I will consider it an indication of Providence that I am not to be a soldier," he wrote his mother.[83]

Teaching turned out to be harder work than Howard had anticipated. Letters and numbers were one thing—a question of patience and application. After all, his adolescent niece in Leeds had taught the Georgia refugee Wash Kemp to read and write. But how could a man who had never been a citizen or a soldier learn virtually overnight to be both? The lessons were contradictory, too. "I have to teach them how to stand erect and call no man master and at the same time obey wholesome rules and laws, and [I have to] regulate all their habits," Howard explained. War's end made the task more urgent. Chief Justice Chase himself, meeting with senior officers and Gideonites in Beaufort, explained that he favored extending the vote to former slaves right away. If nothing else, that would give whites an interest in supporting schooling for the freed people.[84]

Laura Towne and Ellen Murray continued to turn out citizens at a slow, steady rate on Saint Helena Island. Towne's classes read through a history of the United States. Murray's advanced to writing compositions. The scholars recited the Declaration of Independence, sang patriotic songs, and delivered speeches at the Brick Church on the Fourth of July, all of it washed down with water sweetened with molasses.

Those were the best of times, for the coming of peace had not meant the end of hardship, even in the protected reserve of General Saxby's domain. Crops wilted under the relentless sun; hardly a drop of rain fell in June and temperatures climbed into the nineties every day. The outlines of renewed racial conflict were beginning to appear. The Northern volunteers were tiring of their task, much subject, with the collapse of the rebellion, to a condition known among them as the "plantation bitters"—a draught, as one Gideonite defined it, "in the shape of complaints, faithlessness, and general rascality on the part of the 'poor negroes.'"[85] And the old masters were returning. Their mere presence set off alarms throughout the islands

Stephen Elliott reached the Sea Islands two months after Appomattox, his arm still useless, his Beaufort town house and outlying plantations divided among his former slaves. The warmth of their greeting caught him by surprise. So did the resolve behind the warmth.

"They were delighted to see me, and treated me with overflowing affection," Elliott wrote. "They waited on me as before, gave me beautiful breakfasts and splendid dinners but they firmly and respectfully informed me: 'We own this land now. Put it out of your head that it will ever be yours again.'"[86]

The Manigaults' former slaves met them with equal firmness, if less regard. "I flatter myself that I know *The Negro Thoroughly*, for I have owned 200 of them and am well aware of the kind treatment so generally bestowed on them," old Charles Manigault wrote. Yet here was his former driver Frederick playing the master at Marshlands. He had apportioned sections of the plantation to fourteen freedmen to work on shares with him. Frederick managed the enterprise in return for 50 percent of the crop.

"I walked into the fields to view these Negroes who though not belonging to the place were working *on my land*, apparently in full confidence that Frederick owned *everything* there," Manigault wrote. "Several of my Negroes complained to the Provost Marshal that I wanted to turn them off. But he told them to go back & stay there as I had no right to move them."[87]

The patriarch had greater success with Union officers in Charleston. He appealed to General Saxton to evict soldiers quartered in his widowed cousin's house on Meeting Street. Saxton obliged. General Hatch called him to his King Street headquarters to discuss a question of stolen property. The summons alarmed Manigault. "I feared someone had been telling lies about me," he wrote. But Hatch only wanted to return a gold watch, engraved with the Manigault name, that his provost troops had taken off some light-fingered soldier.[88]

Louis Manigault still knew nothing, good or ill, of Gowrie's fate. "I shall reclaim my possessions," he decided, "if not prevented from doing so by the Federal authorities."[89] He applied to take the loyalty oath and swore it on June 19. A letter arrived two days later from his last overseer at Gowrie, J. W. Bandy. He hadn't actually been to Argyle Island since December last. But before he fled he had watched Sherman's troops set fire to the house, the servants' house, the barn, and the rice mill. The main buildings were in ruins, the rice lands abandoned.

"The Negroes before I left cut the Canal bank at the red trunk to make their escape," Bandy wrote him. "The boy Simon and his Wife (Polly) is living somewhere on the plantation and as soon as I can see him I will ascertain the condition of the place and inform you."[90]

The dikes were pierced, the trunks damaged, the rice swamps weed-choked and black with rotting lilies. Sherman had stolen the 1864 harvest and there would be no crop this year. When winter came and the people were cold and hungry Louis might return to Gowrie, negotiate labor contracts, and prepare for 1866. Until then he, Fannie, and the children would have to move in with the bewildered old man in Gibbes Street.

# 8

# Crime, Punishment, Absolution

"WE ARE DAILY EXPECTING SOME ANNOUNCEMENT of conditions on which we can take the oath," prisoner Ewell wrote his wife from Fort Warren. The spirits of the Confederates still detained there seven weeks after Appomattox—ranking officers, blockade runners, the state prisoners Alexander Stephens and John H. Reagan—rose and fell with the regularity of the Boston harbor tides. They searched the newspapers for omens and clues. Would the government let them go eventually, or try them for treason?

"One who is habitually persuaded of the certainty of the more dire event said the other day that there was nothing left but to 'die gracefully,'" Ewell went on. "It is curious to see how the same prognostic of some ignorant penny-a-liner will be interpreted by one man as altogether favorable, another as shutting out all hope."[1]

Ewell felt a little better for substituting tea for coffee and for his daily hobble along the ramparts. A gift of cornstarch, rice, raisins, and anchovy sauce arrived from his sister in Baltimore. His stepson Campbell Brown, now quartered with him, managed to acquire a catalog of the Boston publisher Little, Brown, so he had plenty to read. Everyone, generals and lackeys, helped prepare the meals. "I have large undeveloped talents for cooking and expect to astonish the mess," Campbell wrote his sister Hattie when his turn came around.[2] There were no proper stoves, though, only grates. They kept a coal fire going all the time against the granite chill.

President Johnson ended some of the uncertainty, political and personal, with his amnesty proclamation of May 29, 1865. It promised pardon for Southerners and restoration of property rights except in slaves. Most ex-Confederates could present themselves at the nearest Federal post and swear the oath. But more than a dozen classes of rebels were excluded: those with taxable property worth $20,000; senior civil or diplomatic officers; officers above the rank of colonel in the army and lieutenant in the navy; West Point graduates; politicians who quit the U.S. Congress to join the rebellion; anyone accused of abusing Union prisoners of war. Such cases required direct application to the president, and each would be decided on its merits. Altogether, upwards of 165,000 former Confederates were excepted.[3]

Robert E. Lee led the list of senior Confederates petitioning for pardons. His appeal of June 13 contained a telegraphic account of his military career:

> I graduated at the Mil. Academy at W. Point in June 1829. Resigned from the U.S. Army April '61. Was a General in the Confederate Army & included in the surrender of the Army of N. Va: 9 April '65.[4]

The process was relatively simple, as Lee's application suggests. Johnson saw it as a means of forcing ex-rebels to express *remorse* for their actions, a fitting punishment in his view. "I intended that they should sue for pardon," he said later, "and so realize the enormity of their crime." The pardon may have been a form of penalty, but it had practical advantages, too. It restored a man's political and property rights, and made him immune from prosecution for treason.[5]

News of the proclamation cheered the prisoners at Fort Warren. "I see many signs in the policy of Prest. Johnson to make me hopeful," Campbell Brown wrote Hattie. "Prudence, temperance and firmness now will make him the greatest man in history since Washington." History would judge that; meantime, Ewell sent off his pardon application. Lizinka drafted a new plea of her own. "Two months ago I appealed confidently to the memories of former friendship," she wrote the president, "but as the appeal resulted in my own arrest I presumed I was considered presumptuous." Lizinka remained under house arrest in Saint Louis—charged, she learned after weeks of uncertainty, with demanding rent from black squatters on her Nashville town lots. (The Freedmen's Bureau had seized the lots, along with her plantation lands, as abandoned property.) She evidently had misgivings, though, and held on to the letter. "Remember," the general had cautioned her, "I am completely in the dark. I don't want to work at cross-purposes with you." She could, however, turn to Montgomery Blair, of the Missouri Blairs, a longtime Johnson political ally. He promised to keep the case before the president.[6]

For now, freedom seemed beyond Ewell's reach. Perhaps out of spite, Johnson ignored his application and blocked his release. "General Ewell cannot be paroled or permitted to take the Oath of Amnesty at present," he wrote Edwin Stanton on June 4, though he gave no reason for continuing to hold him.[7]

Ewell counseled patience. "I have everything here—don't expect to be hung for treason—it is pleasant weather—magnificent prospect and no care—but I would be happier out," he wrote Lizinka.[8] The authorities freed thirty lower-ranking Confederates on June 10, but the generals remained, Ewell, William Cabell, John Marmaduke, Dudley DuBose, Henry R. Jackson, along with some of their aides (among them Campbell Brown) and, of course, Stephens and Reagan, kept in solitary confinement in the cold fug of the bare, dungeonlike rooms under Fort Warren's western bastion.

Ewell discovered two sound reasons for letting events run their course. June came in on a Thursday in 1865, and Thursdays were notoriously unlucky for the superstitious general. (He had lost his leg on a Thursday; he had fought Sayler's Creek on a Thursday.) He suspected, too, that if the terms of his parole restricted him to Virginia, as seemed likely, he could be rearrested there and brought to trial for the burning of Richmond.

So he exercised on the ramparts, drank in the sea air, and tended geraniums with Campbell. Ewell had discarded his old, ill-fitting wooden leg; or possibly it had gone the way of his stepson's prayer book, a souvenir for one of Sheridan's troopers. Frail Aleck Stephens, his ninety-four pounds swathed against the onshore breeze, caught sight of him from a distance one evening, lurching along the parapet. Stephens asked his officer-escort why Ewell hadn't ordered a new one.

"Ewell said he was waiting before getting an artificial leg to see if the authorities were going to hang him," Stephens learned. "If he was going to be hung, he did not care to go into the expense;

intended to wait and make out on his crutches until the matter was decided. General Ewell has a sense of humor."[9]

Ewell and Brown followed different strategies of geranium culture. Ewell watered every day and shifted the pots back and forth from sun to shade; his stepson relied solely upon the dews and showers and the open sky, bright or overcast. Possibly it was the geraniums that suggested a postwar vocation to Brown. Possibly it was Blair's advice. "It is far better for any man of sense and courage to take part in the new world opening up here than to loiter his life away in Europe, or throw it away in Mexico or Brazil," he offered. For whatever reason, Brown abandoned the notion of exile and decided, whenever he should be free, to forget the war, return to Tennessee, and rebuild his mother's estate at Spring Hill.

"I have got a definite object in view, and with all the conceit of an untried man am imagining that to be all I need to insure success," he wrote her. "That object is to restore and increase the prosperity of the neighborhood where I settle, as far as it in me lies."[10]

With the Fort Warren adjutant as witness, Ewell signed the loyalty oath on June 16. Four days later, on cue from Andrew Johnson, Stanton lifted most of the restrictions on Lizinka, freeing her to travel anywhere but Tennessee. She left Saint Louis for Washington at once. Reaching the capital by the twenty-fifth, she called on Johnson's daughter, Martha Patterson, and arranged to meet with the president himself two days hence.

Ushered into the White House private quarters, Lizinka found Johnson in bed with what she diagnosed as a hangover. Martha sat by his side. Lizinka raised the subject of her husband right away. It failed as a conversational gambit. "Couldn't you find anybody better to marry than a one-legged man?" the president remarked sourly.[11] He motioned for a comb lying on a table just out of his reach. Lizinka hesitated, then handed it to him. The president absently ran the comb through his sleek hair. After a pause, he gave her to understand that he would sign her pardon and Campbell Brown's, but not Ewell's. Lizinka charged this to Mrs. Johnson, whom she suspected of holding a grudge over some insult, real or fancied, going back to prewar days in Nashville. Johnson did say that all the generals would be let go in due course, and that there would be no treason trials except for one—that of Jefferson Davis. Then he invited her to stay for lunch.

With this slight encouragement, Lizinka resolved to return and try again. "I have much less trouble than you suppose in attaining an audience," she wrote Ewell. "The difficulty is to accomplish anything by it." Lizinka went shopping for a canary bird and shipped it to Boston, thinking it might amuse the prisoners. She and Hattie followed the canary to New England a few days later, prepared to storm the gates of Fort Warren if necessary. Meantime, Johnson had relaxed so far as to hint that Ewell and Brown would go free soon. "If you will visit Washington tomorrow or Monday I will err if some arrangement cannot be made," he wrote her. But Lizinka had left the capital by then. The message only caught up to her in Wakefield, Rhode Island, where she paused for a brief holiday en route to Boston.[12]

The presidential tip was premature. The more important prisoners at Fort Warren—the generals, Stephens, and Reagan—were to be held awhile yet. Jefferson Davis remained mewed up under heavy guard in Fortress Monroe. At the Old Penitentiary in Washington, the Lincoln conspirators anticipated the verdict of the military court.

Lew Wallace, the commission's second-ranking member, had forecast acquittal for three or four of the accused, but that was before he heard the powerful closing argument of John Bingham, an Ohio congressman moonlighting as one of Holt's associate prosecutors. Bingham's fire and eloquence on June 28 and 29 evidently recalled the doubters to their duty.

Bingham dismissed the evidence of a kidnap conspiracy, arguing that all eight conspirators (together with the fugitive John Surratt) intended to "kill and murder" Abraham Lincoln from the start, and to attack Andrew Johnson, William Seward, and Ulysses S. Grant at the same time. Davis himself initiated the murder conspiracy, Bingham charged, as the centerpiece of a broad terror offensive against the North.

Quoting *Phillips on Evidence*, he reminded the commission that all eight of the conspirators were equally guilty, regardless of the roles assigned to any one: " 'It is an established rule that where several persons are proved to have combined together for the same illegal purpose, any act done by one of the party is, in the contemplation of the law, the act of the whole party.' "[13] If Edward Spangler held Wilkes Booth's getaway horse in the alley behind Ford's, the court must find him guilty. If Samuel Mudd sheltered Booth and bound up his injured leg, the court must find him guilty. If Mary Surratt kept a safe house for the plotters, joined in their discussions, and arranged for the post-murder flight, then the court must find her guilty, too.

Were there conflicts in Louis Weichmann's testimony about Mudd's alleged visit to Washington in December or January? "The burden of proof is upon the prisoner to prove he was not in Washington in January last," Bingham announced airily. Were not a knife and revolver found in George Atzerodt's room in the Kirkwood House, and hadn't Atzerodt asked to have the hotel's most prominent guest, Andrew Johnson, pointed out to him in the dining room? Did not Lewis Paine turn up at Mary Surratt's house in the middle of the third night following his attack on Seward? "The mere act of Payne, flying to her house for shelter, would have borne witness against her strong as proofs from the Holy Writ," the prosecutor asserted.[14]

At the end of his long summation (it ran to more than fifty printed pages), Bingham acknowledged the lack of direct proofs linking all the accused with conspiracy, murder, attempted murder, and miscarried murder. For one example, Holt's team presented no evidence that Mary Surratt knew that Booth had dropped the abduction plan and decided to kill Lincoln. But he advised court president Hunter, Wallace, and the others not to let the absence of incontrovertible proof influence their verdict.

"That this conspiracy was entered into by all these parties is thus proved by the acts, meetings, declarations, and correspondence of all these parties beyond a reasonable doubt whatever," Bingham assured the judges. "True, it is circumstantial evidence, but the Court will remember that circumstances can not lie."[15]

To a man, the court agreed. All eight of the defendants were found guilty on June 30. Atzerodt, Herold, Paine, and Mrs. Surratt were sentenced to hang. Arnold, Mudd, and O'Laughlin were sentenced to life imprisonment at hard labor. Spangler, Booth's starstruck lackey, received a six-year prison term. With the convictions, theories of a grand conspiracy guided from Richmond seemed all but forgotten.

"I never knew a trial where there was so little result from so many questions," marveled John Gray in Charleston, who had closely followed the proceedings in the newspapers.[16]

With Andrew Johnson afflicted (a summer cold, flu, catarrh), Joseph Holt did not submit the sentences for presidential confirmation until July 5. By then pleas to spare Mary Surratt on account of her sex were well advanced. Five of the nine members of the court were said to have signed a petition in favor of clemency. The president approved the sentences anyway, and fixed a July 7 execution date.* But even as the gallows were being knocked together, reporters, soldiers on guard duty at the Old Penitentiary, and the hangman himself were certain that Johnson would deliver a last-minute reprieve for Mrs. Surratt.

No one doubted the other three would take the drop. Atzerodt seemed born to be hanged. Herold was Booth's most faithful ally. Paine had savagely attacked the bedfast Seward and his attendants. Arnold, Mudd, O'Laughlin, and Spangler were sufficiently involved to justify their lighter sentences. The times in any case demanded unflinching justice. According to Mudd's family, the wife of one of Johnson's cabinet secretaries reported having overheard a remark from Lew Wallace that doubtless accurately reflected the court's thinking.

"If Booth had not broken his leg," Wallace supposedly said, "we would never have heard the name of Dr. Mudd. The deed is done; somebody must suffer for it, and he may as well suffer as anybody else."[17]

General John Hartranft, in command of the Old Penitentiary, told the prison provost on the evening of July 6 to be ready to execute the capital sentences the next morning. The hangman, a Michigan officer with the expressive name of Christian Rath, sent out for rope—thirty-one-strand, three-quarter-inch Boston hemp—and tied the knots himself, seven for three of the nooses and a labor-saving five for the fourth, for he "fully expected that Mrs. Surratt would never hang," either by reason of a stay or by the intercession of the condemned woman's daughter Anna, who might, if everything else failed, slip her a dose of poison.[18]

Sarah Frances Mudd had said farewell to her prison-bound husband in a large, empty second-floor room earlier in the day. From the window she could see the workmen finishing the gibbet. She re-

---

*Johnson insisted afterward that he had never seen the commission's clemency plea. Given no alternative (or so he claimed), he reluctantly signed Mrs. Surratt's death warrant.

counted her difficulties since Mudd's arrest; soldiers had ransacked the farm, burning fences, dismantling the corncrib, trampling the tobacco and wheat in the fields. Mudd was in shirtsleeves against the heat and wore carpet slippers without socks. The guards seemed to intimidate him and he spoke only of commonplace things. As Mrs. Mudd left she passed Anna Surratt on the way to a last visit with her mother. The president was too ill to hear her plea, Anna said; she and the two priests who attended Mary Surratt had been turned away from the Executive Mansion.

Even so, news reports telegraphed from Washington late on July 6 continued to hint that the president would reprieve Mrs. Surratt. Rath remembered her as calm in Anna's presence. "She bade her daughter to keep up," Rath wrote of their last meeting, "and apparently was stolid as a rock." By other accounts, she collapsed in near hysteria on return to her cell. George Atzerodt, too, dissolved in terror and panic. Only Herold, still flashing his imbecile grin, seemed unconcerned.[19]

Paine was outwardly defiant, shatterproof. During the week he had guarded him Rath found him good-natured, likable, and wholly without remorse. They used to pitch quoits together in the prison yard. It was in the night that Paine's demons rose up to torment him. He had tried a few nights before to knock himself insensible by dashing his head repeatedly against the iron bars of the cell. The guards heard the commotion and subdued him. Now in the hours that remained to him he paced a padded cell, his head wrapped in batting.[20]

Rath turned out the prison garrison early on July 7 and asked for volunteers, promising a dram all around when the thing should be done: three men to bind Atzerodt, Herold, and Paine and lead them to the execution yard; four to place the nooses around the prisoners' necks; and two to knock the posts from the hinged platform under the drops. He assigned an officer as escort for Mrs. Surratt.

They marched to the gallows under a fierce midday sun. Hundreds of witnesses, mostly soldiers, lined the high wall that enclosed the yard. Mary Surratt went first, with her officer attendant and the two priests, Walter and Wigett, swinging crosses and murmuring prayers. She wore a black alpaca dress, a black bonnet, and a thin veil. Walking unsteadily, she listed now into Walter, now into Wigett. Four soldiers followed, with weapons shouldered.

Lincoln conspirators hang from the gibbet in the Old Capitol Prison on July 7, 1865. "I gave the signal," executioner Christian Rath recalled, "the two drops fell with a sickening thud, and, as one, the four bodies shot downward." Mary Surratt is at left. (Library of Congress)

Atzerodt came next, with a Lutheran minister at his side. His chains clanked as he walked. According to Rath, Atzerodt shrank from the sight of the dangling nooses. An Episcopal minister attended Herold. Reality had penetrated at last and he shuddered and quaked with fear. Paine brought up the rear. "He walked," thought the admiring Rath, "like a king about to be crowned." A Baptist parson hurried to keep pace with Paine's long strides.[21]

The prisoners were led to chairs lined up along the edge of the drops. Orderlies held umbrellas over Mrs. Surratt and General Hartranft to shield them from the terrible sun. Hartranft read out the findings and the death warrants. The soldiers pulled white caps over the prisoners' heads and adjusted the nooses. "Don't let me fall," Mary Surratt whispered.[22] Rath himself attended Lewis Thornton Powell, alias Paine.

"Paine, I want you to die quick," he told him, drawing the halter tight.

"You know best, Captain."[23]

General Winfield Scott Hancock, commanding the military District of Columbia, had missed the preliminaries, detained by a habeas corpus petition for Mrs. Surratt—the merest formality, as the wartime suspension remained in force. Now as Hancock approached the platform at last Rath felt certain he carried a reprieve for her. The hangman shot him an inquiring look.

"All is ready, Captain; proceed," Hancock said.

"Her too?"

"Yes."

"I gave the signal," Rath said, "the two drops fell with a sickening thud, and, as one, the four bodies shot downward and hung in midair."[24]

Ten minutes later the surgeons pronounced Mary Surratt, George Atzerodt, David Herold, and Lewis Paine dead. Rath let them hang another ten minutes, then had them cut down and laid in their pine coffins. He arranged Mrs. Surratt in her box with his own hands.

WHERE DID THE ACCIDENTAL PRESIDENT STAND on the issues of restoration? Did the Federal government mean to guarantee political rights and economic opportunity for former slaves? To what extent would ex-rebels be allowed to return to public life? Andrew Johnson had invited Ben Wade, George Julian, and other Radicals to consult the record for his tendencies. As it happened, there wasn't a lot of record to consult. So radicals and conservatives, Northerners and Southerners, hoped for the best from him—or expected the worst.

"As for Johnson, we know but little and that little is not to his credit," John Gray remarked. "He is a drunkard and a boor, and proud of being a boor. He comes from that Western part of North Carolina and East Tennessee which contains the most degraded part of the country, and he has been generally considered a fair representative thereof."[25]

Emma Holmes expressed a widely held South Carolina view, as dismissive as the Bostonian Gray's: Lincoln's successor was "the ex-*tailor* & renegade, who has worked in this state & made clothes for Mr. Hamilton Boykin."[26]

Johnson, fifty-seven years old in 1865, had risen to political prominence as a champion of the common white man. Born into poverty, with a haphazard education and self-conscious about his lack of sophistication, he hardly bothered to conceal his resentment of the privileged classes. "If Johnson were a snake," the rival Tennessee politician Isham Harris once said, "he would lie in the grass to bite the heels of rich men's children."[27] In Congress (the House, 1843–1853; the Senate, 1857–1862), Johnson supported homestead and other legislation benefiting the smallholder class, and opposed tariffs and other forms of government aid for industrial development. In 1860–1861 he was that rare thing, a Southern Unionist, and Lincoln rewarded him for his loyalty with the war governorship of Tennessee.

Owner of a few slaves himself, Johnson defended the Peculiar Institution up to 1861, regretting only that its benefits were not more widely accessible to his poor white constituency. "I wish to God every head of a family in the United States had one slave to take the drudgery and menial service off his family," he once declared.[28] He resisted black political equality as a threat to the white yeomanry, for he believed the old detested planter class would manipulate the black vote in its own interest. By instinct, he regarded African Americans as unfit for a political role, now certainly, and probably for a long time to come.

Yet some Radicals thought they could manage Johnson. The new president kept his first pronouncements deliberately vague. He signaled early on that he meant to treat ordinary ex-rebels generously—with "leniency, conciliation, and amnesty," as he put it in a speech to a delegation of Indiana politicians. He had hard words, though, for the Confederate ruling class, and hinted that he might support confiscation of rebel property to compensate loyalists for their losses. On the other hand, he proposed a swift, conclusive restoration of civil government in the South, on the simple (and simplistic) constitutional premise that the defeated states had never actually been out of the Union, but only suspended their relation to it.[29] He evidently wished to arrange it so that the much talked about 1860 Unionists, men who had opposed secession and only reluctantly cast their lot with the Confederacy, would come to power in the rebellious states on a tide of poor white votes. Julian hardly knew what to make of all this.

"He made us a speech," he wrote his wife Laura at home in Indiana. "*Such* a speech I have seldom heard. In thought, language, grammar, pronunciation, it was an impressive performance. I will tell you what I mean when I see you."[30]

Johnson went so far as to suggest that he might consider limited black suffrage, though only when circumstances seemed right to him. Chief Justice Chase, Senator Sumner, Julian, and others pressed for voting rights for the mass of illiterate and politically unschooled freedmen as a condition of readmitting the rebel states, both as protection for blacks and to assure stable (that is to say, Union/Republican) government in the postwar South. The president somehow left Chase with the impression that the Radicals might eventually argue him around to their view on suffrage.

"Everybody will follow your lead," Chase wrote Johnson, "and I can only repeat my profound conviction that nothing will more exalt your character in the estimation of mankind."[31]

Johnson deflated Radical hopes with his May 29 proclamation (issued together with the amnesty edict) restoring civil rule in North Carolina. It named Raleigh newspaper editor William W. Holden, a Unionist, provisional governor and authorized him to call a convention to draw up a new state constitution. The president made no mention of black suffrage, leaving North Carolina to settle the question for itself.

The North Carolina plan buoyed the hopes of former rebels everywhere. Charlestonian Edward Frost, a former U.S. congressman, led a South Carolina delegation to Washington in late June to lobby for restoration on similar terms. After a period of interim executive rule, a redrafting of the constitution, and the rather minimal obligation of ratifying the Thirteenth Amendment, Johnson offered, South Carolina could choose a governor, a legislature, and representatives to Congress free of Federal interference. "Do you know that I believe I am a better States' Rights man than you are?" he challenged the delegates, who responded with faint, nervous laughter. Frost and his colleagues tentatively proposed several candidates for the governorship: the rice grandee William Aiken, the prewar Unionist Benjamin F. Perry, and three or four lesser names.[32] Judge Frost left the capital rather impressed with the renegade tailor, according to his niece, Emma Holmes.

"Andy Johnson, whom Uncle knew in Congress, behaved much better than reported," Miss Emma wrote in her diary. "Andy left the important item of negro suffrage to be determined by the Legislatures of each state, & of course there is no longer doubt on that point."[33]

South Carolina freedmen could see that plainly enough. Some fifteen hundred of them petitioned President Johnson on June 29 for the right to vote. African Americans made up a majority of South Carolina's population; only the franchise would guarantee the majority protection from unjust legislation. The petitioners asked the president to choose a provisional governor from a list of abolitionists that included onetime Lincoln challenger John C. Frémont and Rufus Saxton.[34]

Whites-only Union meetings sent off their own petitions for restoration. These local caucuses recognized the end of slavery but made no further mention of South Carolina's newest citizens. Given the tone of the Union meetings, James Trotter, on occupation duty in Orangeburg with the Fifty-fifth Massachusetts, considered it unlikely that the United States would grant South Carolina home rule anytime soon.

"Troops are to be scattered all through the state," he wrote his Bostonian friend Kinsley. "This looks like military government for some time. We have given up hope of going home soon."[35]

Johnson issued the South Carolina restoration proclamation on June 30. Within a few weeks, orders reached the Fifty-fifth Massachusetts to head north for mustering out. The presidential edict said nothing about suffrage—as in North Carolina, the state convention would decide who could vote. The president appointed Benjamin Perry, a former rebel judge from up-country Greenville, as provisional governor. No fire-eater, Perry had been a loyal Confederate nevertheless. Johnson was evidently prepared to overlook a great deal in his haste to lift military rule.

With Congress in recess until December, the Radicals were unable to put up much resistance to the initial phase of presidential Reconstruction. Radical representative Thaddeus Stevens, at home in Pennsylvania, could only protest mildly that no Union man he had spoken to yet had endorsed Johnson's evolving policy.

"They believe that 'restoration' as announced by you will destroy our party (which is of but little consequence) and will greatly injure the country," Stevens wrote the president. "Can you not hold your hand and wait the action of Congress and in the mean time govern by military rulers? Profuse pardoning also will greatly embarrass Congress if they should wish to make the enemy pay the expenses of the war or part of it."[36]

Like Stevens, George Julian tracked developments from home. Anxious about his young wife's approaching lying-in,* he was subject again to the familiar afflictions: insomnia, restlessness, headaches. "While I write he is out walking on the pavement to get exercise that will enable him to sleep," Laura Julian wrote her sister. "Poor boy, he is overworked."[37] Yet he canvassed the Burnt District tirelessly, as though this were an election year, alert for the trend of opinion on the president and his works, and on his own feud, personal and political, with Oliver P. Morton, Indiana's powerful war governor.

They had been rivals for fifteen years. Both were natives of Wayne County, both were initiates of the Dark Lyceum, both had practiced law in Centreville. They followed different political paths, Julian a Whig and Free-Soil radical, Morton a conservative Democrat. Morton refused to go along with other district Democrats in 1850 and support the Free-Soiler Julian against the common Whig enemy. Julian lost by seven hundred votes and never forgave him. Now he and Morton were uneasy allies in the party of Lincoln. Morton backed the Johnson political restorations and opposed black suffrage. Through his organ, the *Indianapolis Daily Journal*, he launched a series of attacks on Julian. The congressman accused Morton of using the press and the power of patronage against him in a campaign to destroy his career. The *Journal's* editor took particular issue with a Julian rebuttal of one of Morton's pro-Johnson speeches.

"It is certainly not treason to discuss and criticize a public speech, even of Governor Morton," answered Julian's brother Isaac, editor of the Radical *Indiana True Republican* of Richmond, the chief town of the Burnt District.[38]

Julian accused Morton of favoring a "ghastly policy of arming the white rebels with the ballot and denying it to the negroes." Morton labeled Julian a hypocrite for his silence on the issue of the franchise for Indiana blacks, a not unjust charge. Julian admitted he judged it

---

*She delivered a daughter, Grace, in September.

"impolitic" to raise the question at home. "I confess and deplore the conduct of Indiana toward her colored people," he said; "but if our black laws were a thousand times blacker it would be none the less my duty to plead for negro suffrage in the South." A clause in Indiana's 1850 constitution actually barred blacks from entering the state. Even Julian had to think twice about pushing upstream against so strong a current.[39]

The Fifth Congressional District was quiet for now, whether through exhaustion or indifference Julian could not yet say. The *True Republican* took the optimistic view. "The war is over now," the paper observed, "and the people are getting ready to listen coolly to the truth."[40] Possibly, but the district's farmers and mechanics struck Julian as spent emotionally. Returning soldiers were falling gratefully into the old routines of home and work, harvest time was drawing near, and for idle conversation one could always dish up the case of Amelia Bloomer, of dress reform notoriety. Her husband, an Indianapolis lawyer, had gone to court to dissolve their marriage.

"He had no trouble in getting it, upon the *plea* of *infidelity*," Laura Julian wrote her sister. "He had one of her letters read in court stating that she had met her 'affinity' elsewhere—and loved him far better than she had ever done himself—and never should be his wife again. The court gave him a divorce at once."[41]

Julian knew by now that there would be no such swift resolution of the Radical case for suffrage, land redistribution, and the punishment of rebels. Congress could do nothing before the new session convened, so Radicals looked to General Howard's Freedmen's Bureau to consolidate the revolution.

"His views & plans are practical & right in my judgement," one of Howard's Radical supporters remarked. "He says he will give the freedmen *protection*, *land*, & *schools*, as far & as fast as he can."[42]

As far as he could; but it was clear from the start that Andrew Johnson regarded the bureau's multiple functions—protection, sustenance, and education—as unwarranted Federal intrusion. "The true relief was in work," he told Howard. Let whites and blacks, workers and employers, negotiate their future relations with as little government involvement as possible.[43]

This last was a common enough notion, even among some antislavery veterans. The Sea Island Gideonites had been contending with it since 1862. "We are in danger of *too much* northern management of the negro," Henry Ward Beecher wrote Stanton. "The black man is just like the white, in this—that he should be left, & obliged to take care of himself. I think nursing will only pauperize him. I see in the movements about here a tendency to dandle the black man." Beecher expected the bureau to check those tendencies.[44]

So Commissioner Howard found himself on unfamiliar, treacherous, shifting political terrain. Bogging through the Carolinas would come to seem a simple matter by contrast with the Freedmen's Bureau assignment. Howard had not been prepared for the demands and distractions of high office: bureaucratic conflict, politicians pressing their views, requests for jobs from former staffers, appeals from Confederate West Point classmates for help with their pardon applications, eccentric solicitations.

The editor of the *Soldier's Friend*, for instance, wrote to ask him to help judge a contest offering a $200 prize for "the best specimen of penmanship for left-arm men"—veterans who, like Howard himself, had lost their right arms in battle.[45]

Thomas Jefferson Rawls, M.D., sought Howard's assistance in his bid for the postmastership of Columbia, South Carolina. Rawls had been on duty at the campus hospital the night of February 17 last, attending Union prisoners of war there under the protection of the yellow flag. George Stone, commanding Howard's provost brigade, promised a guard for his empty house. The sentry failed to show and house, office, medical books, furniture, and clothing went up in flames. So he felt a sense of entitlement: would Howard arrange the postal appointment for him?

"It is a new mode of life for you," his brother Rowland wrote. "You must now live among politicians, contractors, officeholders & officeseekers, sycophants & flatterers. May you not 'fall among thieves.' May you not be overrun with selfish corrupt officeseekers & *land* & *cotton speculators*. May you not be bored to death with benevolent but unwise & unpractical clergymen."

From Beaufort, Charles Howard forwarded his commissioner-brother a ringing commendation of Rufus Saxton, together with a warning about the politically unsteady General Gillmore ("He seems suddenly to have changed his policy and to be in favor of the government doing what it can for the Freedmen") and his Department of the South lieutenants John Hatch in Charleston, Edward Potter at Hilton Head, and Cuvier Grover in Savannah—especially Grover, whose sympathies, in Charles's view, lay only too plainly with Savannah's ex-rebels.[46]

"Pro-slavery" soldiers allied with resistant whites were conspiring to undo all of Saxton's good work, Charles wrote. Saxton and his agents were powerless to protect the emancipated people and enforce the law. His solution: give Saxton operational control of troops—Charles's own 128th USCT, for example.

"You know the *execution* of every measure now depends and will for some time depend entirely upon the military," he went on. "It would give him more respect of the existing military authorities and also more deference from the inhabitants."[47]

As ever, Saxton himself dwelt not on the pitfalls of freedom but on the promise of it. He had seen, helped make, the future in the Sea Islands. "So far as I have been able to judge of it," the freed people "only need to be educated and protected in their rights and all will be well with them," he wrote Otis Howard in Washington.[48] Already, though, in remote locales black schools and churches were under attack, blacks were acquiring arms for self-defense, whites were forming nightrider squads, laborers were idle, fields neglected, livestock untended, famine threatening.

The president showed a "steady, though underhand" opposition to the Freedmen's Bureau, according to Howard. At a minimum the Johnson pardons, providing for the immediate restoration of property, would sharply limit the refugee resettlement program. The bureau held only around 800,000 acres of seized or abandoned lands; most of it would now have to be surrendered. In the worst case, Low Country blacks would be chased off their forty-acre farms. Certainly General Gillmore interpreted the amnesty proclamation that way. He revoked Sherman's Special Orders Number 15 as a preliminary to restoration. With Stanton's support, Howard overruled Gillmore. The Sherman lands would be exempt for now, though Howard instructed Rufus Saxton to allow whites to live on the disputed estates while the larger issues were being settled.[49]

With the land question pressing, Howard sent his adjutant, Joseph S. Fullerton, south for a firsthand inspection of Saxton's command. Fullerton had nothing but fault to find in his mid-July report from Hilton Head. Saxton was in Saratoga, New York, on leave by then and could not defend himself. It wouldn't have mattered anyway. Fullerton made no attempt to conceal his lack of sympathy for Saxton and all his works.

"Gen. Saxton has been making such speeches on the subject of suffrage as are likely to make [the freedmen] discontented and to lead them to think that unless they get certain imaginary 'rights' they are not free," he wrote Howard. "I have every reason to believe the reports of the military authorities here that General Saxton pays more attention to such matters than to his legitimate duties as Asst Comsr of the Bureau."[50]

Saxton's henchmen made trouble too—particularly the insolent, pushy Major Martin Delany, one of the army's few African American commissioned officers. Delany incited the freedmen to fight now, and fight hard, for everything they could get: land, seed, mules, tools, rations, schools, political power.

"He has told the negro in public speeches that the lands that they have been working upon belong to them and that they should have it," Fullerton wrote. "This irritates and discontents the negroes and makes them in some cases refuse to work at any price, and in some others causes them to break contracts that have been made."[51]

Fullerton itemized further complaints: slipshod paperwork, mismanagement of a bureau hospital in Beaufort, extravagant demands on the army commissariat for rations, clothing, and transportation. Not that Fullerton intended to prejudge the assistant commissioner.

"I will not make a definite report of Saxton's conduct though until after I have seen him or examined more thoroughly into the workings of his system—if he has any," he wrote Howard.[52]

Saxton had stopped off in Washington on his way north to call on Howard and suspected him of wavering in his commitment. "Rufus does not seem entirely satisfied with his intentions," Willard Saxton remarked in his journal.[53] The commissioner may not have known them himself. He did know that Johnson was hostile to the bureau, and that to carry out its mission he would have to challenge the president, circumvent him, or somehow find a way to convert him.

Howard's Christian beliefs, his humanitarian impulses, were genuine. His sympathies were easily stirred. He continued to take an interest in Wash Kemp, the freedman he and Charles had resettled on their mother's farm in Maine. Howard had, for example, ordered bureau agents to scour Georgia for Kemp's wife and daughters so the family could be reunited. Still, he was a soldier, used to obeying orders. He was young, not yet thirty-five, a novice in political maneuver with a postwar career to advance. "He always tries his very best to do what he has been ordered, and his best, though not wonderful, is good," John Gray once said of him.[54] Even Howard's admirers wondered whether his best would be enough to overcome the president's antagonism.

Howard tried to interpret Johnson's directives in a light most favorable to black settlers. In his Circular No. 13 of July 28, he approved the distribution of bureau-controlled abandoned lands to freedmen in forty-acre plots and advised his agents that the presidential pardons were not to be understood as authorizing the automatic return of abandoned or confiscated property to former owners.

He found a willing accomplice in Rufus Saxton, who returned to Beaufort in early August recharged and ready to renew the battle. Saxton lost a skirmish at sea along the way: his old tormentor John Foster, the senior officer aboard, had ordered the captain of the Hilton Head packet to skip a scheduled call at Fortress Monroe, marooning him there. Saxton reached home late, wrathful and determined to reassert his authority. "He's going to take hold now, & let them know he's at the head of the Bureau here," Willard wrote. He parceled out Edisto Island farmsteads to another 367 black families on the strength of Howard's circular, and struck off one of his own reaffirming the government's promise of land.[55]

"The yankees have instilled into the negroes' minds the belief that the Island country belongs to them," a white landowner complained of Saxton and his agents, "and they throw every obstacle in the way of the planters revisiting their plantations."[56]

It did not last. Howard had issued the July 28 circular without consulting the president. Now Johnson instructed the bureau to draw up a new land policy that reflected the terms of his amnesty proclamation. An August 16 executive order directed Howard's assistant commissioners to return all abandoned lands to owners with presidential pardons with no questions asked, no unreasonable delay, and no compensation to homesteaders other than the growing crops in the fields.[57]

Fullerton supplied Howard, at home in Maine on leave for most of August, with the details. The president had learned through private channels that Saxton and other agents were following their own line. "Mr. Johnson is very kindly disposed toward you & the Bureau," Fullerton wrote him, "but if we attempt to work against him or oppose his policies, then 'look out for breakers.'" This was sound advice, if unwelcome. It gave Howard plenty to think about on the trip back to Washington.

Johnson's cordial greeting heartened him when they met after his return to work. "I have a great deal of perplexing labor still," he wrote Lizzie, "but think I take matters easier than I did at first." His optimism was misplaced. Johnson had not suddenly learned to love the Freedmen's Bureau. Howard's suggestion that he make future pardons conditional on planters' supplying former slaves with small homesteads of five to ten acres only seemed to amuse him. Johnson slipped off the mask of amiability and ordered Howard to release the revised order, Circular Number 15. The commissioner had no choice but to comply.[58]

"Mr. Johnson is giving up the land pretty fast," he wrote Lizzie, "and I begin to tremble with anxiety for the freedmen. This is *entre nous*."[59]

The Low Country felt the impact of Circular Number 15 at once.

"Rufus is overrun with visitors, gentlemen wishing to get their property restored," Willard Saxton observed. "They are fast getting it back & it will all be restored, according to recent orders. This is treason punished."[60]

TWILIGHT OF EVENING, LATE SUMMER DUST thick on brittle leaves, the whir of insects, the faint rattle of a passing team, menace in the hot night air: On the Elmores' Lance's End plantation in the Columbia hinterland, former slaves had staked out their lots and prepared to divide the place among themselves. Then the Yankees told the freedmen they were not to have their forty acres after all.

With the spread of the evil news, the emancipated people looked toward the Sherman lands. "Thousands are abandoning their crops and all they have and making their way to the Coast," Ralph Ely, the Freedmen's Bureau head agent for the Columbia district, reported to Commissioner Howard. Many of those who remained behind were resentful, surly, volatile. Ex-rebel soldier Albert Elmore joined a "vigilant committee" and sent his sister Grace away to a safer Elmore holding in Chester.[61]

"I think we will be like gypsies, always moving," Miss Grace complained. "The Yankees don't care whether we are murdered or not. They even deny us the use of firearms and birdshot. Our hands are tied, we can do nothing in our defense."[62]

Twilight of dawn: Mary Elliott Johnstone rising to mix the bread dough and skim the milk for her children's breakfast. She cut up slabs of beef or bacon for stewing. She learned the number of stitches (120) for a ladies' undershirt. Her daughter Annie helped with the beds and the laundry. There was no money for hired help, and anyhow the cost of servants in up-country Greenville ran to more than wages: "Annie saw some of our dinner set in Main Street for sale a few days ago altho' the key to the cellar is always in my pocket," she wrote her sister Emily.[63] Mary managed to retain but one servant, a little girl who brought water and emptied the slops.

"It is difficult to believe in our utter ruin, and yet present difficulties tell us plainly enough what the future must be," she lamented. "I bless the hard work I have to do for making me weary enough at night to go at once to sleep."[64]

Nights were only a temporary palliative for homesickness, loneliness, and anxiety. She nursed eight-year-old Emma through a terrible asthma attack, brought on, she suspected, by Greenville's choking dust. War had spared her stripling son Elliott; but no one could predict what this disturbed, unsettling, violent peace might bring.

Mary schemed to bring her mother and her sisters Ann and Emily to Greenville, holding out as inducement a severely scaled-down version of amenities the Elliotts used to take for granted. "I am going to get a man and a woman to live in the yard who will for the use of a room do the washing and attend to the cow," she promised. "We will hire a woodcutter once a week and get on finely. Mamma will not suffer from the cold one bit."[65] The board would be simple, though, for the porker that was to have supplied them with spare ribs and sausages for the winter had to be demolished before its time. Mary could no longer afford the cost of its feed.

The scattered, once-powerful Elliotts improvised: Ralph on his smallholding along the Edisto River, the widow Ann Elliott with Emily and Ann on the hired place near Darlington, William convalescing in Beaufort (a recurrence of lung trouble), Thomas trying to put an abandoned farm at Pocotaligo into operation. General How-

Freed people rest in the shade in front of the former slave quarters on an Elliott plantation on Hilton Head Island. The young man at left may be a soldier home on leave, or he may be wearing a cast-off uniform. The Elliotts, prewar South Carolina grandees, struggled to regain their lands and adapt to postwar life. But few of the Elliotts' former slaves would contract to work for them, preferring instead to cultivate their own food crops, and maybe a little cotton for cash. (U.S. Army Military History Institute)

ard's new circular raised hopes for recovery of four contested mainland plantations: The Bluff (700 acres), Middle Place (400 acres), Social Hall (1,700 acres), and the plundered Elliott seat, Oak Lawn.

"I will even, if necessary, take the oath of allegiance on Mama's account," Ralph Elliott announced. "I'd rather die than take it on my own."[66]

He reported a disappointing crop on the Edisto—only five bales of cotton, drought-damaged peas and potatoes, and a balance of six hundred bushels of corn after deductions for labor and other expenses. He planned to send four hundred bushels to Mary in Greenville and to sell the rest, for hard money if possible, with greenbacks falling steadily in value. His survey of the other Elliott properties suggested there would be little else to sustain the family anytime soon.

Former Elliott slaves were in nominal possession of Oak Lawn, unambitiously tending their starveacre plots of corn and yams. Nothing of value remained on the place. The Elliott servants had led the Yankees to all the hiding places, and what the soldiers and their black allies hadn't carried off they smashed. Ralph Elliott took the losses hard.

"It makes me burn with vengeance when I think that those beautiful vessels that used to grace the family board on festive occasions should now be defiled by the touch of vagrant negroes," he wrote Sister Emily. "I am still a rebel, thank God, and these acts, sanctioned by 'the best government the world ever saw,' don't make me the less of one."[67]

The Sea Island plantations, seized for tax arrears or subject to Special Orders Number 15, remained off-limits for now. Thomas Elliott considered settling his family temporarily in one of the Beaufort town houses, but changed his mind after a look around. "The town is not fit for a white lady to stay in," he decided. At the Pocotaligo farm, the sash and shutters were smashed, the kitchen building burned, trees taken down for firewood, fields choked with weeds. At least there were no squatters in sight. He contracted with a freed couple to live on the farm and hired a Yankee to manage it.[68]

Like the Elmores, like whites all over the South, the Elliotts anticipated an explosion of racial violence. Blacks were everywhere arming themselves and drilling for an insurrection, so the rumor went, and nearly everyone believed there would be a mass uprising at Christmas. Up to now, though, the assaults had nearly always been white on black, ambushes of stray freedmen and solitary Yankee black soldiers. "The country is proving generally unhealthy to such as wander beyond the town limits," Ralph Elliott noted with approval. Whites took comfort, too, in the fact that they heavily outgunned the freedmen.[69]

"Could you brush closely against any ragged neighbor without being bruised by his concealed revolver?" Whitelaw Reid had mused during his travels through the South.[70]

Vigilante leaders tapped a vast reservoir of recruits: idle landowners, merchants without stock to sell, lawyers without clients, teamsters without mules, millers without corn to grind, teachers without pupils. "Returned Rebel soldiers lounge about in the hotels," Charles Howard reported, "swearing, chewing tobacco & drinking when they can get liquor and they are perfect desperadoes."[71] The result: a rise to epidemic levels of terror attacks on blacks and black institutions throughout the South.

Whites burned two schools and a church in Mobile on the Gulf Coast. Elsewhere in Alabama a freedman was taken from his bed and hanged; another was chained to a pine tree and set on fire; two others were shot from ambush as they floated down the Tombigbee River in a skiff. Whites attacked a freedwoman named Nancy as she slept and cut off her ears.

"A preacher states in the *pulpit* that the roads in Choctaw County stunk with the dead bodies of servants that had fled from their masters," the Freedmen's Bureau agent in Selma, Alabama, reported.[72]

Similar bulletins reached bureau headquarters from Louisiana, Mississippi, Georgia, and the Carolinas. Whites continued nevertheless to complain to the authorities of secret cabals and midnight preparations for the Christmas insurrection. Jumpy Low Country whites persuaded General Gillmore to seize such weapons as the freedmen possessed. Laura Towne described a black conspiracy on Saint Helena Island of the type that led Gillmore to act:

> A few men united into a company to defend their watermelon patches, and once when they were going their rounds they met a young Captain who has made himself very unpopular since he has lived on the island, and they refused to turn out for his buggy, obliging him to drive around them instead of standing aside for him to pass.

The officer construed this into rebellion. Gillmore ordered a deeply reluctant Charles Howard, now commanding the post at Beaufort, to send out details to collect all the arms on Saint Helena.

"Col. H. told me that he thought the way to make them rebel was to do this," Towne said, "and he would not if he could help it."[73]

Complaints from white mainlanders poured into Saxton's headquarters. Blacks were violating labor agreements; squatters were refusing to leave their patches of land. At the same time, emboldened ex-Confederates ignored Freedmen's Bureau orders and regulations. Charles Howard had no authority on his own to dispatch troops to enforce compliance, and Gillmore hardly ever responded to black complaints against whites.

"I feel at times like damning the whole Southern white race, they act so like brutes and villains to the freedmen," Willard Saxton wrote in his journal. "We need not expect justice from them, except at the point of a bayonet."[74]

The brothers Saxton quarreled anew in the wind-stirred heat of late summer. Matilda Saxton provoked the latest outbreak with a wounding remark about Edward Hooper, Willard's particular friend (and his son Eddie's godfather). Vaguely aware that she had given offense, Tillie escaped the Bay Street hothouse for long gallops on her favorite horse, a charger named General Howard. Rufus naturally took his wife's part. The warring couples finally agreed to break up their long-running ménage. Otis Howard made the parting less awkward with a mid-September order transferring the assistant commissioner's headquarters from Beaufort to Charleston. Amid the upheaval, personal and professional, the brothers looked forward to a mid-month bureau inspection trip into the Georgia interior as a well-timed diversion.

A rebuilt stretch of the Georgia Central Railroad carried the Saxtons forty-five miles into the interior at a spine-jarring ten miles an hour. They changed to an army wagon and pushed on through the pine barrens under an overcast sky. There were few houses, and few people abroad. At dusk they shifted to a covered wagon for the overnight stage. "No sleeping," Willard complained, "except bolt upright."[75]

Another length of restored railroad covered the last thirty miles to Augusta. The brothers checked into the Planters' Hotel around five o'clock in the morning. Rufus turned to bureau business immediately after breakfast. Willard set out alone on a walking tour of the place: the levee, the Cotton Exchange, the ruins of the blown-up Confederate powder mill. "Quite a pretty city, secesh to the core," he found it—and a difficult, dangerous posting for the bureau agent in charge. He looked in later in the day at the military trial of three Georgia young bloods accused of assassinating a Union officer.

"If justice is done, they will be hung," Willard, in no mood for mercy, wrote in his journal that night.[76]

A Northern traveler passing through Augusta around the same time sent his impressions of the place along to Commissioner Howard in Washington. The local people accepted the collapse of the Confederacy and submitted to the Federal occupation with little outward complaint. But they had about them a curiously expectant, knowing air.

"They seem to be waiting for their restoration to the Union, with power to make laws for themselves, & a removal of the military," the traveler reported. "God pity the black man when that takes place."[77]

THE SUMMONS DIRECTED CAPTAIN GEORGE DUTTON, the Veteran Reserve Corps officer last seen guarding the Aqueduct Bridge on the night of the Lincoln assassination, to form a detachment of thirty men, break out thirty days' rations, and be ready to march at a moment's notice. That evening, July 15, an aide led Dutton into a large gaslit room in the Washington Arsenal for an interview with Stanton, Hancock, and Holt, the judge advocate. Hancock had supplied Dutton with a pass to witness the hanging of four of the Lincoln conspirators. Now the war secretary handed him sealed orders to escort the surviving four to prison.

The party filed aboard the steamer *Maine*, with Arnold, Mudd, O'Laughlin, and Spangler in handcuffs and leg irons. Dutton oversaw the prisoners' transfer to the steam warship *Florida* at Fortress Monroe. Mudd and Spangler were violently seasick, though the latter seemed cheerful enough between bouts of mal de mer: "Six years is not so long a time," Spangler would say to no one in particular. Mudd was depressed and overwrought as well as queasy.

"I don't know where they are taking us," he said to Spangler, "but if it is the Dry Tortugas there is no more chance for you than for me; none of us will live more than two years."[78]

That deflated Spangler, for the pestilential Dry Tortugas it proved to be, as Dutton discovered when he opened his orders at sea off Cape Hatteras. The confirmation had the effect of turning Mudd confessional, or so Dutton claimed. Mudd admitted to Dutton that he lied to the court when he swore he hadn't recognized John Wilkes Booth at his door early on the morning after the attack on Lincoln. According to Dutton, Mudd corroborated the damaging testimony of one of the government's chief witnesses, Louis Weichmann.

"Dr. Mudd confessed . . . that he had known Booth for some time, but was afraid to tell of his having been at his house on the 15th of April, fearing that his own and the lives of his family would be endangered thereby," Dutton wrote Benn Pitman, the government clerk who prepared the official account of the trial for publication. "He also confessed that he was at the National Hotel with Booth on the evening referred to by Weichmann in his testimony, that he came to Washington on that occasion to meet Booth by appointment, who wished to be introduced to John Surratt."[79]

The *Florida* plowed southward through heaving seas. Dutton had the prisoners' irons removed during the hottest hours of the day and let them sling their hammocks on deck at night. The ship touched briefly at Key West, then steamed for the Dry Tortugas, seventy miles into the Gulf of Mexico. Fort Jefferson, on its treeless, barren coral rock, swam into view out of the heat haze on July 24. A fever ship lay at anchor in the lee of the island, quarantined.

"There is no hope for me now," Mudd whispered.[80]

Dutton's report of Mudd's "confession" caused a minor sensation. Holt sent to Dutton for a sworn confirmation. Pitman passed it along to the press. The Dutton claim doubtless lightened some consciences—Lew Wallace's, for instance, who had seemed at one point to favor acquittal of the lesser fry. Mudd challenged most of Dutton's claims, though he did finally admit to an accidental meeting with Booth two days before Christmas 1864. From Booth's line of talk, Mudd said, he suspected him at once of being a Union police spy. And he insisted that he had *not* penetrated the disguise of the bewhiskered man who came knocking before dawn on April 15.

"That I confessed to having known Booth while in my house; was afraid to give information of the fact, fearing to endanger my life, or made use of any language in that connection—I positively and emphatically declare to be notoriously false," Mudd insisted.[81]

Fort Jefferson's 550 political prisoners were being released in batches even as the *Florida* cast anchor and prepared to discharge her cargo. President Johnson had finally relented, too, in the case of Richard Ewell and Campbell Brown. In a flying visit to Boston, Lizinka found Ewell haggard, half-blind, all but helpless. She sent off a final embittered appeal to the president.

"You have treated me so harshly and cruelly that I scarcely dare approach you with any petition," she wrote him. "But I am very miserable. A single line from you can give them back to liberty & me to

Dr. Samuel Mudd in a Lew Wallace courtroom drawing. Confident at the trial, Mudd fell into a depression after his conviction and life sentence for conspiracy in the Lincoln assassination. "I don't know where they are taking us," he remarked to fellow convict Edward Spangler as the ship carrying them to prison ploughed southward through the Atlantic, "but if it is the Dry Tortugas . . . none of us will live more than two years." (Indiana Historical Society)

happiness. I am afraid to write more. I could not write less—but if Richard dies in Fort Warren how I will hate you—wicked as it is to hate anyone."[82]

Ewell's spirits ebbed with his physical condition. The canary's failure to sing struck him as an ill omen. "It has seemed on the point of breaking out every minute but is so quiet today one might almost think it sleeping," he wrote morosely. But the general misread the augurs this time. Johnson authorized his release on July 17. Ewell signed a "Form of Parole" two days later, promised to return to Virginia and report weekly to the secretary of war, and posted a $10,000 bond. He and Lizinka spent the night of his release at the Tremont Hotel in Boston. By August 15 they were temporarily settled in Warrenton, Virginia, where Ewell began scouting around for a farm to rent or buy.[83]

The government held a number of politicals still: Davis, Aleck Stephens, John Reagan, Treasury Secretary George Trenholm, and two officers involved with war prisoners—Lucius Northrop, the Confederate commissary general suspected of deliberately starving POWs, and the notorious Captain Wirz, the commandant of Andersonville. George Dutton returned from the Dry Tortugas to take command of the Old Capitol Prison and thus became Henry Wirz's jailer. Lew Wallace, more or less unemployed since the dissolution of the Lincoln court but plunged deep into Mexican intrigue, became Wirz's judge.

Wallace accepted the assignment without enthusiasm. Secretary of State Seward had arranged it to divert Wallace and stop, or anyway curtail, his political-military meddling. Seward opposed any armed activity along the Rio Grande, and Wallace's activities threatened to wreck this Fabian policy. Wallace openly solicited money, arms, and political support for the Juárez Republicans. He conspired with American *filibusteros* along the Rio Grande. He petitioned Johnson, Seward, and Grant to abandon the formal U.S. policy of neutrality and drive the Imperialists out of Mexico.

Mixed motives of altruism, a boyish yearning for adventure, and greed animated Wallace. "When he dies," his wife Susan wrote, "Mexico will be found written on his heart." Wallace doubtless believed in the Monroe Doctrine and Mexican self-determination, just as he believed in his own heroic destiny: himself, braided and beplumed, riding at the head of a Mexican army. There was the matter of money, too. The losses of the spring had been serious. He would never make them good on an officer's salary alone. The Juáristas promised to reward him handsomely. "I must risk myself again," he wrote Susan. "I must put ourselves above the possibility of want." So he plunged into a rather shady colonization scheme known as the United States, European and West Virginia Land and Mining Company of New York. He solicited New York money men for a Mexico bond. He negotiated to buy six of Dr. Gatling's rapid-fire mechanical guns for Juárez's army.[84]

With occupation routines in place in most of the former Confederacy, high U.S. policy makers could shift their attention to the Rio Grande. Grant had wisely declined to employ Wallace in a Texas role. He chose Philip Sheridan to command the fifty thousand strong Army of Observation, with orders to disarm Confederate forces in the Trans-Mississippi, pacify Texas, discourage Maximilian and the French in Mexico, and discreetly aid the Juáristas.

Edmund Kirby Smith removed one complication, surrendering the Trans-Mississippi on May 26. Only a rebel remnant remained at large, a renegade cavalry brigade under Jo Shelby that aimed to clear the Rio Grande, ride into Mexico, and sell its firepower to the highest bidder. Shelby's column approached the frontier at the end of June, just as elements of Sheridan's army, including the all-black Twenty-fifth Corps, were landing along the Texas coast.

Ned Bartlett, Fifth Massachusetts Cavalry, made an uneventful passage from Hampton Roads to the Rio Grande in the steamer *General McClellan*. He fell seasick on the first day out but soon grew accustomed to the plunging motion, the steady tread of the engines, the odor of coal gas and hot machinery, and the blistering sun. The ship rounded Cape Sable at the tip of Florida and passed into Gulf waters "as calm as Walden ever was," in Bartlett's phrase. He slept on deck at night under the unfamiliar southern stars.

The regiment came ashore at Brazos Santiago on July 1. It struck Bartlett as a wasteland at first: blazing hot, salty, and with hardly a living green thing to be seen. Fresh water was scarce, warm, brackish, and expensive—$6 for a hogshead. Bartlett's military duties were light, though, leaving him leisure for long moonlight horseback rides along the hard-packed sand, fishing in the sheltered waters of the laguna, and examining Point Isabel's exotic plant, bird, and aquatic life.

"What a glorious watering place this would be if it were only up in Mass.," he wrote home to Concord. "As far as the eye can reach is one long sand beach on which breakers dash higher than you ever saw them against the rocks of Pigeon Cove."[85]

The Fifth Massachusetts Cavalry shipped without its horses and so drew garrison duty upriver in Brownsville, far from Confederates and Comanches alike. Bartlett's company stayed behind as baggage guard on Brazos Island, encamped on the dazzling sands. The market boats came over from Mexican Bagdad every morning with fresh fish, pineapples, bananas, and sometimes fresh beef; and there were commissary supplements of hard bread, hominy, and potatoes. It was an agreeable, idle existence.

"Do you want to fight the Indians? I hope you won't have to," his sister Annie wrote. "Tis bad enough fighting white men."[86]

Bartlett shot at a pelican one day and missed. He collected the red, purple, and yellow wildflowers that bloomed in the sheltered places in the dunes. He hired someone to row him across to untidy, sunstruck Bagdad one Sunday afternoon and set foot on a foreign shore for the first time in his life. "Every house is a store," he discovered, "and every store a rumshop." The local people spoke a strange language. The women wore scarves rather than bonnets. The men wore odd leather trousers. They amused themselves with "a sort of whirligig," wooden horses going round and round that one could ride for ten cents. Bartlett brought back a sombrero ("a very broad-brimmed hat of white felt, comfortable in the sun") and a pair of Mexican spurs. He witnessed a shipwreck: a schooner loaded with railroad iron (Sheridan's engineers were laying a narrow-gauge line to Brownsville) grounded crossing the Brazos Santiago bar. The crew cut down the masts to keep her from rolling over and two lifeboats from shore lifted the passengers and crew off safely. A heavy surf pounded the vessel to pieces during the night.[87]

That was the high point of Brazos excitement. Time hung heavy and everyone dreamed of home. Some of the men of the Twenty-fifth Corps resented being sent to far-off Texas and a near-mutiny had flared in two units just before the expedition sailed. Bartlett's troopers behaved well, but they were restless, too. "I see by the papers that most of the Mass. regts. are being mustered out of service," he wrote his sister Martha. "I am afraid they will overlook us as being black. Has the 54 and 55th got home yet?"[88] Corps headquarters announced that no officer resignations would be accepted. So Bartlett resigned himself to passing his twenty-third birthday, August 12, on the Rio Grande.

Annie and Martha deepened his growing homesickness with reports of Concord events. A party of Annie's friends had walked over the hills to Walden to go swimming. "They found there a large picnic from Watertown who had come to celebrate Mr. Thoureaux birthday," she wrote him.* "They were more enthusiastic than we are!"[89] He would miss the entire soft Concord summer; he worried, too, that this empty army life would leave him unfit for serious business whenever he finally did get home.

---

*Henry David Thoreau, of course, born July 12, 1817.

"I have what is called a *soft thing*—nothing to do and my own master," he wrote Annie. "Peace soldiering is dull work and a great waste of time."[90]

Things were livelier in the interior. Sheridan's mobile columns pushed inland to bring Yankee order out of the Texas chaos. Local government had collapsed; bushwhackers and horse thieves were operating unchecked; many plantation blacks had not yet learned they were free. Sheridan could handle the military side; but he looked to the Freedmen's Bureau in Washington to manage the social revolution about to burst upon Kirby Smithdom. As elsewhere in the South, white Texans were fighting emancipation with whatever weapons came to hand.

"There are a great many freedmen in Texas; and but few rights will be given these people until you can extend there," Sheridan wrote Commissioner Howard. "We have to keep them on the plantations for their security and welfare, and the planters combine against their rights."[91]

Sheridan's cavalry columns were too late to intercept Jo Shelby. He had denounced Kirby Smith's surrender, called for volunteers, looted the arsenal at Corsicana in northeast Texas (augmenting his troopers' Sharps carbines with 10 Napoleon cannon, 2,000 Enfield rifles, and 40,000 rounds of ammunition), and set out for the Rio Grande, accumulating recruits along the way. By the time he reached Eagle Pass in early July, Shelby had mustered a thousand men.

"We will march into Mexico and reinstate Juárez or espouse the cause of Maximilian," he announced, then put the issue to a vote. The men opted to follow the emperor. In need of specie and not disposed to make a fetish of loyalty to his newfound allegiance, Shelby sold the cannon to the Juárez garrison at Piedras Negras across the river from Eagle Pass for $16,000 in silver and rode south for Monterrey.

Shelby's violent progress (*guerrillero* ambuscades, at least one pitched battle, a rogue raid on a Mexican ranch) ended in an audience with Maximilian in Mexico City in late August. Maximilian prudently declined Shelby's proposal to recruit a tough, battle-tested legion of forty thousand Confederate veterans to keep him on his throne. The brigade dissolved without further incident. Some of the men stayed on as colonists; others took passage for California; a few enlisted in the French army. Shelby himself retired to the new Confederate exile settlement of Carlota, in the Cordoba Valley ninety miles inland from Vera Cruz, to try his luck as a coffee planter.[92]

Lew Wallace, meantime, had turned reluctantly to the Andersonville war crimes trial, convening his court—three major generals, three brigadiers, and three lieutenant colonels—on August 21. Judge Advocate Norton P. Chipman would present the government's case, which charged Wirz with conspiracy "to injure the health and destroy the lives" of thousands of Union captives, and with thirteen individual counts of murder. These last alleged the cold-blooded killings (shootings in most cases, and a beating death in one) of unnamed Andersonville inmates.[93]

"I hear that the prisoner's defense will be that he obeyed orders received from his superiors," Wallace wrote his wife; "in other words, it is expected that out of this investigation will come proof of Jeff Davis' connection with that criminality. *Quien sabe!*"[94]

From the outset, Wallace regarded the bearded, heavily accented, cripple-armed, otherwise nondescript Wirz, forty-two years old, as something of an incarnate freak.

"Wirz is a singular looking genius," he wrote Susan. "He has a small head, retreating forehead, high on the *os frontis* because the hair, light in color, is very thin, threatening him with speedy baldness; prominent ears, small, sharp pointed nose, moustache and beard heavy enough to conceal the mouth and lower face, and of the dirty tobacco-stained color: eyes large, and of mixed blue and gray, very restless, and reminding you continually of a cat's when the animal is excited by the scent of prey: in manner he is nervous and fully alarmed, avoids your gaze, and withers under the knit brows of the court. His complexion is very ashen and bloodless, almost blue. Altogether he was well chosen for the awful duty.

"The prisoner is undoubtedly of the opinion that he is in danger of some kind of punishment," Wallace went on[95]—surely no great advertisement for Wirz's mental powers, as the court president considered the government's case airtight even before he heard a word of it.

For openers there were the thirteen thousand dead, an inconvenient number to account for by natural decrease over a mere fifteen months. As prosecutor Chipman observed, Andersonville lay in fertile, well-watered pine country, yet prisoners starved, suffered from thirst, shivered for lack of shelter and firewood. *Someone* had to answer for that. Just as the trial opened, Stanton ordered the names of Davis, Robert Lee, former war secretary James A. Seddon, and other high Confederates dropped from the conspiracy count. As Chipman noted in retrospect,* echoing Wallace on Dr. Mudd, Henry Wirz was all the government had; they would have to make the best of him.[96]

Defense counsel Otis H. Baker led off with a motion to dismiss the case, arguing that the amnesty terms of the armistice protected Wirz from punishment; that a U.S. military court had no jurisdiction since Wirz had never served in the Union army; and that if Wirz were to be tried at all, a civil court should do the trying. These legal quibbles might answer in a civilian setting. General Wallace sternly rejected them all.

Meeting every day in the hot, overfilled Court of Claims room in the Capitol, the commission heard testimony from rebel soldiers on duty at Andersonville and from about a hundred surviving prisoners. Government witnesses graphically described the disease, hunger, and misery endemic there, and the terrible last hours of many comrades and friends. Most claimed the cruelty had been deliberate.

Ex-prisoner James K. Davidson told the court that he heard Captain Wirz say he was "killing more damned Yankees there than Lee was at Richmond." That was in August 1864. "He was in my wagon at the time," Davidson added. "I had been to the graveyard with the dead men."

Chipman introduced and Wallace admitted masses of hearsay, secondhand evidence, vague claims, imprecise recollections. "I never saw a man shot there," Charles Tibbles testified, "but I heard the guns go off and saw the smoke, and saw the men after they were dead." Witnesses said they had been told that Wirz shot down men for crossing the dead line, allowed dogs to tear a prisoner to pieces, offered furloughs to guards for shooting prisoners who broke the rules.

---

*In his privately published *The Tragedy of Andersonville: The Trial of Captain Henry Wirz* (1911). Chipman wrote it in furious reaction to the Daughters of the Confederacy's sponsorship of a monument to Wirz as an Andersonville victim.

Lew Wallace sketched this scene of a Union prisoner reaching for water across the notorious Dead Line at Andersonville. In a note at the top, he reminds himself that the left arm needs work. When not sketching or dreaming of Mexico, Wallace presided over a show trial with a preordained outcome. Henry Wirz was hanged in Old Capitol Prison in November 1865, the only Civil War participant executed for war crimes. (Indiana Historical Society)

Martin E. Hogan, First Indiana Cavalry, told the court that he saw Wirz knock down an invalid prisoner and kick him. He saw blood streaming from the man's mouth or nose and heard that he died afterward. He couldn't recall the date of the attack, though, or even the victim's name.

Felix de la Baume, Thirty-fifth New York (a deserter, whose real name was Oeser, it turned out), said he saw Wirz shoot two men in a large group of arriving prisoners. One of the wounded men "looked in a dying condition," he said; he never saw the other man again and assumed he had died.

Hugh R. Snee, Thirty-ninth Illinois, testified that he heard six revolver shots as he stood with a large group of prisoners. A rebel subaltern told him later that Wirz had shot two men, one of them fatally.

Horatio B. Terrell, Seventy-second Ohio, said a Connecticut man named Fitzgerald relayed to him the dying statement of a black soldier who claimed that Wirz had shot him in the back. "There was a bullet in his back when he died," Terrell told the court.[97]

"The Comn. gets on bravely," Wallace wrote his wife. "The details are full of horror. Do you read the evidence?"[98]

Chipman entered an extract of the report Dr. Stephen Jones and Louis Manigault had prepared after their inspection of Andersonville in September 1864. Jones's account was unflinching. He faulted nearly every aspect of the sanitary and medical organization at the prison. Like others, though, he blamed the tragedy on conditions substantially beyond Henry Wirz's control. And he protested that Chipman had presented his conclusions selectively.

"The original report contains the excuses which were given by the officers present at Andersonville," Jones emphasized for the record, "and their efforts to better the condition of things."[99]

As Wallace foretold, Wirz offered a just-following-orders defense. "I was only the medium," he tried to explain, "or, I may better say, the tool in the hands of my superiors."[100] Wallace and the court, soldiers all, might have been expected to show a measure of sympathy with the plea. It failed to move Wallace, whose thoughts in any case were usually elsewhere. He made notes for an infantry tactical manual he hoped to sell to the army. He dashed off memos on Mexican recruitment to his colleagues on the court. He commuted to New York City on weekends to raise money for Juárez.

"Consequence is," he admitted to Susan, "I feel sleepy and heavy-handed, and easily disturbed by noises, and the dullest, most pointless cross-examinations of a witness that I ever listened to."[101]

Wallace met with President Johnson on September 18 to discuss his plan to float a large loan to arm the Mexican Republicans. He came away confident that Johnson would block neither the loan nor the colonization scheme (that is to say, the infiltration of mercenaries). "You may rest assured we will have no trouble from that quarter," he wrote José Carvajal, the Juárista envoy. And he assured Carvajal that he could withdraw from the Wirz court at any time should it become necessary.[102]

He passed a note during one interminable session asking General John Geary to raise a corps of volunteers for Mexico from his home state of Pennsylvania. "I will think of it and give answer back tomorrow," Geary replied. During another session, he launched a memo announcing that a Mexican force of nine hundred had fought a Belgian brigade four times its size to a standstill. Wallace wanted to know how many Belgians a thousand Americans could whip. Geary offered an estimate of twenty-two thousand. Chipman, late of the veteran Second Iowa, declined to answer. "I confess to having no stomach for any more fights," he wrote him.[103]

The outline of a large-canvas painting took form in Wallace's imagination as the testimony unfolded. "One of the witnesses testified that a poor prisoner, half dead with thirst, crawled under the dead line and was reaching a cup in the brook when a sentinel shot him dead," he wrote Susan. "That is my idea."[104] He made a rough pen-and-ink sketch in court and liked it well enough to pick up a stock of oils on one of his New York weekends.

The trial soon lost all appearance of fairness and impartiality. Chipman refused to concede an inch to the defense. Wallace helpfully sustained most of his objections and overruled most of defense counsel Baker's. He allowed Chipman to bully defense witnesses. When Wallace suggested at one point that the government might try a little harder to link the evidence and the charges, Chipman was unapologetic.

"Time and place are about the only particulars that can be testified to by these witnesses. They do not recollect names, and some of them hardly remember dates," he told the court.

"They do not even remember the months," Baker broke in.

"I doubt whether you or I would remember anything if we had gone through what they have," Chipman shot back.

"Then you should not attempt to prove it," Baker said.[105]

Chipman rose to challenge even the mildest claims on Wirz's behalf. The Reverend Peter Whelan, a Roman Catholic priest, served as a chaplain at Andersonville from June through September 1864. In his experience, Wirz had been calm and quiet most of the time.

"I have seen him commit no violence," Whelan testified. "He may sometimes have spoken harshly to some of the prisoners. I never heard of his killing a man, or striking a man with a pistol, or kicking a man to death."

"If any such thing occurred must you not have heard of it?" Baker asked.

"It is highly probable that I should have heard of it."[106]

Chipman aggressively cross-examined Whelan about his duties and routines. The priest testified that he reported to the stockade nearly every day, arriving around nine o'clock in the morning and staying until four or five in the afternoon.

"In the morning before going in I would say my prayers and read my office," Father Whelan told the court. "After I came out I continued saying my prayers. I was occupied with my own business and nobody else's."

"How then could you see or know everything that transpired there in reference to Captain Wirz," Chipman pounced, in the tone of a man who knows he has delivered a riposte of Jesuitical neatness and subtlety.

"I did not say that I did," the bewildered priest answered.[107]

Chipman dealt similarly with other efforts on Wirz's behalf. George Stoneman's cavalry raiders destroyed supplies bound for Andersonville and tore up track that could have carried rations there. Could that be accounted an extenuating circumstance? Did Wirz's middling rank absolve him? Could a captain in charge of a distant prison camp compete with senior frontline commanders for scarce supplies? Chipman dismissed such questions. The Wallace court made no effort to develop them. Whatever her husband thought, Sue Wallace felt a stirring of pity for the lone, weak, exposed Swiss jailer.

"I went in one day, the Generals sat up (seven in number) looking very dignified and stately—and the prisoner seemed as if he would be glad to have the mountains fall on him to hide him from the eyes of the court," she wrote her brother. "The man seemed in an agony of terror—almost dying of absolute fear, and it looks to me as if the whole power of the Government has put forth to crush one miserable worm. That Davis and Seddon should be in the place of their wretched tool."[108]

Animated and disputatious at the outset, Wirz grew quiet, almost apathetic, as the trial progressed. He was much subject to headaches and complained of a lack of medical attention. At one point Wallace, impatient to conclude the case, ordered Wirz carried into the courtroom on a stretcher. Baker and his associate, Louis J. Schade, lacked the resources to pay investigators to track down potential defense witnesses and bring them to Washington.

"My conscience is clear," Wirz wrote in an appeal for money and sympathy to the copperhead *New York News*. "I have never dealt cruelly with a prisoner under my charge. If they suffered for want of food, shelter, clothing and necessaries I could not help it—having no control over these things—things which the Confederate government could give only in very limited quantity even to our own men."[109]

The legal machinery ground on toward its foreordained conclusion. The last weeks of summer were dry; Washington was blighted and dusty, the streets dug up for sewers, the canal and the Potomac stagnant and stinking. Wallace met with Grant on Mexican matters on October 15. Rain fell intermittently that day, breaking the drought at last. With the chill overcast, Sue Wallace broke out the guidebooks and dreamed of spiriting her restless husband away to a villa on a Mediterranean island, out of range of cold autumn dews, the frosts and snows of winter, and civil war in Mexico.

"If the loan succeeds Lew will certainly go, and if it fails all fails," she wrote her mother glumly. "A large number of rebel officers have gone into the emperor's service, and eventually there must be a struggle on the Rio Grande."[110]

Wirz awaited the verdict in his cell at the Old Capitol Prison. The turnkey Dutton found him irascible, ill-tempered, repellent. Wirz spoke with a harsh accent; he read books written in German; he swore at his guards and attendants; he seemed tranquil only in the company of the Washington priest, the Reverend F. H. Boyle, who visited him regularly, bringing delicacies (or so Dutton remembered) from copperhead sympathizers in the capital.

Wirz rose early on October 24, the sixty-third day of his trial, to write to one of his supporters, Carrie Furlow, the young wife of an officer of the Andersonville garrison. The prisons were empty of politicals now, except for Jefferson Davis. Wirz was by turns bitterly defiant, submissive, detached.

"Great God," he wrote Miss Carrie, "is it possible that I should suffer for the faults of others? There are moments when I even doubt that I was the Captain Wirz spoken of, that fiend, that devil held up to the just execration of the world.

"If it is decided that I shall be the victim to be sacrificed upon the altar of an offended country, I am satisfied, yea more than satisfied, I shall be proud, the idea that by losing my life the life of other men, better, greater than I am, will be saved enables me to look on calm and patient. God grant that my life will be the last one demanded to pacify the people."

He ended with a malediction on the former prisoners who had lied about him, accused him of unspeakable crimes, covered him with infamy.

"I have cursed them often, & my curse I will leave them as my legacy. It will follow them standing, walking, sitting, eating, sleeping. I will haunt them to their dying hour, like Cain shall they find no rest no peace."[111]

George Dutton pocketed the letter as a souvenir. Carrie Furlow wasn't family, he explained afterward, and it didn't address family matters. Later that morning the Wallace court found Henry Wirz, the self-described "poor, despised prison-keeper of Andersonville," guilty of conspiracy and of eleven of the thirteen counts of murder and sentenced him to hang.

# 9

# Fallow and Neglected Lands

THE LECONTES RALLIED with the coming of autumn. A little money came in from Liberty County, not as much as Joseph LeConte expected, but enough to see the family through to the New Year, when South Carolina College would reopen. "I began to live again somewhat as usual," he wrote in retrospect.[1] As the familiar patterns of private life were reestablished, so, too, did South Carolina public life take on a reassuring shape for LeConte—the immediate consequence of Andrew Johnson's liberal restoration policy. He met some of the officers of the Federal garrison socially, though his wife refused to entertain any Yankee in her home. He knew Governor Perry fairly well. With men of Perry's type in high office, it seemed to him, South Carolina's political future would be secure.

"Perry has been empowered by Johnson to act as he pleases with the exception of remanding the negroes to slavery," Emma LeConte remarked complacently. "Their fine President seems disposed to adopt a conciliatory policy."[2]

Just so: Benjamin Perry, the reluctant secessionist, evidently enjoyed the president's confidence. He had learned of his appointment on the way to Washington to urge Johnson to name someone to the post. Tall and massive, bewigged, with gold-bowed spectacles and a gold-headed cane, Perry cut a conspicuous figure in the capital.

He was, in the words of the new liberal weekly the *Nation*, "a living, moving, smoking, and probably chewing evidence that South Carolina had not been forgotten." He met more than once with Johnson, who held views on state's rights identical to his own and listened sympathetically to his complaints about the African American garrisons.[3]

"The colored troops ought to be removed," Perry advised the president. "They are demoralizing the freedmen & we have serious cause to apprehend an insurrection." In the governor's hometown, Greenville, a party of black soldiers knocked down a white man walking with a lady, and another robbed a wagoner. True, these incidents happened after a local rowdy shot at a black Yankee, wounding him in the knee; but Perry wanted the offending regiment sent away all the same. In mid-September, General Gillmore ordered the withdrawal of all black troops to the coast where, as Perry put it, they could do no further mischief.[4]

Such actions mollified South Carolina whites. "They are *all* anxious to resume their allegiance to the U States & truly sorry for their past rebellion," Perry assured Johnson, laying it on a bit thick. "They will act in good faith hereafter." He promised, too, that the state constitutional convention, called for September 13, would "abolish slavery and carry out the other views we discussed," including a reapportionment that would shift political power from the long-dominant Low Country planters to Johnson's favored class, the up-country yeomanry.[5]

The physical rebuilding of Columbia progressed more slowly than political restoration. Journalist Sidney Andrews, in town to cover the constitutional convention for Boston and Chicago newspapers, found a wilderness of ruins still. But Columbians were industrially clearing away the rubble of the February fire and rows of small, cheap houses were going up apace. Even so, Columbia remained desperately poor. Andrews figured that $20,000 would buy up the entire stock of dry goods, clothing, and groceries in the city's shops.

For those who had struggled through the silent spring and the arid, Yankee-infested summer, though, these mild, quiet early weeks of autumn were a balm. The John LeContes were still working their way through a gift of *real* coffee from Josie's sister Mollie, a luxury unsampled for years. The storekeepers' shelves may have looked bare to the Northerner Andrews, accustomed to plenty. To Josie LeConte, denied so much for so long, they were loaded with treasure.

"There are upwards of seventy stores," she wrote Mollie. "You would call them shanties, but at any rate they have a vast variety of things in them."[6]

The ruins were an inescapable reminder of Columbia's ordeal. Nobody had forgotten the fire; every white Columbian accepted as an article of faith that Sherman had ordered it set. Some senior former Confederates were trying to put together a case against the Yankee anathema, one to be tried in the court of Northern opinion if nowhere else. General D. H. Hill wrote from North Carolina to ask John Le-Conte to collect affidavits from witnesses who had seen Union soldiers starting fires.

"Did Hampton really burn any cotton in Columbia?" Hill wanted to know. "If so, could this have caused the general conflagration? Were there any escaped Federal soldiers in Columbia?"[7]

Hill warned LeConte to proceed with caution. Few Southerners were so wary as Hill in expressing their views ("It is important that my mission should not be known," he wrote LeConte conspiratorially), and hardly anyone recognized a need for sworn statements. The case against Sherman was open and shut. Only the sentence remained to be executed.

"I have been told by dozens of men that he couldn't well walk up the main street of Columbia in the daytime without being shot," Sidney Andrews reported, "and three different gentlemen, residing in different parts of the State, declare that Wade Hampton expresses a purpose to shoot him at sight whenever and wherever he meets him."[8]

As it happened, Hampton had gone to ground at one of the family estates in the North Carolina highlands. His failure to do any damage to Sherman's army the previous winter had cost him none of his personal popularity, and his name still carried immense prestige at home. But Hampton failed to claim his delegate's place at the constitutional convention, and let it be known that he would categorically refuse the governorship, which everyone acknowledged would be his for the taking.

So the convention opened in the undamaged Baptist Church* at noon on September 13, 1865, without Lieutenant General Wade

---

*The secession convention had assembled there in December 1860 before moving on to Charleston.

Hampton in attendance. The shattered Confederacy was well represented nonetheless. Among the 101 delegates were James L. Orr, a former member of the Confederate Senate; Francis W. Pickens, South Carolina's first secession governor; the well-traveled, often-wounded Major General Samuel McGowan, CSA (Fort Sumter, both Manassas battles, Antietam, Fredericksburg, Chancellorsville, the Wilderness campaign); three other generals, six colonels and twenty or so officers of lesser rank; and a dozen delegates to the secession convention of 1860.

No African Americans were invited, but even so (in deference to Andrew Johnson) the delegates were a picture of democratic inclusiveness by the prewar standards of this least democratic of all the once-united states. From colonial times, property qualifications had severely restricted the suffrage in South Carolina; the legislature, not the people, chose the state's governors; and representatives usually voted in secret, so they could veil their actions from their constituents if they chose.

Perry urged the delegates in his opening statement to sweep away those quaint political customs. He instructed them to repeal the ordinance of secession and adopt a constitutional clause formally abolishing slavery. Astonishingly, some delegates came determined to debate this last point, to demand compensation for slave property and to enact a clause restricting former slaves to menial labor. The hard-liners found the governor in no mood for cavil.

"African slavery, which was a cherished institution of South Carolina from her earliest history, is gone, dead forever, never to be revived or hoped for in the future of this state," he told the delegates.

Perry could claim inside of a week that the chief purposes of the convention had been achieved, or soon would be: "The committee has reported in favor of abolishing slavery, equalizing representation, electing the Governor and Presidential electors by the people and voting *viva voce* in the legislature," he wrote the president. Perry did not add that the delegates haggled endlessly over the wording of the abolition amendment, with a view to making it plain the Yankees had forced emancipation upon the state; rejected black suffrage out of hand ("They forget that this is a white man's government, and intended for white men only," the governor himself said of advocates of black voting rights); and expected from now on to be left wholly free of Federal supervision and interference.[9]

"I intend to vote for prohibiting slavery in the constitution, only on the condition that we alone should have the right to manage our own political affinities in our own way," General McGowan announced. "If not, I would prefer martyrdom."[10]

This expressed the temper of the convention pretty faithfully. Joe LeConte followed the deliberations with attention. Writing long afterward, he recalled that he had strongly supported "a franchise *without distinction of color*,"* with property and educational qualifications for everyone. "But that was impossible," he went on, "as the leaders had not 'backbone' enough to propose it and the people were not ready to endorse it."[11] For one thing, a literacy requirement would deny the vote to a lot of whites—perhaps a quarter of South Carolina's voting-age white male population.

True to form, the convention refused to make even a show of decency and accept a petition from Charleston blacks on the question. Sidney Andrews found only four or five men among all those he spoke to over the fifteen-day life of the convention willing to consider so much as a theoretical possibility of suffrage for the 5 percent or so of blacks who could read and write. Emma Holmes's uncle Edward Frost, a Charleston delegate, was virtually the only speaker to address the matter openly.

"We must concede that the negro is a free man, having civil rights, having property rights, having the right to be represented in the body politic, and unquestionably destined at no very distant day to have political rights," Frost said.

This verged on blackest treason. Perhaps only Frost's advanced age and lofty social station saved him from the fate that, from what Andrews had gathered, awaited any Southron who advocated even moderately enlightened views on race; that is to say, "of being found dead some morning—shot from behind, as is the custom of the country."[12]

A DISAPPOINTING COTTON HARVEST in the Sea Islands: A caterpillar infestation followed the drought of early summer, and few farmers managed to raise more than half a crop. The Northern plantation superintendents complained, too, of an outbreak of cotton thieving, a

---

*The italics are LeConte's.

product of hard times—black farmers mixing in stolen seed and marketable fiber with their own modest stocks. "This is the first fruit of making land-owners of the negroes," one of them remarked sourly. These setbacks and frustrations no doubt encouraged Edward Philbrick, the Massachusetts abolitionist-planter, to deliver on his 1864 promise to sell off some of his holdings to the freedmen. He wrote from Boston in October offering "good, arable land" on two of his Saint Helena plantations for $5 an acre.[13]

Andrew Johnson's policy of pardon and restoration touched off a Secesh land rush into the Low Country. Most former Confederates were so confident of regaining their property that they were already making arrangements for next year's planting, seeking hands for the initial task, the early winter collection of marsh grass and mud for fertilizer. The abandoned mainland holdings seemed available for the taking, in spite of Sherman's Special Orders Number 15. And lawyers in Charleston were preparing court challenges to the titles of lands confiscated for nonpayment of taxes and sold in 1863 and 1864. Until now, those titles had been regarded as impregnable.

The Sea Islanders were polite but distant, wary. "The people receive the rebels better than we expected," Laura Towne observed, "but the reason is they believe Johnson is going to put them in their old masters' hands again, and they feel they must conciliate or be crushed."[14] The white refugees of 1861 had lost everything to war and revolution; on their return, some found their former slaves surprisingly solicitous. There were instances of freedmen making small gifts of money and poultry to the old masters. All the same, the freed people were determined to hold onto what they had gained.

The once-powerful Fripps turned up to lay claim to their former holdings on Saint Helena. Clarence Fripp, a physician, set up a medical practice in the village next to his old plantation house, which Towne and Ellen Murray had occupied since 1862. John Fripp approached Philbrick about regaining his land, appealing to the Bostonian's "sense of justice and generosity." Philbrick barely broke even on the 1865 crop, but he and his Massachusetts partners had cleared a profit of $19,000 on 1864 cotton and he had no intention of giving the land away. Philbrick invited Fripp to make an offer. Meantime, he wondered how the new Freedmen's Bureau land policy would play out.

"You may see by the papers that General Howard is sent by the President to see if he can reconcile the claims of the negroes on Edisto and other islands with those of the former owners who clamor to be reinstated in their position," he wrote a friend. "I guess General Howard will have a tough job. I don't envy him."[15]

Petitions reached Howard from every quarter. Mrs. R. S. Cheves wrote to beg for the restoration of family lands on the Ogeechee River below Savannah, saying she and her husband "were impoverished in the last degree." Bureau agents in South Carolina, Georgia, Florida, Alabama, and Mississippi reported up-country blacks as impatiently awaiting their land grants and everywhere refusing to work for the old masters. Northern veterans wrote to inquire about carpetbagging opportunities in the South. The offer of a Regular Army commission had not come through for Charley Morse, late of the Second Massachusetts. He enlisted Major General Francis Barlow, a former brigade commander under Howard, on his and a friend's behalf.

"They are both good officers and good fellows with sound Massachusetts principles, & are just the people whom it is for our good to settle in the South," Barlow wrote the commissioner.[16]

Howard went down to Richmond in mid-September, the start of a two-month Southern inspection tour that would include a stopover in the Sea Islands. As Philbrick noted, President Johnson had ordered Howard to "effect an agreement mutually satisfactory to the freedmen and the land-owners" there—in plain language, to inveigle the freed people out of their homesteads.[17] Restoration of the 800,000 abandoned acres in bureau control was well advanced*; this latest instruction, as Howard understood it, effectively revoked Special Orders Number 15. He saw at once that any deal he could strike would weigh heavily in favor of the returning planters.

"Why did I not resign?" Howard asked long afterward. "Because I even yet strongly hoped in some way to befriend the freed people."[18]

Yet Howard relied too much on faith, too little on good works. "Let me tell you my method of solving the problem," he once con-

---

*Most of those lands would be back in the hands of pardoned Confederates by the end of the year.

fided to a meeting of the Maine Freedmen's Religious Association. "It is, get more of the spirit of Christ." Unfortunately, that proved of little temporal value. The five thousand or so Sea Island families with written possessory titles under the Sherman orders needed more than the operation of the divine spirit to hold onto their farms.[19]

Rufus Saxton and Charles Howard conspired to put some starch into the commissioner—or anyway bring him around to a policy of passive resistance to Johnson. They knew that sentiment existed in Congress for land grants to former slaves. Possibly Thad Stevens, George Julian, and other Radicals could be rallied to the Sea Islanders' cause—and to the larger cause of 4 million landless blacks.

"Let the matter be defended till Congress meets & I am sure a permanent title will be given to the actual settlers on these islands," Charles urged him.[20]

Howard, traveling with his brother Rowland, reached Charleston on October 17. There they met Charles, now seconded to the Freedmen's Bureau as Saxton's chief of staff. Howard spent the night with Rufus and Matilda Saxton at their Meeting Street house, and walked a few doors along the street to bureau headquarters in the morning for a session with rice magnate William Aiken and a delegation of white landowners.

Howard relayed the presidential wishes. Willard Saxton, Charles Howard, and the junior officers tried to eavesdrop. "We are all interested and do not attend to business altogether," Willard confessed in his journal.[21] Howard met later in the day with Charleston's mayor and aldermen. Both meetings went well—too well, in Willard's view.

"'Tis the policy of the President to conciliate, & Gen. Howard is carrying out his orders," he went on. "If all would go as smooth and fair as they [Southerners] talked, there would be no difficulty in the state, & the bureau and the troops might be removed. But the majority of them look upon the freedmen as 'niggers' & they are not to be trusted yet."[22]

Howard set out for Edisto Island on the morning of October 19. Rowland stayed behind, housebound with an attack of diarrhea; Saxton chose not to go. The commissioner, Charles Howard, the planters' representative Colonel William Whaley, and one or two others met a restless crowd of a thousand men and women packed into and around a mid-island church. Everyone on Edisto had known in advance of

Howard's visit, and of its purpose. In the heat, noise, and confusion, a woman began to sing.

> Nobody knows the trouble I feel—
>   Nobody knows but Jesus. . . .

The throng joined in a seemingly endless repetition of the lament. Howard's manners were formal, even stiff on most occasions, but he thoroughly approved of expressions of religious fervor. An evangelical atmosphere loosened him up. When everyone settled down finally, Howard rose to the pulpit to report what President Johnson had said to him before he left Washington, and to convey the gist of his orders. He asked the freed people to consider the fairest way of restoring the planters' lands.

"They did not hiss," Howard recalled, "but their eyes flashed unpleasantly, and with one voice they cried, No, No!"

Amid the uproar, a thickset, powerful freedman shouted down from the gallery, "Why do you take our lands? You take them from us who are true, always true, to the government. You give them to our all-time enemies."[23]

Howard waited for the clamor to subside. The scene moved him. He wanted to help. Perhaps he remembered just then what Charles had suggested about the possibility of congressional intervention. In any case, he offered the islanders what sounded like a fresh promise.

"Congress must meet before any lands can be had and before I can buy any for you," he told them.[24]

The immediate problem remained. At Howard's suggestion the freed people chose three of their number to represent them in talks with the bureau and the planters. The committee promptly reported that the islanders would refuse to work under overseers for their late masters. If they could *rent* the lands they now occupied, they would grudgingly consent to the planters' return. A few might work for wages so long as there were no overseers about, but the general wish was to rent the lands and work them as their own.

Howard set up a supervisory board in which the government, the planters, and the freedmen were equally represented. "The freedmen and the planters could form contracts for rental or for labor with wages, but before the latter could do so his land must be for-

Former slaves with a U.S. government mule cart pose in front of a trim cabin on Edisto Island, South Carolina. Rufus Saxton parceled out hundreds of homesteads to Edisto freedmen before Andrew Johnson intervened. The president sent Freedmen's commissioner Oliver Otis Howard to Edisto in October 1865 to explain that the government had revoked Sherman's promise of land and that islanders would either have to contract with returning landowners or leave their homes. (New-York Historical Society)

mally restored," Howard explained carefully. Once in possession, the planters would be obliged to allow the freed people to stay in their homes so long as they agreed to contract or lease. Freedmen who refused to do one or the other would have two months' notice to leave.[25]

Howard detailed a junior officer, Captain Alexander P. Ketchum, to supervise the restorations, "relieving Rufus," Willard Saxton noted, "of a duty that would have been repulsive to him."[26] That may have been Howard's intent. He admired Saxton. And his heart went out to the islanders. Even so, he returned to Charleston in a complacent mood, a disagreeable duty successfully accomplished.

"They will submit, but with evident sorrow to the breaking of the promise of General Sherman's order," Howard wrote Edwin Stanton. "I am convinced that something must be done to give these people and others the prospect of homesteads."[27]

Howard the soldier had carried out Johnson's wishes almost to the letter. Whaley, the planters' representative, was appreciative at any rate. "I trust that full justice will always be done to the people by the landowners," he wrote the commissioner, "and that you will never have cause to regret it."[28] But Howard's forceful execution of the presidential will caught Stanton the politician by surprise.

"I do not understand that your orders require you to disturb the freedmen in their possession at present, but only to ascertain whether a just, mutual agreement can be made," the war secretary wrote him.[29]

This took Howard aback. He *had* set an eviction process in motion, though he reminded himself that he'd left the freed people a way out: they could rent or contract to work. And he could rely on Saxton and Ketchum to do everything in their power to safeguard the islanders' interests.

By now, though, Saxton's days were numbered. The planters wanted him gone, and neither Stanton nor Howard could protect him much longer. Johnson wired Howard in mid-tour to ask whether he had anyone in mind for a replacement. "Gen. Saxton will probably be removed as he is not satisfactory to the President nor the old citizens of South Carolina—i.e. the whites," Charles Howard observed.[30] The commissioner passed the word to Saxton, probably with kindly intent, to prepare him for the change to come. Johnson would buy Saxton off if possible, sack him if necessary.

"It has been the same as promised that if he would leave this field he could have any position he wanted elsewhere," Willard Saxton wrote. "But he will stay until the order comes. Tis glorious to suffer for truth's sake."[31]

The president's policy would remain in place whether Saxton went quietly or forced Howard to fire him. By Saxton's order, the government on December 9 restored four mainland plantations to Ann Elliott—The Bluff, Middle Place, Social Hall, and Oak Lawn. Her son Ralph took possession at once, duly warning the emancipated people in residence to make contracts or move away. "I do not think there will be any difficulty in getting labor," his brother Thomas advised. "Starvation will bring them to their senses by February at any rate." Saxton rejected the widow Elliott's petition for island property confiscated for tax arrears, directing her to apply to the Treasury Department in Washington for restoration of Shell Point on Saint

Helena, Myrtle Grove on Hilton Head, and Bay Plantation near Beaufort.[32]

Thomas Elliott ventured out from Beaufort to tour the disputed Sea Island plantations. The former slaves were friendly and polite and asked him to send along their best wishes to the family. Hilton Head amazed him. "I was lost in wonder at the vast buildings," he wrote his sister Emily; "the wharf is 1,400 feet long & cost $300,000." While Northern engineering impressed him, he reacted with baffled outrage to Northern business practices. The visit to Myrtle Grove had not gone well.

"I saw the man who hires it from the Govt. & he is like all the rest of the Yankee nation—a skin flint," he complained to Emily. "What will be done by Congress to restore the lands to the former proprietors is impossible to say."[33]

Returning to Washington on November 18, Howard at once recommended to Stanton that the United States purchase the Sherman lands from their prewar owners and rent or sell farmsteads to as many blacks as wanted them.[34] Johnson dismissed the notion out of hand.

Emma Holmes dashed off a cheerful summary of these developments in her diary. The president had risen from drunken tailor to hero in her estimation. "All the lands and houses are being returned to their owners & all negro troops ordered to be disbanded & all negroes ordered to go to work or they are to be sent to Africa," she wrote.[35] This trend had not yet become evident to the freed people. Tens of thousands of former slaves still believed absolutely that the government would sponsor a general division of plantation lands at Christmas—forty acres for every landless adult male, white or black.

With tensions on the rise as the holiday approached, Howard's agents fanned out into the remote regions to let the people know where matters stood. Ralph Ely, the Columbia district sub-assistant commissioner, reached Edgefield late on the raw, overcast afternoon of December 15. The country people streamed into the courthouse square all through the night. They wore their best clothes and were in high spirits in spite of the steady fall of a cold rain.

Village whites looked on apprehensively as the square filled. "Oh, they've come now," the landlord of the tavern opposite the courthouse warned. "Now they're to get their half of the land and the stock." Anything less, he predicted, "and there'll be a hell of a row today." By the time Ely rose to speak, some 2,000 blacks were crowded into the square.[36]

They were free to establish schools for their children, Ely told them, free to meet for religious worship, free to seek work wherever they chose. But they must honor any contracts they made. And any freedman who wanted his own farm must earn the money to buy it. Wartime promises no longer applied, Ely went on; there was no point in striking out for the Sherman tracts, for the government had no land to give away. The crowd let out a long, disappointed groan. To the tavern keep's surprise and perhaps disappointment, they packed up without delay and headed peacefully and quietly homeward.[37]

The islands were in turmoil still. Colonel Whaley's promises about protecting the freedmen's interests turned out to be spurious, at least in Charles Howard's view. Whaley complained bitterly about Ketchum's tendency to take the homesteaders' part, threatening to bring his case against the agent to Stanton in Washington, and he chose to boycott* Howard's land board because the freedmen had elected one of their own to represent them.

"Mr. Whaley's regard for the negro is only a *white wash*," Charles wrote his brother. "He has recently shown the old cloven foot in refusing absolutely to have anything to do with a board having a colored man on it."[38]

The commissioner gave in and replaced the black member with a white bureau agent. He considered removing Ketchum, who was guilty as charged of refusing to compel labor contracts and of pressuring planters to lease or even sell land to freedmen.

Ketchum returned to Edisto with a group of planters in early December. In the aftermath of the October meeting some eighty refugee families had packed up (hoes, seed stocks, and such household belongings as they had been able to accumulate), left their crops in the fields, and trudged back to their home country around Savannah.[39] Anything, they seemed to be saying, was preferable to

---

*The term is an anachronism here, for Captain Charles Boycott did not face ostracism from his Irish tenants until around 1880. Still the Sea Islands dispute had something in common with the Land League agitation in Ireland fifteen years later.

working for or even renting from the returning Secesh. As it happened, Ketchum found things somewhat calmer on Edisto than he expected.

"But many will *never* contract with their old owners," he concluded.[40]

RICHARD EWELL, THE VIRGINIA PAROLEE, applied to General George Meade in mid-October for permission to travel to Philadelphia to be fitted for an artificial leg. Ewell's Second Corps had given Meade, now commanding the Division of the Atlantic, all manner of anxious times at Gettysburg twenty-seven months before, but he granted Ewell's request all the same, and even authorized him to go on from Philadelphia to his wife's estate in Maury County, Tennessee.

So Ewell had completed his rehabilitation. Ned Ripley, the Vermonter who doused the Richmond fires, might regard him as the wanton destroyer of the rebel capital, but the federal authorities never seriously contemplated bringing him to trial. They let him off with fifteen weeks served. In President Johnson's view, the pardon process forced former Confederates to express contrition for the crime of rebellion—sufficient punishment. Looking back on the wartime experience, Ewell felt an occasional stirring of doubt. Had he done the right thing? Yet he could not imagine having acted differently.

"Regret," he used to say, "is not to be confounded with repentance."[41]

Lizinka Ewell's son had taken possession of Spring Hill and the other restored properties at the end of summer. The local bureau agents were helpful, Campbell Brown discovered; they placed no obstacles in his way and he worked like a cart horse to prepare the estate for the Ewells' arrival and the planting season of 1866.[42]

Half the timber still stood in Spring Hill woods, much of it valuable. Brown figured that buying a portable army sawmill would be the cheapest way to supply cordwood and fencing—he estimated the need at 50,000 board feet for outside fencing alone. The Yankees would sell horses and mules, too, if you knew which ones to approach. The houses and cabins were in fair condition and all were tenanted. The stable still stood, though the weatherboards had been stripped off. The main house could be made habitable for General and Mrs. Ewell in six weeks.[43]

Though the president used his pardoning power liberally in the autumn of 1865, two state prisoners remained locked up in Fort Warren. Alexander Stephens had grown despondent as time passed with no change in his or John Reagan's circumstances. Night terrors pursued him, and he dreamed of seeing several Confederate colleagues hanged. Stephens appealed to Grant, to Seward, to Johnson himself, emphasizing his prewar Unionism, his long feud with Jeff Davis, and his earnest attempt to negotiate peace at Hampton Roads. The president agreed to relax the conditions of his imprisonment, permitting him visitors, newspapers, and visits with Reagan. The two messed together now and Stephens had become fond of the rough-mannered, tobacco-chewing Texan. He even forgave his knocking over the spittoon as they sat at a game of piquet one night. The garrison cat adopted him. But no further word came from Johnson.[44]

"I am now satisfied that I am nothing but a sort of political hostage, held without regard to personal merits or demerits," Stephens wrote glumly in his journal. "Here I am held in prison while leading fire-eaters, excepting Mr. Davis and a few others, are at large."[45]

He read of his imminent release in the Boston and New York newspapers, yet nothing happened. Grant spoke up for him. Massachusetts governor Andrew took up his cause. Senator Henry Wilson of Massachusetts sent him a copy of his book, *Anti-Slavery Measures in Congress*. Finally, on October 12, during his twenty-second week in confinement, the guards brought word that Johnson had signed the order for his release. He and Reagan boarded the mailboat for Boston that evening.[46]

Stephens called at the White House on the way home to Georgia. He claimed he told Johnson that he favored limited suffrage for the emancipated people, and a network of schools. These comparatively enlightened views evidently made no impression on the president. Stephens thought he wanted African Americans "removed from the country as the Indians were," perhaps concentrated on reserved lands west of the Mississippi.[47]

If Stephens contemplated a quiet interlude at home, he reckoned without Georgia's restoration legislature, which approached him with the offer of a U.S. Senate seat. Stephens remained under the ban,*

---

*The president would sign Stephens's pardon on February 26, 1866.

though, and Johnson signaled his strong disapproval. He had been the second-ranking officer of the Confederacy, after all, and he believed even now in the principle of secession. ("I opposed secession as a question of policy, and not one of right," he would tell the congressional Joint Committee on Reconstruction. "My convictions on the original abstract questions have undergone no change."[48]) This scheme of sending Stephens to the Senate was an affront, hardly the way to further Johnson's policy of drawing the errant states in easy stages back into the Union.

As one notorious Georgian weighed the prospect of a new career in the U.S. Senate, another shuffled off to the gallows. Henry Wirz was unrepentant to the last. A New York parson, a stranger, wrote him a few days before the end, concluding a long letter of abuse with a list of Bible passages that would prepare him to meet his maker. Wirz struck off a furious reply.

"I consider myself a victim to satisfy just such as you, who cry after my blood, and are too craven-hearted to ask for the punishment of those who are guilty, because they are men who have friends, influence, means at their command, things I unfortunately have not."[49]

The president confirmed the Wallace court's sentence on November 6. George Dutton supervised the hanging of Wirz at the Old Capitol Prison between ten and eleven o'clock on the morning of November 10. When it was done a soldier detail cut the body down and buried it alongside that of George Atzerodt, the Lincoln conspirator.[50]

Neither Alexander Stephens nor any of the other former Confederates chosen for high office in the autumn of 1865 bore any responsibility for Andersonville, even indirectly. Dozens of newly elected officials had blood on their hands even so. True, some of these men, possibly most of them, had spoken out against secession in 1860. Yet most went on to give the Confederacy the best they had in them. Now they anticipated a restoration as near as possible to the Southern world of 1860—less a quarter-million dead Confederate soldiers, of course, and with formal acceptance of the passing of slavery.

Along with Stephens, the South sent four Confederate generals, five colonels, six ex-cabinet officials, and fifty-eight state or Confederate representatives to the U.S. Congress. Not one of these men, whether prewar Unionist or ardent secessionist, could swear the 1862 test oath that he had never borne arms against the United States or held local or national office under the Confederacy. An increasing number, though, could flash presidential pardons. They might fail an ironclad test of loyalty, but the president had absolved them.[51]

In South Carolina, Wade Hampton nearly won the governorship as an unwilling write-in. The defiant General McGowan and ex-governor Aiken were elected to the U.S. House. The legislature sent Provisional Governor Perry, the ex-Confederate judge, to the Senate. Mississippi chose former rebel general Benjamin G. Humphreys as governor. Unpardoned and unapologetic, Humphreys had opposed secession in '61 but went on to command a Confederate infantry brigade at Gettysburg, Chickamauga, and the Wilderness. His onetime division commander Lafayette McLaws, no longer meditating a career in the army of Argentina, won election as clerk of the Superior Court of Richmond County (Augusta), Georgia.

"There seems in many of the elections something like defiance, which is all out of place at this time," Andrew Johnson remarked sourly.[52]

Still, the president could argue that the old fire-eaters had been repudiated. South Carolina might have done worse than Perry and governor-elect James Orr, a former Confederate senator. "He is certainly behind the age but ahead of South Carolina, I think, even now & this is hopeful," Charles Howard said of Perry.[53] The results were troubling to Northerners all the same. As the wartime leadership returned to power with Johnson's approbation, or at least acquiescence, only the occupation forces seemed to stand in the way of a complete restoration of the rebel South.

The freedmen had no say in any of these political arrangements, though not for lack of trying. A freedmen's convention at the Zion Church in Charleston in November petitioned the all-white South Carolina legislature and the U.S. Congress for educational opportunity, the rule of law for all citizens, equal suffrage, and the right to engage in every form of economic enterprise.

"*We are now free*. We are now *all* free," the Charleston convention reminded the South Carolina legislature, then debating a Black Code for former slaves. "We need not assure you with what deep concern we are watching *all* your deliberations, but especially those that have peculiar reference to us."[54]

The Black Codes were a direct outcome of the autumn elections in the South. On one level, they sought to codify the freedmen's rights and responsibilities. Former slaves were permitted to own property, make contracts, testify in court (though only in cases involving other blacks). "At first reading that might seem fair," Charles Howard wrote his brother in Washington. "But it is utterly rejected by the colored people. They claim that the laws of the land for the governance of *whites* are adequate to their cases also and that this legislating against color should *end* with slavery." On a closer reading, Howard saw that the codes contained restrictive clauses that regulated most aspects of social and economic behavior and kept plantation blacks in a state of virtual peonage.[55]

The South Carolina code assessed blacks who sought work as other than farmers or servants annual fees of as much as $100. Blacks were required to sign contracts mandating labor from sunrise to sunset. Vagrancy laws made leaving a plantation without the owner's consent a crime. The town of Opelousas, Louisiana, barred any "negro or freedman" from the corporate limits "without special permission from his employers, specifying the object of the visit and the time necessary for the accomplishment of the same." Louisiana's code provided for the arrest of freedmen who had not signed labor contracts by January 10, 1866. Mississippi's forced apprenticeships on all former slaves younger than eighteen.[56]

President Johnson nonetheless certified all the former Confederate states except Texas as reconstructed. Their leaders might have been Union men in Johnson's view, but they were one with the fire-eaters on the race issue. Even the conservative General James Steedman, commanding Federal occupation forces in Georgia, could see that. "Their political principles, as well as their views on the slavery question, are the same as before the war, and all that can be expected of them is that they will submit to actual necessities from which there is no escape," Steedman reported.[57]

Johnson himself offered the freed people scarcely more than a bare acknowledgment of abolition. "I have but little to say," he told members of the First District of Columbia Volunteers (Colored) at the regiment's mustering out in October, "it being unusual in this Government and in most other Governments to have colored troops in their service." Then he went on to harangue the men about "the glorious privilege of work, of pursuing the ordinary avocations of peace with industry and economy." He omitted any mention of voting rights, but did advise the discharged soldiers to stay out of low saloons and to practice sexual restraint.[58]

Meantime, reports of the *codes noir* were filtering up from the lower South. Congressional Radicals were only too aware of them, and of the election results, too. As the Thirty-ninth Congress prepared to convene in early December, Radicals vowed to block the admission of the rebels-elect and sink Johnson's Reconstruction policy.

George Julian presented the hard-line Radical case in a speech to the Indiana Legislature in Indianapolis on November 17. A speech for the hustings, never intended for wide distribution, it was by turns blunt, funny, and sarcastic. Julian told the mostly Republican crowd that the war had settled but one question absolutely: the military defeat of the Confederacy by numbers and violence.

"All else is in dispute," he said. "There has been no moment, in my judgment, since the beginning of this war so full of peril to the nation as at the present. I may refer to the testimony of Governor Brownlow,* who says the only difference between the rebels of to-day and of 1861 is that a good many of them are under the ground."[59]

Julian offered his nostrum for a permanent settlement: the punishment of rebel leaders, beginning with Davis and Robert Lee ("I would hang liberally, while I had my hand in," he said with candor); confiscation of rebel estates and their parceling out to the poor, white and black; and the ballot for former slaves. He advanced a lively argument for the black franchise on grounds of justice, gratitude, and political expediency. At the same time, he admitted the delicacy of the question in racially conservative Indiana.[60]

"You know how gladly I would avoid the question if I could," Julian told the legislators, who were doubtless shifting uneasily in their seats by now. "Let me say to you, by way of quieting your nerves, that I won't preach in favor of black suffrage to-night, nor white suffrage. All I want is *loyal* suffrage, without regard to color."

He broke the promise a moment later.

---

*William Gannaway "Parson" Brownlow, a former Methodist minister and Tennessee politician. Proslavery and antisecession before the war, he was a ferocious Unionist during and after it.

"Has it never occurred to you, when denouncing the negro, that perhaps the nation lives to-day, and did not perish, because of those black auxiliaries you called into service? When, two or three years ago, the government decided the negro was fit to carry a gun to shoot rebels down, it thereby pledged itself irrevocably to give him the ballot to vote rebels down, when it should become necessary."[61]

Julian sent a copy of the speech along to his abolitionist friend Lydia Maria Child. "Somewhat savage in its justice," Child thought it, but she liked it anyhow. "I hardly knew which to admire most," she wrote him, "its frankness, its wit, or its logic. I have always had a partiality for the western cut-and-thrust style, of which your speech is a felicitous specimen."[62] She agreed with him, too, that with the swift return of the old rebels to power, the nation had reached a new crisis point.

Governor Morton's journalistic mouthpiece saw nothing to admire in Julian's oration. It was, after all, a slap at Morton, who favored a soft peace and a fifteen- to twenty-year probationary period before the privilege of the ballot might be extended to some blacks. The *Indianapolis Daily Journal*'s editor delivered a savage riff of political invective, assigning Julian "the temper of a hedgehog, the adhesiveness of a barnacle, the vanity of a peacock, the vindictiveness of a Corsican, and the duplicity of the devil." Julian usually enjoyed this sort of oratorical battery. At any rate he gleefully reprinted this sample, rather a good one, in his memoirs. But he failed to anticipate a sudden escalation of the political war of words into violence.[63]

Waiting for the Washington train, wrapped in a shawl against the November chill and burdened with a bundle, Julian stood talking with friends at the Richmond, Indiana, depot when Solomon Meredith approached in the half-light. Isaac Julian's newspaper claimed Meredith was drunk. Six feet six inches tall and powerfully built, Meredith had surprise on his side as well as whiskey in his blood. He attacked from the blind side, landing blow after blow to Julian's head, using "iron knuckles," so the *True Republican* alleged, for maximum effect.[64]

Forming an impenetrable circle, a gang of toughs escorting Meredith prevented the crowd from responding to Julian's cries of distress. Entangled in the shawl, he couldn't raise his arms to protect his face, much less strike back. "Ye valyant brigadier, feeling brave under the circumstances, fought him with a great deal more vigor and good will than he ever fought the rebels," Isaac Julian would taunt in that week's paper.* Meredith knocked Julian down, seized him by the hair and tore out a handful by the roots. Then he pulled out a whip. By then, though, Julian lay unconscious in a pool of blood.[65]

What detonated Meredith? Julian had defeated him by seventy-three hundred votes in the 1864 congressional election. He kept a wary eye on his Democratic rival afterward, and just as a precaution spread a story that Meredith had been removed from command of the post at Paducah, Kentucky, on suspicion of disloyalty. Meredith explained that he had attacked the congressman in retaliation for Julian's making trouble for him with the War Department. Julian claimed Meredith and his copperhead allies sought to disable him before the vote on the admission of the Southern representatives to Congress. After all, the two had met many times since Julian's complaint about Meredith's copperhead leanings. Why wait until now for revenge?

Julian recovered in time to travel to the capital for the opening session of Congress. The Republican majority voted on December 4 to pack off the Southern claimants for home, a declaration of open war with Andrew Johnson. Just to make certain they wouldn't try to come back, the Radicals pushed through a resolution two weeks later reaffirming the 1862 Ironclad Oath.

Julian's party colleagues regarded the Meredith attack as nothing less than an assassination attempt. They could not have been more considerate of him, personally and politically. "The affair is tilting powerfully in my favor, & will be of incalculable value to me in our future politics," he wrote Laura at home in Centreville. He realized no immediate benefit, though, for the House Speaker, his fellow Hoosier Schuyler Colfax, denied him the appointment he coveted most: a place on the Joint Reconstruction Committee. And he felt the effects of the larruping for a long time.[66]

"I slept almost none last night," he wrote Laura on December 10. "Ever since my beating I am more nervous. The memory of it comes

---

*Not altogether fair; Meredith was wounded at Gettysburg commanding the famous Iron Brigade, which lost two-thirds of its strength in the battle, and two of his sons died in uniform.

back so vividly that it startles me into restlessness. If I could only forget it I would sleep, but the thought of it & that nobody would answer my cries for help at times almost maddens me. It seems to me I would have gone into the mouth of hell under such circumstances."[67]

Christmas came and went without a mass redistribution of land or an uprising of former slaves in the South. As the New Year of 1866 rang in, Congress and the president were moving fast on diverging courses. Johnson kept up the pressure on Howard's Freedmen's bureau. He continued to mark down for removal agents regarded as too aggressive in the interests of the emancipated people. Thomas Conway in Louisiana had long since been disposed of. Now came Saxton's turn.

There was ice in Meeting Street when Willard Saxton walked across to the bureau office on the morning of January 9. Howard had relieved his brother of his assistant commissionership, he discovered with a shock; he, Willard, was to be mustered out of the army and Rufus returned to duty with the Quartermaster Department in his prewar rank of captain. Charles Howard would be going, too, transferred to bureau headquarters in Washington.[68]

"It has taken us unexpectedly at last. It rather unsettles all things," Willard wrote that night. "It is a triumph of the rebels, which they have long labored to attain; one of the 'compromises' which have been the bane of the nation for years past."[69]

Returning to Charleston after a short leave in Washington, Charles Howard had traveled part of the way in company with Saxton's replacement, Ohioan Robert K. Scott, a veteran of the March to the Sea and the Carolinas campaign. Charles learned on arrival that Saxton meant to light out for Beaufort within a day or so. He hoped to introduce Scott to him before he left to wrap up his affairs in the Sea Islands.

Charles found Saxton bitter and miserable. "He feels that he has been disgraced and unjustly treated," he wrote his brother in Washington. "He really feels it exceedingly disagreeable to *see* these ex-rebels in this state who believe they have triumphed over him." Ex-rebels reserved judgment about Scott; not so the Gideonites, who mistrusted him from the start. Scott struck them as indifferent, cold. "He spoke of the freed people as if they were a herd of cattle," Lizzie

Botume complained. A chastened Saxton made his farewell rounds in late January. "He is so pleasant now, and friendly—as gentlemanly and quiet in his troubles and reverses as he can be," Laura Towne wrote of the abrasive general. "It shows all the nobleness of his nature." Towne's students subscribed their nickels and dimes to a total of $10 and asked her to arrange a gift for Saxton. She sent to her sister in Pennsylvania for a little piece of inscribed silver.[70]

> To
> Our steadfast friend
> Brvt. Maj. Gen. R. Saxton
>    From
> The Freed Children of
> St. Helena Is
> SC
>    February 1866

Congress convened too late to save Saxton, but Radicals in the House were soon moving decisively on the legislative front. "We have just passed the bill granting negro suffrage by 115 to 52," Julian wrote his wife on January 18. "The signs of a storm are very visible," he wrote her a day or two later. "The president is going to betray the country & what the end will be no one knows. Our poor country after all is not sound. What a calamity to have such a president now!"[71]

Anxiety over Johnson's course doubtless contributed to a flare-up of Julian's maladies. The doctor diagnosed a pain in the small of his back as lumbago. Sleep remained elusive. The ravings of one of his fellow boarders, a drunkard in the last stages of *delirium tremens*, kept him awake all night. "His screams last night were terrible," he reported. "I fear we might have to send him to the Asylum." Yet things were going well in Congress. Prospects were good for passage of the proposed Fourteenth Amendment to the Constitution, which would extend laws governing citizenship to blacks and bar active rebels from holding office.[72]

Johnson delivered his response to the suffrage measure at a February 7 meeting with a delegation of black leaders that included Frederick Douglass. He advanced all the well-worn arguments. The freedmen were ignorant, unready. (Julian noted that more than 10 percent of Indiana adults were illiterate.) Congress lacked constitutional authority to legislate voter eligibility for the states. (There was no precedent for appointing provisional state governors, Julian responded, but the president had done it anyhow.) Planters would control the black vote. ("Why, every South Carolinian would be preaching negro suffrage with me if he thought the negroes would vote as he wanted them to," Julian said.)[73]

"Did you ever read such a villainous rigmarole as Andy's speech yesterday to the negroes? We all consider the fight begun," Julian wrote home.[74]

The House in early February passed Julian's Southern Homestead Act, granting blacks and loyal whites preferential access to public lands in the defeated states. Both houses approved Illinois senator Lyman Trumbull's bill extending the life and powers of Howard's Freedmen's bureau. Among other things, it set aside homestead lands for blacks and, delivering on Howard's Edisto Island promise, confirmed the freed people's possessory titles in the Sherman tracts. Johnson returned it to the Senate, calling it unconstitutional and too costly. A few weeks later he vetoed Trumbull's civil rights bill. The vetoes brought congressional moderates and Radicals into close alliance against the president.[75]

In a rambling, self-absorbed speech on Washington's Birthday, Johnson portrayed himself as a lonely defender of the Constitution and a target for Radical assassins. "Cost him his head! They may talk about beheading," Johnson said, not altogether coherently, "but when I am beheaded I want the American people to be the witness." He accused the Radicals—Thaddeus Stevens, Charles Sumner and Wendell Phillips by name—of plotting rebel-like to usurp his powers and destroy the government.[76]

"Have you read his drunken speech to the mob here?" Julian wrote Laura. "We all feel Andy must be ground to powder. We shall have a terrible fight but we will crush him."[77]

SOUTH CAROLINA PLANTERS saw reason for optimism in Northern developments. "Andrew Johnson is struggling almost single handed against the ferocious Black Republicans for the rights of the South and the white man," Emma Holmes noted with approval. With Saxton gone General Daniel E. Sickles, the military governor, assumed effective control of the state. "Matters will immediately assume a much more favorable aspect," Ralph Elliott thought. Sickles might be "a rowdy politician" in Charles Manigault's view, and he did suspend the state's Black Code on January 1, 1866, but he also issued a decree that same New Year's Day requiring plantation blacks to enter into labor agreements within ten days or face eviction.[78]

"We, fortunately, still own our lands," Manigault observed. "The Negroes, on the contrary, own comparatively nothing. Not an acre, or a mule, has been given to them."[79]

With Gowrie plantation "abandoned to the Negroes" for now, Louis Manigault took a job in the countinghouse of the Charleston rice and cotton factor George A. Hopley. But Gabriel planned to return Silk Hope to cultivation in the spring. And the patriarch went to General Sickles for permission to drive off squatting former slaves so a rent-paying white tenant could take over the Marshlands place.

"They are all free now & I have no rights over them," Charles Manigault told Sickles. "Nor have they any rights over *my property*."[80]

The authorities loaned Manigault two government wagons and he set off for Marshlands with Gabriel. They pulled up to the former slave quarters and, moving from cabin to cabin, cleared out the squatters' belongings. After a while the freed people joined in, all of them except a seditionist named Peggy, who threatened to call in the Yankee provost marshal. She backed down in the end, perhaps assuming the wagons, with their government stamps, had been sent on U.S. authority. The Manigaults dumped the contents in a wooded no-man's-land four miles distant and gave the squatters a choice of leaving or making a contract with the lessee.[81]

Mary Johnstone carried on alone in up-country Greenville. She approached a family friend, Robert Barnwell, about enrolling her son Elliott in the reorganized college at Columbia. It reopened in January as the University of South Carolina with Barnwell as chairman of the faculty and Joe LeConte at the head of the School of Chemistry, Pharmacology and Mineralogy—a grand name for a modest operation, as LeConte started with just nine students. "There are only thirty in all for seven professors," Mary wrote her mother in Darlington. Barnwell couldn't accommodate Elliott after all, for a state legislator claimed the place for his son. Elliott's enforced idleness only added to her burden of woe.[82]

Winter came in cold in Greenville. Firewood was scarce and expensive. Mary managed to hire a cook who also did the scullery work and milked the cow, but she could find no one to carry water and wood, chores she regarded as too taxing for the children. As ever, she was the first to do without.

"I pride myself on not having had a fire yet in my bedroom, altho' the thermometer has been as low as 12 degrees," she wrote her mother in early January.[83]

In the Low Country, Ralph Elliott continued to struggle with the bankers, the Federal authorities, the freedmen, and his own ungovernable temper. He met with representatives of Northern banking houses in Charleston in an effort to borrow for animals, tools, and seed. With the insatiable Northern lust for cotton, he figured to be able to drive a good bargain.

"Yankie capitalists are beginning to offer partnerships but so far the planters are loath to yield to their demands requiring a mortgage on their real estate," he wrote his sister Emily, who was with their mother in Darlington. "They are greedy after cotton & will probably come down in a few weeks. If we can get to work by the 20th of February I think it will be time enough."[84]

Ralph posted Emily a box with her dresses and hats and a demijohn of "first-rate Bourbon whiskey." He paid the land taxes on Oak Lawn, though he conceded he could do nothing with the place as yet but try to keep the squatters off. He learned that the family's Beaufort house and the island plantations of Ellis and Myrtle Bank would probably be restored within a month or two, making it possible for Ann Elliott to divide the estate among her children. But he could not hire labor, and he had evidently overestimated the Yankee cotton lust.

"After one month's hard and disgusting work, I am no nearer planting a crop than ever," he wrote his mother. "The southerners have no money & the Yankees will not advance a single cent without a ruinous mortgage. The military and bureau authorities are doing their best to assist the planters but their predecessors in office* have so corrupted the nigger as to make the present efforts unavailing."

He went on, "You may have seen in the papers an advertisement of Clifford & Mathewes to furnish capital to planters. Their terms are ungenerous, grinding & usurious. Unless something turns up by the

---

*Rufus Saxton and Charles Howard.

20th, I am going to get a mule & try for two bags of cotton on my own hook."[85]

Will Elliott took on the task of rebuilding Oak Lawn and The Bluff. Lacking money, seed, tools, expertise, and stamina (lung trouble again, leaving him chronically flushed and feverish), he contracted with two trusted former slaves, familiarly known as Dick and Jacob, to help him at Oak Lawn.

He returned to the home place in early March, reaching the long avenue just at dusk. From the far end he saw, as in a dream, a house, an outbuilding, and a kitchen. Smoke streamed out of the kitchen chimney. "Still," he thought, "there was a strangeness in its appearance. It required a much nearer approach to find that the still erect walls of house & kitchen were but the skeleton that once encased the spirit (forever fled) of the hospitality & refinement of bygone days." Weeds choked the pond. Federal troops had burned all the fences for firewood. The laurels and wild oranges near the house were fire-blackened, but oddly enough, given the Sherman treatment and a full year's neglect, some of the trees in the orchard were in bloom.

The summerhouse stood, though the roof sagged, the walls were damaged, and parts of the floor were rotten. The Yankees had not disturbed the Elliott graveyard. Grass had grown up in the flower beds, but the roses and hyacinths were showing the growth of early spring, and those "plants with the small white flowers," too.

Elliott intended to plant cotton, starting with the home field, overgrown but workable. "I'll do my best be sure," he promised his mother in a letter he headed The Ruins, "though much depends on Dick's arrival." It was a tragicomedy of errors. The cottonseed failed to arrive. The hardware merchant disappointed him about the plows, and sent him eighteen or nineteen hoes when he only asked for a dozen. "He must refund, & I return the surplus, as I need every dollar," Will insisted. He was nearly out of bacon. With the fences down the freedmen's cattle were running wild. The herds would surely trample whatever he put into the ground.[86]

No solution to the labor puzzle presented itself. Even Jacob was being difficult. For the first time in his life he had bargaining power, and he meant to use it.

"He wishes to squat on the place and have the lion's share of everything he may make," Will Elliott complained. "I offered him half of everything if he would plant 5 or 6 acres of Sea Island cotton.

He prefers planting food & having all the provisions he may make for himself—this in consideration to his past importance to the family. I told him I thought the obligation lay the other way. He is eaten up with self-esteem and selfishness."[87]

Elliott finally found two brothers, freedmen named Howard, who agreed to work Oak Lawn for wages of $12 a month with rations, plus four or five acres for their own corn and yams. With Emily due to arrive early in April, he decided to leave the home place to Jacob and the Howard brothers and concentrate his energies on The Bluff.

"The first shock is very great, but the trees and shrubs are very beautiful & I think you can stand it," Miss Emily wrote her mother a day or so after she reached Oak Lawn. "The kitchen could be easily rebuilt; it only wants a floor and a ceiling. The old walls stand well."[88]

It was just as well that Will had moved on to The Bluff. After five catastrophic years Emily Elliott had run out of patience with men: the Secesh who started the rebellion that wrecked the country, the generals who sent a quarter of the South's young male population to their deaths, her brothers (incompetent, obstinate Ralph and weak, consumptive Will) and her officious brother-in-law Gonzales.

Ralph refused to meet the bankers' terms, gave up on planting for the year, and went to work as a night constable in Charleston. William fell weeks behind waiting for cottonseed. Nobody would lend him the $500 he needed for provisions for the hands and feed for the mules. He and Ralph were angling to raise money by selling Social Hall plantation to Gonsie, but they couldn't agree on a purchase price and the negotiations lapsed. Neighbor King already had ten ploughs working; Will could barely manage one.

"It is very well to talk of necessities after four months of idleness," Emily wrote her mother in exasperation. "I know that had I been the fortunate owner of a pair of pantaloons the debts of the Estate would have been paid by this & the lands would remain in hand for the legacies.

"I can not but regret that we were not here in the winter," she went on. "It might have made a great difference in our fortunes. Time and tide won't wait for a man, much less a woman."[89]

A few planters, desperate or visionary, had begun to look to Chinese immigration as a potential solution to the labor problem. Through his Cuban contacts, Gonsie hired a Chinese coolie and sent him with his highest recommendation to Miss Emily at Oak Lawn. The coolie had acquired a Spanish cloak somewhere and cut a super-exotic figure wrapped in it. Emily led him to a plot for a tobacco seedbed and handed him a bag of seed. He appeared not to catch her drift. In time it became clear that he understood English perfectly well—except when the conversation turned to farm labor.

"He does not seem the least inclined to work but roams like a pointer all over the place," Miss Emily complained. "Today he proposed cutting down all of the laurels & large trees to sell in Charleston to make 'too much money.' So ends another attempt to better our fortunes. We expected a man to take a hoe & spade & show the negroes how to work. He *may* be very first rate, but for us & our purposes he's a humbug."[90]

With disaster looming, Emily took charge. She instructed her mother to sell her brooches and bracelets and one of her $500 bonds for what it would bring ($125, she guessed) so she could put the money toward a horse and a small plough and plant tobacco and corn herself. She tried, too, to do her best for William at The Bluff. When he put up his watch for pawn or sale, Emily suggested other baubles that might be surrendered along with it.

"Again let me beg you to have William's sword raffled," she wrote their mother. "His life depends upon his having nutriment. He is now without flour and (lacking a long gun) without the chance for fresh food of any sort. If the money is got, I think I can spend it judiciously for him."[91]

Will Elliott somehow contrived to plant sixty-four acres of long-staple cotton by the end of May. The hands, indifferent, insubordinate, worked at half task. Grass and weeds gained steadily on the young plants. Elliott predicted no more than half a crop for 1866.

"I'm no enchanter & cannot make fresh seed out of old," he confessed.[92]

A new illness lingered upon him, a sort of flu that worsened his tubercular hack. He dosed himself regularly with quinine and prepared to move into the pine barrens (pine needles were said to be good for the lungs) after laying-by time.

THE PROCESS OF MEMORIALIZATION had begun in the victorious North with the Grand Review, triumphal but elegiac, too. The return of the regiments throughout the summer and fall touched off mass celebrations in the capitals of the loyal states—parades, speeches, and presentations of battle flags—and smaller, more intimate commemorations in scores of lesser cities and towns.

The remnants of every Massachusetts regiment, seventy in all, assembled on the Boston Common on December 22, 1865—the cavalry on Park Street, the infantry on Beacon Street. Sixty survivors of the Second Massachusetts turned out, punctilious as ever. Just returned from Brazos Santiago, 120 officers and men of the Fifth Massachusetts Cavalry (Colored) joined the march, as did upwards of 150 veterans of the black Fifty-fourth and Fifty-fifth infantry regiments. The veterans told "a noble tale of war," in the words of one witness. Gaps in the ranks of every Bay State unit told another, sadder tale as the procession wound from Tremont Street to Boylston and Arlington and along Beacon Street for the presentation of the colors to Governor Andrew on the steps of Charles Bulfinch's statehouse.[93]

Grieving families sought and often found comfort in individual memorials, private and unremarked. With Colonel Cogswell's precise directions, Charles and Lydia Storrow retrieved their son's remains from his temporary grave in a farmhouse yard on the Raleigh road in North Carolina. They reburied Lieutenant Samuel Storrow, Second Massachusetts, in Mount Auburn Cemetery, Cambridge, on January 6, 1866.[94]

A town meeting in Concord in March 1866 approved a war monument for the grassy common in front of the Town House. It would be formed of rough granite blocks in the shape of an obelisk and inscribed with the names of Concord's thirty-two war dead, from Major Amiel Whipple, a Regular, to Corporal Charles Hosmer Wright, Eleventh Ohio Volunteers. Ralph Waldo Emerson would be asked to speak at the dedication on Patriot's Day in 1867.

Lew Wallace delivered the keynote address before fifty thousand people at a battle flag ceremony in Indianapolis on the Fourth of July. Wallace, who had begun the war as Indiana's adjutant in charge of raising troops to meet Lincoln's call for 6 regiments from the state, returned the colors of 156 infantry regiments, 13 cavalry regiments, and 26 batteries of artillery to Governor Morton. "In the years to come the soldiers will rally around" the old flags, he said, "to renew their youth, and with each other to fight their battles over again."

Wallace, hieratic, bemedaled, spoke for an hour, his oration packed with romantic tropes and allusions to Persian knights and Agincourt, comforting imagery perhaps more acceptable now that the actual fighting had been over for more than a year.[95]

These memorial tokens were simple, straightforward, and satisfying. Political realities in 1866 were more complex. The Radicals were accusing Andrew Johnson of squandering the hard-fought victory: the vetoes, his opposition to the Fourteenth Amendment, toleration of continuing white suppression of Southern freedmen. Secret vigilante groups—the Pale Faces, the White Brotherhood, and an organization with the sinister and perplexing name of Ku Klux Klan—were terrorizing blacks. White mobs went on the rampage in Norfolk and Memphis, killing and burning in black neighborhoods. Public opinion was difficult to measure. But by the spring of 1866 the Radicals sensed it moving their way.

"All my news from the district is favorable thus far but the war with Andy may be fatal to me," George Julian wrote his wife. "I think not, but at any rate I shall stand by the old flag of freedom."[96]

As Jefferson Davis approached the end of his first year of imprisonment at Fortress Monroe, Julian renewed the call for his trial and execution. By then, though, most Northerners preferred to forget about the Confederate president. Not even Thad Stevens wanted him hanged. The Lincoln assassination case against Davis had collapsed entirely with the exposure of the government's chief witness, Sanford Conover (real name: Charles A. Dunham), as a fraud who had fabricated nearly every detail of the Confederate Grand Conspiracy. But Julian cared little now about the Lincoln crime. It was the future that concerned him. He regarded the punishment of Davis and other leading rebels as a moral, psychological, and political necessity. On April 30, 1866, the day Julian delivered his rebel punishment speech on the House floor, white vigilantes murdered a Freedmen's Bureau agent, Lieutenant J. B. Blanding, in a Grenada, Mississippi, street.

"Without punishment the rebellion itself, instead of being effectually crushed, must find a fresh incentive to renew its life in its impunity from the just consequences of its guilt," Julian told the House in support of his resolution for Davis's speedy trial.

Julian considered treason a crime, not a mere difference of opinion. Yet Andrew Johnson had issued wholesale pardons to leading traitors and allowed them to occupy places of power and profit in the South. He wanted Davis brought before a military court so there would be less likelihood of an acquittal. As for Robert E. Lee, "his spared life has outraged the honest claims of the gallows since his surrender," Julian said. Failure to punish him was a travesty.

"It is to call evil good and good evil," he went on; "and since God is not to be mocked, it must in some form bring down on our heads the retribution which we may only escape by enforcing the penal laws of the nation against the magnificent felons who have sought its life."[97]

Julian rated the speech a crowd-pleaser. "I have no fears at all that its sentiments will be displeasing to the loyal millions," he wrote Laura. "Some may count the speech severe, but its only severity is the truth." In fact, the House heard it without comment and quietly referred Julian's resolution to the Judiciary Committee. The president took no notice at all. He made no move either to free Davis or to bring him to trial.[98]

As spring turned to summer, Julian's views on Reconstruction, regarded as extreme not long before, began to sound reasonable to his moderate congressional colleagues, particularly his call for strict Federal rule of the South so "a Christian civilization and a living democracy" could take root there. Only when the South's political and social structures had been thoroughly transformed should Congress receive the Southern representatives.[99]

Like most visionaries, Julian reacted with ambivalence to the wider acceptance of his ideas. They seemed less heroic somehow when practically everyone endorsed them. Congress overrode Johnson's veto of the Civil Rights measure in April, approved the Fourteenth Amendment over the president's opposition in June, and went over his head in July to give two years of new life to General Howard's Freedmen's Bureau, though the revised bill reduced the amount of homestead lands available to blacks and dropped the clause confirming the Sea Island land warrants. These successes seemed to deflate Julian. Then, too, Governor Morton's opposition at home and Johnson's threat to his patronage (dozens of postmasterships in Fifth Congressional District towns) were cause for anxiety. Tired, depressed, and bilious, he dosed himself with blue pill and oil, a prescription whose galvanic effect left him trembling and listless.

"I grow weary of my political life," he wrote Laura. "It is no life at all. If you could be with me it would all be well. At night, especially when unwell, I am very lonely.[100]

With Congress firm, Johnson worked to discredit the Freedmen's bureau by executive means. For starters, he dispatched two officers he trusted on a tour of the South to report on bureau operations. They were James Steedman, "a rough character with no sympathy for negroes," according to Howard, and bureau staffer Joseph Fullerton, author of the scathing report on Rufus Saxton in the summer of 1865. Commissioner Howard at least had warning of the setup, and through a thoroughly reliable source—Ulysses S. Grant.

"Howard, you must not take too much to heart or as against yourself what may be said or reported before long against your bureau," Grant told him privately on the eve of the Steedman-Fullerton tour.[101]

The inspectors traveled with a claque of sympathetic reporters. "They passed on from city to city and from place to place, visiting military and bureau headquarters in each Southern State, and sent their reports, as critical and adverse as possible, broadcast through the newspapers to the entire country," Howard wrote later. They claimed to uncover corruption, maladministration, and instances of cruelty to freedmen. Howard's agents were establishing a new system of slavery, forcing contracts on freedmen, swindling them, getting rich off them, obliging them to work for pittance wages. The bureau, the inspectors concluded, had ended up doing more harm than good.[102]

The 1865 crop failures led to widespread distress, especially in Arkansas, Alabama, and South Carolina. Around the time Steedman and Fullerton were setting out, a congressional resolution claimed that without a Federal relief program thousands would die of hunger. From June 1865 to April 1866, the Freedmen's Bureau supplied nearly 8 million rations* to destitute Southerners. By the midsummer of 1866 bureau agents were keeping thousands of people of both races from starvation. The inspectors hardly seemed to notice.[103]

---

*A ration was enough beef, pork, or bacon; bread; cornmeal, beans, peas, or hominy; and sugar, salt, pepper and vinegar to sustain one person for a week.

Freedmen queue up to draw rations in Beaufort. The Freedmen's Bureau kept thousands of destitute Southerners from starvation, supplying 8 million rations to poor and refugee whites and blacks from June 1865 to April 1866. The bureau stepped up the level of assistance during the hungry summer of 1866. (U.S. Army Military History Institute)

"They profess to be acting for the Freedmen's Bureau, but manifest no interest in the freed people, nor in what is done or left undone for them," observed Lizzie Botume, who met the inspection party at Port Royal. "They came with fixed opinions, and do not wish to hear or see anything to change these opinions. We decide they are for the President, against the bureau."[104]

Not that there were no grounds for criticism. Some officers were indifferent, cruel, or corrupt. Possibly the Reverend Mansfield French, "Bureau missionary and Superintendent of Marriage Relations," as the inspectors dubbed him, really would realize a 200 to 300 percent gain on his investment in an Edisto Island cotton plantation, though the report contained no evidence of this, only the charge.[105] Some bureau officers did act as agents for the planters. Howard had given in to the president's demand for the removal of Conway, Saxton,

Samuel Thomas in Mississippi, and Edgar Gregory in Texas, the best of his assistant commissioners. And he could have pushed harder for the land program.

Howard meant well, though. His August 23 report to the president challenged the Steedman-Fullerton claims of maladministration as overblown and exaggerated. Besides, even when the charges were true they involved isolated cases. "The effect of this course has been to concentrate the attention of the public upon certain individual acts of officers and agents, or accusations against them carelessly drawn, in such a way as to keep the faults committed, and not the good done, prominently in view." Steedman himself had calculated that the investigation would do more harm "by exposing the abuses and frauds and peculations of its officers" than by attacking the bureau's role as protector of the freed people. Howard charged that the inspectors misrepresented the bureau and its works for purely political purposes. But Johnson knew that already. That was what he had assigned Steedman and Fullerton to do.[106]

The report stirred rumors of Howard's imminent sacking. He evidently judged them credible. Like Saxton before him, he decided to force the president to act rather than follow the politically safe course and quit. "I am not going to resign until I am removed," Howard wrote a friend, "and I probably shall not be removed until after the fall elections." If the balloting went against the president, things still might turn out all right.[107]

A racial explosion in New Orleans gave terrible substance to much of what the bureau's defenders were saying. City police squads, made up mostly of Confederate veterans, attacked a group of two hundred blacks assembling for a political convention on July 30. Thirty-four blacks and three white supporters were killed in what amounted to a police riot. Another one hundred were injured. It looked to many Northerners as though the rebellion had broken out all over again.[108]

With the election drawing near, Johnson decided to take the case for his leave-alone policies directly to the people. Politicians in the 1860s regarded presidential campaigning as undignified. But Johnson had been schooled politically in the rough mountain communities of East Tennessee and he planned to use Tennessee-style electioneering to carry his message from the big seaboard cities through upstate New York and into the old Northwest. One had to be careful, though, of what one said in such comparatively sophisticated outposts as Albany, Buffalo, Cleveland, Chicago, Saint Louis, and Indianapolis. Laura Towne referred to Johnson as a "low cock-pit orator." Even his friends recognized his seemingly limitless capacity for blundering. Wisconsin senator James Doolittle cautioned the president to speak only from a carefully prepared text, and to make no unrehearsed remarks at all.

"*Our enemies your enemies,* have never been able to get any advantage from anything *you ever wrote,*" Doolittle reminded him. "But what you have said extemporaneously in answer to some question or interruption has given them a handle to use against us."[109]

Johnson embarked on his "Swing around the Circle" on August 28 with an entourage of Secretary of State Seward, Navy Secretary Gideon Welles, Admiral David G. Farragut, and General Grant. Hecklers turned out at every stop. Goaded by hostile crowds, Johnson lashed back, savagely attacking his opponents and offering himself as a martyr, abused and misunderstood. He was soon comparing himself to the crucified Christ.[110]

The president opened quietly in Cleveland on the evening of September 3. He evidently forgot his instructions, though, and before long he lit into the Radicals as a "subsidized gang of hirelings and traducers," remarks surely not part of his prepared speech. "Don't get mad, Andy!" a warning voice rang out. When someone in the crowd called out for the hanging of Jefferson Davis, Johnson suggested stringing up Wendell Phillips and Thad Stevens instead. "I have been fighting the South, and they have been whipped and crushed," he explained, "and now, as I go around the circle, having fought the traitors at the South, I am prepared to fight the traitors at the North. He who is opposed to the restoration of this Government and the reunion of the States is as great a traitor as Jeff Davis or Wendell Phillips." He went on in this vein for awhile, to mingled cheers and catcalls.

"Is this dignifed?" somebody wanted to know.

"I care not for dignity," Johnson shot back. "There is a portion of your countrymen who will always respect their fellow-citizens when they are entitled to respect, and there is a portion of them who have no respect for themselves and consequently have no respect for others."

"Traitor!" a voice called out from the shadows.

"I wish I could see that man," Johnson shouted. By now he had worked himself into a tantrum. "I would bet you now, that if the light fell on your face, cowardice and treachery would be seen in it. Show yourself. Come out here where I can see you. If you ever shoot a man you will do it in the dark, and pull the trigger when no one is by to see you."[111]

So it went. The swing continued on to Chicago, then to Saint Louis, where the president developed the Christ/Judas Iscariot theme and accused the Radical Congress of inciting the New Orleans riot. Local newspapers reported his performances in excruciating detail. "A crowning disgrace," the *Chicago Tribune* called the Saint Louis speech. "I know the great Northern heart is boiling," Lew Wallace wrote his wife, "yet when I see such men as Grant and Farragut, and a host of lesser lights, military and civil, honoring him with their presence and company, I hardly know what to think of the result." Johnson's tormentors only grew fiercer. In Terre Haute, Indiana, a mob tried to derail his train. The presidential party fled eastward, reaching Indianapolis safely on the evening of September 10.[112]

A surly crowd estimated in the thousands lined the route to the Bates House and hundreds of Chinese lanterns cast an eerie light into the streets. Johnson reached the hotel without incident. After a while he appeared on the balcony with Grant and Farragut. There were roars of approval for the war heroes. Solomon Meredith—"ye valyant brigadier," George Julian's assailant—introduced Johnson. Hisses drowned out the president when he tried to speak, forcing him to retire behind a curtain. One of his aides (his "bottleholder," someone suggested) leaned over the railing and called out, "Hush! You d——d set of ignorant Hoosiers!" With the reprimand, the throng chanted all the louder for Grant and Farragut.[113]

Johnson reappeared to a cacophony of "cheers, groans and the rattle of drums," according to an account in the *Daily Journal,* Governor Morton's newspaper. (By now even Morton had turned against Johnson. "No man in public life ever brought such magnificent resources to the support of both sides of a question," Julian would say of the governor.) Johnson bowed and again began to speak in a hoarse voice, but could not be heard for cries of "Memphis!" and "New Orleans!" He waved a handkerchief, wiped his eyes, and withdrew once again behind the curtain. Fighting broke out in the streets, with Radicals and Johnson supporters trading punches and blazing away with pistols. At least five men were shot; one died of his wounds and the surgeons expected to take off the leg of another.[114]

Senator Doolittle estimated later that the Swing around the Circle cost Johnson and his mostly Democratic allies a million votes.[115] Presidential Reconstruction was probably doomed anyway. Republicans campaigned hard against it, and for the Fourteenth Amendment. Maine voted first, in early September, and went Republican by a big majority. After a short rest, Julian began canvassing the Burnt District. He found that even conservatives were supporting him now. Isaac Julian's *True Republican* commented on the phenomenon:

> General Browne said in his speech at Connorsville last Saturday, that he went into the army a conservative, but every bombshell that exploded in our ranks, and every bullet that whizzed past his ear made him feel radical, and he kept growing worse, until at last he consented to support Mr. Julian for Congress, and would do the same thing this year.[116]

Special half-fare trains carried Republicans to mass rallies called to "sustain the Reconstruction policy of Congress." Julian, Morton, and Indiana-born General Ambrose E. Burnside were lined up to speak at a great rally in Centreville on September 20. The party laid on a free dinner for Union veterans at the Fireman's Hall. Heavy rains kept the crowds down and forced the speeches inside Town Hall, but did nothing to extinguish Julian's fire.

He "scathingly reviewed the treacherous acts of our imbecile executive," Isaac's sheet reported, charging that Johnson planned to bring the excluded unrepentant rebels into the House and Senate while keeping loyal freedmen in subjection. "Should the grayback who shot off your arm or leg at Chickamauga or Gettysburg wield four times the influence in the government he tried to destroy and you fought to save?" Julian asked the veterans in the crowd.[117]

The Radicals Carl Schurz and Henry Warmoth, a Northerner resettled in riotous New Orleans, campaigned on his behalf. Warmoth gave a hair-raising account of the New Orleans massacre "and distinctly fathered it upon Andrew Johnson," according to the *True Republican*. Julian ventured outside his home territory to speak for Republican candidates in Indiana's Tenth and Eleventh Congressional Districts.

Confident he would outpoll Solomon Meredith, his Democratic opponent, Julian made negligible political use of the attack at the Richmond railroad station nine months before. He barely mentioned it during a long interview with a reporter from the *Cincinnati Gazette*. "I fancied he possessed some of that Quaker sternness which bends lily-like to the breeze, but stands straight in the storm," the journalist wrote, obviously impressed. Julian won reelection on October 9 by around sixty-two hundred votes—slightly behind the state ticket in the Burnt District but a brilliant Radical victory withal, the *True Republican* trumpeted, for "here the whole gospel of equal rights to all men has been unhesitatingly preached."[118]

Despite party friction over Julian's advocacy of black suffrage, Republicans carried Indiana by a majority of fifteen thousand, taking eight of eleven congressional seats and both houses of the state legislature. Julian left immediately after the vote to campaign for Republicans in Illinois, Minnesota, and Iowa. The party claimed a massive victory at the end of the election season in November. Republicans carried twenty states altogether. With a veto-proof majority in the Fortieth Congress, they could dismantle Andrew Johnson's Reconstruction policy if they chose. Already some Radicals were beginning to talk of impeachment.

THE ELMORE PLANTATION YIELDED twenty-five small bales of cotton in the autumn of 1866, only 650 pounds. In the old days, in Grace Elmore's recollection, a good harvest would run to sixty to seventy-five bales, hundreds of bushels of wheat, corn for the livestock, and corn, bacon, and other provisions to feed two hundred slaves. The Elmores used to slaughter hundreds of hogs every year. They butchered the last twenty hogs on the place in the autumn of 1866. The corn had been stripped from the fields before it ripened, so there would be no provisions for the hands in 1867—if any hands could be hired.[119]

William Elliott gathered in a meager cotton crop at The Bluff, far smaller than he had hoped even with his late start, but possibly just enough to cover expenses. But possibly not: the need for immediate cash forced him to sell at a calamitous seven cents a pound. He began to fear entrapment in a cycle from which there would be no recovery: the eternal paying down of this year's debts with money for next year's crop.

Sister Emily approached him about making preparations for their mother's belated return from Darlington. Could he get a suitable room ready for her for the winter? "Perhaps Mama would be less shocked by The Bluff than by Oak Lawn," she suggested in mid-November.[120] By then, though, William Elliott, age thirty-four, had sickened for his last illness. He died early in 1867.

# Coda

# 1876–1877

E DWARD BARTLETT LIVED IN USEFUL OBSCURITY in 1876, America's centennial year. He began postwar life with a capital of $100 in banknotes, his father's gift. Dr. Bartlett had tucked the money away in an old notebook in 1862, in case he should need it to bring his youngest child's body home to Concord. In the event, Ned Bartlett survived camp life, the entry into Richmond, and the Texas expedition to be mustered out of the Fifth Massachusetts Cavalry and collect the $100 for himself.

Bartlett managed Lewis's Wharf in Boston, supervising the loading, discharging, and temporary storage of seaborne cargoes. He remained a citizen of Concord, deeply involved in the town's affairs. Bartlett turned out with the volunteer company to fight the fire that badly damaged Emerson's home in July 1872. He served on the Sleepy Hollow Cemetery board. He and his wife Sarah (they married in 1873) raised two children, a girl and a boy, in a cottage along Academy Lane. His gardens were the admiration of the neighborhood.

Charley Fox, Fifty-fifth Massachusetts Infantry, was a partner in the civil engineering firm of Holbrook & Fox in 1876, with offices in Post Office Square, Boston. He, his wife, Mary, and their two daughters lived on Milton Avenue in suburban Dorchester. Fox made a brief foray into politics, representing Dorchester in the Massachusetts legislature as a Republican. But public life disagreed with him, and he resigned before the end of his term.

His brother John, Second Massachusetts, maintained a small architectural practice in Post Office Square. Business, slack through the first postwar decade, had picked up in the previous year or so. "I hope it is a permanent improvement," he wrote Charles Morse, his old regimental commander. "If so, I look forward in the course of a year to getting a house for myself and still better a wife."[1] For the time being, John Fox kept bachelor's hall in Clapp Street, Dorchester. His sister Fairy taught kindergarten in the Boston public schools, and lived at home still.

Charley Morse, Second Massachusetts, abandoned the idea of setting up as a carpetbagging cotton planter and pushed west to find a niche in America's booming postwar railroad industry. Superintendent of the Burlington & Missouri River Railroad in Nebraska in the early '70s, Morse had moved on by the centennial year to the Atchison, Topeka & Santa Fe in Kansas, with multifarious duties: he once arranged a buffalo hunt with officers of the Fort Dodge garrison for Baron Rothschild.

James Monroe Trotter, Fifty-fifth Massachusetts, settled in Hyde Park, Dorchester, after the war. Boston's African American community of around twenty-five hundred encountered fewer legal bars than existed elsewhere; schools were nominally integrated, and an 1865 state law prohibited racial discrimination on public conveyances and in many public places. Proud and sensitive as ever, Trotter resented any slight; and as time went by and others in the post office were promoted ahead of him he imagined it was on account of his race. His work life, however unsatisfactory, at least left him the energy to collect and evaluate material for a study of black musicians. He would publish it as *Music and Some Highly Musical People.*

Trotter married Virginia Isaacs, an Ohioan whose mother had been a slave, in 1868. Their first two children died in infancy. The third, William Monroe Trotter, born in 1872, would survive to become a prominent journalist and militant civil rights leader.[2]

LIZINKA BROWN EWELL died on January 22, 1872, at Spring Hill, Maury County, Tennessee, of pneumonia she contracted while nursing her failing husband. The eccentric lieutenant general died on the twenty-fifth, a Thursday, ever his unlucky day. They were buried together in a Nashville cemetery.

Richard Ewell had passed his last years in easy circumstances. Spring Hill prospered under Campbell Brown's management. The old Richmond arson charge followed Ewell into retirement, though, and he put up as vigorous a defense of his actions of April 2–3, 1865, as his enfeebled health would allow. And he made his peace with the old flag.

"Let nothing disrespectful to the United States be put on my tomb," he murmured as he lay dying.[3]

Lafayette McLaws enjoyed a tranquil postwar existence. When the occupation authorities removed him from his elected position as Augusta Superior Court clerk in 1865, Andrew Johnson restored him to office. The Fourteenth Amendment, ratified in 1868 with the readmission of four ex-rebel states under Radical rule, put him under the ban again; he regained his full political rights with the congressional amnesty of 1872. McLaws held two comfortable patronage appointments in Savannah in 1876, postmaster and collector of internal revenue.

Ann Elliott died at Oak Lawn plantation in 1877 at age seventy-four. She outlived her daughter Caroline (d. 1862), her husband William (d. 1863), her son William (d. 1867), her daughter Hattie (died of the yellow jack in Cuba in 1869), and her son Thomas (died at Ball's plantation in the centennial summer). The spinster sisters Emily and Ann carried on at Oak Lawn, bucking long odds in trying to restore a semblance of antebellum glory to the estate. Ralph Elliott, irascible, quick-tempered, never much good at anything, held a job at a sawmill at Altman's Station, South Carolina. Straightened circumstances forced the widow Mary Elliott Johnstone to migrate northward. The land-poor Elliotts could offer her scant assistance and in 1876 she worked at the Edgeworth School, a boarding school for girls, in Baltimore.

Edward Stephens, a former Elliott slave, sent the family a box of oranges as a gift for Christmas 1876.

OLIVER OTIS HOWARD SURVIVED as head of the Freedmen's Bureau until the agency's dissolution at the end of 1868. He helped found the black university in Washington, D.C., that bears his name today, serving as its president until 1874. The bureau's enemies pursued Howard into the 1870s, accusing him of misapplying government funds during his term as commissioner, a trumped-up charge of which Congress eventually exonerated him.

General Howard's army career prospered. He negotiated a treaty with the Apache Chief Cochise in 1872 that seemed to promise peace in the southwestern territories. Broken government pledges wrecked the accord. Howard moved on to the Pacific Northwest in 1874 to command the Department of the Columbia. His son Guy, just graduated from Yale, joined him there in 1876 as a newly commissioned second lieutenant in the Twelfth Infantry.

He made war on the Nez Percé Indians in the summer and early autumn of 1877. It was ironic, perhaps, that earnest, well-meaning Christian Howard should have been so closely associated with two of the more sordid episodes of his time, the Edisto Island evictions of 1865 and the expulsion from their Wallowa Valley homeland of Chief Joseph and the Nez Percé a dozen years later. Yet so he was.

Ranchers coveted the Wallowa Valley for grazing lands. Howard proposed a government buyout of the land and a move of the Nez Percé to the Lapwai reservation in Idaho. The tribe rejected the offer; war parties carried out a series of hit-and-run attacks on settlers. Howard took the field in a three-month pursuit of the Nez Percé that covered thirteen hundred miles from the valley across the Bitterroots to the Canadian frontier. With winter coming on, two U.S. columns trapped the tribal remnant along the Snake River in the Bear Paw Mountains. "They were covered with dirt, their clothing was torn," Howard wrote later, "and their ponies, such as they were, were thin and lame."[4] As part of the surrender terms, Howard agreed to escort the surviving Nez Perce to the Idaho reservation. General Sherman overruled him and ordered the tribe's forced resettlement in distant, alien Kansas.

Washington Kemp, the Howard brothers' Georgia protégé, worked a hardpan farm in Leeds, Maine, in 1876. His wife and daughters had been restored to him with Freedmen's Bureau help, but things hadn't worked out on the Howard family farm. Striking out on his own, Kemp achieved local fame as a minstrel in 1870s Maine, touring the state with the "Kemp Family from the Sunny Old South."[5]

Wartime Port Royal governor Rufus Saxton had vanished into Regular Army anonymity. He held the post of deputy quartermaster general in 1876, with the rank of lieutenant colonel. "Many millions of money passed through his hands during his long career as a disbursing officer," a nineteenth-century biographical sketch said of him kindly; but it omitted any mention at all of "General Saxby's" heroic effort in the Sea Islands from 1862 to 1865.[6]

George Julian, radical of Radicals, served on the House committee of seven that drew up the first articles of impeachment against Andrew Johnson in 1867. The president eventually was tried on a second set, a shaky case—one of Johnson's alleged high crimes involved the use of profane and disrespectful language in reference to Congress. The accidental president defended himself ably and escaped conviction in his highly politicized Senate trial by a single vote. He left office quietly on the expiration of his term in 1869.

Julian proposed a constitutional amendment granting the franchise to women in 1868. After all, for him the abolition of slavery meant "simply the introduction and prelude to the emancipation of all races from all forms of servitude."[7] The amendment died on the House floor. He opposed large government land grants to railroads, arguing that public domain should be reserved for the poor, white and black. The lands went to the railroad barons. His congressional career ended in 1870, when Oliver Morton's conservative Republican faction turned him out of office at last. Indiana's Burnt District knew George Julian no more.

He broke with his party to campaign for Horace Greeley and the Liberal Republicans against President Grant in 1872, even though Greeley's movement pledged a federal withdrawal from the volatile reconstructed South. He knew the president to be intemperate, inexperienced in government, tolerant of corruption. "I could not aid in the re-election of Grant without sinning against decency and my own self-respect," Julian explained.[8] Grant won anyway, with an enormous outpouring of southern black votes.

Julian's Southern Homestead Act would not survive white "redemption" of the South. Public lands in the former Confederate states were in any case mostly swampy or heavily forested—wilderness tracts earlier waves of settlers had rejected. Only a few thousand black families claimed homesteads under the act.[9] The lands were, however, immensely valuable to speculators and timber companies. A more conservative Congress's repeal of Julian's act after 1876 opened them to widespread exploitation.

LOUIS MANIGAULT'S FIRST GOWRIE TENANT died a few weeks after taking on the dilapidated plantation. He found a second lessee in early 1867, one from whom he expected much, the former Confederate general George P. Harrison. Manigault went down to Argyle Island during the third week of March to meet Harrison, his first postwar visit to the place.

Jack Savage, "the well known notorious Rascal," had returned, though he'd made no visible effort to mend the trunks and gates that regulated the flow of water to the rice fields. Manigault met him, incorrigible as ever, in company with a dozen or so freedmen, a brief encounter that left him confused and unhappy. "That former mutual & pleasing feeling of Master towards Slave and vice versa is now a dream of the past," he saw. Gowrie, once a village, was now a virtual wilderness. Even the fire-blackened bricks had been carted off and sold.[10]

Harrison divided Gowrie's 640 acres into five sections and, with Freedmen's Bureau approval, hired a foreman to manage each section. The foremen—four of whom had been Manigault slaves—procured the hands, ten for each section. Harrison himself had little or no contact with the laborers. After all expenses were paid, Harrison would keep half the profits. The foremen and the hands would divide the rest.

Harrison gave up after two seasons. Daniel Heyward leased Gowrie for several years, paying as much as $3,500 a year in rent. But he refused to carry out promised improvements, even though he boasted later that he had made money every year on the place. Manigault finally decided to manage Gowrie himself, with help from his cousin James Heyward. He found the plantation "a perfect wreck" when he took charge on January 1, 1876.

All the bridges were down, either dismantled or rotted away. The once-sturdy houses in the former slave quarters had fallen in. A boisterous and turbulent group of around fifty blacks lived in the Gowrie settlement. "It seemed that Mr. Daniel Heyward regarded Gowrie as a kind of Botany Bay, and just the proper place for all bad characters," Manigault decided. Cousin James ruthlessly cleared out the quarters, replacing undesirables with sober, willing tenants. Manigault hired a gang of two dozen Irishmen to rebuild Gowrie's drainage system.

"They are first-class ditchers and are superior in all canal and bank work," he observed of the Irish. "There is no talking, as with negroes, no trifling but the work goes on rapidly and in a serious manner."[11]

Manigault built a kitchen and privy and replastered the inside of the overseer's house, which he had taken for himself. By early spring seventy-five hands were at work hoeing off the rice stubble. In June, when Manigault returned to Charleston for the summer, the young plants stood 10 inches high, promising a bumper rice crop for 1876. He anticipated a harvest of at least fourteen thousand bushels—and a good thing, too, for he had used up all his ready cash in fixing up the place.

The months from June 1876 through the harvest in the fall and the eventual sale of the crop in April 1877 brought unrelieved disaster. A treaty with the Sandwich Islands removed the duty from imported island rice. With the market saturated, rice prices plunged. A June flood badly damaged the Gowrie crop. Political disruption across the Savannah River in South Carolina, where the former Confederate general Wade Hampton had launched a violent campaign to seize control of the state from the Radical Republicans, unsettled everyone: planters, laborers, and the moneymen whose credit kept it all going from season to season.

Day after day the rains lashed down, filling the rivers, streams, and swamps. The Savannah rose to 23 feet above flood stage at Augusta on June 16 and crested at 31 feet 9 inches two days later. The freshet came at a time when the rice plants were most vulnerable. Gowrie's entire 640 acres were flooded; some fields lay under as much as 5 feet of water.

By June 24 the river had returned to its banks and the fields were drying. Heyward roused out all the hands. They hoed every square inch of cultivated land and thus, with immense labor, managed to save part of the crop. Even so, fifty acres were destroyed entirely and another fifty substantially. Some fields would yield only fifteen bushels to the acre, nowhere near enough to cover the cost of cultivation.

"I did not go into the business blindly," a dejected but resigned Manigault recorded in the Gowrie journal.[12]

The 1876 harvest totaled seventy-seven hundred bushels, half of what Manigault had projected in the spring. Rice prices fell to six or seven cents a pound, down from thirteen cents in 1865–1866. Gowrie rice sold for as little as four cents a pound. Manigault realized barely $12,000 on his $16,000 investment in the 1876 crop. With the net loss, his Savannah factors advised that they would probably decline to advance him money for the 1877 planting season.

Manigault owed $8,000 to his sisters and $4,500 to a Savannah lending agent named Smith. He could borrow no more, so he leased Gowrie plantation to James Heyward. Cousin James agreed to meet all the expenses of planting and divide the profits equally. Manigault's share of the 1877 crop came to $131.18.

JOE LECONTE TRIED TO STAY CLEAR of racial politics. He tried to ignore the Radical ascendancy in South Carolina in the spring of 1868, when federal occupation forces oversaw the adoption of a new state constitution and Republicans with overwhelming support from the black majority won the governorship and control of the legislature. "It brings to my mind the disgusting fact that I am in the power of these black rascals," he wrote. His wife, however, developed a "small political mania," according to their daughter Emma, and scolded him for his apathy.[13]

"Last night there was a magnificent Democratic torchlight procession, with quantities of fireworks, transparencies etc., and a live Goddess of Liberty," Emma wrote her fiancé Farish Furman, a Georgia planter and lawyer. "This morning at breakfast mother gave a glowing description of the whole affair and a synopsis of all the speeches. Gen. Hampton spoke in the most absolutely confident manner in regard to the success of the Democrats. He does not seem to entertain the smallest shadow of a doubt on the subject."[14]

Discounting Hampton's prophecy, John and Josie LeConte decided against risking an unfavorable election outcome. John accepted a teaching job at the newly established University of California and took his family across country to the east shore of San Francisco Bay. He offered to scout around there for an academic post for Joe.

"It is almost amusing to hear mother," Emma wrote her husband-to-be. "One moment she is sure the Democrats will succeed and after all thinks it much better to stay where we are while in the next breath she anticipates a war in the winter and is more anxious than ever to quit the country forever and take refuge in California."[15]

Southern blacks were decisive in electing Grant to the presidency in 1868. Radical Republicans settled into the statehouse in Columbia; 75 of 124 members of the House in the special session of 1868 were African American, among them Prince Rivers, the onetime slave coachman and Union army recruiter in the Sea Islands.[16]

The state's new rulers moved tentatively to open the University of South Carolina to blacks. LeConte dreaded the prospect of admitting marginal students into his sections, forgetting perhaps that he had taught remedial classes to ill-prepared Confederate veterans without complaint. "The affairs of the university are in an awful condition," he lamented. "Everybody seems to think that it is on its last legs."[17] With the appointment of blacks to the university's board of trustees early in 1869, he resolved to leave as soon as John could arrange an appointment to the California faculty.

"There are seven trustees altogether and all radicals," Miss Emma explained. "It is supposed that when they meet in May they will ask the present corps of professors to resign & fill their places with their own creatures."[18]

LeConte followed his brother to California in August 1869 to become professor of geology at the year-old university. Resettlement meant a painful and permanent parting from Emma, now married and living on Farish Furman's plantation near Milledgeville, Georgia. She had fretted all through their courtship about her fitness for the role of planter's wife. Her health and strength were unreliable; she had always been a student, never yet a doer. "When the occasion requires you can and will display any requisite amount of 'quiet energy,'" Furman assured her. "I know you well enough to feel that there is nothing to fear, and that you can and will be useful as well as ornamental."[19] Emma remained ambivalent. She thought she loved Farish Furman, but felt misgivings about marriage. She was only twenty-one; she was deeply attached to her father; and after all she knew Furman mostly through his letters. Her cousin Johnnie had teased her mercilessly as the wedding day approached. Her eyes, he told her, were big as saucers with fear.

"How I would look forward to next month were you not coming with such designs on my freedom and did not that terrible vow of '*obeying*' and visions of frightful slavery float in my mind," she wrote her fiancé a few weeks before the ceremony.[20]

Miss Emma never adapted fully to her new life in Georgia. She missed her family terribly, her father in particular. She felt weak and listless a lot of the time. She miscarried with twins in 1870 and although she successfully bore two daughters later on (Kate in 1872 and Bess in 1874), she began to live as a semi-invalid. A long visit to Berkeley in 1875–1876 only seemed to deepen her melancholy.

Joe LeConte returned to the suffering South as a visitor in the centennial summer of 1876. His Syfax plantation had not shown a profit since 1863–1864. A call at Woodmanston, his father's place, his boyhood home, caused him to regret ever having come back to Liberty County. Woodmanston seemed to him a metaphor for all that had gone wrong since 1861.

"Before the war the plantation for a mile in every direction was a continuous plain of waving green," he wrote. "I found instead only a little garden patch, half cultivated, about each one of the negro cabins—all else a wilderness, cotton houses, corn houses and negro cabins decaying and tumbling down, the gardens all gone to ruins."[21]

Only his father's camellia trees flourished. Some of them now measured more than a foot in diameter at the bole.

IMPERSONAL ECONOMIC FORCES, insubordinate labor, bad management, ill luck—all contributed to the decline of the planters' fortunes. Louis Manigault complained bitterly of Radicals fomenting unrest among the emancipated people. There were strikes in the South Carolina Low Country in the summer of 1876, with bands of "armed negroes" marching from plantation to plantation inciting the hands. Some planters were forced to pay double wages or risk the loss of their crops. Gabriel Manigault's Silk Hope and the Marshlands place were hardly worth the trouble of cultivating. Gowrie, as it happened, was exempt from the disturbances—mostly, Manigault remarked with gratitude, because Georgia had long since been "redeemed."[22]

Redemption: the white South's term (the connotation of a holy crusade intentional) for the overthrow of multiracial Radical Republican state governments. Whites redeemed Georgia in 1872 (the Democratic governor, James M. Smith, advised the freedmen to forget politics and "get down to honest hard work"), then Tennessee, Virginia, and North Carolina. Mississippi was violently redeemed in 1875–1876. By the centennial summer only Louisiana, Florida, and South

Carolina remained under Radical rule. Louis Manigault admitted readily that he knew nothing of politics. He held strong views on alleged South Carolina misrule all the same.

"Every class of white man has been affected either in one way or another," he wrote. "Taxes have been enormous, assessments upon real estate equally so, money in every form and shape stolen by the dominant party, the State legislature composed in great part of ignorant negroes many of whom could neither read nor write, and even they enriching themselves."[23]

Such notions travestied Radical Reconstruction. There was graft, sure, but politicians everywhere stole in the 1870s—Tammany's Boss Tweed raked down tens of millions in New York City alone. South Carolina Radicals funded a public school system, built asylums and orphanages, paved roads, distributed relief to the destitute, and promoted economic development, particularly in the form of railroads. The state even pursued a modest program of land distribution. By 1876, the South Carolina land agency had settled fourteen thousand black families on small farms of their own.

The issue wasn't corruption—two prominent Redeemers, the former Confederate generals Matthew Calbraith Butler (last seen skirmishing with Howard's van along Congaree Creek in February 1865) and Martin W. Gary (he led the Confederate rear guard out of Richmond in April 1865) would show themselves to be spoilsmen of the top class.[24] It wasn't economic development. It wasn't schools or railroads or handouts to the poor. It was race. South Carolina whites were in no way prepared to accept a democratic solution, to share power and perquisites with the state's black majority.

The Sea Islands were sheltered from the fiercest of mainland political storms. Laura Towne and Ellen Murray pursued their life's work at the Penn School on Saint Helena untroubled for the most part. Hundreds of black farmers had been able to confirm their wartime titles and hold onto their land after all. The islands in 1876 remained a protected pocket of black political and economic self-sufficiency.

Still, times were hard. What the Gullahs called a "dry drought" seared the Low Country in the summer of 1875, parching the corn, stunting the potatoes, shriveling the cotton bolls. "The poor people think it a judgment and that we are going to have 'a famish,'" Towne wrote her sisters at Oakshade in Pennsylvania. So they did: islanders experienced serious hardship into the winter and spring of 1876.

Towne and Murray supplied two pecks of grits a week that cruel spring to the family of a drowned Saint Helena fisherman. They handed out weekly rations to very old people, to orphans, to large families—to around fifty families altogether, with help from northern charities. For the first time in her fifteen-year experience in the islands people were coming to her and saying, " 'Miss Town, I hongry,'" she wrote, "real nice people, who never asked a thing before."[25]

Laura Towne's vision had never failed. She never quaffed "plantation bitters," nor lost faith in the Penn School's mission and achievement. It was the islands' secondary school, and a normal school, too, for the training of teachers for posts elsewhere. The exertion never seemed more valuable to her, more worthwhile, than during exhibition time in early summer.

"Just imagine the ferment our young people are in," Towne wrote. "When they go to praise or parties the whole evening is taken up with going over exhibition lessons and pieces—they seem to think and dream of nothing else. We are, therefore, happy as we are busy."[26]

Towne and Murray had long since left the Oaks, whose former owner reclaimed it a year or so after the war. Laura bought Frogmore, an abandoned plantation house, in 1867. They lived comfortably on her "dowry money," on Ellen's $45 a month salary from a northern benevolent society, and, after 1875, on a bequest from Laura's older brother Henry. The legacy allowed her to decline her $65 monthly teaching stipend so it could be used elsewhere.

"I thank Henry more for this than for any other thing I could get with his money—that is, for being able to live here, keep up this home, to feel sure of Ellen's staying and of the school not being turned over to some teacher I could not agree with, or to some set of Trustees who would do with it exactly what we wouldn't like," she wrote her sisters.[27]

As ever, Towne offered counsel, aid, and friendship to the islanders. She dispensed medical and legal advice. She led the Band of Hope temperance society. "I was asked to 'gie name' to a baby the other day and I named it Matilda Saxton," she reported happily. She kept up with the Saint Helena gossip. "Did I write that George Wood has eloped with the light-house keeper's youngest daughter?"[28]

The islands were her home now. Towne's people in Pennsylvania saw her so infrequently that her sister Tadie wrote to request a photograph. Laura demurred, saying she did not photograph well and citing the evidence of many encounters with camera and flash over the years: "Such a gallery of shying, vicious horses, grim bulldogs, starving maniacs, strong-minded women and idiotic, simpering old maids. I want idealizing badly."[29]

She and Ellen kept mostly to themselves. They met planter-class whites now and then and found them charming, though irrelevant. "The other day I met young Rhett in Beaufort and he apologized for not calling at Frogmore long ago," Towne wrote. "He seems a very pleasant youth for a southerner, yet I did not invite him to come, for our ways are not their ways, and it is bothersome to know them."[30] In some places, especially in the interior, it had become dangerous, too, especially for those with views like Towne's. The political season of 1876 touched off something very like the war that Bessie LeConte had so dreaded eight years before.

The Redeemers meant to carry South Carolina in 1876—peacefully if possible, by fraud, intimidation, and violence if necessary. Wade Hampton pledged to protect the civil rights of blacks and preserve conditional black suffrage. Most of Hampton's allies, Butler and Gary prominent among them, were sworn to restore white supremacy. The Republicans and their leader, Massachusetts-born carpetbagger Governor Daniel Chamberlain (a veteran of the Fifth Massachusetts Cavalry, so it happened), though badly split along racial lines, were prepared to fight to retain their hold on power. An outrage in Hamburg, in Aiken County, set the tone for the campaign.

Hamburg's black militia company assembled in the streets for a drill session on the Fourth of July. Two white passersby, Thomas Butler and Henry Getson, complained to the company commander, Dock Adams, that his militiamen were blocking their right of way. Adams, a Union army veteran, had moved to Hamburg two years before from Augusta in Redeemed Georgia because blacks there, he explained, could no longer "exercise their political opinion, and I did not wish to be oppressed in that way."[31] His men were in a bystreet, Adams told Butler and Getson; they could easily detour around them. The whites insisted and Adams relented after a short argument. He ordered the company to stand aside and let the carriage pass.

The travelers were not appeased. Tensions had been building between blacks and whites in Hamburg; whites passing through the mostly black town complained of harassment from the constabulary, and of having been turned away from the public water fountain. Then and there, Butler and Getson decided to take a stand for white rights. They laid their complaint before the county judge, Prince Rivers, who had returned to his native Aiken County from the Sea Islands after the war. Rivers summoned Dock Adams into his court on July 8, a Saturday, to answer the charge of obstructing the road.

Black citizen-soldiers drifted into Hamburg all through the day. Calbraith Butler appeared in Rivers's courtroom in the morning as counsel for the plaintiffs, armed with his law books. The magistrate granted his request for a delay. Butler dropped out of sight for a few hours, then reappeared with more than a hundred armed men, a field-piece, and a demand that the Hamburg militiamen surrender their weapons. He gave Captain Adams thirty minutes to comply.

Adams refused and withdrew with forty or so of his men into the company's brick barracks. Center Street filled rapidly with white irregulars, Butler overseeing the deployment from a buggy. The vigilantes captured a slow-footed militiaman, Jim Cook, in the street, confiscated his double-barreled shotgun, and led him away under guard.

Judge Rivers tried to negotiate a peaceful end to the standoff. What, he asked Butler, could be done to avoid bloodshed? "There is nothing that will satisfy me but the surrender of these guns & the officers to go to Robert Butler* and apologize for what they have done," the general told him. Adams again refused to hand over the weapons. Rivers volunteered to box them up himself and ship them off to Governor Chamberlain in Columbia. "It is best for those men to give up the guns," Butler told him icily, "for if I have to start into it, I will not stop this side of November. I'll have the damn town in ashes."

The shooting commenced around suppertime. Adams's men returned a desultory fire from the barricaded drill room. A stray shot struck and killed McKie Meriwether, one of Butler's vigilantes. In retaliation, one of the general's people cut out Jim Cook's tongue and forced it into his hand. Scattered firing continued after sunset.

---

*The plaintiff's father.

Someone in the street called for a keg of powder to blow up the barracks. The militiamen, outnumbered and outgunned, decided to run for it. Adams told them to slip singly out the back door and melt into the gathered dusk.

Pompey Curry sprinted into the open and drew a fusillade. A slug struck him in the knee and he limped off into the woods. Frank Robinson crept down to the railroad yard unseen and hid among the stacked crossties. He heard someone shout, "Boys, there's some damn negroes in this yard." A moment later two whites pulled him from his hiding place and took him to an improvised prison pen in Center Street. Brown Anderson managed to skip across the lane without being hit. He ducked into a darkened building and squeezed off a retaliatory shot. By now a lopsided moon had risen. Anderson stepped out into the bright moonlight and directly into the path of a patrol of irregulars.

One of Butler's sharpshooters saw John Parker clearly in the moon glow as he scampered across a yard. A rifle ball struck him in the fleshy part of his back and knocked him down. A moment later the vigilantes were upon him. "I surrender like a man," Parker said to one of his captors, Joe Gussie Twiggs. "Please don't let them hurt me." Twiggs marched him away to the house Butler had taken for a field headquarters.

"Is that one of them damn rascals?" Butler queried. "God damn you," he said, turning to Parker, "are you one of the company?"

Parker admitted he was. Tom Butler shoved a pistol into his ribs and volunteered to finish him off. The general waved Tom away. Joe Gussie Twiggs asked yet another Butler, Pierce, a medical man, to probe for the ball in Parker's back. "Give me a gun with a bayonet on it and I'll probe for it," the doctor volunteered. Twiggs asked an irregular named Bice Pemble to bring water for the wounded man.

"I did not come here to wate on negroes," Pemble spat out. "I came here to kill negroes."

Brown Anderson recognized several Butlers in the moonlight. Pierce Butler offered to shoot Anderson then and there, but cooler heads prevailed. They led him away to the prison ring, where twenty or so black captives were being held at gunpoint.

"Someone asked Genl Butler what should be done with prisoners," Anderson said later. "Someone then call the roll, he called A. J.

Attaway. Attaway was taken out and 15 or 20 shots was fired. Then they came back and taken David Phillips in the same direction, then Hamp Stephens, next Minyard. Would not have taken Minyard but John Lamar said there is another son of a b. to be linched."

The shooting stopped after a few minutes. The remaining prisoners were told to scatter and the firing started up again as they fled. Anderson escaped without injury and spent the rest of the night in hiding. He saw two bodies in the deserted street on Sunday morning, including that of Jim Cook, tongueless, who "looked like he had been beat in the face." Three other corpses were sprawled down by the South Carolina Railroad tracks: those of Stephens, Phillips, and Attaway. Minyard was still alive, though wounded in several places. Pompey Curry emerged from the woods after sunrise, using a rake handle as a crutch. He saw Jim Cook dead in the street, the other four, too.

Governor Chamberlain reported the Hamburg Massacre as a political attack, and called upon President Grant to reinforce the federal garrison in the state. Butler and six others were indicted for murder and summoned to Aiken, the county seat, for trial in late July. Butler denied he had selected prisoners for the firing squad and claimed he had left the scene before anyone was killed. A large party of his irregulars massed in Aiken, all wearing red flannel shirts—the origin, the Butler family would later boast, of Wade Hampton's private political army. Armed Red Shirts monitored the proceedings from the courtroom gallery. They did not like what they heard, so they adjourned the trial and freed the defendants after just two days of testimony.[32]

General Butler was thus free to place Hampton's name in nomination for the governorship at the Democratic state convention in August. Hampton presented himself as a cooperationist and appealed for black votes. At the same time, he accepted Red Shirt support with few questions asked. In one of their first operations, several hundred Red Shirts turned out on August 12 to "observe" a Radical Republican rally in Edgefield. The meeting broke up with hardly a speech delivered.

Hampton distanced himself from extremists such as Martin Gary, who called for a concerted campaign of beatings and killings to prevent blacks from voting. But he exploited the Red Shirts, and Gary's rifle companies for that matter, for their power to intimidate.

Hampton delivered fifty-seven speeches in thirty-one of South Carolina's thirty-two counties from September to November, often with hundreds of armed Red Shirts mounted on mules as escort.

He brought his Redeemer campaign to the hostile venue of Bay Street, Beaufort, in October. Laura Towne came over from Saint Helena for the speech. Hampton did not draw a large crowd and his listeners were mostly white, "the broad-brimmed, long-haired, sallow kind," according to Towne. "They all seemed much excited and very *nervous*, but there was no enthusiasm observable."[33] He began to speak with his hat on. After the first scattered cheers, and the waving of handkerchiefs by some of the white ladies in the audience, he removed it. Towne thought he looked far better so.

"He is a stout, good-looking man with a good voice and moderate manner—cautious manner, I should say," she wrote. "He addressed himself mostly to the negroes—told them not to regard any oaths they might have taken nor any pledges they might have made to act with the Republican party—that they were all void. He spoke to them as if he had absolving power. He said to them that they were a small part of South Carolina—and if they were Republicans to a man, they nevertheless saw before them their future governor—for *that* he was *sure* to be."[34]

With a decisive assist from the Red Shirts, Hampton won by 1,100 votes out of 183,000 cast. Mart Gary claimed a seat in the state senate. The new legislature would reward Butler with election to the U.S. Senate. Without question, the carpetbagger Chamberlain would have won an honest canvass. The Democratic vote for Hampton in Edgefield County alone exceeded the local white population by 2,000.[35]

Hampton's legions operated more subtly in the Sea Islands, but they were effective all the same. The Democrats, reported Towne, used such "horrid nasty tricks" as slipping among the good tickets many counterfeit ones headed "Union Republican" with no presidential candidate listed, Hampton alone on the ballot for governor, and the familiar Republican names for local officers lower down. Hundreds voted unintentionally for Hampton.[36]

Nationally, Democrat Samuel J. Tilden of New York outpolled Ohio Republican Rutherford B. Hayes by around 250,000 votes on November 7, 1876. Tilden collected 184 electoral votes, one short of a majority; Hayes had 165. Twenty votes—all those of South Carolina, Florida, and Louisiana and one of Oregon's—were contested. Claiming fraud, Chamberlain refused to cede the South Carolina governorship. Claiming victory, Hampton formed a shadow government and kept his private army in the field. The Republicans cast around for a way to secure the 20 electoral votes in the contested states—all 20, for Tilden needed but one to win.

In the long term, the presidential outcome would mean little either way to the South's four million African Americans. Hayes and Tilden had both pledged to withdraw the U.S. garrisons from the South and leave whites free to deal with racial issues as they chose. Republicans manipulated the electoral college result so that their man won the presidency. Oregon's lone contested ballot went to Hayes. So, after many weeks of uncertainty, did the eight disputed electoral votes of South Carolina, Louisiana's seven votes, and Florida's four.

Lew Wallace always believed that in an honest election the Republicans would have taken the three southern states anyway. Appointed to a panel of "visiting statesmen" to monitor the fairness of the count in the contested states, he found himself in the middle of an electoral stricken field when he reached Tallahassee, Florida, on November 21. Both sides, it seemed to him, were equally corrupt.

"It is terrible to witness their determination to win," he wrote Susan at home in Indiana. "Conscience offers no restraint. Nothing is so common as the resort to perjury, unless it is violence. In short, I do not know who to believe."[37]

Political civil war could not help but recall Mexico to Wallace's mind. His dream of leading a nationalist army south of the Rio Grande had exploded in a cloud of recrimination against the Juáristas. The association brought him neither wealth nor honors, though it did lead to something tangible after all: a historical novel called *The Fair God*, published in 1873, set in the time of the Spanish conquest of the Aztecs and packed with battles, sudden death, magniloquent speeches and unpronounceable names. *The Fair God* sold well, seven thousand copies in the first year after publication—preparing the ground for Wallace's *Ben Hur* (1880), which would become the best-selling novel of the nineteenth century, outpacing *Uncle Tom's Cabin*.[38]

Wallace soon concluded that much of what he heard in Tallahassee at the end of 1876 was fiction, and that the Democrats' inventions were even more fantastic than those of their opponents.

He wrote Susan, "All the lawyers in the state but two are of the rebel persuasion. Money and intimidation can obtain the oath of white men as well as black to any required state of facts. A ton of affidavits could be carted into the state house tomorrow and not a word of truth in them except the names of the parties and their ages and places of residence."[39]

Wallace and his fellow visiting statesman Edward F. Noyes, a former governor of Ohio, certified a small Florida majority for Hayes.* South Carolina and Louisiana were decided for the Republican, too. In return, Hayes (now dubbed "Rutherfraud") fulfilled his campaign promise to withdraw the U.S. garrisons and hand over Louisiana, Florida, and South Carolina to the Redeemers.

Wade Hampton claimed the statehouse in Columbia in April 1877. He made an effort to honor some of his promises to blacks, appointing quite a respectable number to minor offices, for instance. Blacks continued to vote, though in steadily declining numbers. The Sea Islander Robert Smalls held onto his congressional seat into the 1880s. Gradually, though, black political gains were rolled back in South Carolina as everywhere in the old Confederacy. The Redeemers established and their descendants extended the unnatural, oppressive, and wicked system of racial subordination known as Jim Crow. Generations would pass before the ruins of it could be cleared away.

LAURA TOWNE DIED in 1901, in her seventy-fifth year. Several hundred Sea Islanders, many of them former Penn School students, trailed the mule cart that carried her body down to the Port Royal Ferry for the journey north to a Philadelphia burying ground. With Ellen Murray's retirement a few years later the Penn School became a very different sort of place, a vocational school on the Booker T. Washington model—farming for the boys, domestic arts for the girls.

---

*As a reward, Noyes won appointment as U.S. minister to France. Hayes offered Bolivia to Wallace. He turned it down.

Islanders haven't grown long-staple cotton since the boll weevil infestation of the 1920s. Small farms on Saint Helena, Port Royal, and Edisto produce mostly vegetables and soybeans nowadays. Beaufort is a busy year-round tourist center on the Intracoastal Waterway. Hilton Head sinks slowly under the weight of its golf courses and condominiums. There are quiet places on Saint Helena Island still: the remains of the Chapel of Ease (built 1740, burned 1886) and the Brick Church, with the simple stone memorials to the misses Towne and Murray in the oak-shaded yard. The legend REVELATION 14, VERSE 13 is inscribed at the base.

> And I heard a voice from heaven saying unto me, Write, Blessed are the dead which die in the Lord from henceforth: Yea, saith the spirit, that they may rest from their labors; and their works do follow them.

# Notes

For the reader's convenience, manuscript and published sources are cited in full at their first use in each chapter; subsequent citations are shortened. All sources appear in full in the Bibliography. The following abbreviations have been used in the Notes:

CFPL     Concord Free Public Library, Concord, Massachusetts
GHS      Georgia Historical Society, Savannah
IHS       Indiana Historical Society, Indianapolis
ISL       Indiana State Library, Indianapolis
OR       U.S. War Department, *The War of the Rebellion: A Compilation of the Official Records of the Union and Confederate Armies* (Washington, D.C.: 1880–1891)
MHS     Massachusetts Historical Society, Boston
MLS     Massachusetts State Library, Boston
SCL      South Caroliniana Library, University of South Carolina, Columbia
SHC     Southern Historical Collection, Wilson Library, University of North Carolina at Chapel Hill
UCB     Bancroft Library, University of California at Berkeley

## —— 1. Honey Hill ——

1. Edwin S. Redkey, *A Grand Army of Black Men: Letters from African-American Soldiers in the Union Army, 1861–1865* (New York: Cambridge University Press, 1992), 208; Ira Berlin and Leslie S. Rowland, eds., *Families and Freedom: A Documentary History of African-American Kinship in the Civil War Era* (New York: New Press, 1997), 86–87.

2. William L. Logan to Edward W. Kinsley, August 25, 1864, Edward W. Kinsley Papers, Special Collections Library, Duke University.

3. James M. Trotter to Edward W. Kinsley, November 21, 1864, Kinsley Papers, Duke.

4. Charles B. Fox to Mary Fox, November 21 and 24, 1864, in "Extracts from Letters to His Wife," vol. 3, Charles B. Fox Papers, MHS.

5. *New York Times*, December 9, 1864, 1.

6. OR, ser. 1, vol. 44, 421–422.

7. Ibid., 425–426.

8. Ibid., 416–417, 906.

9. Alfred S. Hartwell to Edward W. Kinsley, December 4, 1864, Edward W. Kinsley Papers, MHS; OR, ser. 1, vol. 44, 431–432.

10. Luis F. Emilio, *A Brave Black Regiment: History of the Fifty-fourth Regiment of Massachusetts Volunteer Infantry, 1863–1865* (Salem, N.H.: Ayer, 1990), 246.

11. OR, ser. 1, vol. 44, 433; Charles Fox to Mary Fox, December 24, 1864, Charles B. Fox Papers, MHS.

12. OR, ser. 1, vol. 44, 424; Emilio, *A Brave Black Regiment*, 252; Charles Fox to Mary Fox, December 15, 1864, Charles B. Fox Papers, MHS; Charles C. Soule, "Battle of Honey Hill," *Philadelphia Weekly Times*, May 10, 1884, in *Voices of the 55th*, by Noah A. Trudeau (Dayton, Ohio: Morningside Press, 1996), 214.

13. Charles Fox to Mary Fox, December 2, 1864, Charles B. Fox Papers, MHS.

14. OR, ser. 3, vol. 4, 1027; Elizabeth Ware Pearson, ed., *Letters from Port Royal, 1862–1868* (1906; reprint, New York: Arno Press, 1968), ii.

15. Worthington C. Ford, ed., *A Cycle of Adams Letters* (Boston: Houghton Mifflin, 1920), 1:10.

16. Charles Francis Adams Jr., *Charles Francis Adams, 1835–1915: An Autobiography* (Boston: Houghton Mifflin, 1916), 125.

17. Ibid., 133.

18. Ford, *Cycle of Adams Letters*, 1:112.

19. Ibid., 1:117.

20. Ibid., 1:172.

21. Laura M. Towne, *The Letters and Diary of Laura M. Towne*, ed. Rupert S. Holland (1912; reprint, New York: Negro Universities Press, 1969), 143.

22. Quoted in Willie Lee Rose, *Rehearsal for Reconstruction: The Port Royal Experiment* (New York: Vintage, 1967), 218.

23. George Sheldon, *A History of Deerfield, Massachusetts* (1896; reprint, Somersworth, N.H.: New Hampshire Publishing Co., 1972), 281–283.

24. Whitelaw Reid, *After the War: A Tour of the Southern States, 1865–1866*, ed. C. Vann Woodward (1866; reprint, New York: Harper & Row, 1965), 80.

25. Pearson, *Letters from Port Royal*, 83.

26. Arthur Sumner to J. H. Clark, January 23, 1863, Arthur Sumner Manuscripts, Penn School Papers, SHC.

27. S. Willard Saxton to A. S. Hitchcock, September 25, 1864, Letterbook 1, Rufus and S. Willard Saxton Papers, Manuscripts and Archives, Yale University Library.

28. Laura Towne to her sister, February 8, 1863, Laura Towne Letters, Penn School Papers, SHC.

29. S. Willard Saxton journal, January 23, 1863, Saxton Papers, Yale.

30. Elizabeth Hyde Botume, *First Days Amongst the Contrabands* (1893; reprint, New York: Arno Press, 1968), 109.

31. Botume, *First Days*, 57; Pearson, *Letters from Port Royal*, 209.

32. Towne, *Letters and Diary*, 98; Laura Towne to her sisters, April 25, 1862, Towne Letters, SHC.

33. Laura Towne to her sisters, April 25, 1862, Towne Letters, SHC.

34. Towne, *Letters and Diary*, 33.

35. Ford, ed., *Cycle of Adams Letters*, 1:111.

36. Charlotte Forten, "Life on the Sea Islands," *Atlantic Monthly* 13 (May 1864): 588.

37. Pearson, *Letters from Port Royal*, 17–18.

38. Towne, *Letters and Diary*, 141.

39. Laura Towne to her sisters, August 26, 1862, Towne Letters, SHC.

40. Towne, *Letters and Diary*, 141.

41. Pearson, *Letters from Port Royal*, 289–290.

42. John C. Gray Jr. and John C. Ropes, *War Letters, 1862–1865*, ed. Worthington C. Ford (Boston: Houghton Mifflin, 1927), 421; OR, ser. 1, vol. 44, 445.

43. Charles Izard Manigault, notes on his will, Manigault Family Papers, SHC.

44. James M. Clifton, ed., *Life and Labor on Argyle Island* (Savannah, Ga.: Beehive Press, 1978), xxii–xxiii.

45. Samuel Miller, "In Andersonville Prison" (S2955), typescript memoir, Manuscript Section, ISL.

46. Oscar F. Curtis, ed., "The Civil War Diary of Asbery Stephen," typescript booklet, 16, IHS.

47. Louis Manigault to Fannie Manigault, September 18, 1864, Manigault Family Papers, SHC; OR, ser. 3, vol. 8, 599–600.

48. Henry Sparks diary (SC20), March 28, 29, and 30, 1864; June 7, 11, and 12, 1864; July 17, 1864; August 9, 1864, IHS.

49. Sparks diary, August 17, 1864, IHS.

50. OR, ser. 3, vol. 8, 599.

51. Nathaniel P. Chipman, *The Tragedy of Andersonville: The Trial of Captain Henry Wirz, the Prison-Keeper* (Sacramento, Calif.: Privately published, 1911), 101.

52. Louis Manigault to Fannie Manigault, September 18, 1864, Manigault Family Papers, SHC.

53. Curtis, ed., "Civil War Diary of Asbery Stephen," 17, 21, IHS.

54. Sparks diary, April 10, 1864, IHS.

55. OR, ser. 3, vol. 8, 603; Gabriel Manigault to Charles Manigault, September 8, 1864, Louis Manigault Papers, Special Collections Library, Duke University; Louis Manigault to Fannie Manigault, September 18, 1864, Manigault Family Papers, SHC.

56. Louis Manigault, Plantation Journal, Manigault Family Papers, SHC.

57. Ibid.

58. Clifton, *Life and Labor on Argyle Island*, 348.

59. Ibid., 356.

60. Ibid., 350.

61. Charles Fox to Mary Fox, December 4, 1864, Charles B. Fox Papers, MHS.

62. Ibid.

63. Charles Bowditch to his mother, February 10, 1864, in "War Letters of Charles P. Bowditch," *Proceedings of the Massachusetts Historical Society* 57 (1923–1924): 471.

64. James Trotter to Francis J. Garrison, August 2, 1864, quoted in Trudeau, *Voices of the 55th*, 143.

65. Ibid., 141.

66. Ibid.

67. James Trotter to Edward W. Kinsley, November 21, 1864, Kinsley Papers, Duke.

68. Olivia Bowditch to Edward W. Kinsley, February 7, 1865, Kinsley Papers, Duke.

69. Redkey, *Grand Army of Black Men*, 39.

70. Gray and Ropes, *War Letters*, 422.

## ___ 2. The Laws of War ___

1. John A. Fox to the Reverend Thomas B. Fox, December 14, 1864, Fox Family Papers, MHS.

2. OR, ser. 1, vol. 44, 702, 728.

3. Charles Morse to Ellen Morse, December 18, 1864, Charles Fessenden Morse Papers, MHS.

4. Charles W. Wills, *Army Life of an Illinois Soldier* (Carbondale: Southern Illinois University Press, 1996), 320.

5. Henry Hitchcock, *Marching with Sherman*, ed. M. A. deWolfe Howe (New Haven, Conn.: Yale University Press, 1927), 165; John C. Gray Jr. and John C. Ropes, *War Letters, 1862–1865* (Boston: Houghton Mifflin, 1927), 424, 428.

6. Hitchcock, *Marching with Sherman*, 161; William T. Sherman, *Memoirs of General W. T. Sherman* (New York: Library of America, 1990), 670.

7. Samuel Storrow to Lydia Storrow, December 18, 1864, Samuel Storrow Papers, MHS.

8. Henry Sparks diary (SC20), November 10, 1864, IHS.

9. Samuel Storrow to Lydia Storrow, December 24, 1864, Storrow Papers, MHS.

10. Wills, *Army Life*, 330; Hitchcock, *Marching with Sherman*, 142.

11. Charles Morse to Robert Morse, December 24, 1864, Morse Papers, MHS; OR, ser. 1, vol. 44, 676.

12. OR, ser. 1, vol. 44, 940, 942, 955.

13. John Fox to Feroline Fox, December 26, 1864, Fox Family Papers, MHS; Samuel Storrow to Charles S. Storrow, December 25, 1864, Storrow Papers, MHS.

14. Samuel Storrow to Charles S. Storrow, October 12, 1862, Storrow Papers, MHS.

15. Ibid., Samuel Storrow to Charles and Lydia Storrow, May 12, 1863, Storrow Papers, MHS.

16. John Fox to George Fox, November 1, 1864, Fox Family Papers, MHS; Samuel Storrow to Lydia Storrow, October 27, 1864, Storrow Papers, MHS.

17. OR, ser. 1, vol. 38, pt. 5, 793.

18. Hitchcock, *Marching with Sherman*, 140.

19. Sherman, *Memoirs*, 673.

20. OR, ser. 1, vol. 44, 110–111; Sherman, *Memoirs*, 674.

21. Hitchcock, *Marching with Sherman*, 189.

22. OR, ser. 1, vol. 44, 701–702.

23. Elizabeth Howard to Oliver O. Howard, December 18, 1864, Oliver Otis Howard Papers, Bowdoin College.

24. Hitchcock, *Marching with Sherman*, 187, 191; William T. Sherman, *Home Letters of General Sherman*, ed. M. A. deWolfe Howe (New York: Scribner's, 1909), 322.

25. Samuel Storrow to Lydia Storrow, November 16, 1862, Storrow Papers, MHS.

26. John Fox to Thomas Fox, July 18, 1863, and John Fox to Thomas B. Fox, July 29, 1863, Fox Family Papers, MHS.

27. John Fox to George Fox, January 3, 1865, Fox Family Papers, MHS.

28. Sparks diary, November 21, 1864, IHS.

29. Walt Whitman, *Complete Poetry and Collected Prose*, ed. Justin Kaplan (New York: Library of America, 1982), 765; George W. Julian, *Political Recollections, 1840 to 1872* (Chicago: Jansen, McClung, 1884), 239.

30. OR, ser. 1, vol. 44, 279–280.

31. Charles H. Howard to his mother, Charles H. Howard Papers, Bowdoin College.

32. Charles Morse to Robert Morse, December 24, 1864, Morse Papers, MHS.

33. Ibid., and Charles Morse to Robert Morse, January 2, 1865, Morse Papers, MHS.

34. Charles Morse to Robert Morse, January 2, 1865; Sherman, *Memoirs*, 694; W. T. Sherman to Ellen Sherman, January 5, 1865, in Sherman, *Home Letters*, 326.

35. Charles Morse to his father, January 31, 1865, Morse Papers, MHS; Lafayette McLaws to Emily McLaws, December 24, 1864, Lafayette McLaws Papers, SHC; Emma Manigault to Louis Manigault, January 10, 1865, Louis Manigault Papers, Special Collections Library, Duke University.

36. Charles Howard to his mother, December 27, 1864, C. H. Howard Papers, Bowdoin; E. A. Nason to Oliver O. Howard, January 12, 1865, O. O. Howard Papers, Bowdoin.

37. Oliver O. Howard to Elizabeth Howard, December 26, 1864, O. O. Howard Papers, Bowdoin.

38. Lafayette McLaws to Emily McLaws, December 27, 1864, McLaws Papers, SHC.

39. Lafayette McLaws to Emily McLaws, December 27, 1864, McLaws Papers, SHC; Sherman, *Memoirs*, 715.

40. Cameron McRae to Oliver O. Howard, December 24, 1864, O. O. Howard Papers, Bowdoin.

41. John Fox to Feroline Fox, December 26, 1864, Fox Family Papers; Thomas W. Osborn, *The Fiery Trail: A Union Officer's Account of Sherman's Last Campaigns*, ed. Richard Harwell and Philip N. Racine (Knoxville: University of Tennessee Press, 1986), 80.

42. Samuel Storrow to Lydia Storrow, December 18, 1865, Storrow Papers, MHS.

43. Samuel Storrow to Lydia Storrow, January 15, 1863, Storrow Papers, MHS.

44. Lafayette McLaws to Emily McLaws, January 12, 1865, McLaws Papers, SHC.

45. Charles Morse to Robert Morse, December 24, 1864, Morse Papers, MHS.

46. Oliver Otis Howard, *The Autobiography of Oliver Otis Howard* (New York: Baker & Taylor, 1907), 2:96; Gray and Ropes, *War Letters*, 434.

47. Wills, *Army Life*, 336.

48. Emma Manigault to Louis Manigault, December 21, 1864, Louis Manigault Papers, Duke; Louis Manigault, Plantation Journal, Manigault Family Papers, SHC.

49. Emma Manigault to Louis Manigault, January 10, 1865, Louis Manigault Family Papers, Duke.

50. "Testimony by a Georgia Freedman before the Southern Claims Commission," in *The Destruction of Slavery*, ser. 1, vol. 1 of *Freedom: A Documentary History of Emancipation*, ed. Ira Berlin et al. (New York: Cambridge University Press, 1985), 144.

51. OR, ser. 1, vol. 44, 385; Berlin et al. *Destruction of Slavery*, 150.

52. Berlin et al., *Destruction of Slavery*, 149.

53. Joseph LeConte, *The Autobiography of Joseph LeConte*, ed. William Dallam Armes (New York: D. Appleton, 1903), 6.

54. Ibid., 179.

55. Emma LeConte, *When the World Ended: The Diary of Emma LeConte*, ed. Earl S. Miers (Lincoln: University of Nebraska Press, 1987), 9.

56. Ibid., 16.

57. Ibid., 22.

58. Joseph LeConte, "A Journal of Three Months Personal Experience during the Last Days of the Confederacy," manuscript notebook in the Joseph LeConte

Papers, SCL. The University of California Press published the journal as '*Ware Sherman* in 1937.

59. Joseph LeConte, "Journal," 19, 20–25, 33–34, 37, 59–60, 84, SCL.

60. Charles Fox to Mary Fox, January 15, 1865, Charles B. Fox Papers, MHS; James M. Trotter to Edward W. Kinsley, January 29, 1865, Edward W. Kinsley Papers, Special Collections Library, Duke University.

61. John Fox to Thomas B. Fox, August 5, 1863, Fox Family Papers, MHS.

62. Charles Fox to Mary Fox, January 21, 1865, and January 31, 1865, Charles B. Fox Papers, MHS.

63. John Fox to Thomas B. Fox, January 24, 1865, Fox Family Papers, MHS.

64. Ibid.

65. Charles Fox to Mary Fox, January 17, 1865, Charles B. Fox Papers, MHS.

## —— 3. The Sherman Lands ——

1. Charles Morse to Robert Morse, January 2, 1865, Charles Fessenden Morse Papers, MHS; John C. Gray Jr. and John C. Ropes, *War Letters, 1862–1865* (New York: Houghton Mifflin, 1927), 436.

2. Gray and Ropes, *War Letters*, 427.

3. Ibid., 444, 424; Charles Morse to Robert Morse, January 2, 1865, Morse Papers, MHS.

4. William T. Sherman, *Memoirs of General W. T. Sherman* (New York: Library of America, 1990), 677; OR, ser. 1, vol. 47, pt. 2, 36.

5. W. T. Sherman to Ellen Sherman, December 25, 1864, in William T. Sherman, *Home Letters of General Sherman*, ed. M. A. deWolfe Howe (New York: Scribner's, 1909), 319.

6. Henry Hitchcock, *Marching with Sherman*, ed. M. A. deWolfe Howe (New Haven, Conn.: Yale University Press, 1927), 202.

7. OR, ser. 1, vol. 47, pt. 2, 37–41.

8. Ibid., 41.

9. Ibid., 60–62; Sherman, *Memoirs*, 726–727.

10. Laura Towne to her sister, December 18, 1864, Laura Towne Letters, Penn School Papers, SHC.

11. Laura Towne to her sister, December 25, 1864, Towne Letters, SHC; OR, ser. 1, vol. 44, 787.

12. OR, ser. 3, vol. 4, 1030; Elizabeth Ware Pearson, ed., *Letters from Port Royal, 1862–1868* (1906; reprint, New York: Arno Press, 1968) 108, 122.

13. Elizabeth Hyde Botume, *First Days Amongst the Contrabands* (1893; reprint, New York: Arno Press, 1969), 180.

14. Ira Berlin et al., *The Destruction of Slavery*, ser. 1, vol. 1 of *Freedom: A Documentary History of Emancipation* (New York: Cambridge University Press, 1985), 140–141.

15. OR, ser. 3, vol. 4, 1029–1030.

16. Edward Pierce to Laura Towne, April 18, 1864, Towne Letters, SHC.

17. Rufus Saxton to Prince Rivers, January 18, 1864, Letterbook 2, Rufus and S. Willard Saxton Papers, Manuscripts and Archives, Yale University Library.

18. George Julian, *Speeches on Political Questions* (1872; reprint, Westport, Conn.: Negro Universities Press, 1970), 269; Willie Lee Rose, *Rehearsal for Reconstruction: The Port Royal Experiment* (New York: Vintage, 1967), 27.

19. OR, ser. 3, vol. 4, 1025–1026.

20. Rufus Saxton to Charles Sumner, December 6, 1863, Letterbook 1, Saxton Papers, Yale.

21. Arthur Sumner to Joseph Clark, January 23, 1863, and Arthur Sumner to Nina Hartshorn, December 13, 1864, Arthur Sumner Manuscripts, Penn School Papers, SHC; Rufus Saxton to Edward Philbrick, June 15, 1864, Letterbook 2, Saxton Papers, Yale.

22. Towne is quoted in Rose, *Rehearsal for Reconstruction*, 174.

23. Laura Towne to her sister, October 23, 1864, Towne Letters, SHC.

24. Pearson, *Letters from Port Royal*, 15; Botume, *First Days*, 236.

25. Arthur Sumner to Joseph Clark, January 23, 1863, and June 15, 1863, Sumner Manuscripts, SHC.

26. Laura M. Towne, *The Letters and Diary of Laura M. Towne*, ed. Rupert S. Holland (1912; reprint, New York: Negro Universities Press, 1969), 101.

27. Pearson, *Letters from Port Royal*, 300–301.

28. Ibid., 303.

29. Botume, *First Days*, 78, 83.

30. Ibid., 117; Towne, *Letters and Diary*, 149.

31. Laura Towne to her sister, February 19, 1865, Towne Letters, SHC.

32. Laura Towne to Dear G, January 8, 1865, Towne Letters, SHC.

33. Botume, *First Days*, 107–108.

34. Charlotte Forten, "Life on the Sea Islands," *Atlantic Monthly* 13 (May 1864): 589.

35. Oliver O. Howard to Elizabeth Howard, January 20, 1865, Oliver Otis Howard Papers, Bowdoin College.

36. Oliver O. Howard to Elizabeth Howard, January 13, 1865, O. O. Howard Papers, Bowdoin.

37. S. Willard Saxton journal, January 23, 1865, Saxton Papers, Yale.

38. Thomas Wentworth Higginson, "Leaves from an Officer's Journal," *Atlantic Monthly* 15 (January 1865): 71; Hitchcock, *Marching with Sherman*, 328.

39. Arthur Sumner to Nina Hartshorn, February 4, 1865, Sumner Manuscripts, SHC.

40. Willard Saxton journal, January 4, 1865, Saxton Papers, Yale.

41. Oliver O. Howard to Elizabeth Howard, December 26, 1864, and January 13, 1865, O. O. Howard Papers, Bowdoin.

42. Oliver O. Howard to Elizabeth Howard, January 6, 1865, and January 27, 1865, O. O. Howard Papers, Bowdoin; Pearson, *Letters from Port Royal*, 30–32.

43. Gray and Ropes, *War Letters*, 440; 420.

44. Whitelaw Reid, *After the War: A Tour of the Southern States, 1865–1866*, ed. C. Vann Woodward (1866; reprint, New York: Harper & Row, 1965), 117; Hitchcock, *Marching with Sherman*, 226–227.

45. Gray and Ropes, *War Letters*, 442.

46. Willard Saxton journal, January 15, 1865, Saxton Papers, Yale.

47. Botume, *First Days*, 115.

48. Willard Saxton journal, January 15, 1865, Saxton Papers, Yale.

49. OR, ser. 1, vol. 47, pt. 2, 187.

50. Willard Saxton journal, January 15, 1865, Saxton Papers, Yale.

51. Oliver Otis Howard, *The Autobiography of Oliver Otis Howard* (New York: Baker & Taylor, 1907), 2:100–102.

52. Quoted in *A Southern Reader*, ed. Willard Thorp (New York: Knopf, 1955), 232.

53. Ralph Elliott to Ann Elliott, December 11, 1864, Elliott and Gonzales Papers, SHC.

54. Harriet Gonzales to Emily Elliott, February 1865, Elliott and Gonzales Papers, SHC.

55. William Elliott to Ann Elliott, February 2, 1865, Elliott and Gonzales Papers, SHC.

56. Emily Elliott to Ann Elliott, January 29, 1865, Elliott and Gonzales Papers, SHC.

57. Willard Saxton journal, January 22, 1865, Saxton Papers, Yale.

58. Oliver O. Howard to Rufus Saxton, January 29, 1865, O. O. Howard Papers, Bowdoin.

59. Charles Morse to Robert Morse, January 16, 1865, Morse Papers, MHS; Samuel Storrow to Lydia Storrow, January 22, 1865, Samuel Storrow Papers, MHS.

60. Charles Morse to Robert Morse, January 15, 1865, and January 25, 1865, Morse Papers, MHS.

61. Charles F. Morse, *Letters Written during the Civil War* (Boston: Privately published, 1898), 24.

62. Charles Morse to Robert Morse, January 15, 1865, Morse Papers, MHS; Gray and Ropes, *War Letters*, 450.

63. Joshua T. Owen to Oliver O. Howard, January 30, 1865, O. O. Howard Papers, Bowdoin; Rowland Howard to Oliver O. Howard, January 1, 1865, O. O. Howard Papers, Bowdoin.

64. Morse, *Letters*, 91.

65. Ibid., 105; Russell Duncan, ed. *Blue-Eyed Child of Fortune: The Civil War Letters of Robert Gould Shaw* (Athens: University of Georgia Press, 1992), 306.

66. John Fox to Thomas B. Fox, July 28, 1863, Fox Family Papers, MHS.

67. John Fox to Feroline Fox, January 3, 1865, Fox Family Papers, MHS.

68. Charles Morse to Ellen Morse, January 8, 1865, Morse Papers, MHS.

69. Charles Morse to his father, January 31, 1865, Morse Papers, MHS.

70. Ibid.; Thomas W. Osborn, *The Fiery Trail: A Union Officer's Account of Sherman's Last Campaigns*, ed. Richard Harwell and Philip N. Racine (Knoxville: University of Tennessee Press, 1986), 83.

71. E. B. Webb to Oliver O. Howard, January 9, 1865, O. O. Howard Papers, Bowdoin.

72. Oliver O. Howard to Elizabeth Howard, January 27, 1865, O. O. Howard Papers, Bowdoin.

#### —— 4. The Smoky March ——

1. Daniel Oakey, "Marching through Georgia and the Carolinas," *Battles and Leaders of the Civil War* (New York: Century, 1887), 4:675; Samuel Storrow to Charles S. Storrow, January 22, 1865, Samuel Storrow Papers, MHS.

2. Charles Morse to his father, January 31, 1865, Charles Fessenden Morse Papers, MHS.

3. William T. Sherman to Maria Sherman Fitch, January 19, 1864, quoted in *Sherman: A Soldier's Passion for Order*, by John F. Marszalek (New York: Free Press, 1993), 309.

4. Henry Hitchcock, *Marching with Sherman*, ed. M. A. deWolfe Howe (New Haven, Conn.: Yale University Press, 1927), 251.

5. Thomas W. Osborn, *The Fiery Trail: A Union Officer's Account of Sherman's Last Campaigns*, ed. Richard Harwell and Philip N. Racine (Knoxville: University of Tennessee Press, 1986), 102.

6. Hitchcock, *Marching with Sherman*, 242; Samuel Storrow to his father, January 22, 1865, Storrow Papers, MHS.

7. Oliver O. Howard to Elizabeth Howard, January 27, 1865, and January 29, 1865, Oliver Otis Howard Papers, Bowdoin College.

8. John C. Gray Jr. and John C. Ropes, *War Letters, 1862–1865*, ed. Worthington C. Ford (Boston: Houghton Mifflin, 1927), 456.

9. Ibid., 436.

10. Ibid., 447.

11. Osborn, *Fiery Trail*, 98.

12. Ibid., 95.

13. Hitchcock, *Marching with Sherman*, 252.

14. OR, ser. 1, vol. 47, pt. 1, 683.

15. Ibid., 640.

16. Henry Slocum, "Sherman's March from Savannah to Bentonville," *Battles and Leaders of the Civil War* (New York: Century, 1887), 4:685–686n.

17. Charles Morse to Robert Morse, January 2, 1865, Morse Papers, MHS.

18. Charles W. Wills, *Army Life of an Illinois Soldier* (Carbondale: Southern Illinois University Press, 1996), 341; Osborn, *Fiery Trail*, 110.

19. Oliver Otis Howard, *The Autobiography of Oliver Otis Howard* (New York: Baker & Taylor, 1907), 2:110–111; William T. Sherman, *Memoirs of General W. T. Sherman* (New York: Library of America, 1990), 756.

20. OR, ser. 1, vol. 47, pt. 1, 21; 197–198.

21. Wills, *Army Life*, 349; Osborn, *Fiery Trail*, 126.

22. OR, ser. 1, vol. 47, pt. 1, 1048.

23. J. B. Ray to Lafayette McLaws, January 21, 1865, Lafayette McLaws Papers, SHC; OR, ser. 1, vol. 47, pt. 1, 1047, 1049.

24. Lafayette McLaws to Emily McLaws, February 22, 1865, McLaws Papers, SHC.

25. Louis Manigault to William H. Huger, April 10, 1865, Manigault Family Papers, SHC.

26. Emma LeConte, *When the World Ended: The Diary of Emma LeConte*, ed. Earl S. Miers (Lincoln: University of Nebraska Press, 1987), 12.

27. Grace B. Elmore diary, February 7, 1865, SCL.

28. Ibid., February 10, 1865.

29. Ibid., February 7, 1865, and February 13, 1865.

30. Emma LeConte, *When the World Ended*, 31.

31. Joseph LeConte, "A Journal of Three Months Personal Experience during the Last Days of the Confederacy," 85, manuscript notebook in the Joseph LeConte Papers, SCL.

32. Emma LeConte, *When the World Ended*, 31–34; Joseph LeConte, "Journal," 86, Joseph LeConte Papers, SCL; Josephine LeConte to Julian LeConte, February 28, 1865, LeConte Family Papers (C-B 1014), UCB.

33. OR, ser. 1, vol. 47, pt. 1, 1048; Sherman, *Memoirs*, 759–760; Marion B. Lucas, *Sherman and the Burning of Columbia* (College Station: Texas A&M University Press, 1976), 65; OR, ser. 1, vol. 53, 1050.

34. Lucas, *Sherman and the Burning of Columbia*, 67; Elmore diary, February 21, 1865, SCL; OR, ser. 1, vol. 47; pt. 1, 198.

35. OR, ser. 1, vol. 47, pt. 1, 199, 227, 243, 265; Sherman, *Memoirs*, 760; Osborn, *Fiery Trail*, 128.

36. Lucas, *Sherman and the Burning of Columbia*, 27; OR, ser. 1, vol. 47, pt. 1, 243; Elmore diary, February 10, 1865, SCL.

37. Wills, *Army Life*, 350.

38. Josephine LeConte to Julian LeConte, February 28, 1865, LeConte Family Papers, UCB.

39. Elmore diary, February 21, 1865, SCL.

40. Ibid.

41. Emma LeConte, *When the World Ended*, 45.

42. Charles Howard to his mother, April 1, 1865, Charles H. Howard Papers, Bowdoin College; John G. Barrett, *Sherman's March through the Carolinas* (Chapel Hill: University of North Carolina Press, 1956), 85; OR, ser. 1, vol. 47, pt. 1, 228, 265, 310.

43. Emma LeConte, *When the World Ended*, 56.

44. Osborn, *Fiery Trail*, 134; Emma LeConte, *When the World Ended*, 57.

45. OR, ser. 1, vol. 47, pt. 1, 22; Slocum, "Sherman's March," 686; Sherman, *Memoirs*, 767.

46. Elmore diary, February 21, 1865, SCL.

47. Emma LeConte, *When the World Ended*, 60.

48. Ibid., 61.

49. Howard, *Autobiography*, 2:124; Sherman, *Memoirs*, 768.

50. Emma LeConte, *When the World Ended*, 54.

51. Joseph LeConte, "Journal," 94, Joseph LeConte Papers, SCL.

52. Ibid., 145.

53. Ibid., 150.

54. Ann Elliott to her daughters, February 3, 1865, Elliott and Gonzales Papers, SHC.

55. Ann Elliott to her daughters, February 10, 1865, Elliott and Gonzales Papers.

56. Louis Manigault, "Book," Manigault Family Papers, SHC.

57. Gray and Ropes, *War Letters*, 459; Henry S. Tew, "An Eye-witness Account of the Occupation of Mount Pleasant," *South Carolina Historical Magazine* 66 (January 1965): 8–10.

58. Charles Manigault, "Some Things Relating to Our Family Affairs," undated manuscript, Manigault Family Papers, SHC; Charles Manigault to Louis Manigault, April 10, 1865, Manigault Family Papers, SHC.

59. Charles Manigault, "Some Things," Manigault Family Papers, SHC.

60. Ibid.

61. Charles Manigault, "Close of the War," Manigault Family Papers, SHC.

62. Ibid.

63. Louis Manigault to William Huger, April 10, 1865, Manigault Family Papers, SHC.

64. Charles Fox to Mary Fox, March 19, 1865, Charles B. Fox Papers, MHS.

65. Charles Fox to Mary Fox, February 20, 1865, Charles B. Fox Papers, MHS.

66. Charles Fox to Mary Fox, February 23, 1865, Charles B. Fox Papers, MHS.

67. Charles Fox to Mary Fox, March 13, 1865, Charles B. Fox Papers, MHS.

68. Osborn, *Fiery Trail*, 139.

69. OR, ser. 1, vol. 47, pt. 2, 505–506, 544; Osborn, *Fiery Trail*, 147n, 153; Wills, *Army Life*, 355.

70. Howard, *Autobiography*, 2:130; OR, ser. 1, vol. 47, pt. 2, 544, 546, 567, 568; OR, ser. 1, vol. 47, pt. 1, 318–319.

71. Slocum, "Sherman's March," 687; Wills, *Army Life*, 357, 365.

72. Emma Holmes, *The Diary of Miss Emma Holmes*, ed. John F. Marszalek (Baton Rouge: Louisiana State University Press, 1979), 413.

73. Ibid., 402.

74. Wills, *Army Life*, 357; Osborn, *Fiery Trail*, 166–167.

75. Osborn, *Fiery Trail*, 171; Wills, *Army Life*, 358.

76. Oakey, "Marching through Georgia and the Carolinas," 677–678; OR, ser. 1, vol. 47, pt. 2, 728.

77. Osborn, *Fiery Trail*, 187; Charles F. Morse, *Letters Written during the Civil War* (Boston: Privately published, 1898), 212–213.

78. Charles Morse to Robert Morse, March 12, 1865, Morse Papers.

79. John Fox to Feroline Fox, March 12, 1865, Fox Family Papers, MHS.

80. Slocum, "Sherman's March," 689.

81. Oliver O. Howard to Elizabeth Howard, March 15, 1865, O. O. Howard Papers, Bowdoin; OR, ser. 1, vol. 47, pt. 2, 803.

82. Osborn, *Fiery Trail*, 182; OR, ser. 1, vol. 47, pt. 2, 779.

83. Oakey, "Marching through Georgia and the Carolinas," 679.

84. J. W. Hastings to Charles S. Storrow, March 25, 1865, Samuel Storrow Papers, MHS.

85. William Cogswell to Charles S. Storrow, March 24, 1865, Samuel Storrow Papers, MHS.

86. Ibid.

87. OR, ser. 1, vol. 47, pt. 2, 919.

88. Sherman, *Memoirs*, 786.

89. OR, ser. 1, vol. 47, pt. 2, 950.

90. Howard, *Autobiography*, 2:150.

91. Lafayette McLaws to Emily McLaws, March 25, 1865, Lafayette McLaws Papers, SHC.

92. Ibid.; OR, ser. 1, vol. 47, pt. 2, 1454.

93. Sherman, *Memoirs*, 788.

94. Rowland Howard to Oliver O. Howard, February 14, 1865, O. O. Howard Papers, Bowdoin.

95. Rowland Howard to Oliver O. Howard, March 27, 1865, O. O. Howard Papers, Bowdoin.

96. Rowland Howard to Oliver O. Howard, March 31, 1865, O. O. Howard Papers, Bowdoin.

## —— 5. The Shell of Rebellion ——

1. OR, ser. 1, vol. 46, pt. 1, 1293.

2. Charles M. Blackford, *Letters from Lee's Army*, ed. Susan L. Blackford (New York: Scribner's, 1947), 290.

3. OR, ser. 1, vol. 46, pt. 2, 1254, 1258, 1265; Blackford, *Letters from Lee's Army*, 276.

4. John B. Jones, *A Rebel War Clerk's Diary*, ed. Earl S. Miers (New York: Sagamore Press, 1958), 487, 492, 497, 505.

5. Blackford, *Letters from Lee's Army*, 279.

6. Thomas Conolly, *An Irishman in Dixie*, ed. Nelson D. Lankford (Columbia: University of South Carolina Press, 1988), 37–38.

7. Ibid., 48.

8. Letter fragment to "Dear Marshall" (probably Lee's military secretary, Lieutenant Colonel Charles Marshall), March 30, 1865, Richard S. Ewell Papers, SHC.

9. Quoted in Douglas Southall Freeman, *Lee's Lieutenants: A Study in Command*, vol. 3 (New York: Scribner's, 1946), 331.

10. Ibid., 332.

11. Conolly, *Irishman in Dixie*, 84.

12. OR, ser. 1, vol. 46, pt. 1, 1293.

13. Ibid., 1293; J. B. Kershaw to Campbell Brown, October 9, 1865, Ewell Papers, SHC.

14. Campbell Brown, ms. note or affidavit, April 14, 1865, Ewell Papers, SHC.

15. Edward M. Boykin, *The Falling Flag* (New York: E. T. Hale & Son, 1874), 15.

16. Edward Bartlett to Martha Bartlett, March 30, 1865, Edward J. Bartlett Letters, MHS.

17. Ibid.

18. Annie Bartlett to Edward Bartlett, May 26, 1864, Annie Keyes Bartlett/Edward J. Bartlett Collection, CFPL.

19. Edward Bartlett to Martha Bartlett, May 14, 1864, Bartlett Letters, MHS.

20. Ibid.

21. Edward Bartlett to Annie Andrews, January 5, 1865, Bartlett Letters, MHS.

22. Charles F. Adams to his father, November 2, 1864, in *A Cycle of Adams Letters*, ed. Worthington C. Ford (Boston: Houghton Mifflin, 1920), 2:218–219.

23. Edward Bartlett to Martha Bartlett, November 20, 1864, Bartlett Letters, MHS.

24. Edward Bartlett to Martha Bartlett, January 25, 1865, and February 5, 1865, Bartlett Letters, MHS.

25. Charles F. Adams to his father, June 28, 1862, in Ford, *Cycle of Adams Letters*, 1:160.

26. Charles F. Adams to his father, December 18, 1864, in Ford, *A Cycle of Adams Letters*, 2:234–236.

27. Edward Bartlett to Ripley Bartlett, March 29, 1865, Bartlett Letters, MHS.

28. Martha Bartlett to Edward Bartlett, April 2, 1865, Bartlett Family Papers, CFPL.

29. Edward Bartlett to Martha Bartlett, April 3, 1865, Bartlett Letters, MHS.

30. "Entry into Richmond," in "Memoirs of Concord Veterans of the Civil War, 1861–1865," vol. 1 (unpublished typescript, Concord, Mass., 1910), CFPL.

31. Edward Bartlett to Martha Bartlett, April 3, 1865, Bartlett Letters, MHS.

32. OR, ser. 1, vol. 46, pt. 3, 509.

33. Ibid., 535.

34. Lizzie Ewell to Richard Ewell, April 13, 1865, Ewell Papers, SHC.

35. Edward Bartlett to Martha Bartlett, April 3, 1865, Bartlett Letters, MHS.

36. Charles F. Adams to his father, April 10, 1865, in Ford, *Cycle of Adams Letters*, 2:261–262.

37. George Cary Eggleston, *A Rebel's Recollections* (New York: G. P. Putnam's Sons, 1878), 237.

38. Boykin, *Falling Flag*, 48.

39. R. T. W. Duke, "Burning of Richmond," *Southern Historical Society Papers* 30 (1897):137.

40. Campbell Brown, postscript to accounts of the Richmond evacuation and Sayler's Creek, *Southern Historical Society Papers* 13 (1885):258.

41. OR, ser. 1, vol. 46, pt. 3, 610; OR, ser. 1, vol. 46, pt. 1, 1295.

42. Quoted in Freeman, *Lee's Lieutenants*, 3:707.

43. Quoted in Shelby Foote, *The Civil War: A Narrative* (New York: Random House, 1974), 3:919.

44. Thomas Gantt to Lizinka Ewell, April 9, 1865, Ewell Papers, SHC.

45. Edward Bartlett to Martha Bartlett, April 4, 1865, Bartlett Letters, MHS.

46. Edward H. Ripley, *The Capture and Occupation of Richmond* (New York: G. P. Putnam's Sons, 1907), 23–24.

47. Lincoln is quoted in Benjamin P. Thomas and Harold M. Hyman, *Stanton: The Life and Times of Lincoln's Secretary of War* (New York: Knopf, 1962), 393; Ripley, *Capture and Occupation*, 23–24.

48. Ripley, *Capture and Occupation*, 14, 28.

49. Charles F. Adams to his father, April 10, 1865, in Ford, *Cycle of Adams Letters*, 2:263.

50. OR, ser. 1, vol. 46, pt. 3, 575, 684.

51. Ibid., 619.

52. Ibid., 663.

53. Charles A. Dana, *Recollections of the Civil War* (New York: D. Appleton, 1898), 269; OR, ser. 1, vol. 46, pt. 3, 574.

54. Susan Wallace to Delia Wallace, March 10, 1865, Lew Wallace Papers (M292), IHS.

55. Lydia Maria Child to George W. Julian, April 8, 1865, Joshua R. Giddings Papers, microfilm, ISL.

56. Laura Julian to her sister, January 8, 1865, George W. Julian Papers (L81), ISL.

57. George Julian, *Political Recollections, 1840 to 1872* (Chicago: Jansen, McClung, 1884), 69.

58. Ibid., 100.

59. "George W. Julian's Journal—the Assassination of Lincoln," *Indiana Magazine of History* 2 (1915):327.

60. George W. Julian to Laura Julian, April 9, 1865, Julian Papers, ISL.

61. "George W. Julian's Journal," 331.

62. George W. Julian to Laura Julian, April 11, 1865, Julian Papers, ISL.

63. "George W. Julian's Journal," 333.

64. John Ropes to John Gray, March 31, 1865, in John C. Gray Jr. and John C. Ropes, *War Letters, 1862–1865*, ed. Worthington C. Ford (Boston: Houghton Mifflin, 1927), 465.

65. S. Willard Saxton journal, April 3, 1865, and April 9, 1865, Rufus and S. Willard Saxton Papers, Manuscripts and Archives, Yale University Library.

66. Charles Fox to Mary Fox, April 15, 1865, Charles B. Fox Papers, MHS.

67. Willard Saxton journal, February 6, 1865, and February 27, 1865, Saxton Papers, Yale.

68. Laura Towne to her sisters, March 3, 1865, Laura Towne Letters, Penn School Papers, SHC.

69. Elizabeth Ware Pearson, ed., *Letters from Port Royal, 1862–1868* (1906; reprint, New York: Arno Press, 1968), 308.

70. Laura Towne to her sisters, March 3, 1865, Towne Letters, SHC.

71. Pearson, *Letters from Port Royal*, 308.

72. Willard Saxton journal, March 17, 1865, Saxton Papers, Yale.

73. Willard Saxton journal, March 24, 1865, Saxton Papers, Yale.

74. Laura Towne to S, April 23, 1865, Towne Letters, SHC.

75. Laura Towne to her sister, April 23, 1865, Towne Letters, SHC.

76. Quoted in Foote, *The Civil War*, 3:971.

77. Willard Saxton journal, April 14, 1865, Saxton Papers, Yale.

78. William Lloyd Garrison is quoted in the *Dictionary of American Biography*, vol. 7 (New York: Scribner's, 1931), 171; Laura Towne to S, April 23, 1865, Towne Let-

ters, SHC; John Gray to Elizabeth Gray, April 17, 1865, in Gray and Ropes, *War Letters*, 469.

79. Quoted in John Thomas, *The Liberator: The Life of William Lloyd Garrison* (Boston: Little, Brown, 1963), 430.

80. Ibid., 431; Charles Howard to Oliver O. Howard, April 22, 1865, Oliver Otis Howard Papers, Bowdoin College.

81. Willard Saxton journal, April 15, 1865, Saxton Papers, Yale.

## —— 6. Booth and His Crime ——

1. "George W. Julian's Journal—the Assassination of Lincoln," *Indiana Magazine of History* 2 (1915): 334.

2. OR, ser. 1, vol. 46, pt. 3, 752, 756, 770, 773.

3. C. C. Augur to George W. Dutton, April 14, 1865, George Wendell Dutton Papers, MHS; George Dutton to C. C. Augur, April 15, 1865, Dutton Papers, MHS.

4. OR, ser. 1, vol. 46, pt. 3, 773, 770.

5. Ibid., 781, 785; *New York Times*, May 2, 1865, 1.

6. OR, ser. 1, vol. 46, pt. 3, 756, 769.

7. George W. Julian to Laura Julian, April 15, 1865, George W. Julian Papers, ISL.

8. "George W. Julian's Journal," 335.

9. George W. Julian, *Political Recollections, 1840 to 1872* (Chicago: Jansen, McClung, 1884), 243.

10. "George W. Julian's Journal," 335.

11. Ibid.; George W. Julian to Laura Julian, April 27, 1865, Julian Papers, ISL.

12. George W. Julian to Laura Julian, April 19, 1865, Julian Papers, ISL.

13. Ibid.

14. George W. Julian to Laura Julian, April 17, 1865, Julian Papers, ISL; Thomas R. Turner, *Beware the People Weeping: Public Opinion and the Assassination of Abraham Lincoln* (Baton Rouge: Louisiana State University Press, 1982), 26, 50.

15. OR, ser. 1, vol. 47, pt. 3, 301.

16. Richard Ewell to Ulysses S. Grant, April 1865, Richard S. Ewell Papers, SHC.

17. Edward H. Ripley, *The Capture and Occupation of Richmond* (New York: G. P. Putnam's Sons, 1907), 20; *New York Times*, April 24, 1864, 1; Richard S. Ewell, note or affidavit dated April 14, 1865, Ewell Papers, SHC.

18. *New York Times*, April 24, 1865, 2.

19. Harriot Brown to Lizinka Ewell, April 19, 1865, Ewell Papers, SHC.

20. Campbell Brown to Harriot Brown, April 23, 1865, Ewell Papers, SHC.

21. Thomas Gantt to Lizinka Ewell, April 21, 1865, Ewell Papers, SHC.

22. Leroy P. Graf et al., eds., *The Papers of Andrew Johnson* (Knoxville: University of Tennessee Press, 1986), 7:560.

23. Ibid., 7:561, 597.

24. Harriot (Brown) Turner, "Recollections of Andrew Johnson," *Harper's Monthly* 120 (January 1910): 174.

25. Lizinka Ewell to Montgomery Blair, May 24, 1865, Ewell Papers, SHC; Lizinka Ewell to Richard Ewell, May 25, 1865, Ewell Papers, SHC.

26. OR, ser. 2, vol. 8, 507; Lizinka Ewell to Richard Ewell, May 25, 1865, Ewell Papers, SHC.

27. OR, ser. 1, vol. 47, pt. 3, 220–221.

28. Henry Hitchcock, *Marching with Sherman*, ed. M. A. deWolfe Howe (New Haven, Conn.: Yale University Press, 1927), 298.

29. Daniel Oakey, "Marching through Georgia and the Carolinas," *Battles and Leaders of the Civil War* (New York: Century, 1887), 4:679.

30. OR, ser. 1, vol. 47, pt. 3, 221.

31. Ibid., 245.

32. William T. Sherman, *Memoirs of General W. T. Sherman* (New York: Library of America, 1990), 837.

33. OR, ser. 1, vol. 47, pt. 3, 237.

34. Charles W. Wills, *Army Life of an Illinois Soldier* (Carbondale: Southern Illinois University Press, 1996), 371.

35. Oliver O. Howard to Elizabeth Howard, April 18, 1865, Oliver Otis Howard Papers, Bowdoin College.

36. Elizabeth Howard to Oliver O. Howard, April 15, 1865, O. O. Howard Papers, Bowdoin.

37. Oliver O. Howard to Elizabeth Howard, April 18, 1865, O. O. Howard Papers, Bowdoin; Sherman, *Memoirs*, 839–840.

38. OR, ser. 1, vol. 47, pt. 3, 345.

39. Ibid., 266.

40. Ibid., 843.

41. Thomas W. Osborn, *The Fiery Trail: A Union Officer's Account of Sherman's Last Campaigns*, ed. Richard Harwell and Philip N. Racine (Knoxville: University of Tennessee Press, 1986), 211.

42. OR, ser. 1, vol. 47, pt. 3, 294.

43. Ibid., 312.

44. Oliver O. Howard to Elizabeth Howard, April 29, 1865, O. O. Howard Papers, Bowdoin.

45. "George W. Julian's Journal," 337; Julian, *Political Recollections*, 258.

46. *New York Times*, April 24, 1865, 4.

47. OR, ser. 1, vol. 47, pt. 3, 302; Sherman, *Memoirs*, 853–854, 856.

48. Wills, *Army Life*, 373.

49. Ibid., 374; Osborn, *Fiery Trail*, 219; Charles Morse to Robert Morse, June 4, 1865, Charles Fessenden Morse Papers, MHS.

50. Oliver O. Howard to Lizzie Howard, April 29, 1865, O. O. Howard Papers, Bowdoin.

51. Wills, *Army Life*, 377, 379.

52. Ibid., 375, 379.

53. Charles Howard to Oliver O. Howard, April 22, 1865, O. O. Howard Papers, Bowdoin; Oliver O. Howard to Elizabeth Howard, April 7, 1865, O. O. Howard Papers, Bowdoin; Oliver Otis Howard, *The Autobiography of Oliver Otis Howard* (New York: Baker & Taylor, 1907), 2:207–208.

54. Oliver O. Howard to Elizabeth Howard, May 14, 1865, O. O. Howard Papers, Bowdoin.

55. Whitelaw Reid, *After the War: A Tour of the Southern States, 1861–1865*, ed. C. Vann Woodward (New York: Harper & Row, 1965), 32.

56. *New York Times*, June 1, 1865, 2; John C. Gray Jr. and John C. Ropes, *War Letters, 1862–1865*, ed. Worthington C. Ford (Boston: Houghton Mifflin, 1927), 481.

57. Gray and Ropes, *War Letters*, 481.

58. Emma LeConte, *When the World Ended: The Diary of Emma LeConte*, ed. Earl S. Miers (Lincoln: University of Nebraska Press, 1987), 51.

59. Grace B. Elmore diary, March 4, 1865, SCL.

60. Emma LeConte, *When the World Ended*, 83, 90, 93, 97, 100, 104.

61. Louis Manigault to Charles Manigault, April 3, 1865, Manigault Family Papers, SHC.

62. Charles Manigault to Louis Manigault, April 10, 1865, Manigault Family Papers, SHC.

63. Charles Manigault to Louis Manigault, April 30, 1865, Manigault Family Papers, SHC.

64. Charles Fox to Mary Fox, May 2, 1865, Charles B. Fox Papers, MHS.

65. Elizabeth Ware Pearson, *Letters from Port Royal 1862–1868* (1906; reprint, New York: Arno Press, 1968), 311.

66. Laura Towne to her sister, April 23, 1865, Laura Towne Letters, SHC.

67. Pearson, *Letters from Port Royal*, 311.

68. Quoted in Edwin S. Redkey, *A Grand Army of Black Men: Letters from African-American Soldiers in the Union Army, 1861–1865* (New York: Cambridge University Press, 1992), 60.

69. Emma LeConte, *When the World Ended*, 105.

70. Quoted in Irving McKee, *"Ben-Hur Wallace": The Life of General Lew Wallace* (Berkeley: University of California Press, 1947), 92.

71. Lew Wallace to Susan Wallace, February 17, 1865, Lew Wallace Papers, IHS.

72. Lew Wallace to Susan Wallace, February 24, 1865, Wallace Papers, IHS.

73. Lew Wallace to Ulysses S. Grant, February 22, 1865, Wallace Papers, IHS.

74. Charles Worthington to Lew Wallace, March 7, 1865, Wallace Papers, IHS.

75. Lew Wallace to Ulysses S. Grant, March 14, 1865, Wallace Papers, IHS; Lew Wallace to Susan Wallace, March 14, 1865, Wallace Papers, IHS.

76. Wallace to Grant, March 14, 1865, Wallace Papers, IHS.

77. Lew Wallace to Susan Wallace, March 14, 1865, Wallace Papers, IHS.

78. John Walker to James Slaughter, March 27, 1865, copy in Wallace Papers, IHS.

79. OR, ser. 1, vol. 46, pt. 3, 967, 1072.

80. Prentiss Ingraham, "Capture and Death of John Wilkes Booth," *Century* 39 (1890):446. Other sources suggest Booth shot the horses. In any case, their carcasses were never found.

81. Ibid., 43, 445–464, 448.

82. OR, ser. 1, vol. 46, pt. 1, 1320.

83. Ibid., 1321.

84. Gray and Ropes, *War Letters*, 483.

## —— 7. Exile and Return ——

1. Charles W. Wills, *Army Life of an Illinois Soldier* (Carbondale: Southern Illinois University Press, 1996), 382.

2. S. Willard Saxton journal, May 29, 1865, Rufus and S. Willard Saxton Papers, Manuscripts and Archives, Yale University Library.

3. Charles Howard to his mother, May 23, 1865, Charles H. Howard Papers, Bowdoin College.

4. William T. Sherman to Oliver O. Howard, May 17, 1865, Oliver Otis Howard Papers, Bowdoin College.

5. Ibid.

6. Walt Whitman, *Complete Poetry and Collected Prose*, ed. Justin Kaplan (New York: Library of America, 1982), 770.

7. William T. Sherman, *Memoirs of General W. T. Sherman* (New York: Library of America, 1990), 865–866.

8. Noah Brooks, *Washington in Lincoln's Time*, ed. Herbert Mitgang (New York: Rinehart, 1958), 278; Sherman, *Memoirs*, 866.

9. Charles Morse to Robert Morse, June 4, 1865, Charles Fessenden Morse Papers, MHS.

10. Sherman, *Memoirs*, 869–870.

11. Shelby Foote, *The Civil War: A Narrative* (New York: Random House, 1974), 3:1040.

12. Adjutant General's Office, Special Orders Number 227, May 13, 1865, copy in Morse Papers, MHS.

13. Charles Morse to Robert Morse, May 23, 1865, Morse Papers, MHS.

14. Charles Morse to Robert Morse, June 4, 1865, Morse Papers, MHS.

15. Charles Morse to Robert Morse, June 10, 1865, Morse Papers, MHS.

16. Alonzo H. Quint, *The Record of the Second Massachusetts Infantry, 1861–1865* (Boston: J. P. Walker, 1867), 290.

17. Wills, *Army Life*, 370–371.

18. John C. Gray Jr. and John C. Ropes, *War Letters, 1862–1865*, ed. Worthington C. Ford (Boston: Houghton Mifflin, 1927), 467.

19. Ibid., 491.

20. Ibid., 476.

21. Annie Bartlett to Edward Bartlett, April 20, 1865, Annie Keyes Bartlett/ Edward J. Bartlett Collection, CFPL.

22. Edward Bartlett to Martha Bartlett, May 7, 1865, Edward J. Bartlett Letters, MHS.

23. Annie Bartlett to Edward Bartlett, April 20, 1865, Bartlett Collection, CFPL; Ralph Waldo Emerson, *The Works of Ralph Waldo Emerson* (Boston: Houghton Mifflin, 1878), 11:307.

24. Annie Bartlett to Ned Bartlett, May 7, 1865, and April 19, 1865, Bartlett Collection, CFPL.

25. Edward Bartlett to Martha Bartlett, June 3, 1865, Bartlett Letters, MHS.

26. Charles Francis Adams Jr., *Charles Francis Adams, 1835–1915: An Autobiography* (Boston: Houghton Mifflin, 1916), 167.

27. Charles M. Blackford, *Letters from Lee's Army*, ed. Susan L. Blackford (New York: Scribner's, 1947), 295.

28. Ibid.

29. Emma Holmes, *The Diary of Miss Emma Holmes*, ed. John F. Marszalek (Baton Rouge: Louisiana State University Press, 1979), 439.

30. Benjamin Yancey to General Mequisa, May 24, 1865, Lafayette McLaws Papers, SHC.

31. Charles Manigault, "Close of the War," Manigault Family Papers, SHC.

32. Stephen Elliott to William Elliott, May 20, 1865, Elliott and Gonzales Papers, SHC.

33. Ibid.

34. Joseph LeConte, *The Autobiography of Joseph LeConte*, ed. William Dallam Armes (New York: D. Appleton, 1903), 230; Emma LeConte, *When the World Ended: The Diary of Emma LeConte*, ed. Earl S. Miers (Lincoln: University of Nebraska Press, 1987), 107.

35. A. S. Hartwell, General Orders Number 12, June 9, 1865, Alfred S. Hartwell Papers, MSL.

36. Emma LeConte, *When the World Ended*, 116.

37. Official proclamation, May 20, 1865; A. S. Hartwell to Nathaniel Haughton, June 9, 1865; General Orders Number 12, June 9, 1865; Official proclamation, June 9, 1865, Hartwell Papers, MSL.

38. Emma LeConte, *When the World Ended,* 110; C. Vann Woodward and Elisabeth Muhlenfeld, eds., *The Private Mary Chesnut* (New York: Oxford University Press, 1984), 261; Grace B. Elmore diary, July 13, 1865, SCL.

39. Woodward and Muhlenfeld, *Private Mary Chesnut,* 256.

40. Holmes, *Diary,* 445, 446, 453, 461, 462.

41. Grace Elmore diary, June 25, 1865, SCL.

42. Sidney Andrews, *The South Since the War* (1866; reprint, New York: Arno Press, 1969), 99.

43. A. S. Hartwell to L. B. Perry, August 7, 1865, Hartwell Papers, MSL.

44. Elizabeth Ware Pearson, ed., *Letters from Port Royal, 1862–1868* (1906; reprint, New York: Arno Press, 1968), 309; Charles Fox to Mary Fox, May 22, 1865, Charles B. Fox Papers, MHS; James M. Trotter to Edward W. Kinsley, July 1, 1865, Edward W. Kinsley Papers, Special Collections Library, Duke University.

45. James M. Trotter to Edward W. Kinsley, July 1, 1865, Kinsley Papers, Duke.

46. Charles Fox to Mary Fox, May 22, 1865, Charles B. Fox Papers, MHS.

47. Quoted in Edwin S. Redkey, *A Grand Army of Black Men: Letters from African-American Soldiers in the Union Army, 1861–1865* (New York: Cambridge University Press, 1992), 184.

48. Ibid., 185.

49. Emma LeConte, *When the World Ended,* 114.

50. Ibid., 121.

51. Jane Harden to John LeConte, October 26, 1865, LeConte Family Papers, UCB.

52. William Jones to Joseph and John LeConte, July 3, 1865, LeConte Family Papers, UCB.

53. *New York Times,* May 14, 1865, 5; Lew Wallace, *The Autobiography of Lew Wallace* (New York: Harper & Brothers, 1906), 2:851.

54. Brooks, *Washington in Lincoln's Time,* 238–239; Benjamin Perley Poore, *Perley's Reminiscences of Sixty Years in the National Metropolis* (Tecumseh, Mich.: A. W. Mills, 1886), 2:184–185.

55. Gray and Ropes, *War Letters,* 493, 497.

56. Edmund Kirby Smith to Lew Wallace, May 7, 1865; Lew Wallace to Ulysses S. Grant, May 16, 1865, Lew Wallace Papers, IHS.

57. Lew Wallace to José Carvajal, May 19, 1865, Wallace Papers, IHS.

58. Ibid.

59. Susan Wallace to her mother, August (?) 1865, Wallace Papers, IHS.

60. *New York Times,* May 15, 1865, 1.

61. Willard Saxton journal, May 16, 1865, Saxton Papers, Yale.

62. Charles A. Dana, *Recollections of the Civil War* (New York: D. Appleton, 1898), 282; Gray and Ropes, *War Letters,* 493.

63. Benn Pitman, ed. *The Assassination of President Lincoln and the Trial of the Conspirators* (Cincinnati: Moore, Wilstach & Boldwin, 1865), 28.

64. Ibid., 70–72.

65. Ibid., 84.

66. Gray and Ropes, *War Letters,* 486.

67. David Branson to Lew Wallace, June 2, 1865, Wallace Papers, IHS.

68. Lew Wallace to Susan Wallace, June 26, 1865, Wallace Papers, IHS.

69. Pitman, *Assassination,* 85.

70. Ibid., 115–116.

71. Ibid., 124, 127.

72. *New York Times,* May 14, 1865, 5.

73. Pitman, *Assassination*, 172.

74. Ibid., 175–176.

75. Ibid., 177.

76. Lew Wallace to Susan Wallace, June 21, 1865, Wallace Papers, IHS.

77. Lew Wallace to Susan Wallace, June 26, 1865, Wallace Papers, IHS.

78. Whitelaw Reid, *After the War: A Tour of the Southern States, 1865–1866*, ed. C. Vann Woodward (1866; reprint, New York: Harper & Row, 1965), 114.

79. Ibid., 105.

80. Quoted in Francis B. Simkins and Robert H. Woody, *South Carolina during Reconstruction* (1932; reprint, Gloucester, Mass.: P. Smith, 1966), 228; Reid, *After the War*, 123.

81. Reid, *After the War*, 88.

82. Charles Howard to his mother, May 23, 1865, C. H. Howard Papers, Bowdoin.

83. Charles Howard to Rowland Howard, May 7, 1865, C. H. Howard Papers, Bowdoin; Willard Saxton journal, July 3, 1865, Saxton Papers, Yale; Charles Howard to his mother, May 10, 1865, C. H. Howard Papers, Bowdoin.

84. Charles Howard to his mother, May 23, 1865, C. H. Howard Papers, Bowdoin; Charles Howard, "Reminiscences of the Civil War," unpublished manuscript, C. H. Howard Papers, Bowdoin.

85. Pearson, *Letters from Port Royal*, 310.

86. Quoted in Willie Lee Rose, *Rehearsal for Reconstruction: The Port Royal Experiment* (New York: Vintage, 1967), 347–348.

87. Charles Manigault, "Close of the War," Manigault Family Papers, SHC.

88. Ibid.

89. James M. Clifton, ed., *Life and Labor on Argyle Island* (Savannah, Ga.: Beehive Press, 1978), 350.

90. J. W. Bandy to Louis Manigault, June 18, 1865, Manigault Family Papers, SHC.

## —— 8. Crime, Punishment, Absolution ——

1. Richard Ewell to Lizinka Ewell, May 27, 1865, Richard S. Ewell Papers, SHC.

2. Campbell Brown to Harriot Brown, May 8, 1865, Ewell Papers, SHC.

3. Paul H. Bergeron et al., eds., *The Papers of Andrew Johnson* (Knoxville: University of Tennessee Press, 1989), 8:129–130.

4. Ibid., 8:232.

5. Eric L. McKitrick, *Andrew Johnson and Reconstruction* (Chicago: University of Chicago Press, 1960), 143–146.

6. OR, ser. 2, vol. 8, 582; Lizinka Ewell to Andrew Johnson, May 30, 1865, Ewell Papers, SHC; Richard Ewell to Lizinka Ewell, May 19, 1865, Ewell Papers, SHC.

7. Lizinka Ewell to Richard Ewell, May 29, 1865, Ewell Papers, SHC; Bergeron et al., *Papers of Andrew Johnson*, 8:180.

8. Richard Ewell to Lizinka Ewell, June 5, 1865, Ewell Papers, SHC.

9. Alexander H. Stephens, *Recollections of Alexander H. Stephens*, ed. Myrta Lockett Avary (New York: Doubleday Page, 1910), 220.

10. Campbell Brown to Lizinka Ewell, June 9, 1865, Ewell Papers, SHC.

11. Harriot (Brown) Turner, "Recollections of Andrew Johnson," *Harper's Monthly* 120 (January 1910):175.

12. Lizinka Ewell to Richard Ewell, June 28, 1865, Ewell Papers, SHC; Andrew Johnson to Lizinka Ewell, July 7, 1865, Ewell Papers, SHC.

13. Benn Pitman, ed., *The Assassination of President Lincoln and the Trial of the Conspirators* (Cincinnati: Moore, Wilstach & Boldwin, 1865), 372.

14. Ibid., 385, 394.

15. Ibid., 395.

16. John C. Gray Jr. and John C. Ropes, *War Letters, 1862–1865*, ed. Worthington C. Ford (Boston: Houghton Mifflin, 1927), 493.

17. Nettie Mudd, *The Life of Dr. Samuel A. Mudd* (1906; reprint, Saginaw, Mich.: Privately published, 1962), 38.

18. John A. Gray, "The Fate of the Lincoln Conspirators," *McClure's* 37 (1911): 635.

19. *New York Times*, July 7, 1865, 1; Gray, "Fate of the Lincoln Conspirators," 634.

20. Gray, "Fate of the Lincoln Conspirators," 633.

21. Ibid., 636.

22. *New York Times*, July 8, 1865, 1.

23. Gray, "Fate of the Lincoln Conspirators," 636.

24. Ibid., 636.

25. Gray and Ropes, *War Letters*, 472.

26. Emma Holmes, *The Diary of Miss Emma Holmes*, ed. John F. Marszalek (Baton Rouge: Louisiana State University Press, 1979), 456.

27. Harriot Turner, "Recollections of Andrew Johnson," 170.

28. Quoted in Kenneth M. Stampp, *The Era of Reconstruction, 1865–1877* (New York: Knopf, 1965), 87.

29. Leroy P. Graf et al., eds., *The Papers of Andrew Johnson* (Knoxville: University of Tennessee Press, 1986), 7:613.

30. George Julian to Laura Julian, April 21, 1865, George W. Julian Papers, ISL.

31. Bergeron et al., *Papers of Andrew Johnson*, 8:29.

32. Ibid., 8:281; *New York Times*, June 25, 1865, 5.

33. Holmes, *Diary*, 461.

34. Bergeron et al., *Papers of Andrew Johnson*, 8:317–318.

35. James Trotter to Edward Kinsley, Edward W. Kinsley Papers, Special Collections Library, Duke University.

36. Bergeron et al., *Papers of Andrew Johnson*, 8:365.

37. Laura Julian to her sister, September 4, 1865, Julian Papers, ISL.

38. *Indiana True Republican*, November 16, 1865.

39. George W. Julian, *Political Recollections, 1840 to 1872* (Chicago: Jansen, McClung, 1884), 267; *Indianapolis Daily Journal*, November 3, 1865; George W. Julian, *Speeches on Political Questions* (1872; reprint, Westport, Conn.: Negro Universities Press, 1970), 282.

40. *Indiana True Republican*, November 9, 1865.

41. Laura Julian to her sister, August 13, 1865, Julian Papers, ISL.

42. Quoted in William S. McFeely, *Yankee Stepfather: General O. O. Howard and the Freedmen* (New Haven, Conn.: Yale University Press, 1968) 16.

43. Oliver Otis Howard, *The Autobiography of Oliver Otis Howard* (New York: Baker & Taylor, 1907), 2:227.

44. Henry Ward Beecher to Edwin Stanton, May 3, 1865, Oliver Otis Howard Papers, Bowdoin College.

45. William O. Bourne to Oliver O. Howard, November 21, 1865, O. O. Howard Papers, Bowdoin.

46. Charles Howard to Oliver O. Howard, May 24, 1865, and June 9, 1865, O. O. Howard Papers, Bowdoin.

47. Charles Howard to Oliver O. Howard, June 9, 1865.

48. Rufus Saxton to Oliver O. Howard, May 24, 1865, O. O. Howard Papers, Bowdoin.

49. Howard, *Autobiography*, 2:228, 233; McFeely, *Yankee Stepfather*, 97.

50. J. S. Fullerton to Oliver O. Howard, July 20, 1865, O. O. Howard Papers, Bowdoin.

51. Ibid.

52. Ibid.

53. S. Willard Saxton journal, July 16, 1865, Rufus and S. Willard Saxton Papers, Manuscripts and Archives, Yale University Library.

54. Gray and Ropes, *War Letters*, 452.

55. Willard Saxton journal, August 6, 1865, Saxton Papers, Yale; Rufus Saxton, Circular Number 2, August 16, 1865, in *Report of the Joint Committee on Reconstruction at the First Session, Thirty-ninth Congress* (1866; reprint, Westport, Conn.: Negro Universities Press, 1969), 230.

56. Quoted in Willie Lee Rose, *Rehearsal for Reconstruction: The Port Royal Experiment* (New York: Vintage, 1967), 356.

57. Edward McPherson, *The Political History of the United States of America during the Period of Reconstruction* (1871; reprint, New York: DaCapo, 1972), 13.

58. Oliver O. Howard to Elizabeth Howard, September 2, 1865, O. O. Howard Papers, Bowdoin; Howard, *Autobiography*, 2:235–236; McPherson, *Political History*, 12.

59. Oliver O. Howard to Elizabeth Howard, September 9, 1865, O. O. Howard Papers, Bowdoin.

60. Willard Saxton journal, September 30, 1865, Saxton Papers, Yale.

61. Ralph Ely to Oliver O. Howard, September 22, 1865, Edward Stoeber Papers, SCL; Grace B. Elmore diary, October 3–4, 1865, SCL.

62. Elmore diary, October 3–4, 1865, SCL.

63. Mary Johnstone to Emily Elliott, November 3, 1865, Elliott and Gonzales Papers, SHC.

64. Mary Johnstone to Ann Elliott, September 5, 1865, Elliott and Gonzales Papers, SHC.

65. Johnstone to Elliott, November 3, 1865.

66. Ralph Elliott to Emily Elliott, October 15, 1865, Elliott and Gonzales Papers, SHC.

67. Ibid.

68. Thomas Elliott to Emily Elliott, December 19, 1865, Elliott and Gonzales Papers, SHC.

69. Ralph Elliott to Ann Elliott, July 11, 1865, Elliott and Gonzales Papers, SHC.

70. Whitelaw Reid, *After the War: A Tour of the Southern States, 1865–1866*, ed. C. Vann Woodward (New York: Harper & Row, 1965), 422.

71. Charles Howard to Oliver O. Howard, September 24, 1865, O. O. Howard Papers, Bowdoin.

72. Carl Schurz, *A Report of Conditions in the South* (1865; reprint, New York: Arno Press, 1969), 73.

73. Laura Towne to her sister, August 3, 1865, Laura Towne Letters, Penn School Papers, SHC.

74. Willard Saxton journal, September 16, 1865, Saxton Papers, Yale.

75. Willard Saxton journal, September 19, 1865, Saxton Papers, Yale.

76. Willard Saxton journal, September 20 and 21, Saxton Papers, Yale.

77. C. W. Strickland to Oliver O. Howard, August 22, 1865, O. O. Howard Papers, Bowdoin.

78. George Dutton, "War Memories," newspaper clipping, n.d. (probably 1880s), in Civil War scrapbook, George Wendell Dutton Papers, MHS.

79. George Dutton to Benn Pitman, August 14, 1865, Dutton Papers, MHS.

80. Dutton, "War Memories."

81. Mudd, *Life of Dr. Samuel A. Mudd*, 42.

82. Lizinka Ewell to Andrew Johnson, July 13, 1865, Ewell Papers, SHC.

83. Richard Ewell to Lizinka Ewell, July 16, 1865, Ewell Papers, SHC; Bergeron et al., *Papers of Andrew Johnson*, 8:442.

84. Lew Wallace to Susan Wallace, September 1, 1865, Lew Wallace Papers, IHS.

85. Edward Bartlett to Martha Bartlett, July 16, 1865, and July 30, 1865, Edward J. Bartlett Letters, MHS.

86. Annie Bartlett to Edward J. Bartlett, July 17, 1865, Annie Keyes Bartlett/Edward J. Bartlett Collection, CFPL.

87. Edward Bartlett to Martha Bartlett, July 9, 1865, Bartlett Letters, MHS.

88. Edward Bartlett to Martha Bartlett, July 23, 1865, Bartlett Letters, MHS.

89. Annie Bartlett to Edward Bartlett, July 17, 1865.

90. Edward J. Bartlett to Annie Bartlett, August 20, 1865, Bartlett Letters, MHS.

91. Philip H. Sheridan to Oliver O. Howard, August 3, 1865, O. O. Howard Papers, Bowdoin.

92. The Shelby material is drawn from Daniel O'Flaherty, *General Jo Shelby, Undefeated Rebel* (Chapel Hill: University of North Carolina Press, 1954).

93. *New York Times*, August 22, 1865, 1; *Trial of Henry Wirz*, House Exec. Doc. 23, 40th Cong., 2nd sess. (Washington, D.C.: Government Printing Office, 1866), 3–8.

94. Lew Wallace to Susan Wallace, August 18, 1865, Wallace Papers, IHS.

95. Lew Wallace to Susan Wallace, August 21, 1865, Wallace Papers, IHS.

96. *New York Times*, August 24, 1865, 1; Nathaniel P. Chipman, *The Tragedy of Andersonville: The Trial of Captain Henry Wirz, the Prison-Keeper* (Sacramento, Calif.: Privately published, 1911), 30.

97. *Trial of Henry Wirz*, 142, 297, 89, 282, 353, 175.

98. Lew Wallace to Susan Wallace, September 1, 1865, Wallace Papers, IHS.

99. *Trial of Henry Wirz*, 640.

100. Chipman, *Tragedy of Andersonville*, 45.

101. Lew Wallace to Susan Wallace, September 1, 1865, Wallace Papers, IHS.

102. Lew Wallace to José Carvajal, September 18, 1865, Wallace Papers, IHS.

103. Lew Wallace to John Geary, September (?) 1865, Wallace Papers, IHS; Lew Wallace to Wirz Commission members, October 7, 1865, Wallace Papers, IHS.

104. Lew Wallace to Susan Wallace, September 4, 1865, Wallace Papers, IHS.

105. *Trial of Henry Wirz*, 150.

106. Ibid., 429.

107. Ibid.; *New York Times*, September 27, 1865, 1.

108. Susan Wallace to William F. Elston, September 30, 1865, Wallace Papers, IHS.

109. Reprinted in the *New York Times*, August 30, 1865, 5.

110. Susan Wallace to her mother, October 15, 1865, Wallace Papers, IHS.

111. Henry Wirz to Carrie Furlow, October 24, 1865, Dutton Papers, MHS.

## —— 9. Fallow and Neglected Lands ——

1. Joseph LeConte, "A Journal of Three Months Personal Experience during the Last Days of the Confederacy," manuscript notebook in the Joseph LeConte Papers, SCL.

2. Emma LeConte, *When the World Ended: The Diary of Miss Emma LeConte*, ed. Earl F. Miers (Lincoln: University of Nebraska Press, 1987), 119.

3. *Nation* 1 (August 31, 1865): 262.

4. Paul H. Bergeron et al., eds., *The Papers of Andrew Johnson* (Knoxville: University of Tennessee Press, 1989), 8:651; *New York Times*, September 20, 1865, 1.

5. Bergeron et al., *Papers of Andrew Johnson*, 8:651.

6. Josephine LeConte to her sister, September 17, 1865, LeConte Family Papers, UCB.

7. D. H. Hill to John LeConte, n.d. (by contents, summer 1865), LeConte Family Papers, UCB.

8. Sidney Andrews, *The South Since the War* (1866; reprint, New York: Arno Press, 1969), 31.

9. *New York Times*, September 20, 1865, 1; Andrews, *South Since the War*, 45–46.

10. *New York Times*, September 28, 1865, 1.

11. Joseph LeConte, *The Autobiography of Joseph LeConte*, ed. William Dallam Armes (New York: D. Appleton, 1903), 256.

12. Andrews, *South Since the War*, 385.

13. Elizabeth Ware Pearson, ed., *Letters from Port Royal, 1862–1868* (1906; reprint, New York: Arno Press, 1968), 322–323.

14. Laura M. Towne, *The Letters and Diary of Laura M. Towne*, ed. Rupert S. Holland (1912; reprint, New York: Negro Universities Press, 1969), 167.

15. Pearson, *Letters from Port Royal*, 317.

16. Francis Barlow to Oliver O. Howard, September 17, 1865, Oliver Otis Howard Papers, Bowdoin College.

17. General Orders Number 145, October 9, 1865, in Andrews, *South Since the War*, 208.

18. Oliver Otis Howard, *The Autobiography of Oliver Otis Howard* (New York: Baker & Taylor, 1907), 2:238.

19. *Nation* 1 (August 31, 1865): 263; Martin Abbott, *The Freedmen's Bureau in South Carolina* (Chapel Hill: University of North Carolina Press, 1967), 62.

20. Charles Howard to Oliver O. Howard, September 24, 1865, O. O. Howard Papers, Bowdoin.

21. S. Willard Saxton journal, October 18, 1865, Rufus and S. Willard Saxton Papers, Manuscripts and Archives, Yale University Library.

22. Willard Saxton journal, October 18, 1865, Saxton Papers, Yale.

23. Howard, *Autobiography*, 2:238–239.

24. Quoted in William McFeely, *Yankee Stepfather: O. O. Howard and the Freedmen* (New Haven, Conn.: Yale University Press, 1968), 143.

25. Howard, *Autobiography*, 2:240.

26. Willard Saxton journal, October 24, 1865, Saxton Papers, Yale.

27. Howard, *Autobiography*, 2:240.

28. William Whaley to Oliver O. Howard, October 19, 1865, O. O. Howard Papers, Bowdoin.

29. Quoted in Abbott, *Freedmen's Bureau in South Carolina*, 58.

30. Charles Howard to his mother, October 23, 1865, Charles H. Howard Papers, Bowdoin College.

31. Willard Saxton journal, October 24, 1865, Saxton Papers, Yale.

32. Richard De Treville to Ann Elliott, November 9, 1865, and December 12, 1865, Elliott and Gonzales Papers, SHC; Thomas R. S. Elliott to Emily Elliott, December 19, 1865, Elliott and Gonzales Papers, SHC.

33. Thomas R. S. Elliott to Emily Elliott, Elliott and Gonzales Papers, SHC.

34. Howard, *Autobiography*, 2:241.

35. Holmes, *The Diary of Miss Emma Holmes*, ed. John F. Marszalek (Baton Rouge: Louisiana State University Press, 1979), 477–478.

36. *Nation* 2 (January 11, 1866): 48.

37. Ibid.

38. Charles Howard to Oliver O. Howard, November 25, 1865, O. O. Howard Papers, Bowdoin.

39. McFeely, *Yankee Stepfather,* 147.

40. Charles Howard to Oliver O. Howard, December 6, 1865, O. O. Howard Papers, Bowdoin.

41. Harriot (Brown) Turner, "Recollections of Andrew Johnson," *Harper's Monthly* 120 (January 1910):176.

42. Freedmen's Bureau orders, September 8, 1865, and September 14, 1865, Richard S. Ewell Papers, SHC.

43. Campbell Brown to Lizinka Ewell, August 31, 1865, Ewell Papers, SHC.

44. Alexander H. Stephens, *Recollections of Alexander H. Stephens,* ed. Myrta Lockett Avary (New York: Doubleday, Page, 1910), 506–507, 512.

45. Ibid., 508.

46. Edward McPherson, *The Political History of the United States of America during the Period of Reconstruction* (1871; reprint, New York: DaCapo, 1972), 14.

47. Stephens, *Recollections,* 537.

48. *Report of the Joint Committee on Reconstruction at the First Session, Thirty-ninth Congress* (1866; reprint, Westport, Conn.: Negro Universities Press, 1969), 167–168.

49. Henry Wirz to C. B. Smyth, October 29, 1865, George Wendell Dutton Papers, MHS.

50. *Trial of Henry Wirz,* House Exec. Doc. 23, 40th Cong., 2nd sess. (Washington, D.C.: Government Printing Office, 1866), 813; 814–815.

51. Michael Perman, *Reunion without Compromise: The South and Reconstruction, 1865–1868* (Cambridge, Engl.: Cambridge University Press, 1973), 164.

52. Paul H. Bergeron et al., eds., *The Papers of Andrew Johnson* (Knoxville: University of Tennessee Press, 1991), 9:434.

53. Charles Howard to Oliver O. Howard, September 24, 1865, O. O. Howard Papers, Bowdoin.

54. Philip S. Foner and George E. Walker, eds., *Proceedings of the Black State Conventions, 1840–1865* (Philadelphia: Temple University Press, 1980), 2:301.

55. Eric Foner, *Reconstruction: America's Unfinished Revolution, 1863–1877* (New York: Harper & Row, 1988), 199; Charles Howard to Oliver O. Howard, November 29, 1865, O. O. Howard Papers, Bowdoin.

56. Foner, *Reconstruction,* 200; Carl Schurz, *A Report of Conditions in the South* (1865; reprint, New York: Arno Press, 1969), 92; John T. Trowbridge, *The South: A Tour of Its Battle-fields and Ruined Cities* (Hartford, Conn.: L. Stebbins, 1866), 370; 408.

57. Shurz, *Conditions in the South,* 52; Trowbridge, *The South,* 228.

58. *New York Times,* October 11, 1865, 1.

59. George W. Julian, *Speeches on Political Questions* (1872; reprint, Westport, Conn.: Negro Universities Press, 1970), 265.

60. Ibid., 268.

61. Ibid., 273.

62. Lydia Maria Child, to George Julian, January 22, 1865, Joshua Giddings Papers, Library of Congress (microfilm, ISL).

63. *Indianapolis Daily Journal,* November 18, 1865.

64. *Indiana True Republican,* November 30, 1865.

65. Ibid.

66. McPherson, *Political History,* 110; George Julian to Laura Julian, December 5, 1865, and December 15, 1865, George W. Julian Papers, ISL.

67. George Julian to Laura Julian, December 10, 1865, Julian Papers, ISL.

68. Ralph Elliott to Ann Elliott, January 13, 1865, Elliott and Gonzales Papers, SHC; Willard Saxton journal, January 9, 1865, Saxton Papers, Yale.

69. Willard Saxton journal, January 9, 1865, Saxton Papers, Yale.

70. Charles Howard to Oliver Otis Howard, January 19, 1865, O. O. Howard Papers, Bowdoin; Elizabeth Hyde Botume, *First Days Amongst the Contrabands* (1893; reprint, New York: Arno Press, 1968), 220; Towne, *Letters and Diary*, 169; Laura Towne to her sister, February 23, 1866, Laura Towne Letters, Penn School Papers, SHC.

71. George Julian to Laura Julian, January 20, 1866, Julian Papers, ISL.

72. George Julian to Laura Julian, January 28 and 29, 1866, and February 8, 1866, Julian Papers, ISL.

73. McPherson, *Political History*, 52–55; Julian, *Speeches on Political Questions*, 280.

74. George Julian to Laura Julian, February 8, 1866, Julian Papers, ISL.

75. Foner, *Reconstruction*, 246, 249–250; Lyman Trumbull to Oliver O. Howard, February 19, 1866, O. O. Howard Papers, Bowdoin; Davis Tillson to Oliver O. Howard, February 21, 1866, O. O. Howard Papers, Bowdoin.

76. McPherson, *Political History*, 61.

77. George Julian to Laura Julian, February 20, 1866, and February 22, 1866, Julian Papers, ISL.

78. Holmes, *Diary*, 485; Ralph Elliott to Ann Elliott, January 13, 1866, Elliott and Gonzales Papers, SHC; Abbott, *Freedmen's Bureau in South Carolina*, 61.

79. Charles Manigault, "Close of the War," Manigault Family Papers, SHC.

80. Louis Manigault, Plantation Journal, Manigault Family Papers, SHC; Charles Manigault, "Close of the War," Manigault Family Papers, SHC.

81. Charles Manigault, "Close of the War," Manigault Family Papers, SHC.

82. Joseph LeConte to the Reverend C. Bruce Walker, December 20, 1865, Joseph LeConte Papers, SCL; Mary Elliott Johnstone to Ann Elliott, January 24, 1866, Elliott and Gonzales Papers, SHC.

83. Mary Elliott Johnstone to Ann Elliott, January 10, 1866, Elliott and Gonzales Papers, SHC.

84. Ralph Elliott to Emily Elliott, January 28, 1866, Elliott and Gonzales Papers, SHC.

85. Ralph Elliott to Ann Elliott, February 8, 1866, Elliott and Gonzales Papers, SHC.

86. William Elliott to Ann Elliott, March 13–14, 1866, Elliott and Gonzales Papers, SHC; William Elliott to Ralph Elliott, April 2, 1866, Elliott and Gonzales Papers, SHC.

87. William Elliott to Ann Elliott, March 25, 1866, Elliott and Gonzales Papers, SHC.

88. Emily Elliott to Ann Elliott, April 7, 1866, Elliott and Gonzales Papers, SHC.

89. Emily Elliott to Ann Elliott, May 1, 1866, Elliott and Gonzales Papers, SHC.

90. Emily Elliott to Ann Elliott, April 15, 1866, Elliott and Gonzales Papers, SHC.

91. Ibid.

92. William Elliott to Ann Elliott, May 25, 1866, Elliott and Gonzales Papers, SHC.

93. (?) Dewhurst to Edward Stoeber, December 22, 1865, Edward Stoeber Papers, SCL; *Boston Herald*, December 23, 1865, 2.

94. Alonzo H. Quint, *The Record of the Second Massachusetts Infantry, 1861–1865* (Boston: J. P. Walker, 1867), 506.

95. *Indianapolis Daily Journal*, July 6, 1866.

96. George Julian to Laura Julian, February 10, 1866, Julian Papers, ISL.

97. Julian, *Speeches on Political Questions*, 320–321.

98. George Julian to Laura Julian, May 1, 1866, Julian Papers, ISL; *New York Times*, May 1, 1866, 1.

99. Foner, *Reconstruction*, 273.

100. George Julian to Laura Julian, June 6, 1866, Julian Papers, ISL.

101. Howard, *Autobiography*, 2:297.

102. Ibid., 2:297, 298–308; *New York Times*, August 10, 1866, 1.

103. *New York Times*, May 2, 1866, 1; McPherson, *Political History*, 69.

104. Botume, *First Days*, 227–228.

105. *New York Times*, June 13, 1866, 1.

106. Howard, *Autobiography*, 2:298, 307–308; Paul H. Bergeron et al., eds., *The Papers of Andrew Johnson* (Knoxville: University of Tennessee Press, 1992), 10:627.

107. Oliver O. Howard to Eliphalet Whittlesey, August 30, 1866, O. O. Howard Papers, Bowdoin.

108. Foner, *Reconstruction*, 262.

109. Paul H. Bergeron et al., eds., *The Papers of Andrew Johnson* (Knoxville: University of Tennessee Press, 1994), 11:153.

110. Foner, *Reconstruction*, 265.

111. McPherson, *Political History*, 134–136.

112. Ibid., 137; Lew Wallace to Susan Wallace, September 11, 1866, Lew Wallace Papers, IHS.

113. *Indianapolis Daily Journal*, September 11, 1866.

114. Ibid.; George W. Julian, *Political Recollections, 1840 to 1872* (Chicago: Jansen, McClung, 1884), 270.

115. Foner, *Reconstruction*, 265.

116. *Indiana True Republican*, August 2, 1866.

117. *Indiana True Republican*, September 27, 1866.

118. *Indiana True Republican*, September 13, 1866, and October 18, 1866.

119. Grace B. Elmore diary, SCL.

120. Emily Elliott to William Elliott, November 16, 1866, Elliott and Gonzales Papers, SHC.

## ___ Coda: 1876–1877 ___

1. John Fox to Charles Morse, May 12, 1877, Charles Fessenden Morse Papers, MHS.

2. Stephen R. Fox, *The Guardian of Boston: William Monroe Trotter* (New York: Atheneum, 1970), 8–9.

3. Harriot (Brown) Turner, "Recollections of Andrew Johnson," *Harper's Monthly* 120 (January 1910):176.

4. Oliver Otis Howard, *My Life and Experiences among Our Hostile Indians* (Hartford, Conn.: A. D. Worthington & Co., 1907), 299.

5. William McFeely, *Yankee Stepfather: General O. O. Howard and the Freedmen* (New Haven, Conn.: Yale University Press, 1968), 212–213.

6. Rufus Saxton entry, *National Cyclopedia of American Biography*.

7. George W. Julian, *Political Recollections, 1840 to 1872* (Chicago: Jansen, McClung, 1884), 372.

8. Ibid., 335.

9. Eric Foner, *Reconstruction: America's Unfinished Revolution, 1863–1877* (New York: Harper & Row, 1988), 246.

10. Louis Manigault, Plantation Journal, Manigault Family Papers, SHC.

11. Louis Manigault, "Season of 1876," Manigault Family Papers, SHC.

12. Ibid.

13. Francis B. Simkins and Robert H. Woody, *South Carolina during Reconstruction* (1932; reprint, Gloucester, Mass.: P. Smith, 1966), 109–110; Joseph LeConte to Josephine LeConte, July 28, 1868, LeConte Family Papers, UCB.

14. Emma LeConte to Farish Furman, July 28, 1868, LeConte-Furman Papers, GHS.

15. Ibid.

16. Thomas Holt, *Black over White: Negro Political Leadership in South Carolina during Reconstruction* (Urbana: University of Illinois Press, 1977), 97.

17. Joseph LeConte to John LeConte, March 16, 1869, LeConte Family Papers, UCB.

18. Emma LeConte to Farish Furman, March 10, 1869, LeConte-Furman Papers, GHS.

19. Farish Furman to Emma LeConte, July 27, 1868, LeConte-Furman Papers, GHS.

20. Emma LeConte to Farish Furman, February 21, 1869, LeConte-Furman Papers, GHS.

21. Joseph LeConte, "A Journal of Three Months Personal Experience during the Last Days of the Confederacy," 157–158, manuscript notebook in the Joseph LeConte Papers, SCL.

22. Louis Manigault, "Season of 1876," Manigault Family Papers, SHC.

23. Ibid.

24. Holt, *Black over White*, 196.

25. Elizabeth Hyde Botume, *First Days Amongst the Contrabands* (1893; reprint, New York: Arno Press, 1968), 260; Laura Towne to her sisters, May 21, 1876, Laura Towne Letters, Penn School Papers, SHC.

26. Laura Towne to her sister, June 17, 1875, Towne Letters, SHC.

27. Laura Towne to her sisters, July 5, 1875, Towne Letters, SHC.

28. Laura Towne to her sisters, February 10, 1867, Towne Letters, SHC.

29. Laura Towne to her sister, July 2, 1876, Towne Letters, SHC.

30. Laura Towne to her sister, October 29, 1876, Towne Letters, SHC.

31. Quoted in Foner, *Reconstruction*, 570.

32. Sources for this account of the Hamburg Massacre are the manuscript trial notes in the Martin W. Gary Papers, SCL, and the Butler Family Scrapbooks, also in the SCL.

33. Laura Towne to her sister, October 29, 1876, Towne Letters, SHC.

34. Ibid.

35. Holt, *Black over White*, 174.

36. Laura Towne to an unnamed correspondent, November 8, 1876, Towne Letters, SHC.

37. Lew Wallace to Susan Wallace, November 26, 1876, Lew Wallace Papers, IHS.

38. Robert E. Morsberger and Katharine M. Morsberger, *Lew Wallace: Militant Romantic* (New York: McGraw-Hill, 1980), 447.

39. Lew Wallace to Susan Wallace, November 27, 1876, Wallace Papers, IHS.

# Bibliography

## —— Manuscript Collections ——

Bartlett Family Papers, Concord Free Public Library, Concord, Massachusetts.

Annie Keyes Bartlett/Edward J. Bartlett Collection, Concord Free Public Library, Concord, Massachusetts.

Edward J. Bartlett Letters, Massachusetts Historical Society, Boston.

Butler Family Scrapbooks, South Caroliniana Library, University of South Carolina, Columbia.

George Wendell Dutton Papers, Massachusetts Historical Society.

Elliott and Gonzales Papers, Southern Historical Collection, Wilson Library, University of North Carolina at Chapel Hill.

Grace B. Elmore Diary, South Caroliniana Library, University of South Carolina.

Richard S. Ewell Papers, Southern Historical Collection, Wilson Library, University of North Carolina at Chapel Hill.

Charles B. Fox Papers, Massachusetts Historical Society.

Fox Family Papers, Massachusetts Historical Society.

Martin W. Gary Papers, South Caroliniana Library, University of South Carolina.

Alfred S. Hartwell Papers, Massachusetts State Library, Boston.

Charles H. Howard Papers, Bowdoin College, Brunswick, Maine.

Oliver Otis Howard Papers, Bowdoin College.

George W. Julian Papers, Indiana State Library, Indianapolis.

Edward W. Kinsley Papers, Special Collections Library, Duke University, Durham, North Carolina.

Edward W. Kinsley Papers, Massachusetts Historical Society.

LeConte Family Papers, Bancroft Library, University of California at Berkeley.

Joseph LeConte Papers, South Caroliniana Library, University of South Carolina.

LeConte-Furman Papers, Georgia Historical Society, Savannah.

Lafayette McLaws Papers, Southern Historical Society Collection, Wilson Library, University of North Carolina at Chapel Hill.

Manigault Family Papers, Southern Historical Collection, Wilson Library, University of North Carolina at Chapel Hill.

Louis Manigault Papers, Special Collections Library, Duke University.

Charles Fessenden Morse Papers, Massachusetts Historical Society.
New England Freedman's Aid Society Papers, Massachusetts Historical Society.
Rufus and S. Willard Saxton Papers, Manuscripts and Archives, Yale University Library, New Haven, Connecticut.
Henry Sparks Diary, Indiana Historical Society, Indianapolis.
Samuel Storrow Papers, Massachusetts Historical Society.
Arthur Sumner Manuscripts, Penn School Papers, Southern Historical Collection, Wilson Library, University of North Carolina at Chapel Hill.
Laura Towne Letters, Penn School Papers, Southern Historical Collection, Wilson Library, University of North Carolina at Chapel Hill.
Lew Wallace Papers, Indiana Historical Society, Indianapolis.

## —— Books, Memoirs, Articles ——

Abbott, Martin. *The Freedmen's Bureau in South Carolina.* Chapel Hill: University of North Carolina Press, 1967.
Adams, Charles Francis Jr. *Charles Francis Adams, 1835–1915: An Autobiography.* Boston: Houghton Mifflin, 1916.
Andrews, Sidney. *The South Since the War.* 1866. Reprint, New York: Arno Press, 1969.
Barrett, John G. *Sherman's March through the Carolinas.* Chapel Hill: University of North Carolina Press, 1956.
Bergeron, Paul H., et al., eds. *The Papers of Andrew Johnson.* Vols. 8–11. Knoxville: University of Tennessee Press, 1989–1994.
Berlin, Ira, and Leslie S. Rowland, eds. *Families and Freedom: A Documentary History of African-American Kinship in the Civil War Era.* New York: New Press, 1997.
Berlin, Ira, et al., eds. *The Destruction of Slavery.* Ser. 1, vol. 1 of *Freedom: A Documentary History of Emancipation.* New York: Cambridge University Press, 1985.
Blackford, Charles M. *Letters from Lee's Army.* Edited by Susan L. Blackford. New York: Scribner's, 1947.
Botume, Elizabeth Hyde. *First Days Amongst the Contrabands.* 1893. Reprint, New York: Arno Press, 1968.
Bowen, James. *Massachusetts in the War.* Springfield, Mass.: C. W. Bryan, 1889.
Boykin, Edward M. *The Falling Flag.* New York: E. T. Hale & Son, 1874.
Brooks, Noah. *Washington in Lincoln's Time.* Edited by Herbert Mitgang. New York: Rinehart, 1958.
Chipman, Nathaniel P. *The Tragedy of Andersonville: The Trial of Captain Henry Wirz, the Prison-Keeper.* Sacramento, Calif.: Privately published, 1911.
Clifton, James M., ed. *Life and Labor on Argyle Island.* Savannah, Ga.: Beehive Press, 1978.
Conolly, Thomas. *An Irishman in Dixie.* Edited by Nelson D. Lankford. Columbia: University of South Carolina Press, 1988.
Creel, Margaret W. *A Peculiar People: Slave Religion and Community-Culture Among the Gullahs.* New York: New York University Press, 1988.
Dana, Charles A. *Recollections of the Civil War.* New York: D. Appleton, 1898.
Duke, R. T. W. "Burning of Richmond." *Southern Historical Society Papers* 30 (1897).
Duncan, Russell, ed. *Blue-Eyed Child of Fortune: The Civil War Letters of Robert Gould Shaw.* Athens: University of Georgia Press, 1992.
Dusinberre, William. *Them Dark Days: Slavery in the American Rice Swamps.* New York: Oxford University Press, 1996.

Eggleston, George Cary. *A Rebel's Recollections.* New York: G. P. Putnam's Sons, 1878.

Emilio, Luis F. *A Brave Black Regiment: History of the 54th Regiment of Massachusetts Volunteer Infantry, 1863–1865.* Salem, N.H.: Ayer, 1990.

Faust, Drew Gilpin. *Mothers of Invention: Women of the Slaveholding South in the American Civil War.* Chapel Hill: University of North Carolina Press, 1996.

Fellman, Michael. *Citizen Sherman.* New York: Random House, 1995.

Foner, Eric. *Reconstruction: America's Unfinished Revolution, 1863–1877.* New York: Harper & Row, 1988.

Foote, Shelby. *The Civil War: A Narrative.* 3 vols. New York: Random House, 1958–1974.

Ford, Worthington C., ed. *A Cycle of Adams Letters.* 2 vols. Boston: Houghton Mifflin, 1920.

Forten, Charlotte. "Life on the Sea Islands." *Atlantic Monthly* 13 (May 1864).

———. *The Journal of Charlotte Forten.* Edited by Ray A. Billington. New York: Norton, 1981.

Fox, Stephen R. *The Guardian of Boston: William Monroe Trotter.* New York: Atheneum, 1970.

Freeman, Douglas Southall. *Lee's Lieutenants: A Study in Command.* Vol 3. New York: Scribner's, 1946.

Furgurson, Ernest. *Ashes of Glory: Richmond at War.* New York: Knopf, 1996.

Gannet, W. C. "The Freedmen at Port Royal." *North American Review* 101 (July 1865).

"George W. Julian's Journal—the Assassination of Lincoln." *Indiana Magazine of History* 2 (1915).

Graf, Leroy P., et al., eds. *The Papers of Andrew Johnson.* Vol. 7. Knoxville: University of Tennessee Press, 1986.

Gray, John C. Jr., and John C. Ropes. *War Letters, 1862–1865.* Edited by Worthington C. Ford. Boston: Houghton Mifflin, 1927.

Hanchett, William. *The Lincoln Murder Conspiracies.* Urbana: University of Illinois Press, 1983.

Higginson, Thomas Wentworth. "Leaves from an Officer's Journal." *Atlantic Monthly* 15 (January 1865).

———. *Massachusetts in the Army and Navy during the War of 1861–1865.* 2 vols. Boston: Wright & Potter, 1896.

Hinkley, Julian W. *A Narrative of Service with the Third Wisconsin Infantry.* Madison: Wisconsin Historical Commission, 1912.

Hitchcock, Henry M. *Marching with Sherman.* Edited by M. A. deWolfe Howe. New Haven, Conn.: Yale University Press, 1927.

Holmes, Emma. *The Diary of Miss Emma Holmes.* Edited by John F. Marszalek. Baton Rouge: Louisiana State University Press, 1979.

Holt, Thomas. *Black over White: Negro Political Leadership in South Carolina during Reconstruction.* Urbana: University of Illinois Press, 1977.

Howard, Oliver Otis. *The Autobiography of Oliver Otis Howard.* 2 vols. New York: Baker & Taylor, 1907.

———. *My Life and Experiences among Our Hostile Indians.* Hartford, Conn.: A. D. Worthington & Co., 1907.

Ingraham, Prentiss. "Capture and Death of John Wilkes Booth." *Century* 39 (1890).

Jarrell, Hampton. *Wade Hampton and the Negro.* Columbia: University of South Carolina Press, 1949.

Jones, John B. *A Rebel War Clerk's Diary.* Edited by Earl S. Miers. New York: Sagamore Press, 1958.

Julian, George. *Political Recollections, 1840 to 1872.* Chicago: Jansen, McClung, 1884.
———. *Speeches on Political Questions.* 1872. Reprint, Westport, Conn.: Negro Universities Press, 1970.
Kirkland, Edward C. *Charles Francis Adams Jr., the Patrician at Bay.* Cambridge, Mass.: Harvard University Press, 1965.
LeConte, Emma. *When the World Ended: The Diary of Emma LeConte.* Edited by Earl S. Miers. Lincoln: University of Nebraska Press, 1987.
LeConte, Joseph. *The Autobiography of Joseph LeConte.* Edited by William Dallam Armes. New York: D. Appleton, 1903.
———. *'Ware Sherman: A Journal of Three Months Personal Experience in the Last Days of the Confederacy.* Berkeley: University of California Press, 1937.
Lucas, Marion B. *Sherman and the Burning of Columbia.* College Station: Texas A & M University Press, 1976.
McFeely, William. *Yankee Stepfather: General O. O. Howard and the Freedmen.* New Haven, Conn.: Yale University Press, 1968.
McKee, Irving. *"Ben Hur Wallace": The Life of General Lew Wallace.* Berkeley: University of California Press, 1947.
McKitrick, Eric L. *Andrew Johnson and Reconstruction.* Chicago: University of Chicago Press, 1960.
McPherson, Edward. *The Political History of the United States of America during the Period of Reconstruction.* 1871. Reprint, New York: DaCapo, 1972.
Marszalek, John F. *Sherman: A Soldier's Passion for Order.* New York: Free Press, 1993.
Marvel, William. *Andersonville: The Last Depot.* Chapel Hill: University of North Carolina Press, 1994.
Morsberger, Robert E., and Katharine M. Morsberger. *Lew Wallace: Militant Romantic.* New York: McGraw-Hill, 1980.
Morse, Charles F. *Letters Written during the Civil War.* Boston: Privately published, 1898.
Mudd, Nettie. *The Life of Dr. Samuel A. Mudd.* 1906. Reprint, Saginaw, Mich.: Privately published, 1962.
Nichols, George W. *The Story of the Great March from the Diary of a Staff Officer.* New York: Harper & Brothers, 1865.
Oakey, Daniel. "Marching through Georgia and the Carolinas." *Battles and Leaders of the Civil War.* Vol. 4. New York: Century, 1887.
O'Flahery, Daniel. *General Jo Shelby, Undefeated Rebel.* Chapel Hill: University of North Carolina Press, 1954.
Osborn, Thomas W. *The Fiery Trail: A Union Officer's Account of Sherman's Last Campaigns.* Edited by Richard Harwell and Philip N. Racine. Knoxville: University of Tennessee Press, 1986.
Pearson, Elizabeth Ware, ed. *Letters from Port Royal, 1862–1868.* 1906. Reprint, New York: Arno Press, 1968.
Perman, Michael. *Reunion without Compromise: The South and Reconstruction, 1865–1868.* Cambridge, Eng.: Cambridge University Press, 1973.
Pierce, Edward L. "The Freedmen of Port Royal." *Atlantic* 12 (September 1863).
Pitman, Benn, ed. *The Assassination of President Lincoln and the Trial of the Conspirators.* Cincinnati: Moore, Wilstach & Boldwin, 1865.
Powers, Bernard E. Jr. *Black Charlestonians: A Social History, 1822–1895.* Fayetteville: University of Arkansas Press, 1994.
Quint, Alonzo H. *The Record of the Second Massachusetts Infantry, 1861–1865.* Boston: J. P. Walker, 1867.

Rable, George. *Civil Wars: Women and the Crisis of Southern Nationalism.* Urbana: University of Illinois Press, 1989.

Redkey, Edwin S. *A Grand Army of Black Men: Letters from African-American Soldiers in the Union Army, 1861–1865.* New York: Cambridge University Press, 1992.

Reid, Whitelaw. *After the War: A Tour of the Southern States, 1865–1866.* Edited by C. Vann Woodward. 1866. Reprint, New York: Harper & Row, 1965.

*Report of the Joint Committee on Reconstruction at the First Session, Thirty-ninth Congress.* 1866. Reprint, Westport, Conn.: Negro Universities Press, 1969.

Riddleberger, Patrick. *1866: The Critical Year Revisited.* Carbondale: Southern Illinois University Press, 1979.

———. *George Washington Julian, Radical Republican.* Indianapolis: Indiana Historical Bureau, 1966.

Ripley, Edward H. *The Capture and Occupation of Richmond.* New York: G. P. Putnam's Sons, 1907.

Rose, Willie Lee. *Rehearsal for Reconstruction: The Port Royal Experiment.* New York: Vintage, 1967.

Royster, Charles. *The Destructive War: William Tecumseh Sherman, Stonewall Jackson and the Americans.* New York: Knopf, 1991.

Schurz, Carl. *A Report of Conditions in the South.* 1865. Reprint, New York: Arno Press, 1969.

Sherman, William T. *Home Letters of General Sherman.* Edited by M. A. deWolfe Howe. New York: Scribner's, 1909.

———. *Memoirs of General W. T. Sherman.* New York: Library of America, 1990.

Simkins, Francis B., and Robert H. Woody, *South Carolina during Reconstruction.* 1932. Reprint, Gloucester, Mass.: P. Smith, 1966.

Slocum, Henry. "Sherman's March from Savannah to Bentonville." *Battles and Leaders of the Civil War.* Vol. 4. New York: Century, 1887.

Stampp, Kenneth M. *The Era of Reconstruction, 1865–1877.* New York: Knopf, 1965.

Stephens, Alexander H. *Recollections of Alexander H. Stephens.* Edited by Myrta Lockett Avary. New York: Doubleday, Page, 1910.

Stephens, Lester D. *Joseph LeConte: Gentle Prophet of Evolution.* Baton Rouge: Louisiana State University Press, 1982.

Tew, Henry S. "An Eye-Witness Account of the Occupation of Mount Pleasant." *South Carolina Historical Magazine* 66 (January 1965).

Thomas, Benjamin P., and Harold M. Hyman. *Stanton: The Life and Times of Lincoln's Secretary of War.* New York: Knopf, 1962.

Tidwell, William A. *April '65: Confederate Covert Action in the American Civil War.* Kent, Ohio: Kent State University Press, 1995.

Towne, Laura M. *The Letters and Diary of Laura M. Towne.* Edited by Rupert S. Holland. 1912. Reprint, New York: Negro Universities Press, 1969.

*Trial of Henry Wirz.* House Exec. Doc. 23. 40th Cong., 2nd sess. Washington D.C.: Government Printing Office, 1866.

Trowbridge, John T. *The South: A Tour of Its Battle-Fields and Ruined Cities.* Hartford, Conn.: L. Stebbins, 1866.

Trudeau, Noah A. *Like Men of War: Black Troops in the Civil War.* Boston: Little, Brown, 1998.

———. *Voices of the 55th.* Dayton, Ohio: Morningside Press, 1996.

Turner, Harriot (Brown). "Recollections of Andrew Johnson." *Harper's Monthly* 120 (January 1910).

Turner, Thomas R. *Beware the People Weeping: Public Opinion and the Assassination of Abraham Lincoln.* Baton Rouge: Louisiana State University Press, 1982.

U.S. War Department. *The War of the Rebellion: A Compilation of the Official Records of the Union and Confederate Armies.* Washington, D.C.: Government Printing Office, 1880–1891.

Wallace, Lew. *The Autobiography of Lew Wallace.* 2 vols. New York: Harper & Brothers, 1906.

Whitman, Walt. *Complete Poetry and Collected Prose.* Edited by Justin Kaplan. New York: Library of America, 1982.

Wills, Charles W. *Army Life of an Illinois Soldier.* Carbondale: Southern Illinois University Press, 1996.

Woodward, C. Vann, and Elisabeth Muhlenfeld, eds. *The Private Mary Chesnut.* New York: Oxford University Press, 1984.

# Index

*Note:* Page numbers in *italics* indicate illustrations.

## DATE DUE

| | | | |
|---|---|---|---|
| | | | |
| | | | |
| | | | |
| | | | |
| | | | |
| | | | |
| | | | |
| | | | |
| | | | |
| | | | |
| | | | |
| | | | |
| | | | |
| | | | |
| | | | |
| | | | |
| | | | |
| | | | |